EARTH SHELTERED RESIDENTIAL DESIGN MANUAL

Underground Space Center
University of Minnesota

Prepared by:

Dr. Raymond Sterling
William T. Farnan
John Carmody

Prepared for:

U.S. Department of Housing and Urban Development
Office of Policy Development and Research
Project Number: H-5266 CA

VAN NOSTRAND REINHOLD COMPANY
NEW YORK CINCINNATI TORONTO LONDON MELBOURNE

The work that provided the basis for this
publication was supported by funding under a
Grant/Cooperative Agreement with the U.S.
Department of Housing and Urban
Development. The substance and findings of
that work are dedicated to the public. The
author is solely responsible for the accuracy of
the statements and interpretations contained in
this publication and such interpretations do not
necessarily reflect the views of the Government.

Copyright © 1982 by the University of Minnesota

Library of Congress Catalog Card Number 82-2658

ISBN 0-442-28678-3

ISBN 0-442-28679-1 (pb)

Printed in the United States of America

Designed by John Carmody

Published by Van Nostrand Reinhold Company Inc.
135 West 50th Street
New York, NY 10020

Van Nostrand Reinhold Publishers
1410 Birchmount Road
Scarborough, Ontario M1P 2E7, Canada

Van Nostrand Reinhold Australia Pty. Ltd.
17 Queen Street
Mitcham, Victoria 3132, Australia

Van Nostrand Reinhold Company Limited
Molly Millars Lane
Wokingham, Berkshire, England

16 15 14 13 12 11 10 9 8 7 6 5 4 3 2 1

Library of Congress Cataloging in Publication Data

Sterling, Raymond

    Earth sheltered residential design manual.

    Bibliography: p. 239
    Includes index.
    1. Earth sheltered houses—Design and construction.
I. Carmody, John. II. University of Minnesota. Underground Space Center. III. Title.
TH4819.E27S735   690.8   82-2658
ISBN 0-442-28678-3   AACR2
ISBN 0-442-28679-1 (pbk.)

Preface

This study provides the technical information necessary to evaluate the suitability of an earth sheltered residence, considers the factors influencing its overall design, and evaluates the appropriateness of materials and construction techniques. This information should be of value both in developing the design for an earth sheltered residence and in analyzing a completed design to determine whether it is suitable. Although other publications, notably *Earth Sheltered Housing Design* [1.1], deal with design considerations and examples of earth sheltered houses, there is a need for more specific technical information that can help to clarify and solve problems in the design and construction of these buildings. This book attempts to provide this information while complementing and elaborating on these other publications.

The information in this manual has been developed by the staff of the Underground Space Center at the University of Minnesota for the U.S. Department of Housing and Urban Development. The Underground Space Center has completed numerous research projects and publications on earth sheltered housing and is in contact with hundreds of architects, engineers, builders, owners, code officials, and finance officers involved in the design, construction, use, and evaluation of earth sheltered homes. In addition, consultation and review was provided by several experts on earth sheltered design and construction in different regions of the country.

In the past, the term *earth sheltering* has sometimes been a source of confusion. It would seem to be generally accepted that •

a standard frame house resting on a flat floor slab is not earth sheltered and that a space totally underground, connected to the surface by only a tunnel or shaft, is earth sheltered. Between these two extremes, however, is a continuum that includes standard homes with basements, walkouts, split-entries, split-levels; earth-bermed houses; homes with earth on the roof; and earth-covered homes that have only the most minimal aboveground exposure. Although the exact degree or percentage of earth covering—the line that separates the exact number of square feet of cover required for a structure to be considered earth sheltered or not earth sheltered—is relevant for some types of tax and code matters, it is not the primary concern here. Therefore, a more performance-oriented definition seems appropriate. For this study earth sheltering shall mean the deliberate use of the mass of the earth placed in contact with a structure to benefit the environment of a habitable space. These benefits may be ecological, aesthetic, economic, and/or related to land use.

It is only fair to state at the beginning the assumptions and limitations of this study. The first limitation is time. Technical knowledge, social attitudes, and economic conditions are changing very rapidly. Both the specific data and the attitudes and assumptions on which this study is based could become outdated in a relatively short period of time. Therefore, information is presented here with the caution that it is not a body of unchanging truth, but rather a state-of-the-art study that will require periodic updating, rethinking, and revision.

The second limitation is situational.

Although every effort has been made to make this study as specific and detailed as possible, often the right option in one situation is wrong in another. Therefore, whenever a specific recommendation is made, the reader is advised to temper that recommendation with his or her own firsthand knowledge of the situation to which it is to be applied, as some conditions may exist that were not considered when the general recommendation was made. In cases where many alternatives appear to be possible, this study provides a means to evaluate these variables, listing the advantages and disadvantages of each option rather than suggesting a specific choice.

The third limitation is the inability to present information at a level appropriate to all potential members of the audience. Obviously, the background of each reader will be different; some readers will have had no previous experience in construction, whereas others may have worked in construction for a number of years. This study does not aspire to teach readers everything about construction; it is aimed at the reader who already has a thorough working knowledge of the standard construction techniques and wishes to supplement that knowledge with specific information related to earth sheltering. The manual assumes that the reader is a professional architect or engineer designing an earth sheltered residence, a contractor building such a residence, or a code enforcement official or finance officer evaluating an earth sheltered housing project. Although many others will certainly find the manual useful, no book can replace the years of education and experience of a professional. Nonprofessionals are cautioned that the information presented here is intended to be evaluated in the light of a professional judgment of the particular circumstances of its application.

This manual is organized into three major parts, which are further subdivided into ten chapters in an order that is intended to reflect the sequence of the design and construction process. In practice, most of the components of the process in design and construction simultaneously interact with each other. The first part of the book provides a general assessment of earth sheltered housing. Included in this part are an introduction to earth sheltered housing, as well as chapters on regional suitability of and economic considerations for these structures. These first three chapters introduce the concept of earth sheltered housing and provide information that will be useful in evaluating its feasibility for a particular situation and formulating general design concepts. The second part of the manual, which consists of design and technical information, is divided into six chapters: *Site Design and Building Form; Soils; Structural Systems; Waterproofing; Heating, Cooling and Insulation;* and *Landscape Design.* The third part of the manual, *Integration of Design Technology*, consists of only one chapter, which presents and discusses typical design problems and details. Whereas the second part of the book presents technical information in a number of detailed areas, the third part illustrates the coordination of these various systems.

Credits

Authors:

Principal Investigator:

Dr. Raymond Sterling
Director
Underground Space Center
Assistant Professor
Department of Civil and
     Mineral Engineering
University of Minnesota

Project Coordinator:

William T. Farnan
Architect
Underground Space Center
University of Minnesota
Currently in private practice:
William T. Farnan, A.I.A.
White Bear Lake, Minnesota

Associate Project Coordinator:

John Carmody
Research Coordinator
     and Architect
Underground Space Center
University of Minnesota

Chapter 9—Landscape Design:

Gail Elnicky
Assistant Professor
Department of Architecture
     and Landscape Architecture
University of Minnesota

Book Design:

Graphics, illustrations, page layout, and cover design by John Carmody with assistance from Mark Heisterkamp and Katherine Carmody. Sketches in chapter 10 by Mark Heisterkamp.

Special Assistance

As members of the Underground Space Center staff, the following people contributed to and reviewed portions of the manual.

Brent Anderson
Division 7 Corporation
Bloomington, Minnesota

Dr. George Meixel
Research Associate
Underground Space Center
University of Minnesota

Charles Lane
Private Consultant
Shoreview, Minnesota

Glenn Strand
Edwards Sales Corp.
Minneapolis, Minnesota

Consultants and Reviewers:

Dr. Thomas Bligh, Assoc. Professor
Department of Mechanical Engineering
Massachusetts Institute of Technology
Cambridge, Massachusetts

Dr. Lester L. Boyer, Professor
Department of Architecture
Oklahoma State University
Stillwater, Oklahoma

Steve Heibein
National Concrete Masonry Association
Herndon, Virginia

Dr. Ernst Keisling, Chairman
Department of Civil Engineering
Texas Tech University
Lubbock, Texas

Kenneth Labs
Undercurrent Design Research
New Haven, Connecticut

William Morgan
William Morgan Architects
Jacksonville, Florida

David Scott, Professor
Department of Architecture
Washington State University
Pullman, Washington

Ralph Spears
Portland Cement Association
Skokie, Illinois

David Wright
Solar Energy Architect Group
Nevada City, California

Contents

Acknowledgments

The conceptualization, writing, and illustrating of this Design Manual required the time, talents and commitment of a number of people. The project was initially conceived by the Office of Policy Development and Research at the Department of Housing and Urban Development. Ron Morony, in his role of project officer for HUD, encouraged and facilitated our staff in the development of the manual.

Although most of the chapters in the book were jointly written by the three authors, there is one exception. Chapter 9, Landscape Design, was written entirely by Gail Elnicky, an assistant professor at the School of Architecture and Landscape Architecture at the University of Minnesota. We appreciate not only her contribution but also the cooperation of her department in allowing her to participate in this study.

A design manual that presents technical information concerning a constantly evolving new building form must be carefully scrutinized so that it represents the most current thought and practice. Two groups provided valuable assistance in critically reviewing the manual, providing suggestions and contributing material from their own work. The first group consisted of members of the Underground Space Center staff: Brent Anderson, Dr. George Meixel, Jr., Glenn Strand, and Charles Lane. Brent Anderson, in particular, contributed his time as well as some valuable material and his field experience in preparing the chapters on waterproofing and insulation. Dr. George Meixel, Jr. reviewed the chapter on heat transfer, an area in which he is continuing to develop much needed design guidelines.

In addition to the Underground Space Center staff, the manual was reviewed in its final stages by a group of very experienced professionals in the field of earth sheltered buildings. The contribution of this group (listed on the credits page) was extremely valuable and is greatly appreciated by the authors.

Finally, we would like to thank several members of the Underground Space Center staff who contributed their time and effort in the production of the manual. Mark Heisterkamp provided his skill in drawing or assisting with all of the illustrations in the book, and Katherine Carmody did the keylining as well as contributed to the graphic design. Donna Ahrens devoted considerable time and energy to the editing of the text. The extensive typing and retyping of the manual was done primarily by Penny Bader with assistance from Arlene Bennett and Andrea Spartz.

PART ONE:

GENERAL ASSESSMENT OF EARTH SHELTERED HOUSING

1. INTRODUCTION TO EARTH SHELTERED HOUSING
2. REGIONAL SUITABILITY
3. ECONOMIC CONSIDERATIONS

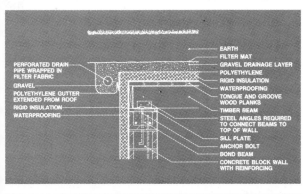

PERFORATED DRAIN PIPE WRAPPED IN FILTER FABRIC
GRAVEL
POLYETHYLENE GUTTER EXTENDED FROM ROOF
RIGID INSULATION
WATERPROOFING

EARTH
FILTER MAT
GRAVEL DRAINAGE LAYER
POLYETHYLENE
RIGID INSULATION
WATERPROOFING
TONGUE AND GROOVE WOOD PLANKS
TIMBER BEAM
STEEL ANGLES REQUIRED TO CONNECT BEAMS TO TOP OF WALL
SILL PLATE
ANCHOR BOLT
BOND BEAM
CONCRETE BLOCK WALL WITH REINFORCING

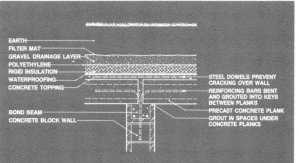

EARTH
FILTER MAT
GRAVEL DRAINAGE LAYER
POLYETHYLENE
RIGID INSULATION
WATERPROOFING
CONCRETE TOPPING
BOND BEAM
CONCRETE BLOCK WALL

STEEL DOWELS PREVENT CRACKING OVER WALL
REINFORCING BARS BENT AND GROUTED INTO KEYS BETWEEN PLANKS
PRECAST CONCRETE PLANK
GROUT IN SPACES UNDER CONCRETE PLANKS

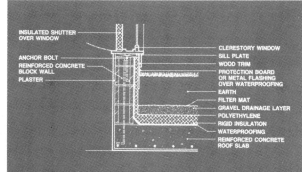

INSULATED SHUTTER OVER WINDOW
ANCHOR BOLT
REINFORCED CONCRETE BLOCK WALL
PLASTER

CLERESTORY WINDOW
SILL PLATE
WOOD TRIM
PROTECTION BOARD OR METAL FLASHING OVER WATERPROOFING
EARTH
FILTER MAT
GRAVEL DRAINAGE LAYER
POLYETHYLENE
RIGID INSULATION
WATERPROOFING
REINFORCED CONCRETE ROOF SLAB

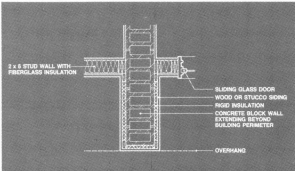

2 x 6 STUD WALL WITH FIBERGLASS INSULATION

SLIDING GLASS DOOR
WOOD OR STUCCO SIDING
RIGID INSULATION
CONCRETE BLOCK WALL EXTENDING BEYOND BUILDING PERIMETER
OVERHANG

CHAPTER 1

INTRODUCTION TO EARTH SHELTERED HOUSING

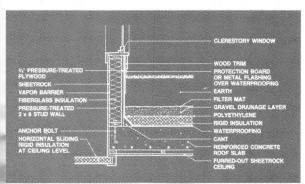

CLERESTORY WINDOW

¾" PRESSURE-TREATED PLYWOOD
SHEETROCK
VAPOR BARRIER
FIBERGLASS INSULATION
PRESSURE-TREATED 2 x 6 STUD WALL

ANCHOR BOLT
HORIZONTAL SLIDING RIGID INSULATION AT CEILING LEVEL

WOOD TRIM
PROTECTION BOARD OR METAL FLASHING OVER WATERPROOFING
EARTH
FILTER MAT
GRAVEL DRAINAGE LAYER
POLYETHYLENE
RIGID INSULATION
WATERPROOFING
CANT
REINFORCED CONCRETE ROOF SLAB
FURRED-OUT SHEETROCK CEILING

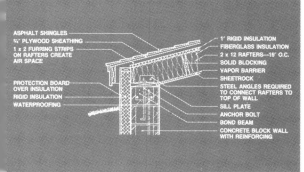

ASPHALT SHINGLES
¼" PLYWOOD SHEATHING
1 x 2 FURRING STRIPS ON RAFTERS CREATE AIR SPACE
PROTECTION BOARD OVER INSULATION
RIGID INSULATION
WATERPROOFING

1" RIGID INSULATION
FIBERGLASS INSULATION
2 x 12 RAFTERS—16" O.C.
SOLID BLOCKING
VAPOR BARRIER
SHEETROCK
STEEL ANGLES REQUIRED TO CONNECT RAFTERS TO TOP OF WALL
SILL PLATE
ANCHOR BOLT
BOND BEAM
CONCRETE BLOCK WALL WITH REINFORCING

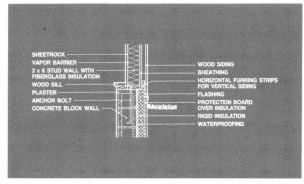

SHEETROCK
VAPOR BARRIER
2 x 6 STUD WALL WITH FIBERGLASS INSULATION
WOOD SILL
PLASTER
ANCHOR BOLT
CONCRETE BLOCK WALL

WOOD SIDING
SHEATHING
HORIZONTAL FURRING STRIPS FOR VERTICAL SIDING
FLASHING
PROTECTION BOARD OVER INSULATION
RIGID INSULATION
WATERPROOFING

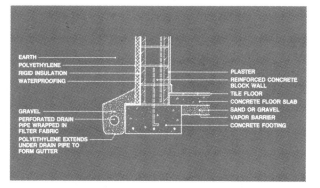

EARTH
POLYETHYLENE
RIGID INSULATION
WATERPROOFING

GRAVEL
PERFORATED DRAIN PIPE WRAPPED IN FILTER FABRIC
POLYETHYLENE EXTENDS UNDER DRAIN PIPE TO FORM GUTTER

PLASTER
REINFORCED CONCRETE BLOCK WALL
TILE FLOOR
CONCRETE FLOOR SLAB
SAND OR GRAVEL
VAPOR BARRIER
CONCRETE FOOTING

Introduction

The purpose of this chapter, which
includes a brief description of the benefits
of building earth sheltered houses, is
threefold. First, it introduces the concept of
earth sheltered housing to those who are
unfamiliar with it. Second, it serves as a
necessary component of the general
assessment of earth sheltered housing
provided in the first three chapters of this
manual. In order to assess the suitability
of earth sheltered structures on a regional
basis or the feasibility in economic terms,
it is necessary to clarify the wide range of
issues involved in such assessments.
Finally, it is important to state the reasons
for building earth sheltered houses,
because they should be clearly reflected in
both the general conceptual design
decisions and the details of the structure.
By clarifying and assigning priorities to
various reasons for building an earth
sheltered house, the designer can use the
technical information in parts two and three
of this manual in a consistent and
appropriate way to successfully achieve the
desired effects.

Potential Benefits of Earth Sheltered Construction

Aesthetics

One of the great attractions of the concept of earth sheltering—and, for some people, the major reason for designing earth sheltered buildings—is the aesthetic potential of earth shelter design. Building a structure partially or completely below grade with earth-covered walls and roof offers opportunities for integrating a building with the surrounding landscape to a degree that is simply not possible with conventional buildings.

The houses shown are good examples of the unique aesthetic possibilities with earth sheltering. The form of the Clark-Nelson house (built in 1972) unites far more harmoniously with its site than most houses (fig. 1-1). In the Winston house (1972), the white, man-made geometrical precision of the patios and the structure contrasts with the unmowed grasses growing wild around it and on its roof (fig. 1-2).

The relationship of any building to its site is one of the key elements of the aesthetics of the building. Earth sheltering offers many opportunities for the skillful designer to explore and reinterpret this relationship, as well as many perils for the careless designer working with idioms from a different design language. Successful earth sheltering can yield visual pleasure and delight for the intellect, both through the blending of building and site and in the forms that can be created through simple grading and innovative use of shells and other structural elements particularly suited to earth sheltered construction. In addition, plant materials can be used as a design element in ways not possible with

1-1: Clark-Nelson House

Architect: Michael McGuire
Stillwater, Minnesota

1-2: Winston House

Architect: Don Metz
Lyme, New Hampshire

other types of construction. The aesthetic opportunities will be an exciting area for designers, owners, and observers to explore as the art of earth shelter design matures.

The opportunities to create an aesthetically successful earth sheltered house are limited only by the skill of the designer and, in some cases, the potential of the individual site. Although appropriate designs can be developed for almost any site, sites that have varied landforms and a substantial growth of native plant materials may offer the most dynamic design opportunities for earth sheltered building.

Land-Use Benefits

A number of potential land-use benefits are associated with earth sheltered buildings. With regard to land use, perhaps the most important characteristic of earth sheltered construction is its ideal suitability to sloping sites. Some sites that might be considered unbuildable using conventional construction—because they slope too much or because they are too high or too low in relationship to the street—may be well suited for earth sheltering. Generally, the steeper the slope, the more densely it can be developed with earth sheltered construction, whereas the inverse is usually true with conventional construction. It is possible to build earth sheltered housing on slopes up to 50 percent, provided that the soils are appropriate.

In densely developed surburban or urban environments, earth sheltering can make the difference between having little or no "greenspace" and having a significant planted area. As the density increases, the importance of having such a greenspace

also increases: even a very small planted area is highly valued in a densely developed neighborhood. A coordinated development of multiple earth sheltered units offers the opportunity to combine these rooftop spaces into a network of natural amenities.

Earth sheltering can be of value in preserving open space even apart from consideration of the natural, living environment. Cities usually contain densely developed areas where more development is contemplated. Underground construction makes it possible to use this valuable land without further reducing already limited open space. In certain situations a greater area of a particular parcel of land can be used by subsurface rather than conventional construction, because some earth sheltered areas are usable both as interior space (areas below the roof of the structure) and exterior greenspace. A valuable site can be carefully designed to house more people while simultaneously providing adequate privacy and landscaped outdoor areas.

Another land-use benefit of earth sheltered construction is the potential development and enhancement of urban sites that are normally considered undesirable. Some land in the urban environment is convenient to services and employment but is not considered suitable for residential or other types of development because it has no natural features (for example, vegetation) or because it is adjacent to incompatible uses such as airports, freeways, railways, or industry. Earth sheltered structures can be used on such sites because they can be designed to reduce the effects of outside noises and views, as well as to enhance and restore vegetation to barren sites.

The potential for taking advantage of these various land-use benefits depends on a number of factors. Efficient land use generally is most beneficial in more densely populated areas. Sloping sites or sites that are considered unusable because of excessive noise nearby are the best examples of the land-use advantages associated with earth sheltering. If one of the reasons for building earth sheltered structures is to increase open space or densities by using the rooftop areas of the structures, the project must be designed to achieve this goal. For example, earth-covered roofs usually must be flat and accessible; otherwise, their impact will be only visual.

Environmental Benefits

Some home owners and designers see earth sheltering as a means of preserving the environment. Techniques for accomplishing this goal range from recessing some of the walls into a hillside, so that the volume of the house has less visual impact, to covering the entire roof with plant material growing out of the earth, thereby using carbon dioxide and generating oxygen, absorbing rainwater (rather than draining it off), and providing a habitat for plants and animals. If the total impact on the environment and use of resources is a concern, then these benefits must be weighed against the energy and resources expended in the manufacture, transportation, and installation of the additional building materials required for earth sheltered construction.

A rural area may provide great incentive to preserve a functioning ecosystem, since one of the primary reasons for living in a rural area is to be in close proximity to the natural environment. Whatever can be done to reduce the impact of human habitation on that environment is usually perceived as desirable. In a more urban setting, earth sheltered buildings may offer an opportunity to restore plant and animal life, thus improving the air and water quality. These environmental benefits, which relate directly to the aesthetic and land-use benefits discussed above, are difficult to quantify.

Acoustical Isolation

Another benefit of earth sheltered buildings is the dampening effect of the weight of the structure and the earth on noise and vibration. The ability of the structure to reduce outside noises depends on the amount of earth mass surrounding and covering the house. In an earth sheltered house that has large window and exposed wall areas, acoustical isolation will be minimized. Protection from a specific noise source, such as a busy freeway, can, however, be achieved by placing earth berms adjacent to the freeway and opening the windows and doors of the housing away from it. Protection from outside noises is most useful in dense urban settings, particularly on sites adjacent to freeways, railways, airports, or other localized noise sources. An example of an actual project using earth for noise protection on a site adjacent to a busy freeway is a twelve-unit town house project in Minneapolis, Minnesota, shown in the adjacent photograph (fig. 1-3). As noted above, this ability to use these otherwise undesirable sites also results in more efficient land use than is possible with conventional structures.

1-3: Seward Town Houses

Architect: Mike Dunn, Close Associates
Minneapolis, Minnesota
Photograph: Jerry Mathiason

Reduced Maintenance

One often cited advantage of earth sheltered houses is reduced maintenance in comparison to conventional wood-frame houses. This assumption is based on the durability of concrete structures and the protection of much of the exterior surface by the earth mass. Materials buried beneath the earth are not exposed to cycles of freezing and thawing, the intense heat and ultraviolet radiation of the sun, or other severe effects of the local climate.

Reduced maintenance is very dependent on the detailed design of the building. For example, waterproofing, insulation, and other buried elements of the house must be properly installed and of long-lasting, high-quality materials in order to be considered truly low maintenance. Similarly, unless the exposed elements of the house (for example, siding and window frames) have low-maintenance characteristics, the house will differ only slightly from a conventional house in terms of maintenance required.

Fire Protection

Fires can start anywhere. Careless smokers, children, inattentive cooks, and improper use of flammable materials cannot be designed out of any house. The increased use of wood-burning stoves has also brought about an increase in fires, which are usually caused by improper installation and use of the stoves. In an earth sheltered house built of concrete, masonry, or heavy timber, the spread of a fire may be limited and structural damage minimized. It is important to realize, however, that even the furnishings in a room can generate enough smoke for a

fatal fire, without any involvement of the structure. Fires can also be caused by lightning; and some homes, particularly in parts of California and in wilderness areas, are destroyed by brush or forest fires. It may be difficult to get assistance in time to save a conventional home located in a remote area, either because of the distance from help or because the fire may cover an extensive area. Earth sheltering a house greatly reduces its exposure to lightning, sparks, and flying brands, and makes the wetting down of the exposed part of the structure a much more manageable operation than it is for a conventional house.

In comparison to a conventional house, the structure of an earth sheltered house is likely to be less damaged in a fire; however, the furnishings will be equally vulnerable. Because the interior of the house can easily fill up with smoke, proper design of fire exits according to building codes is essential for safety. Although fire protection benefits are important in all structures regardless of location, they may be most critical in rural areas where fire department response is slow or in areas that are constantly exposed to brush or forest fires.

Protection from Earthquakes

The heavier and stronger structural systems of earth sheltered buildings can also offer protection from the damaging forces of earthquakes. Heavily reinforced walls placed in the earth are generally less likely to be destroyed by these violent lateral forces than are surface structures, which are shaken by their foundation. Although some cracking may occur, the walls and roof can usually be protected

from failure by proper engineering. The mass of an earth-covered roof can be a disadvantage, however. Roofs must be well anchored to the walls so that the earthquake forces do not cause a disastrous collapse of the heavy roof. Earthquakes can also cause soil on steeper hillsides to slide. Although earth sheltered structures built into steep slopes may help provide normal slope stability, they may be vulnerable to sliding caused by soil liquefaction or movement under earthquake conditions. Nevertheless, earth sheltered construction offers some potential for mitigating structural damage from earthquakes, provided these potentially damaging effects are considered in site selection and design.

Protection from Nuclear Attack and Fallout

Just as it provides protection from earthquake forces, the heavier, stronger structure of an earth sheltered building can also protect it from damage from nearby explosions. Moreover, in the case of a nuclear blast, earth berms can offer greater protection from radiation, and the lowered levels of infiltration in an earth sheltered house could reduce the effects of fallout. Of course, because exposed walls and windows in an earth sheltered house behave no differently from those in a conventional structure, the house must be properly designed in order to provide effective protection. A totally enclosed, windowless space within the house surrounded by massive walls that is designed to serve as a place of refuge could provide this protection. The overall design of the house could also help minimize the effects of a nuclear blast. For example, a house that has earth berms on four sides and windows facing a central atrium would provide more protection than a house that has extensive areas of exposed glass (see fig. 1-4).

Storm and Tornado Protection

Earth sheltering tends to reduce storm damage significantly, because less of the exterior of the structure is exposed to hail and wind and the structure is designed to support heavier loads than is a conventional house. A large section of a tree that would crash through a wood-frame wall or conventional roof might have no effect on a structure designed to resist the massive weight of the earth, especially if there is a thick layer of dirt on the roof to absorb and distribute the impact. Hail can do little damage to a roof and walls covered with vegetation.

Probably the most awesome storm is the tornado. A study of residential structural failures caused by tornadoes in conventional wood-frame houses during 1969 and 1970 examined roof failures, in which the decking and rafters detached, leaving the bottom cord and ceiling in place; wall-to-roof connection failures, in which the entire roof and ceiling assembly detached from the walls; and foundation failures, in which the house was pulled from the foundation. The study found that in many instances these connections had depended largely on gravity and were not constructed even to the extent required by the codes, so that the structural features were unable to resist uplifting forces. It appears that stronger connections would greatly assist conventional houses in resisting the forces of a tornado. These

1-4: Bordie Residence

Architect: Coffee and Crier
Austin, Texas

types of stronger connections are intrinsic in earth-bermed and earth-covered homes, where they are necessary to help the structure resist the lateral forces of the earth against the walls. Normally, a roof heavy enough to resist the wind forces likely to be encountered during a tornado can be designed. For a conventional roof, a steep pitch, minimal overhangs, proper venting, and appendages such as dormers and gables all assist somewhat in withstanding wind damage.

Generally, the most effective strategies for resisting winds are below-grade construction, minimal glazing, strong connections of exterior walls to floor and roof, short-span refuge compartments, and interior partitions that are securely fastened to the structure above. All of these

conditions are usually met in earth sheltered houses, except for minimal glazing, since a passive solar design incorporates significant glazing on the south side. A large amount of glazing facing in the direction of an approaching storm would be the greatest hazard because wind-driven debris shatters glass and thus figures as one of the most frequent causes of injury and damage. On the other hand, an atrium-type design as shown in figure 1-4, with all windows facing a protected courtyard, would present less of a problem. A study of houses struck by a tornado that approached from the southwest found that hallways that had a window on the south or west end were particularly hazardous, as they acted as a wind tunnel after the window was blown out. Small, windowless, below-grade rooms on the north side of the house were the ideal refuge [1.2]. Most earth sheltered houses have a bathroom, storage area, utility room, or closet that meets these criteria. It appears that at least some portion of an earth sheltered house should provide excellent protection for the inhabitants, while the house itself should suffer much less damage than a conventional wood-frame structure if a tornado occurs. The regional importance of tornado protection offered by earth sheltered structures is discussed in more detail in chapter 2.

Increased Security

For some people the psychological feeling of security is as important as any actual physical protection. Because earth sheltered structures often have fewer windows, doors, and walls exposed to the outside, as well as more limited, controlled points of access, they are frequently perceived as being more secure than a conventional above-grade house. It is generally assumed that the durable construction materials, less visible structure, and perhaps, the less familiar type of layout and means of entry and exit will contribute to fewer attempts at break-ins or vandalism. It should be noted, however, that these same qualities of limited entry and less visibility may also make a house an attractive target for a break-in because burglars may remain undetected if they use secluded points of entry, such as a private courtyard. A successful design that provides increased security depends on the specific house and site design, as well as on the relationship of the house to neighboring structures and spaces.

Costs

One reason that many people are attracted to the concept of earth sheltered housing is that the life-cycle cost (initial cost plus operating expenses) will be lower for an earth sheltered structure than for a conventional building. Based on the first few examples of earth sheltered housing that have been built, initial construction costs for these houses appear to be higher than for conventional wood-frame housing. Specific cost comparisons are difficult to make, however, because the costs of both earth sheltered and conventional houses not only cover a broad range, but also differ substantially in different regions of the nation. One of the most frequently quoted generalizations is that earth sheltered houses cost about 10 percent more than a custom-designed and -built conventional house. Budgets for several recent projects in the Minnesota area seem to confirm this estimate. It should be noted, however, that some earth sheltered homes have cost the same as, or even less than, conventional houses.

Operating costs, which include energy for heating, cooling, and maintenance, are lower for a properly designed earth sheltered house than for a conventional house. Chapter 3 deals with the rather complex evaluation of all the economic factors that are involved in comparing costs of earth sheltered and conventional houses.

Energy Conservation

Anticipation of substantial energy savings for heating and cooling is the primary factor responsible for the great recent interest in earth sheltered housing. The potential for such savings is based on several physical characteristics of these structures, which are substantially set into and often covered by earth. The first of these characteristics is the reduction of heat loss or heat gain caused by transmission of heat through the building envelope. The amount of heat conducted through the envelope of the structure is a function of the thermal transmission coefficient, or U-value, and the temperature difference between the inside and outside of the wall. Although the thermal resistivity of earth is lower than that of typical insulation products, enough earth frequently can be added to the walls of the structure to achieve R-values equal to or greater than those typically associated with common insulation materials. On the roof, however, the relatively thin layer of earth that it is economically feasible to support does not have a substantial resistance to conduction and additional insulation is normally required.

In an aboveground structure, the temperature differential is completely dependent on the outside temperature. Because the daily and seasonal temperature fluctuations on the surface are never completely felt below grade, however, the transmission loss for an earth sheltered structure is reduced. In addition to the dampening effect of the soil on temperature, energy performance is improved by a "thermal lag" effect, which increases as the soil depth increases. The thermal lag effect results from the soil temperature lagging behind the surface temperature: because the soil in effect carries some coolness from winter into summer and some stored heat from summer into winter, cooling and heating needs for the house are reduced at the beginning of those respective seasons.

Another important characteristic of earth sheltered structures is the reduced heat loss resulting from infiltration. A conventional above-grade house loses a significant portion of its heat through cracks in the structure, particularly those around windows and doors. This heat loss is accelerated when the wind blows. With proper siting, the earth can provide protection from wind and considerably reduce the general infiltration. Infiltration also increases the summertime cooling load, by permitting both heat and humidity to enter the structure.

A final characteristic of earth sheltered housing is the thermal mass of the structure and the surrounding earth—that is, the heat storage capacity of a building. A house with a larger thermal mass, especially one with a concrete shell, can absorb heat from the air or from direct solar insolation. At night, when a net heat loss occurs, this heat is radiated back into the space. This process can be slow enough in a structure that has a large mass to supply adequate heat to the house for several hours. A conventional house, on the other hand, can store very little excess heat gain and loses whatever heat it has relatively rapidly if a heat source is interrupted.

An advantage accruing to earth sheltered houses from their high thermal mass is their ability to maintain a steady or slowly dropping temperature when power outages or shortages occur. This characteristic can prevent damage to plumbing in freezing weather, as well as impart a sense of security and independence to the occupants. The thermal mass of earth sheltered housing can also be well integrated with other energy systems that provide heat on a fluctuating basis; it is

particularly compatible with passive solar collection, wood-burning fireplaces, and use of nonpeak electrical heat. The slow temperature change provides a consistency of comfort uncommon in conventionally heated houses, which have hot and cold areas governed by thermostat control cycles.

The effects of these physical characteristics can be simply stated. Given proper design, earth sheltered housing can result in very low energy consumption and high comfort levels during both heating and cooling cycles. Additional information on the impact of energy conservation on the form of the building is included in chapter 4; chapter 8 provides a more detailed discussion of energy use and insulation placement.

Selecting Appropriate Energy Conservation Strategies

Although people build earth sheltered houses for a wide variety of reasons, energy conservation remains the most widely publicized and important reason for many people. It is also, however, a complex and confusing issue, partially because an understanding of how best to analyze and achieve energy conservation underground is still evolving. If energy conservation is the major or only reason for deciding to build a house into the earth, it is particularly important for the designer/builder to be aware that energy use is affected by a number of factors and that earth sheltered houses can vary greatly in terms of energy-efficient design and in energy consumption. Contact with the earth must be regarded as one of a group of energy-conserving strategies that

include proper orientation and site planning, as well as optimal window and insulation placement.

It is also important to remember that an earth sheltered design is not always the only or best choice for achieving energy conservation. Sometimes the site conditions or climate will make it more economically feasible to select another of the energy-efficient housing alternatives such as passive or active solar, superinsulated, or double-envelope houses. In reality, the earth sheltered concept is not totally separate from these other strategies but is often combined with them. The following brief description of these other housing types is included in order to clarify the nature of these alternatives, which may be either integrated with or used in place of earth sheltered housing under appropriate conditions.

active solar systems

For many people the first thing that comes to mind when energy-efficient housing is mentioned is adding active solar panels to a house. This association is natural because the concept is readily understandable, the panels can be added without changing the other parameters of a proposed or existing house, and the idea of active solar is compatible with the approach developed over the past thirty years: simply adding mechanical devices to heat or cool a building. But, despite many advances in selective absorbent coatings, high-transmission glazing, and microprocessor controls and despite many highly successful installations, the energy conservation movement has not resulted in as much activity in active solar as was once anticipated.

Like most other beneficial things, active solar systems have their drawbacks. One drawback is expense. Active systems require solar panels, a storage medium, a means of getting the heat into storage, a means of reclaiming the heat, and a system for connecting and controlling all of these components. Elements of an active solar system are all likely to be extra features that serve no other purpose and would not otherwise be in the structure. This means that all the money spent on the system is additional capital expenditure (beyond the cost of the house itself). Many of the components incorporate relatively expensive metal, glass, and mechanical equipment.

passive solar houses

Because passive solar features are more easily integrated with the structure, passive solar is more likely to be seen not as an alternative to other energy conservation strategies, but rather as an amplification and enhancement of other measures. When other energy-conserving strategies are being considered, difficulties in making decisions about which strategy to use may arise because the limited number of construction dollars usually available will pay for only one type of strategy. Such decision-making problems are less likely to occur when earth sheltering and passive solar features are incorporated into the design, because a single, mostly glazed exposure and a structure having substantial mass are basic to both strategies. Thus, if site conditions, house orientation, and the owner's tastes permit it, many of the same elements can be used for both energy-conserving measures at little or no additional cost.

double-envelope houses

A double-envelope house may be considered to be a passively heated home that incorporates convection circulation between the inner and outer skin. Studies have indicated that the convection should be augmented by a fan. The main question with regard to this strategy, however, is whether the extra cost of a double skin is justified by the benefits gained, or whether fans could circulate the air through other paths less expensively while the insulation advantage of the double wall could be matched by a well-insulated earth-covered or single wall. The answer to this question will vary with the efficiency of the design in achieving the second envelope, as well as with the suitability of the site for other strategies such as earth sheltering.

superinsulated houses

A superinsulated house is based on a different principle. Instead of gaining heat from the environment, it is cut off from the environment as much as possible in order to contain the heat that is generated within the house. Superinsulated houses can be built anywhere that a house normally can be built, without unusual concerns about subsoil conditions or solar access. Periods of cloudy weather have little effect on the energy performance of such houses. Superinsulated houses can be made to look very conventional, although they may have less window area than many people are accustomed to. Much of the technology is the same as that applied in constructing conventional houses; the major difference is that more insulation is used. Great care is usually taken to insulate everywhere, prevent heat wicks, and close every hole and crack against infiltration.

Superinsulated homes also have some potential disadvantages. For example, some superinsulated designs may become aesthetically confining, separating the inhabitants from the light, space, view, and stimulation of their environment, as well as from its temperature variations. A hidden cost of both double-envelope and superinsulated houses is the floor space consumed by the added thickness of the walls. Three inches of extra wall thickness on a 24-foot by 48-foot house would consume 48 square feet—about the size of a typical full bathroom. Another drawback to superinsulated, as well as earth sheltered, houses is that a house can be sealed too tightly. When this occurs, adequate fresh air cannot enter unless measures are taken to introduce the air in a controlled manner. People, pets, combustion from cooking and heating, and even products emitted from objects used to build and furnish homes all contribute to indoor air pollution, which builds up if not exhausted and replaced with fresh air. Heat exchangers have now been developed to exhaust the stale air while using the heat from it to temper the incoming cold air. Indoor air purity is discussed more thoroughly in chapter 8.

Each of these energy conservation strategies is appropriate in certain situations and each has some application in conjunction with earth sheltered homes. It is important not to approach design with the attitude that any one idea will produce the only "right" solution, but rather to evaluate the merits and drawbacks of each in light of the particular situation. Only by doing so will the designer achieve an integrated solution, in which each component is in harmony with the others from both a functional and an aesthetic standpoint.

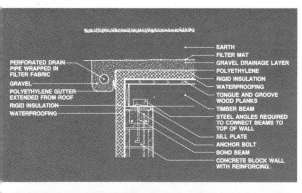

EARTH
FILTER MAT
GRAVEL DRAINAGE LAYER
POLYETHYLENE
RIGID INSULATION
WATERPROOFING
TONGUE AND GROOVE
WOOD PLANKS
TIMBER BEAM
STEEL ANGLES REQUIRED
TO CONNECT BEAMS TO
TOP OF WALL
SILL PLATE
ANCHOR BOLT
BOND BEAM
CONCRETE BLOCK WALL
WITH REINFORCING.

PERFORATED DRAIN
PIPE WRAPPED IN
FILTER FABRIC
GRAVEL
POLYETHYLENE GUTTER
EXTENDED FROM ROOF
RIGID INSULATION
WATERPROOFING

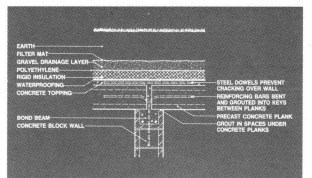

EARTH
FILTER MAT
GRAVEL DRAINAGE LAYER
POLYETHYLENE
RIGID INSULATION
WATERPROOFING
CONCRETE TOPPING

BOND BEAM
CONCRETE BLOCK WALL

STEEL DOWELS PREVENT
CRACKING OVER WALL
REINFORCING BARS BENT
AND GROUTED INTO KEYS
BETWEEN PLANKS
PRECAST CONCRETE PLANK
GROUT IN SPACES UNDER
CONCRETE PLANKS

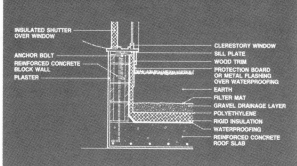

INSULATED SHUTTER
OVER WINDOW

ANCHOR BOLT
REINFORCED CONCRETE
BLOCK WALL
PLASTER

CLERESTORY WINDOW
SILL PLATE
WOOD TRIM
PROTECTION BOARD
OR METAL FLASHING
OVER WATERPROOFING
EARTH
FILTER MAT
GRAVEL DRAINAGE LAYER
POLYETHYLENE
RIGID INSULATION
WATERPROOFING
REINFORCED CONCRETE
ROOF SLAB

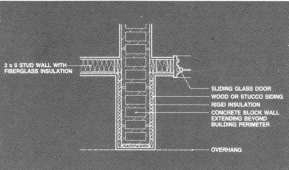

2 x 6 STUD WALL WITH
FIBERGLASS INSULATION

SLIDING GLASS DOOR
WOOD OR STUCCO SIDING
RIGID INSULATION
CONCRETE BLOCK WALL
EXTENDING BEYOND
BUILDING PERIMETER

OVERHANG

CHAPTER 2

REGIONAL SUITABILITY

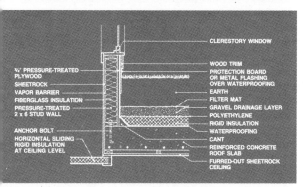

CLERESTORY WINDOW
WOOD TRIM
PROTECTION BOARD
OR METAL FLASHING
OVER WATERPROOFING
EARTH
FILTER MAT
GRAVEL DRAINAGE LAYER
POLYETHYLENE
RIGID INSULATION
WATERPROOFING
CANT
REINFORCED CONCRETE
ROOF SLAB
FURRED-OUT SHEETROCK
CEILING

¾" PRESSURE-TREATED
PLYWOOD
SHEETROCK
VAPOR BARRIER
FIBERGLASS INSULATION
PRESSURE-TREATED
2 x 6 STUD WALL

ANCHOR BOLT
HORIZONTAL SLIDING
RIGID INSULATION
AT CEILING LEVEL

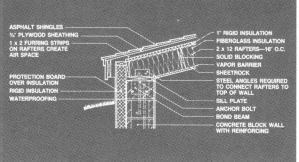

ASPHALT SHINGLES
¾" PLYWOOD SHEATHING
1 x 2 FURRING STRIPS
ON RAFTERS CREATE
AIR SPACE

PROTECTION BOARD
OVER INSULATION
RIGID INSULATION
WATERPROOFING

1" RIGID INSULATION
FIBERGLASS INSULATION
2 x 12 RAFTERS—16" O.C.
SOLID BLOCKING
VAPOR BARRIER
SHEETROCK
STEEL ANGLES REQUIRED
TO CONNECT RAFTERS TO
TOP OF WALL
SILL PLATE
ANCHOR BOLT
BOND BEAM
CONCRETE BLOCK WALL
WITH REINFORCING

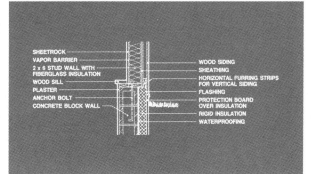

SHEETROCK
VAPOR BARRIER
2 x 6 STUD WALL WITH
FIBERGLASS INSULATION
WOOD SILL
PLASTER
ANCHOR BOLT
CONCRETE BLOCK WALL

WOOD SIDING
SHEATHING
HORIZONTAL FURRING STRIPS
FOR VERTICAL SIDING
FLASHING
PROTECTION BOARD
OVER INSULATION
RIGID INSULATION
WATERPROOFING

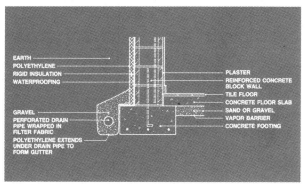

EARTH
POLYETHYLENE
RIGID INSULATION
WATERPROOFING

PLASTER
REINFORCED CONCRETE
BLOCK WALL
TILE FLOOR
CONCRETE FLOOR SLAB
SAND OR GRAVEL
VAPOR BARRIER
CONCRETE FOOTING

GRAVEL
PERFORATED DRAIN
PIPE WRAPPED IN
FILTER FABRIC
POLYETHYLENE EXTENDS
UNDER DRAIN PIPE TO
FORM GUTTER

Introduction

The previous chapter clearly demonstrates that earth sheltered houses are built for a wide variety of reasons. These can be classified into two basic categories, the first of which includes reasons that are almost universally applicable—aesthetics or lower maintenance, for instance. The advantages associated with these reasons are available in any location under almost any circumstances, provided that the house is properly designed to enhance or optimize the appropriate features. Other reasons for earth sheltering, such as energy conservation or tornado protection, are not universally applicable. For example, in the case of energy use, the effects of earth sheltering on energy performance can vary considerably, depending on the local climate.

Although the potential benefits of earth sheltered buildings can be examined with respect to a particular characteristic, such as cooling performance, it is not appropriate to generalize—for example, by indicating that earth sheltered buildings are definitely suitable in one area of the country and not another. Such a statement would be overly simplistic because there are simply too many design variations, as well as varying combinations of reasons for building these structures. General assessments of suitability must remain basically an individual decision based on the perceived importance of the many variables, together with the particular requirements of site and program. The purpose of this chapter is to assist in this decision-making process by examining the characteristics of earth sheltered housing that can be scientifically quantified and discussed in a regional context. These characteristics are the climatic variations that affect energy use for heating and cooling and the occurrence of tornadoes and earthquakes. By examining these effects, it is possible to indicate in which regions the most benefits can be derived from building an earth sheltered house. With regard to climate, some general indications of the most useful design strategies, as well as the greatest potential problems in a particular region, are provided. These regional variations and various nonclimatic reasons for building earth sheltered houses are combined in a chart (fig. 2-11) at the end of the chapter that summarizes the regional suitability for earth sheltered houses.

Energy Conservation: Climatic Variations

Climate is the most significant factor in determining the regional suitability of earth sheltered structures; it determines the magnitude and the type of potential energy-conserving benefits that can generally be associated with earth sheltered structures in a given region. This section, which evaluates climate information for sixteen regions of the United States in terms of its impact on earth sheltered buildings, is followed by a summary of this information and other suitability factors.

When energy conservation is the primary motivation for considering an earth sheltered house, it is important to remember that earth sheltered housing is neither the only nor always the best way to conserve energy. Therefore, it is useful to consider its performance relative to other alternative types of buildings such as aboveground superinsulated and active and passive solar houses. At the same time, it is also important to understand that earth sheltered housing is not a single type of housing characterized by a rigid set of specific features. For example, the amount and configuration of earth cover can vary significantly. Furthermore, earth sheltered houses nearly always include a combination of energy-efficient strategies—passive solar features in particular, but also active solar and superinsulation. These other strategies are discussed further in chapter 4.

The term *climate* encompasses a wide range of effects that can all directly or indirectly affect human comfort and thus, energy use in buildings. The main heat transfer mechanisms that determine climate and our response to it are air temperature, radiation, moisture and humidity, heat conduction, and convection. These factors are all interrelated in determining local climate.

Solar radiation is the primary force behind all climatic effects. Radiation from the sun strikes the ground surface and warms the ground, which then heats the air around it by conduction. The warm air rises by convection, thereby cooling and eventually condensing the water vapor contained in the air into clouds and/or rain. Because clouds can block much of the sun's radiation from reaching the ground surface, the climate can be altered significantly when cloud cover is prevalent. Rainfall or the presence of water increases evaporation rates, which in turn causes evaporative cooling. But the more humid the air already is, the less the ability of the air to absorb water and, hence, to provide additional cooling. Differences in topography and relationships between land and oceans also affect these interrelationships of the various climatic factors and can cause large variations in climate for regions at the same latitude.

On a smaller scale, the same factors affect human comfort in the everyday environment. Direct radiant heat to the body can compensate for a lower air temperature; conversely, a cool nearby surface can provide comfort when air temperatures are high. Ventilation provides a mechanism for the air to carry additional heat away from the body by convection. Although ventilation is beneficial for cooling, it must be kept to a minimum for comfort in winter. In dry climates the body can lose a significant amount of heat by evaporation, but the potential for evaporative cooling is reduced when humidity is high. Other local sources of evaporation, such as fountains and vegetation, can also provide relief from the heat [2.1].

Conduction of heat through a material under normal climatic conditions is dependent not only on the conductivity of the material but also on its specific heat. A material that has a higher specific heat will absorb more heat when the temperature rises than will a material that has a lower specific heat. Thus, a material that has a high specific heat will cause a delay in the transfer of temperature variations from one side of the material to the other because the material stores some of the heat energy that would otherwise be transmitted through it. This property is most valuable in maintaining relatively even temperatures when climate conditions change rapidly.

Climate Regions in the United States

Research by the American Institute of Architects (AIA) Research Corporation in conjunction with the National Climatic Center of the National Oceanic and Atmospheric Administration (NOAA) has resulted in the identification of sixteen general climate regions in the United States (see fig. 2-1), based on heating and cooling needs, solar usefulness in a 50° to 65°F range, wind usefulness in a 75° to 85°F range, diurnal temperature impact, and low humidity impact for natural heating and cooling of homes [2.2, 2.3, 2.4]. In the remainder of this chapter, data are provided for one city in each region, in order to indicate the scope of the climatic factors in that area. It should be noted that because many of the figures are averages, they may not fully delineate all the trends and variations associated with that particular location. In addition, it must be emphasized that because no region has climates that are completely uniform or bounded by a straight black line, there are climate variations within a region, and the climate of some border areas may be more similar to that of an adjacent region than to the climate of the city listed for their assigned regions. Information on the climatic data for most major American cities can be obtained from the National Oceanic and Atmospheric Administration, National Climatic Center, Asheville, NC 28801 [2.5, 2.6].

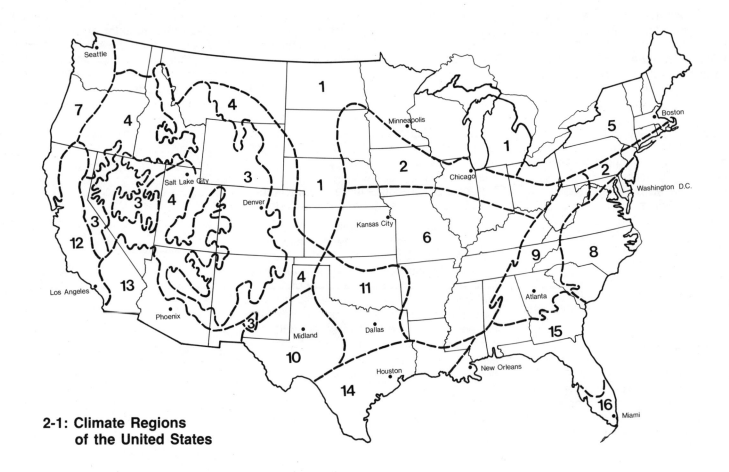

2-1: Climate Regions of the United States

The climatic data for the cities within the sixteen regions are presented in four tables, two related to heating loads (figs. 2-3 and 2-4) and two to cooling loads (figs. 2-5 and 2-6). The temperatures recorded in the heating tables are spread over a 102°F range, from the minimum comfort temperature of 68°F to the lowest recorded temperatures for these cities (–34°F). The cooling tables cover a much narrower temperature range, from the maximum comfort temperature of 78°F to a record high of 118°F.

Human Comfort

The building bioclimatic chart shown in figure 2-2—which is developed from the standard psychrometric chart—helps illustrate the variables involved in heating and cooling to achieve human comfort. The horizontal axis represents dry bulb temperature; the vertical axis represents pounds of water per pound of dry air. Lines of humidity curve down from upper right to lower left. The top curve is the dew point or saturation temperature at which condensation occurs. The area on the left side of the chart is too cool for comfort, the area on the right side is too warm, and the comfort zone is in the middle. In the areas shown on the chart (with the exception of a small area below the comfort zone, which represents the condition of adequate temperature but inadequate moisture), the only way of achieving comfort under the "too cool" condition is to add some form of heat. Within the areas shown as too warm for comfort, however, are some areas that can be made comfortable by use of dehumidification, ventilation, radiation, evaporative cooling, combinations of these strategies, and finally, removal of some of the heat by mechanical means.

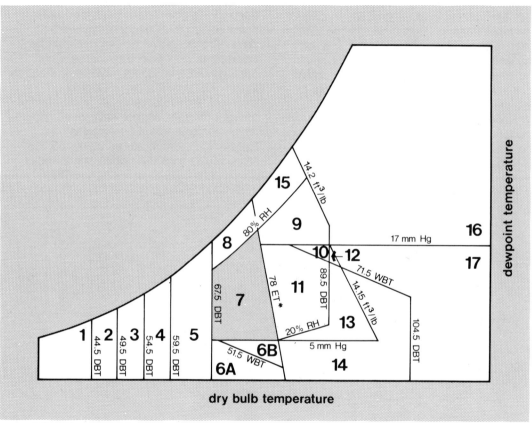

2-2: Bioclimatic Chart

Chart based on work by Baruch Givoni
See *Man, Climate and Architecture* (2.7).

Heating Season Data

The first heating table (fig. 2-3) is based on annual figures representing the total heating degree days over the year, using a 68°F base temperature. The cities are ranked on the basis of this figure, starting with the coldest climate (the city that has the most heating degree days). The annual heating degree day figure is the sum of the amount that the temperature is below the base temperature (68°F in this case) for each day of the year. For example, a day when the average temperature is 46°F would contribute 22 (68 minus 46) to the total of annual degree days. Because the heating degree day figure is based on averages, the effects of temperature extremes are muted; however, the table lists the record low temperature for each city in order to indicate the maximum temperature severity. The percentage of hours that the temperature is below 68°F—times when some source of heat from either an active or passive source is needed—is also listed. Each percentage point equals 87.6 hours, or about 3.65 days. These figures do not necessarily coincide in rank with the degree days because an area could have temperatures in the 50s and 60s (which would be included in this percentage) a substantial amount of time, yet not have many degree days. For example, Los Angeles experiences temperatures below 68°F more of the time than does Minneapolis.

These percentage figures are useful for each region when they are compared with the amount of time that cooling is required and the amount of time that the area has temperatures in the comfort zone. The percentage of hours below 50°F and the mean number of days when the maximum temperature is less than 32°F help give a more complete picture of the scope of the heating requirements. The final column in the chart shows the percentage of time the area is in the comfort zone, that is, periods when the climate is not too warm, too cold, too damp, or too dry.

The second heating table (fig. 2-4) provides data on the month of January, which is ordinarily the peak heating month. The regions are ranked in the same order

City	Region	degree days 68°F base	% hours less than 68°F	% hours less than 50°F	number of days with high temp. less than 32°F	record low temp. (°F)	% possible sun annual basis	% hours in comfort zone
Minneapolis	1	8159	79.4	53	84	-34	58	10.7
Chicago	2	6127	73.7	48	45	-23	57	12.5
Denver	3	6016	79.1	49	21	-30	70	9.3
Salt Lake City	4	5983	75.5	50	24	-30	70	11.0
Boston	5	5621	79.6	47	27	-18	60	10.8
Kansas City	6	5357	64.2	40	28	-22	67	13.6
Seattle	7	5185	92.7	52	3	0	49	6.0
Washington	8	4211	66.4	37	9	1	58	12.4
Atlanta	9	3095	59.3	26	3	-9	61	12.5
Midland	10	2621	53.4	25	2	-11	—	16.9
Dallas	11	2382	48.8	21	3	-8	68	12.7
Los Angeles	12	1819	80.3	7	5	23	73	15.2
Phoenix	13	1552	44.7	15	0	16	86	12.9
Houston	14	1434	39.0	7	1	5	57	6.6
New Orleans	15	465	41.6	11	0	7	59	9.3
Miami	16	206	15.7	1	0	26	67	18.1

Data and analysis on charts in figures 2-3 through 2-6 is taken from *Climatic Design for Home Building* by Donald Watson and Kenneth Labs [2.5] and *Regional Analysis of Ground and Above Ground Climate* by Kenneth Labs [2.6]. The number of years in the data base available is not uniform between cities. The data base was compiled in 1980.

2-3: Annual Climate Data for Heating

as they were in figure 2-3; the table indicates the average daily temperature for January, as well as average highs and lows. The difference between the high and low temperatures is also indicated, because one of the ways earth sheltering helps conserve energy is by storing the heat available from the higher temperature, which in turn moderates the lower temperature. This process tends to bring both high and low temperature extremes nearer to a constant median temperature. The magnitude of this temperature differential does not appear to be related to the coldness of the climate.

Figure 2-4 also presents information on ground temperatures near the surface and deeper in the soil, where an earth-covered home would probably be built. It should be noted that these figures are intended only to indicate trends and should not be considered absolute values. They represent undisturbed ground temperatures, expressed as averages over different depth ranges; these figures have been estimated by computer modeling. Ground temperature will vary with the amount of moisture in the soil and type of ground cover. The placement of an earth sheltered house changes the temperature conditions of a previously undisturbed site: the house tends to raise the temperature of the site over a period of time as the heat from the house warms the earth around it.

Even though the presence of such a structure may change the ground temperature figures given in figure 2-4, the temperatures listed are useful in illustrating how the earth dampens the effects of the climate extremes and usually provides an environment that will tend to moderate the air temperature toward comfort. For example, even before a building would have time to warm the soil around it, the relatively cold soil temperature in Minneapolis would still be almost 39°F warmer than the average daily low temperature in January. The temperature differential between the average low temperatures and the undisturbed ground temperature at 2- to 12-foot depths is an indication of how much benefit can be gained by covering a building with earth instead of exposing it to the air.

City	Region	average temp. (°F)	average high (°F)	average low (°F)	average high minus low (°F)	ground temp. A 0-6 feet (°F)	ground temp. B 2-12 feet (°F)	ground temp. B minus average low	average daily solar radiation (BTU/sf) vertical, south-facing	average daily solar radiation (BTU/sf) horizontal surface	% possible sun	% relative humidity midnight	% relative humidity midday	mean wind speed	wind direction
Minneapolis	1	12.2	21.2	3.2	18.0	33	42	38.8	921	464	51	76	66	10.4	N.W.
Chicago	2	24.3	31.5	17.0	14.5	38	46	29.0	921	507	44	71	65	11.5	W
Denver	3	29.9	43.5	16.2	27.3	42	50	33.8	1440	840	72	63	45	9.1	S
Salt Lake City	4	28.0	37.4	18.5	18.9	41	50	31.5	1129	639	48	77	69	7.7	SSE
Boston	5	29.2	35.9	22.5	13.4	40	47	24.5	878	475	54	66	58	14.2	N.W
Kansas City	6	27.1	35.7	18.4	17.3	42	50	31.6	1098	648	58	71	64	10.7	—
Seattle	7	38.2	43.5	33.0	10.5	44	48	15.0	559	262	21	79	74	10.1	SSW
Washington	8	35.6	43.5	27.7	15.8	43	51	23.3	959	572	49	66	54	10.0	N.W
Atlanta	9	42.4	51.4	33.4	18.0	52	59	25.6	1041	718	48	75	60	10.5	N.W
Midland	10	43.6	57.8	29.4	28.4	58	65	35.6	1496	1081	—	61	45	10.2	S
Dallas	11	44.8	55.7	33.9	21.8	58	65	31.1	1164	821	56	74	60	11.2	S
Los Angeles	12	54.5	63.5	45.4	18.1	61	66	20.6	1353	926	70	70	55	6.6	W
Phoenix	13	51.2	64.8	37.6	27.2	61	67	29.4	1472	1021	78	56	44	5.2	E
Houston	14	52.1	62.8	41.5	21.3	66	72	30.5	1014	772	42	85	66	8.3	NNW
New Orleans	15	52.9	62.3	43.5	18.8	60	66	22.5	1097	835	44	83	67	9.5	—
Miami	16	67.2	75.6	58.7	16.9	68	72	13.3	1236	1057	48	81	60	9.4	NNW

2-4: January Climate Data

Cooling Season Data

The annual cooling table (fig. 2-5) ranks the regional cities by cooling degree days. The annual cooling degree day figure is the sum of the amount that the temperature is above the base temperature (78°F in this case). Also listed for each city is the percentage of hours that are too warm for comfort. These hours are in turn broken down into those that can be made comfortable by using ventilation, those that can be made comfortable only through the use of nonpassive methods of mechanical cooling and dehumidification, and those that require nonventilating passive methods such as evaporative cooling or radiation.

The use of humidification only (area 6 on the bioclimatic chart), which is not included in any of the above figures, is usually a very minor issue. Use of dehumidification only is included under the nonpassive category, but not as part of the total cooling category. These psychrometric zones are based on the assumption that a person is inactive, lightly clad, and able to benefit from moving air. It is important to note that there are often times when more activity is necessary or when heavier clothing (such as suit and tie) may be worn, than comfort or climate would normally dictate. It is also important to consider that, while ventilation may suffice for comfort from a temperature and humidity standpoint, it may be considered impractical from the occupant's viewpoint for a number of other reasons. For example, some areas of the country are so dusty that the residents do not open windows. Other people may find open windows impractical because of the need for privacy, noise from outside, or security reasons.

Information on July climate data, shown in figure 2-6, indicates some data for peak summer conditions. The cities are marked in the same order as in the previous chart. Average July temperatures, shown in the first column, correlate well with the cooling degree day ranking, as do the undisturbed ground temperatures. The diurnal temperature differential and the temperature differential between the ground

City	Region	degree days 78°F base	% hours more than 78°F	% hours ventilation is effective	% hours requiring mechanical cooling	% hours requiring dehumidification	total % hours requiring nonpassive cooling	% hours passive cooling other than ventilation is effective	number of days with high temp. more than 90°F	record high temp. (°F)
Seattle	7	19	1.2	1.1	0.0	0.0	0.0	0.1	3	100
Los Angeles	12	28	2.0	1.5	0.0	1.4	1.4	0.4	0	110
Boston	5	127	6.0	5.3	0.2	3.5	3.7	0.3	12	104
Denver	3	145	7.1	3.1	0.0	0.0	0.0	4.0	33	105
Minneapolis	1	160	7.2	6.3	0.6	2.5	3.1	0.3	15	108
Chicago	2	241	10.0	8.5	0.4	3.9	4.3	0.7	21	105
Salt Lake City	4	276	10.2	4.5	0.0	0.0	0.0	5.7	58	107
Washington	8	322	14.2	10.9	1.5	8.0	9.5	0.5	37	103
Atlanta	9	397	17.2	14.2	0.5	12.2	12.7	1.0	22	103
Kansas City	6	496	17.9	14.1	1.2	4.6	5.8	1.9	40	113
Midland	10	731	23.7	15.2	0.1	2.4	2.5	8.6	92	109
New Orleans	15	772	33.5	19.2	1.6	28.0	29.5	0.3	68	102
Houston	14	998	40.4	22.9	0.3	31.2	31.5	0.0	88	108
Miami	16	1045	50.2	35.4	0.6	30.0	30.6	0.1	30	100
Dallas	11	1051	31.9	21.5	3.0	8.1	11.1	5.3	92	112
Phoenix	13	1554	35.7	13.6	2.1	0.7	2.8	19.8	165	118

Note: The dehumidification category includes areas 8 and 15 on the Bioclimatic Chart (fig. 2-2). Area 8 is not included in total cooling hours, since only dehumidification is required. To avoid duplication, area 15 is listed in the dehumidification column but not the cooling column of the nonpassive category. In regions where the sum of ventilating cooling, passive nonventilating cooling and nonpassive cooling exceed total cooling, the discrepancy is equal to area 8, dehumidification.

2-5: Annual Climate Data for Cooling

temperature and the average high temperature appear to be related to other factors, however. In the colder climates, the presence of heated walls all winter tends to raise the temperature of the soil above the undisturbed soil temperature shown. This phenomenon would slightly reduce any possibility of condensation. In a warmer climate such as that of Miami, the undisturbed winter soil temperature is 72°F and the summer temperature is 78°F. Since these temperatures are approximately equal to the winter and summer design temperatures, the ground temperature in these areas would probably change very little regardless of whether a house is located on the site.

This July chart also includes more extensive information on humidity than does the winter chart because of concerns about dampness and condensation in earth sheltered construction. The mean daily minimum, average, and maximum dew point temperatures for July 21 were compiled from records collected over a thirty-year period. The dew point temperature usually peaks twice each day, ordinarily three to four hours after sunrise and three to four hours after sunset. The likelihood of condensation occurring on the wall can be projected from these figures, in a general way, based on the fact that condensation will occur if the wall surface temperature is below the dew point temperature of the room. There are, however, a number of variables that will influence the actual occurrence of condensation in an individual building (for example, insulation, ventilation, and the amount of moisture added by household activities such as cooking).

In most cases, adequate insulation and/or ground warming will prevent the the wall surface temperature from falling below the dew point temperature. Although some areas need dehumidification much of the time regardless of the type of construction used, an analysis of likely wall surface temperatures will assist in determining strategies for borderline cases. Under normal circumstances wall surface temperatures of structures that have good internal air circulation and are occupied year-round will rarely be more than 4°F cooler than indoor air temperatures [2.8].

City	Region	average temp. (°F)	average high (°F)	average low (°F)	average high minus low (°F)	ground temp. A 0-6 feet (°F)	ground temp. B 2-12 feet (°F)	ground temp. B minus average high	average daily solar radiation (BTU/sf) vertical, south-facing	average daily solar radiation (BTU/sf) horizontal surface	% possible sun	July 21st minimum dew point temp. (°F)	July 21st average dew point temp. (°F)	July 21st maximum dew point temp. (°F)	% relative humidity midnight	% relative humidity midday	mean wind speed	wind direction
Seattle	7	64.5	75.1	53.8	21.3	59	54	21.1	405	2248	65	49.6	52.9	55.7	67	49	8.4	S
Los Angeles	12	68.5	74.8	62.1	12.7	74	68	6.8	993	2307	80	57.8	59.8	61.2	83	69	7.6	W
Boston	5	73.3	81.4	65.1	16.3	63	56	25.1	940	1749	66	57.0	61.7	65.4	76	56	10.9	S
Denver	3	73.0	87.4	58.6	28.8	65	56	31.4	1130	2273	71	36.9	44.5	50.5	57	36	8.5	S
Minneapolis	1	71.9	82.4	61.4	21.0	62	53	26.4	1140	1970	71	58.8	62.9	67.6	75	54	9.3	S
Chicago	2	74.7	84.4	65.0	17.4	65	56	28.4	1026	1944	70	60.2	64.9	68.8	72	55	8.4	S
Salt Lake City	4	76.7	92.8	60.5	32.3	65	56	36.8	1328	2590	84	37.5	44.8	50.5	41	26	9.4	S
Washington	8	78.7	88.2	69.1	19.1	68	60	28.2	884	1817	63	63.3	66.9	70.9	76	52	8.2	S
Atlanta	9	78.0	86.5	69.4	17.1	75	68	18.5	775	1812	62	66.1	69.1	72.1	87	63	7.4	S
Kansas City	6	77.5	88.0	68.9	19.1	69	60	28.0	1034	2102	81	64.5	67.6	70.8	73	53	8.5	
Midland	10	82.3	95.0	69.5	25.5	77	70	25.0	989	2389	—	56.8	61.0	65.4	55	41	10.8	S
New Orleans	15	81.9	90.4	73.3	17.1	78	73	17.4	728	1813	57	70.9	74.1	76.7	89	66	6.2	—
Houston	14	83.3	93.8	72.8	21.0	84	79	14.8	734	1828	67	74.0	75.8	77.3	89	58	6.5	S
Miami	16	82.3	89.1	75.5	13.6	83	78	11.1	677	1763	74	70.3	73.3	75.5	82	65	7.8	S
Dallas	11	84.8	95.5	74.0	21.5	81	74	21.5	893	2122	78	64.4	68.5	72.1	67	49	9.4	S
Phoenix	13	91.2	104.8	77.5	27.3	78	72	32.8	1059	2406	85	56.1	60.7	65.6	33	28	7.2	S

2-6: July Climate Data

Tornado Protection

Tornado protection, like energy conservation, is a potential benefit of earth sheltered housing that is clearly related to location. An understanding of some of the basic characteristics of tornadoes can provide helpful background for examining the patterns of tornado occurrence and their effects on the regional suitability of earth sheltered housing. Because the localized nature, great force, and short duration of tornadoes have made them difficult to study, controversy, myth, and misinformation regarding their effects abound.

No data appear to be available on how much area tornadoes actually cover in an average year. In the United States, an average of 703 tornadoes strike per year, causing 93 related deaths and many more injuries (the record annual number of tornadoes was 1,109 in 1973). A tornado may barely touch ground or may cover 200 miles or more. The average length of a tornado's path is estimated to be 16 miles, although there is some controversy over whether this distance refers to multiple funnels or to skipping or intermittent tornadoes that have actual average lengths of 3 to 8 miles. On the average, tornadoes are 150 to 200 yards wide, although damage paths up to 5 miles wide have been reported for some tornadoes. The tornadoes that have the longest paths also tend to exert the greatest force and wreak the most destruction per mile. Once a strong tornado is formed, it can continue moving regardless of topography, crossing lakes and rivers, ripping through forests, and even moving down 4,000-foot-high mountains [2.9].

Tornadoes can be classified by strength from F0 (characterized by 40- to 72-mph winds) through F6 (winds of 319 mph or greater). Ninety percent of tornadoes in the United States are classified as F-2 or less; these tornadoes have wind speeds of 157 mph or less. Seven percent are F-3 strength (158 to 206 mph), and only 2 to 3 percent are F-4 or F-5, having wind speeds exceeding 207 mph. The effects of atmospheric pressure changes causing structural "explosions" seem subject to popular exaggeration. Most researchers apparently agree that the pressure changes are relatively small and that, although they may contribute to some structural failures, most of the destruction is attributable to the accompanying wind.

The likelihood of a tornado striking varies widely throughout the country. Although they have occurred in all fifty states, the collision of cool, dry air coming over the Rocky Mountains with warmer, moist air coming up from the Gulf of Mexico makes the Great Plains area of the country particularly susceptible to tornadoes. Because a tornado is a highly localized storm, sometimes only a few yards wide, in most areas of the country the chances of a house being struck by a tornado are considered infinitesimal. Nevertheless, the incidence of tornadoes is high enough in some areas of the United States to bear consideration before house design begins.

Figure 2-7 shows a map of the continental United States divided into 1° squares. Although the size of the squares varies, each 1° square represents an average area of approximately 3,650 square miles.

The total number of tornadoes over a twelve-year period (1955-1967) was divided by the area to obtain the odds of a tornado hitting any one-square-mile area during a twelve-year period. This number in turn was divided by twelve to find the probability of a tornado hitting in any square-mile area in any one year. It should be noted that this method assumes an equal distribution over the twelve years of the total number of tornadoes. It also assumes an equal distribution of tornadoes over an entire area, whereas, in reality, many factors may cause them to be more or less frequent in a particular area (for example, the warmth generated by a city may offer some protection from tornadoes). For simplicity, these figures also assume that each tornado covers a one-square-mile area. (These figures may vary from state to state and according to the data and method used for calculation. For example, Howe estimated that the area covered by a tornado averaged .96 square miles for the entire region east of the Rockies, ranging from 1.49 square miles in Oklahoma to .12 square miles in New England. Skaggs finds an average area of 1.82 square miles in the twelve states that had the most tornadoes from 1950 to 1964. The areas ranged from 5.38 square miles in Minnesota, 3.12 in Kansas, 2.82 in Iowa and 2.6 in Michigan, to 0.54 in New York and Pennsylvania [2.9]).

In order to estimate the odds that the structure would be hit at some time during its projected useful life, the value for the likelihood of a tornado occurring in any one year was then multiplied by an

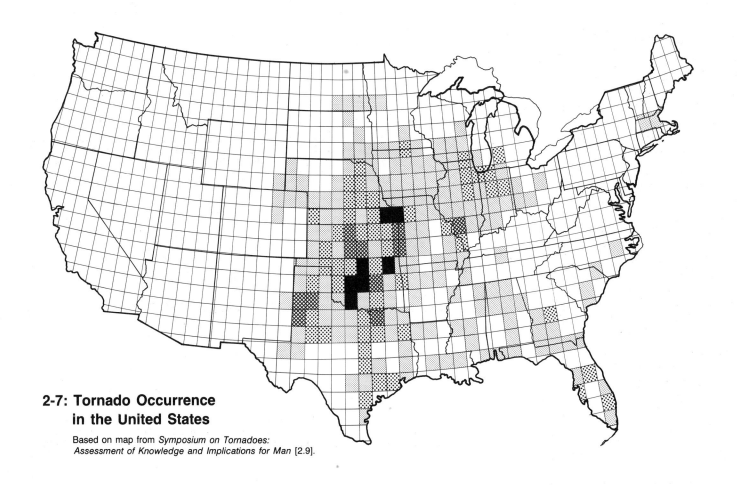

2-7: Tornado Occurrence in the United States

Based on map from *Symposium on Tornadoes: Assessment of Knowledge and Implications for Man* [2.9].

**number of tornadoes
(1955-1967)**

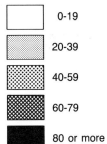

	0-19
	20-39
	40-59
	60-79
	80 or more

number of tornadoes	approximate odds of a tornado occurring in one square mile	
	in one year	in eighty years
20	1:2200	1:28
40	1:1100	1:14
60	1:730	1:9
80	1:550	1:7

assumed life expectancy of eighty years for a structure. These values were found to be quite high for some areas. In evaluating these data, it is important to remember that the largest number of tornadoes are not those characterized by the highest velocities and that many buildings do not sustain substantial damage from the lower-velocity tornadoes.

Because the number of fatalities from tornadoes does not necessarily correlate with the frequency of tornadoes, the frequency of tornadoes is not the only consideration for home builders. When a list of states hit by more than 160 tornadoes in the five years from 1975 to 1979 (fig. 2-8) is compared to a list of states where more than twenty deaths occurred during the same period (figure 2-9), Texas is the only state that appears on both lists.

It can be seen from these tables that—both in absolute numbers and relative to the number of tornadoes—substantially more deaths occur in a band across Arkansas, Mississippi, and Alabama. Population densities could affect this figure; nevertheless, it appears that although this part of the country is struck by fewer tornadoes than are areas to the west and north, the tornadoes in the southern states are more likely to be the more violent types, characterized by higher ranges of wind speeds. It is also possible that in areas subject to more frequent tornadoes, the population is more likely to support a more extensive warning system and to take the proper action to protect itself in the event of a tornado.

state	number of tornadoes	number of deaths	deaths per 100 tornadoes	persons per sq. mi. (1970)
Texas	712	68	9.5	41.9
Florida	379	8	2.1	116.0
Nebraska	234	4	1.7	19.2
Oklahoma	188	16	8.5	36.6
Iowa	166	13	7.8	50.2

2-8: States with More Than 160 Tornadoes (1975-79)

Data in figures 2-8 and 2-9 from *Insurance Facts* [2.10].

state	number of tornadoes	number of deaths	deaths per 100 tornadoes	persons per sq. mi. (1970)
Texas	712	68	9.5	41.9
Alabama	131	25	19.1	36.3
Arkansas	156	21	13.5	66.8
Mississippi	116	21	18.1	46.5

2-9: States with More Than 20 Tornado Deaths (1975-79)

Resistance to Earthquake Damage

The potential for reducing structural damage from earthquake forces is another benefit of earth sheltered structures, assuming proper site selection and design. Like tornadoes, the frequency and magnitude of earthquakes vary from region to region. Thus, threat of damage from earthquakes can also be considered a component in assessing regional suitability of earth sheltered housing. The map in figure 2-10 indicates various zones of seismic risk in the continental United States.

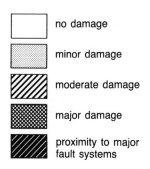

no damage

minor damage

moderate damage

major damage

proximity to major fault systems

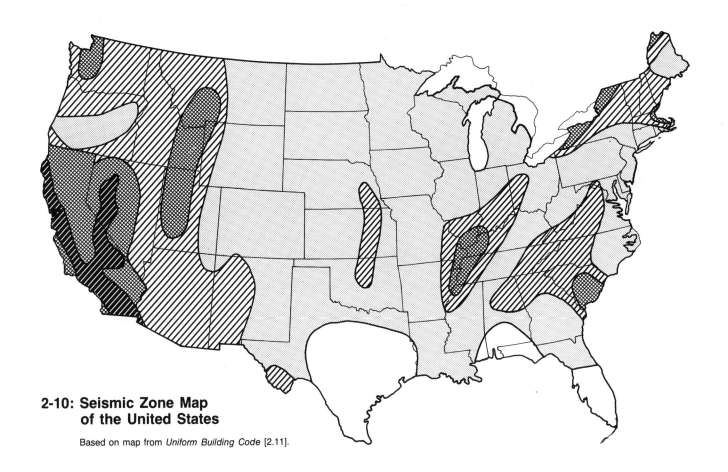

2-10: Seismic Zone Map of the United States

Based on map from *Uniform Building Code* [2.11].

Summary of Regional Suitability

Figure 2-11 summarizes some of the main reasons that home owners may choose to build earth sheltered homes. The reasons are rated for each region, according to the significance of each aspect in that region, on a scale from 0 to 4 (4 = "Very Important," i.e., would have a deciding influence on the house). The reasons are divided into two groups: those related specifically to the energy effects in the climate zones discussed and those related to other factors.

The relative importance of many of the issues that are not specifically climate related is very subjective. Consequently, low-maintenance and aesthetics factors were rated equal for all regions. The land-use category relates to several issues. In the most densely populated regions, land-use issues take on the most importance because preservation of amenities and open space is crucial in areas with high concentrations of people. It is in these same areas that building earth sheltered houses on land not suitable for other uses is most important. Also rated somewhat higher in this category are areas that have more sloping terrain or differentiated natural features; the Great Plains states, characterized by broad open spaces, were not rated as highly.

With regard to fire protection, less densely populated areas were rated higher than more densely populated areas on the assumption that the denser areas were closer to fire fighters, whereas the less dense areas might be quite distant from such service. The exception was California, where brush fires commonly cover large areas and destroy suburban neighborhoods that lie in their paths.

The potential for earthquake damage relates to the geological features below the surface rather than to climatic features. Although the sixteen regions correlate somewhat with earthquake zones, the information given on the seismic risk map (fig. 2-10) is more specific. The information from figure 2-7 was used to determine the degree of regional importance for the tornado category.

The criteria for rating the importance of reasons listed in the climate-related portion of the chart are somewhat more specific. The importance of heating was judged on two issues: heating degree days and percentage of hours when temperatures are below 50°F. A "Very Important" (4) rating was assigned to areas where there were more than 5,000 degree days (DD) and the temperature was below 50°F 40 percent or more of the time. "Important" (3) was used in areas with more than 4,000 DD and temperatures below 50°F 30 percent or more of the time. "Moderately Important" (2) was assigned to areas with 3,000 DD and temperatures below 50°F 25 percent or more of the time; "Slightly Important" (1) to areas with 2,000 DD and 20 percent or more hours below 50°F; and "No Importance" (0) to areas where heating values were less than the above figures.

Because of the different nature of the cooling process, the cooling analysis is divided into two parts. The first considers passive cooling techniques in assessing whether cooling is necessary and whether earth sheltering is appropriate. The second analyzes the need for active, mechanical cooling, which can be assisted by the high mass and low infiltration of earth

sheltering, as well as by evaporative cooling and shading of plant material on the roof of an earth sheltered structure.

Passive cooling was first evaluated in terms of need, based on cooling degree days (i.e., above the 78°F base) and percentage of hours above 78°F. The importance of passive cooling in regions that had more than 900 cooling degree days (DD) and temperatures above 78°F more than 40 percent of the time was rated (4), "Very Important." In regions with more than 600 DD and temperatures above 78°F more than 20 percent of the time, passive cooling was rated (3), "Important." Areas having more than 200 DD and temperatures above 78°F more than 10 percent of the time received a (2) "Moderately Important," rating; those with more than 100 DD and temperatures above 78°F more than 5 percent of the time received a (1) "Slightly Important," rating. A (0) "No Importance," rating was assigned to areas where passive cooling values were less than the above figures.

This analysis established the maximum rating for each region. The regions were then evaluated for the July temperature differentials between the average high air temperature and the average low air temperature, and between the average high air temperature and the undisturbed ground temperature in the 2- to 12-foot depths. These two figures were then added together for each region and rated (see fig. 2-12). The temperature differential was selected as a criterion because one of the principal ways that passive cooling works is by the thermal flywheel effect, which counteracts the heat of the summer day with what is, in effect, coolness stored from the nighttime and winter.

2-11: Regional Suitability

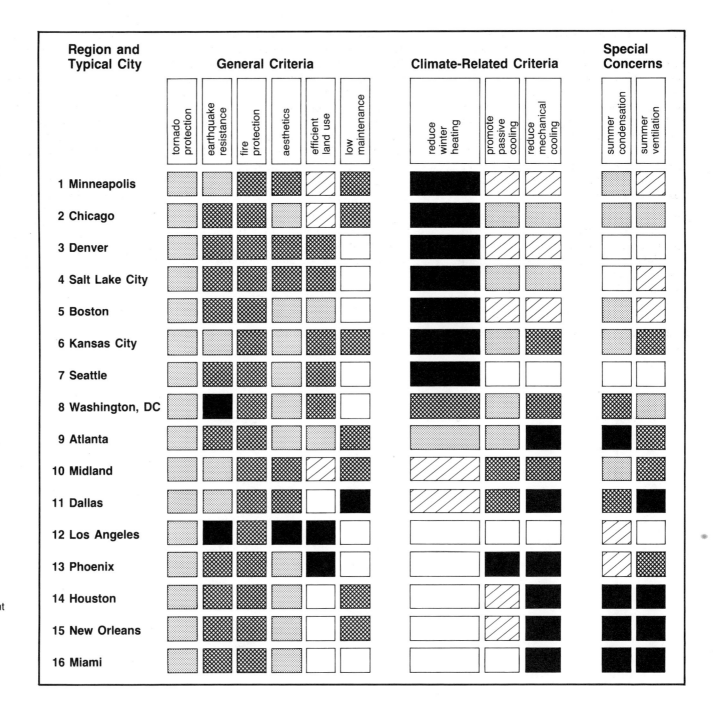

Region and Typical City	General Criteria						Climate-Related Criteria			Special Concerns	
	tornado protection	earthquake resistance	fire protection	aesthetics	efficient land use	low maintenance	reduce winter heating	promote passive cooling	reduce mechanical cooling	summer condensation	summer ventilation
1 Minneapolis	Moderately Important	Moderately Important	Important	Important	Slightly Important	Important	Very Important	Slightly Important	Slightly Important	Moderately Important	Slightly Important
2 Chicago	Moderately Important	Important	Important	Moderately Important	Slightly Important	Important	Very Important	Moderately Important	Moderately Important	Moderately Important	Moderately Important
3 Denver	Moderately Important	Important	Important	Important	Important	Not Important	Very Important	Slightly Important	Slightly Important	Not Important	Not Important
4 Salt Lake City	Moderately Important	Important	Important	Important	Important	Not Important	Very Important	Important	Important	Not Important	Slightly Important
5 Boston	Moderately Important	Important	Important	Moderately Important	Moderately Important	Not Important	Very Important	Slightly Important	Slightly Important	Moderately Important	Slightly Important
6 Kansas City	Moderately Important	Important	Important	Important	Important	Important	Very Important	Moderately Important	Important	Moderately Important	Important
7 Seattle	Moderately Important	Important	Important	Moderately Important	Moderately Important	Not Important	Very Important	Not Important	Not Important	Not Important	Not Important
8 Washington, DC	Moderately Important	Very Important	Important	Important	Important	Not Important	Important	Important	Important	Important	Important
9 Atlanta	Moderately Important	Important	Important	Moderately Important	Moderately Important	Important	Moderately Important	Moderately Important	Very Important	Very Important	Important
10 Midland	Moderately Important	Important	Important	Important	Slightly Important	Important	Slightly Important	Important	Important	Moderately Important	Important
11 Dallas	Moderately Important	Important	Important	Not Important	Very Important	Slightly Important	Important	Important	Important	Very Important
12 Los Angeles	Moderately Important	Very Important	Important	Very Important	Very Important	Not Important	Not Important	Not Important	Not Important	Slightly Important	Not Important
13 Phoenix	Moderately Important	Important	Important	Moderately Important	Very Important	Not Important	Not Important	Very Important	Very Important	Slightly Important	Important
14 Houston	Moderately Important	Important	Important	Moderately Important	Not Important	Important	Not Important	Slightly Important	Very Important	Very Important	Very Important
15 New Orleans	Moderately Important	Important	Important	Moderately Important	Not Important	Important	Not Important	Slightly Important	Very Important	Very Important	Very Important
16 Miami	Moderately Important	Important	Important	Moderately Important	Not Important	Not Important	Not Important	Not Important	Very Important	Very Important	Very Important

Key:

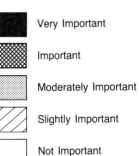

- Very Important
- Important
- Moderately Important
- Slightly Important
- Not Important

Humidity was also examined for each region, because high humidity works against the evaporative cooling of rooftop plants and excessive humidity causes concern about dampness and condensation on cool surfaces. The regions were rated on two criteria: average maximum dew point temperature for July 21 and percentage of time that dehumidification is required. If a region did not meet both requirements (fig. 2-12), it was listed in the next drier category.

The temperature differential rating and the humidity rating were added together to obtain a rating indicating the suitability of the climate for passive cooling by earth sheltering. The ratings for the need for passive cooling and for the suitability of passive cooling were then compared, and the lower rating was used in figure 2-11. Rating based on this method shows that Denver, which has a high temperature differential (4) and low humidity (4),

making it ideal for earth cooling, still received a low rating because it has so little need for cooling (1). Miami has a high need for cooling (4) but also has a low temperature differential (0) and high humidity (0); therefore, it also received a low rating (0). Because Phoenix has a high cooling need (4), high temperature differential (4), and low humidity (3), it received a very high rating (4).

If a residence uses mechanical cooling and dehumidification, earth sheltering will assist in reducing the load on the mechanical cooling system in much the same way that it reduces the load on the heating system: by surrounding the building with an earth mass so that the structure is not as subject to extreme temperature swings as is unprotected construction, as well as by reducing infiltration. The percentage of hours that passive cooling (other than ventilation) and nonpassive

cooling would be required were added together. When the sum exceeded 12 percent, reducing mechanical cooling loads was rated "Very Important" (4); over 7 percent, "Important" (3); over 4.5 percent, "Moderately Important" (2); over 3 percent, "Slightly Important" (1); and less than 3 percent, "Not Important" (0). Nonventilating passive cooling was included because it was judged to represent a somewhat idealized situation, in which all conditions must be just right to make the cooling acceptable. This condition was most noticeable in Phoenix, where, according to the figures, mechanical air conditioning is required only 2.8 percent of the year (less than Minneapolis's 3.1 percent). In comparison, nonventilating passive cooling is adequate 19.8 percent of the year in Phoenix, even though the temperature exceeds 90°F an average of 165 days annually.

rating	total temperature differential (°F)	humidity
0	less than 30°	dewpoint temperature above 72° and dehumidification required more than 10% of time
1	30° to 40°	dewpoint temperature above 70° and dehumidification required more than 6% of time
2	40° to 46°	dewpoint temperature above 65° and dehumidification required more than 2% of time
3	46° to 55°	dewpoint temperature above 60° and dehumidification required more than 5% of time
4	more than 55°	dewpoint temperature below 60° or dehumidification required less than .5% of time

2-12: Rating of Suitability for Earth Sheltered Passive Cooling

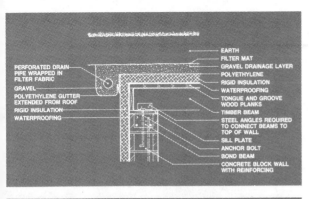

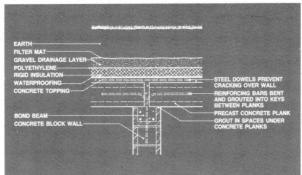

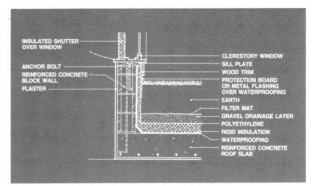

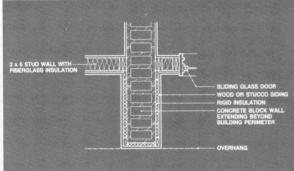

CHAPTER 3

ECONOMIC CONSIDERATIONS

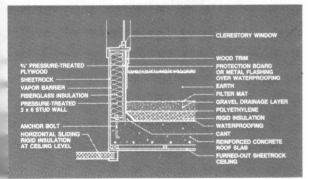

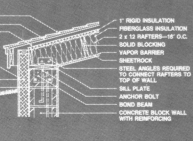

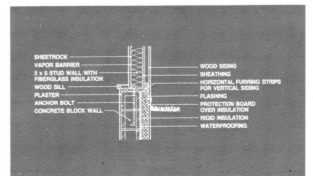

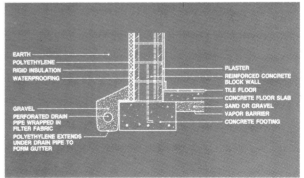

Introduction

It takes more than warm earth and cold nights to build an earth sheltered home. It takes more than knowledge and experience. It takes money. Besides representing a decision about life-styles and goals, housing is a financial decision. Very few people can ignore the financial aspects of buying or building a home; for most people they are the deciding factors. Yet while factors of climate can be measured, analyzed, and projected under the reasonably constant laws of nature, the laws of economics are subject to the more capricious actions of people, changes of policy, political pressures, and even the optimism or pessimism of the public, all of which affect the movement of money from one place to another. It is often difficult to generalize about economic factors because overriding considerations can invalidate the normal economic criteria. For example, it does not make economic good sense to build on a site where the soil will not support reasonable construction loads—*unless* the proximity of the site to some amenity invests it with great enough value to offset its shortcomings. The balance between cost and value is constantly changing as cities grow, attitudes change, new technologies are invented, and costs fluctuate.

In spite of all the seemingly intangible and imprecise aspects of cost and value, it is important to attempt to indicate the economic considerations for earth sheltered houses so that their relative costs can be compared with other options. The following discussion of the economics of earth sheltering addresses the initial costs of constructing a home, the availability and costs of financing, tax-related benefits, and operating costs such as energy, insurance, and maintenance. Each of these costs involves myriad variables. In order to deal with this wide range of variables, the final section of this chapter examines a case that is reasonable under existing conditions and discusses how changes in the cost components will affect the financial aspects of earth sheltering over the life cycle of the building.

Initial Construction Costs

Cost of Land

A number of variations are possible even in the very first costs associated with home-building. Some homes will be built on premium lots. Landowners who have realized that many buyers want a south-sloping lot are pricing these lots accordingly. In some parts of the country, it is already commonplace to see lots advertised as "earth home lots." On the other hand, earth sheltered homes can also be successfully designed for many lots that are unsuitable for conventional construction because of noise, a steep slope, or an unpleasant view—and those lots generally cost less than ordinary lots. As noted earlier, one reason for building into the earth is to rehabilitate normally unusable sites while simultaneously preserving unspoiled sites.

Design Costs

Most conventional houses are built without the professional design assistance of an architect or engineer. The structural aspects of such houses are well understood because they have evolved over a long period of time and thousands of standard plans are available. In building an earth sheltered home, however, it is a very rare amateur who can successfully integrate the needs for access, light, air, and egress into an attractive and efficient design that is detailed to deal properly with the forces and movements of earth, water, and heat. Furthermore, many financial institutions require professional certification of plans for their protection, and many code officials also insist on professional design before they will issue a building permit. Therefore, even if a home owner is theoretically willing to take the substantial risk of building a home that has not been designed and engineered by someone who has professional credentials, in reality the option to take that risk may not exist.

The design professional, in turn, may view earth sheltering as a rapidly developing—but still relatively new—construction type. Not all designers, contractors, laborers, and suppliers are aware of all that is required for sound construction on an earth sheltered home. More research, more detailed drawings, and more checking may be necessary than is typical in conventional house construction. For example, the great forces induced by heavy loads of earth require careful structural calculations. Moreover, the design professional may also be concerned about greater exposure to liability because he or she is working in a rapidly developing field, rather than one in which standard practices are well established. Adequate compensation for this professional time, effort, and expertise is money paid out before construction begins, in contrast to the often hidden costs of poor design that will be paid out over the life span of many conventional structures.

Actual Cost of Construction

In terms of actual construction, earth sheltering is associated with both extra costs and extra savings. Although the greatest extra costs are usually for structure and waterproofing, items such as deeper excavations, shoring, extra drain tile, special backfill, hand placement of earth on the roof, landscaping, retaining walls, and the added expense of dealing with concrete and masonry on the interior for furring, wiring, and plumbing can all add to the construction costs. On the other hand, earth sheltering reduces the amount of exterior siding, finishing, and painting required. If exposed masonry is used on the inside of the structure, earth sheltering can reduce the amount of interior gypsum board, taping, and sanding required.

Although there are exceptions, the extra costs usually are greater than the extra savings with an earth sheltered house. Specific cost comparison figures for earth sheltered and conventional houses can vary widely but most fall in the general range of 0 to 30 percent more expensive for the earth sheltered house. It should be noted that some of the increased costs associated with single-family detached earth sheltered houses can be reduced in multiple-unit developments and as more efficient building techniques are developed. In houses with conventional roofs and earth-bermed walls, however, the extra costs are diminished since many of the largest cost items—additional roof structure, larger foundations, and waterproofing—are associated with an earth-covered roof. Analysis and comparisons of cost figures for earth sheltered homes must be done extremely cautiously, as a number of factors tend to distort some of the figures. These factors—explained in the remainder of this section—include discrepancies between costs for owner-built and contractor-built houses, contractor attitudes, and inconsistent assumptions about including basements and garages in the comparisons.

owner-built homes

In any new type of housing such as earth sheltering, many of the first examples are built by their owners, who are experimenters and pioneers. Unfortunately, these houses do not generally produce consistent or reliable cost information. For example, a number of small, inexpensive, owner-built homes, finished to the simple requirements of a cabin, have been built. At the same time, other people have built huge earth sheltered homes that include indoor swimming pools, expensive finishes, and exotic gadgets. For some houses the home owner has done a substantial amount of labor, contracted out only very small portions of it, and shopped carefully for the least expensive materials. Occasionally, an owner will accept a level of finish and comfort that others would find unacceptable. Some homes have been built in areas lacking code or zoning restrictions that would have required additional construction and expense had they been built elsewhere. Many earth sheltered home owners take great pride in having constructed their homes for a very low cost per square foot; however, it should be noted that in some cases these cost savings have been achieved by valuing the cost of the owner's labor at nothing.

cost estimates by contractors

Although construction costs based on the bid of a professional contractor are generally considered to more accurately reflect the true cost of a home than figures from owner-built houses, contractor bids are also subject to many variables. Perhaps the most difficult cost to pinpoint is the cost of uncertainty in the minds of the contractor and subcontractor. The cost of any project will vary with the way that overhead, profit, and contingencies are figured. A contractor who is building according to a familiar or repetitive type of construction does not need to include a large sum for contingencies: because the scope of the project is well known, the amount of work to be covered by profit and overhead is also well known. Another factor influencing cost is the eagerness of the contractor to work on the building. A contractor who is not busy, is eager to get started and establish a reputation in a new building type, or is simply intrigued with a concept may be willing to figure the profit and overhead more closely and to seek out favorable sub-bids more diligently than a contractor who is not convinced that the project is well thought out, is quite busy with other, more familiar projects, or simply does not want to have to put up with unanticipated difficulties. When this possible reluctance—with its concomitant cost increases—is multiplied by each of the subcontractors, the construction price may be so distorted that it bears little or no relationship to the true cost of building the structure.

the bidding process

Bidding on a conventional house may involve little or no uncertainty; with an innovative house, however, uncertainty may well lead to a higher bid—especially in situations when the bidder may feel it is either not possible or unnecessary to clarify, economize, and compete. Indeed, a number of design professionals have found that a particularly important part of their role in earth sheltered construction involves clarifying the plans during bidding to contractors who may have greater concern than is warranted about the difficulty of earth sheltered construction, as well as reviewing the final bids when they appear to be higher than justified. A carefully prepared, accurate estimate is very helpful in this bid review process.

The experience of a Florida architect designing innovative earth sheltered shell structures is a good example of the importance of overseeing the bidding process. On one job he received three masonry bids ranging from $5,200 to $12,000. After reviewing the actual materials and labor required for the job with the low bidder, the masonry subcontractor was willing to do the job for $3,400. In another instance, the concrete for a job was bid on the basis of 50 cubic yards of concrete, when no more than 30 cubic yards were actually required [3.1, 3.2].

Knowing what the cost should be also can help alert the architect to the subcontractor who has erroneously bid too low, as when an electrical contractor has not included the cost of running conduit through masonry walls and, to compensate later, may either want to increase the contract price or may be less willing to put the normal amount of effort into the job. In some regions contractors and subcontractors are unable or unwilling to do the required careful analysis of materials and find it difficult to estimate the amount of labor for an unusual job; their solution is simply to use the customary price for what seems to be a similar job, add a safety margin, and submit that figure as their bid. The Florida architect referred to above found that by sitting down with contractors and subcontractors to review the amount of labor and materials in the project, bids that had been 50 percent over the estimate could be brought to within 5 percent of the estimate, with only minor changes made in the work to be done.

basement or other auxiliary spaces

The presence of a basement in conventional houses often makes direct cost comparisons to earth sheltered houses difficult or invalid since they have no basement but provide some alternative space for typical basement functions. In colder regions of the U.S., Minnesota for example, the building code requires that frost footings for conventional structures extend at least 42 inches below grade. A basement can be completed with very little additional construction, thereby substantially increasing the floor area of the house at very little extra cost. Basement space is generally not prime living space, however, because it usually has few windows and little finishing and is not integrated into the rest of the spaces in the house. Basements are usually considered primarily utilitarian space to be used for furnaces, water heaters, laundry facilities, and storage, and sometimes as workshop, playroom, or auxiliary recreation space. The size of the area is not determined by the space needed for the activities, but rather simply by whatever size the house above is, whether that amount of space is actually needed or not.

If a basement the same size as that in a conventional house was designed to be placed below a comparable earth sheltered house, it would provide space and utility equivalent to that of the conventional house, but it is not equivalent in other ways. The basement would be the cheapest space to build in the conventional house. In the earth sheltered house, however, it would be the most expensive space because the additional depth complicates the excavation and requires a much stronger wall to resist the much greater forces encountered at the greater depth. It would be much more advisable to incorporate a laundry room, furnace room, and storage room into a nonprime area of the earth sheltered house, against an earth sheltered north wall.

garage space

Another factor that must be considered in cost comparisons is the way in which the cost of a garage is figured. Because the garage frequently is a relatively large space requiring only a minimal level of finishing, including it in the overall cost figures for the house can throw off the average-cost-per-square-foot figure. For example, if the owner builds a 1,200-square-foot house with an 800-square-foot garage at a cost of $70 per square foot for the house and $20 per square foot for the garage, the cost of the 2,000-square-foot building can be calculated at a cost of $50 per square foot. Someone building a similar house without a garage would be mistaken, however, to expect to build it for $60,000 instead of $84,000.

In comparing the costs of earth sheltered and conventional houses, particular attention should be paid to the effect of the garage on costs. A wood-frame garage attached to a wood-frame house will be far less expensive than a reinforced concrete, waterproofed underground garage attached to an earth sheltered house. In order to avoid increasing the cost of the garage and distorting cost differences, the value of a garage, its design relative to the house, and possible future uses should be carefully examined.

additional factors affecting costs

It is important to remember that the sometimes exorbitant costs of one particular earth sheltered house may not hold true for other houses of similar size. If an error is made with reinforced concrete, whether masonry, precast, or cast-in-place, it is likely to be much more expensive to fix than would be the case for a wood-frame house. This is one of the reasons why careful planning by knowledgeable people is so important in an earth sheltered project.

With respect to speculative earth sheltered homes, the cost of the shell, with the attendant structural reinforcement and waterproofing required, is another factor that can raise the cost above that of a similar-sized conventional home. Realizing this, the developer may decide to increase the quality of the finishes to a higher level as well, reasoning that purchasers who are paying more will expect higher-quality finishes. Doing so, of course, raises the cost of the house still further, so that it may appear to cost substantially more than a typical house of the same size. In fact, only part of that extra cost may be due to the earth sheltering; the rest is the result of adding other, more traditional—and more visible—amenities to help justify the somewhat higher structural cost.

Finally, many of the first earth sheltered homes were designed and built by people who sought to incorporate the best energy conservation measures available. A number of these same people carried this pursuit of excellence over into the entire house, seeking a level of perfection in the design, materials, and craftsmanship beyond what many builders require. In some instances this high level of quality also accounts for the higher cost of the earth sheltered house.

Financing and Tax-Related Considerations

Availability and Cost of Financing

The financing of earth sheltered construction may still vary from region to region, depending on the attitudes of the representatives of financial institutions in the area. In the past, some financial officers who have been uncomfortable with the concept of earth sheltering have been inclined to require higher down payments or greater financial stability of the owner. It seems that as more information is made available to financial officers and presented in a professional, businesslike manner, and as a more extensive track record is established, earth sheltered housing is coming to be evaluated for financing purposes in much the same manner as other housing. Earth sheltered homes are acceptable for such programs as FHA (Federal Housing Administration) financing. If the initial cost of the earth sheltered home is greater than the initial cost of a comparable conventional home, the cost of financing that difference must be considered in the life-cycle cost analysis, although part of that cost will be offset by income tax savings on the extra interest paid [3.3].

Government Incentives

Another factor in the cost of energy-efficient housing is government incentives, which may be offered at the federal, state, or local level. Because these incentives vary depending on the jurisdiction, the policies in effect, and the funds available, and will also change from time to time as these other variables change, it is best to check on programs operating at the time and location of construction.

One of the most common means of establishing an incentive is the tax credit, which often reduces the amount of income tax due by some portion of the amount of money spent for energy conservation. Although some features are clearly intended solely for energy conservation purposes (solar panels and rock heat storage bins, for instance), many components of both earth sheltered construction and passive solar heating serve several functions. In many cases designating exactly which expenses should qualify for tax credits is a difficult job, because the various technologies and features often cannot be easily and clearly explained in a few sentences of tax law. Many laws therefore take a somewhat conservative approach, allowing tax credits only for items intended unmistakably for energy conservation but not for features that are difficult to differentiate from other elements of the structure, even though they may be equally important to an energy conservation strategy.

For example, the Internal Revenue Code allows the taxpayer to claim a credit against tax due of 40 percent, up to a maximum of $4,000, provided that certain conditions are met. One of these conditions is that the parts of the system for which credit is claimed must relate solely to the functioning of the active or passive solar energy system. Thus, if a house uses a load-bearing masonry wall as a heat sink, the owner pays the full cost of the wall and receives no tax credit for using the wall in a passive system as heat storage. If a similar house is built with a load-bearing masonry wall and uses a rock bed for heat storage, however, the owner still pays 100 percent of the cost of the wall, pays 60 percent of the cost of the rockbed, and receives a government tax credit to pay for the remaining 40 percent of the rockbed.

States have different rules for tax credits; in some instances, the rules include specific credits for earth sheltering. It is prudent to review the definition of earth sheltering for the particular jurisdiction early in the project, to determine whether the project qualifies for a tax credit and/or whether it is advantageous to design it to qualify.

Another strategy used to encourage conservation is to allow home owners to exempt the extra value of the house resulting from conservation measures from the property tax. Without this provision an energy-efficient house would presumably be taxed more heavily than a house that was similar in every way except that it used more energy and did not carry the initial additional investment.

Operating Costs

Energy Costs

Often the primary economic reason for building an earth sheltered home is the potential energy savings over the life of the structure. While much research remains to be done on exactly how heat flows into and out of an earth sheltered house, the energy loss can be calculated with sufficient accuracy to compare the heat flow to that of a conventional house. Based on these calculations, the current energy rates in the area where the house will be built can be used to determine the energy cost for the house. In projecting this cost, the biggest variable is the relative costs of energy in the future. Even the overall rate of inflation (or deflation) in the economy is difficult to predict. Energy costs are subject not only to the same forces as the general economy, but also to the political interactions of foreign energy producers, as well as to the political pressures for domestic regulatory and tax policies. Conservation measures, new discoveries of oil supplies, and developments of alternative energy sources such as wind, geothermal energy, and photovoltaic cells may also affect future energy costs.

Although some developments may cause costs to rise more rapidly while others may tend to moderate costs, it seems safe to make several general observations. First, fossil fuels are a finite resource. The most easily and therefore most cheaply extracted fossil fuels have largely been used up, thus leading us to turn to sources from which fuels are progressively more difficult—and therefore more expensive—to extract. Second, many alternative energy strategies are becoming feasible primarily because the high cost of obtaining energy from current sources is catching up with the costs of developing new energy sources. Finally, conservation is a strategy that can only continue to accumulate savings for the home owner after the original cost of the conservation measures has been recouped.

Although data was analyzed for a thirty-year period, the life-cycle cost analysis in the following section concentrates on the first twelve years, on the assumption that predictions become progressively less accurate as they look further into the future. These calculations are based on a thirty-year, fixed-rate mortgage, which, as of this writing, appears to be a decreasingly available option for home buyers. But it seems safe to assume that higher interest rates will be tied to higher inflation, which in turn is likely to correlate with higher energy costs; hence, the relative paybacks would not change to a great degree. A significant portion of the interest cost is also offset by the tax deduction for interest, assuming no changes in tax policy over the life of the mortgage.

Maintenance Costs

Although low maintenance usually seems to be a high priority on every home owner's wish list, the cost of maintenance is always difficult to project for any house. One reason for the higher initial cost of an earth sheltered home is the obvious requirement that the buried portion of the house be as maintenance-free as possible. The owner of a conventional house can compromise on the maintenance requirements in order to reduce the initial cost—by selecting lower-quality materials and finishes, for example—and such compromises are commonly made on the average house. This option is not open to the owner of an earth sheltered house, the exterior materials for which must be carefully selected in order to resist the moisture and chemicals that are constantly present in the soil. Attempting to scrimp on these materials in an earth sheltered house will likely produce disastrous results.

Insurance

Because earth sheltered homes tend to be less susceptible to storm damage and more fire resistant than conventional houses, a good case can be made for lower insurance rates for earth sheltered homes. Although a number of earth sheltered home builders have been successful in negotiating lower rates on their homes with their insurers, most insurance rates are calculated with data based on broad averages of the factors involved, and these data are simply not yet available for earth sheltered houses. It would appear that lower rates are a possibility on a case-by-case basis, but at this time only a few companies seem to offer a rate reduction on a regular basis for earth sheltering. It seems reasonable to expect that as earth sheltered houses become more common and more data on them become available, more insurance companies will adjust their rates accordingly.

Life-Cycle Cost Analysis

To better understand this mosaic of land costs, professional fees, construction costs, insurance, financing, government incentives, maintenance, and energy costs, it is useful to study an example that compares the costs of a conventional house to those of an earth sheltered house. The basic conventional house is assumed to have a total initial puchase price of $90,000, a $30,000 down payment, and a thirty-year mortgage of $60,000 at 14 percent. Energy costs are assumed to be $800 per year and insurance costs are $500 per year. It is further assumed that the annual rate of inflation is 12 percent (except for energy costs, which rise at a rate of 20 percent per year) and that the owner is in the 35 percent incremental tax bracket. The earth sheltered house is assumed to cost a total of $100,000 and to have the same down payment and the same terms on a

$70,000 mortgage as the conventional home. If both homes are built on equivalent $13,000 lots, the construction cost of the earth sheltered house would be 13 percent more than the cost of the conventional house. Energy costs for the earth sheltered house are assumed to be $240 per year, or 30 percent of the energy costs for a conventional house. All other factors are assumed to be the same for the two houses.

Figures 3-1 and 3-2 provide cost figures for the two houses for the first twelve years. The two columns in figure 3-3, labeled Cash Savings, compare the figures in figures 3-1 and 3-2. Based on the assumptions noted above, the cash payback for the earth sheltered house—the time at which total cash paid out for the earth sheltered house is less than total cash paid out for the conventional

house—occurs in the seventh year. But the cash payback is only part of the total picture. Given these assumptions, the cash flow for the earth sheltered house is negative only for the first three of those seven years, varying from $31 per month the first year to $10.66 per month the third year. In percentages the cash flow for the earth sheltered house is 5.4 percent greater than for the conventional house for the first year and only 1.7 percent greater by the third year. Figures in this range are statistically insignificant, because it cannot be presumed that they are accurate to within two to three percentage points.

Taking into account the likelihood of reduced insurance premiums and maintenance costs for earth sheltered homes improves the cost analysis for these houses. To analyze the effects of these factors, this study assumed that the

year	energy	insurance	principal	interest	total mortgage	tax saving	year total cash out	cumulative total cash out
1	800	500	139	8,391	8,531	2,936	6,894	6,894
2	960	560	160	8,370	8,531	2,929	7,121	14,015
3	1,152	627	184	8,346	8,531	2,921	7,388	21,404
4	1,382	702	212	8,318	8,531	2,911	7,703	29,108
5	1,658	786	243	8,287	8,531	2,900	8,074	37,185
6	1,990	881	280	8,250	8,531	2,887	8,514	45,700
7	2,388	986	322	8,208	8,531	2,873	9,032	54,734
8	2,866	1,105	370	8,160	8,531	2,856	9,645	64,380
9	3,439	1,237	425	8,105	8,531	2,836	10,370	74,752
10	4,127	1,386	489	8,041	8,531	2,814	11,229	85,983
11	4,953	1,552	562	7,968	8,531	2,789	12,247	98,230
12	5,944	1,739	646	7,884	8,531	2,759	13,455	111,685

3-1: Cost for Conventional House

year	energy	insurance	principal	interest	total mortgage	tax saving	year total cash out	cumulative total cash out
1	240	500	163	9,789	9,952	3,426	7,266	7,266
2	288	560	187	9,765	9,952	3,417	7,383	14,649
3	345	627	215	9,737	9,952	3,408	7,516	22,167
4	414	702	247	9,705	9,952	3,396	7,672	29,840
5	497	786	284	9,668	9,952	3,383	7,852	37,693
6	597	881	327	9,625	9,952	3,369	8,061	45,756
7	716	986	376	9,576	9,952	3,351	8,303	54,059
8	859	1,105	432	9,520	9,952	3.332	8,584	62,643
9	1,031	1,237	496	9,456	9,952	3,309	8,911	71,554
10	1,238	1,386	570	9,382	9,952	3,289	9,293	80,847
11	1,486	1,552	656	9,296	9,952	3,253	9,737	90,584
12	1,783	1,739	754	9,198	9,952	3,219	10,255	100,839

3-2: Costs for Earth Sheltered House

Year	Cash Savings		Difference in Net Assets Accumulated	
	for year	cumulative	for year	cumulative
1	-372	-372	852	852
2	-262	-634	1,109	1,961
3	-128	-763	1,408	3,307
4	31	-732	1,752	5,059
5	222	-508	2,151	7,210
6	453	-56	2,615	9,825
7	729	679	3,151	12,976
8	1,061	1,737	3,776	16,752
9	1,459	3,198	4,502	21,254
10	1,936	5,136	5,345	26,599
11	2,510	7,646	6,332	32,931
12	3,200	10,846	7,483	40,414

Positive value indicates earth sheltered cost is less than conventional.
Negative value indicates earth sheltered cost is more than conventional.
Assumptions: Conventional energy cost is $800 per year.
Earth sheltering represents 70% savings in energy.

3-3: Comparison of Earth Sheltered House to Conventional House

insurance premiums would be 10 percent less for the earth sheltered home and that the conventional home would cost $200 more to repaint every five years and $1,000 more to reroof every twenty years (both in constant first-year dollars). The study found that by amortizing maintenance costs over twenty years and adjusting for inflation, costs were reduced to slightly less than $20 per month more for earth sheltering the first year and less than $10 per month more the second year. In the third year, a positive cash flow was achieved. In this case the cash payback period for the earth sheltered house was reduced from seven to five years.

With or without savings on insurance and maintenance, any government tax credits or other incentives associated with earth sheltering could further reduce or eliminate the initial negative cash flow. It is interesting to note that in the case discussed above, even without the insurance and maintenance differential or government incentives, the earth sheltered home owner's total cost is never more than $800 greater than the conventional home owner's cost.

The discussion above is based entirely on a consideration of cash flow. Because a house is the largest expenditure for most families, however, it serves not only as shelter, but also as a means of investment. Decisions about housing affect both the amount of money that will be available for various needs each month and the long-term accumulation of assets. The high rate of inflation in the past several years, combined with long-term commitments made by financial institutions in the past, have led these institutions to seek to participate in the accumulation of equity. A number of possible ways of doing so are now being tried, and some time must elapse before it becomes clear to what extent financers will participate in the equity and what means will be acceptable mechanisms for achieving this participation. Because of this continuing uncertainty about the financer's role, the above example is based on the traditional system, in which interest rates remain constant over a long term and gains in dollar value resulting from inflation accrue to the home owner.

In the example a 12 percent annual inflation rate was assumed. This rate would apply to the value of the house as well as to the costs. It can be argued that the owner's return on the additional $10,000 cost of the earth sheltered house is in the future reduced energy bills. It could also be argued that since the owner never invests more than $800 in out-of-pocket cash, only that $800 sum should be used in figuring appreciation. Additional criteria must be considered, however. One such factor is the replacement cost, the

year	mortgage balance	value of house	year's inflation equity increase	year's net gain in assets	cumulative net gain in assets
1	59,861	100,800	10,800	4,045	4,045
2	59,701	112,896	12,096	5,135	9,180
3	59,517	126,444	13,548	6,344	15,524
4	59,303	141,617	15,173	7,682	23,206
5	59,062	158,611	16,994	9,132	32,338
6	58,782	177,644	19,033	10,799	43,137
7	58,460	198,961	21,317	12,607	55,744
8	58,090	222,836	23,875	14,600	70,344
9	57,665	249,576	26,740	16,795	87,139
10	57,176	279,525	29,949	19,209	106,348
11	56,614	313,068	33,543	21,858	128,206
12	55,968	350,636	37,568	24,759	152,965

3-4: Gain in Assets for Conventional House

cost of buying or building an equivalent house. Although future technological breakthroughs may occur and increased experience and familiarity with earth sheltering on the part of the building team may bring costs down somewhat, in the interests of keeping the comparisons equal, these possibilities were not included in the calculations.

A second factor is the return a new purchaser can expect on the money he or she has invested. If both the earth sheltered and conventional homes were sold at the end of twelve years and a 12 percent annual inflation rate was applied to the initial cost for each, and if equal down payments were required (approximately 30 percent of the purchase price of the earth sheltered home) along with the same type of thirty-year, 14 percent mortgage, the new purchaser of the conventional house (again, in the 35 percent bracket) would pay out $33,276 in pretax payments the first year, or $21,793 in net payments. Added to yearly energy costs of $5,944 ($800 per year, assuming a 20 percent inflation rate for twelve years), this would create a net cash outflow of $27,737. The new purchaser of the earth sheltered home would pay $38,772 in pretax payments, amounting to $25,393 after tax, and $1,783 in energy costs, for a net cash outflow of $27,176. Therefore, even though the $100,000 earth sheltered house has appreciated to $389,600 while the conventional $90,000 house has appreciated to $350,600, the purchaser of the earth sheltered house can afford to pay the higher cost and still pay out $561 less in the first year. If the house is sold before twelve years have passed, the savings to the new owner would be less than $561; or the new owner might have to wait a short period before achieving payback, just as the first owner did.

If the effect of this 12 percent annual appreciation on the $100,000 house versus the $90,000 house is included in the financial analysis, the owner of the conventional house pays out $6,894 in cash the first year and achieves an increase in assets of $4,045 (see fig. 3-4), while the earth sheltered house owner pays out $7,266 in cash and achieves an increase in assets of $4,897 (see fig. 3-5); hence, the earth sheltered home owner pays out $372 more in cash, but accumulates $852 more in assets. Although this gain in assets is a gain "on paper," which is not liquid and is not available until the house is sold, it is still a real gain. For those willing to balance the gain in assets against the cash outflow, the earth sheltered house can be economically more advantageous from the start.

Because this analysis is based on a large number of variables, all of which are subject to changes in the future, it is

year	mortgage balance	value of house	year's inflation equity increase	year's net gain in assets	cumulative net gain in assets
1	69,873	112,000	12,000	4,897	4,897
2	69,650	125,440	13,440	6,244	11,141
3	69,435	140,493	15,053	7,752	18,893
4	69,188	157,352	16,859	9,434	28,327
5	68,904	176,234	18,859	11,314	39,641
6	68,577	197,382	21,148	13,414	53,055
7	68,201	221,067	23,685	15,758	68,813
8	67,769	247,595	26,528	18,376	87,189
9	67,273	277,307	29,712	21,297	108,486
10	66,703	310,584	33,277	21,554	133,040
11	66,047	347,855	37,271	28,190	161,230
12	65,293	389,598	41,743	32,242	193,472

3-5: Gain in Assets for Earth Sheltered House

useful to examine some of the possible variations in the basic conditions. For example, because energy costs were such an important factor in the preceding life-cycle cost analysis, the following figures compare different energy costs for conventional and earth sheltered homes. In order to limit the number of examples, the following tables reduce both the energy required for the conventional house, assuming it is located in a milder climate, and the efficiency advantage of the earth sheltered house (it is reduced from the 70 percent savings used in the initial example).

Figure 3-6 assumes that the conventional house requires only $600 for energy in the first year and that the earth sheltered house saves 60 percent of that energy. All other factors are the same as in the initial example. In this case the cash flow for the earth sheltered house becomes positive in the seventh year and cash payback occurs at the end of the tenth year, but payback with equity included occurs in the first year. First-year cash flow is $48 per month more for the earth sheltered than for the conventional house, $35 per month more in the third year, and $16 more in the fifth year. It is interesting to note that energy costs for a house with a $600 annual energy bill will surpass $800 per year in less than two years, given the 20 percent annual energy inflation rate assumed in these examples. The maximum total cash differential between the two houses is slightly over $2,000.

Figure 3-7 lowers the energy cost for a conventional home to $500 per year and lowers the energy savings achieved with the earth sheltered house to 52 percent. Again, other factors remain the same as in the previous example. Cash flow becomes favorable to earth sheltering in the ninth

Year	Cash Savings		Difference in Net Assets Accumulated	
	for year	cumulative	for year	cumulative
1	-572	-572	652	652
2	-502	-1,074	869	1,521
3	-416	-1,490	1,120	2,641
4	-314	-1,804	1,407	4,048
5	-192	-1,996	1,737	5,785
6	-44	-2,040	2,118	7,903
7	133	-1,907	2,555	10,458
8	345	-1,562	3,060	13,518
9	600	-962	3,643	17,161
10	905	-57	4,440	21,601
11	1,272	1,215	5,094	26,695
12	1,714	2,929	5,997	32,692

3-6: Comparison of Earth Sheltered House to Conventional House

Positive value indicates earth sheltered cost is less than conventional.
Negative value indicates earth sheltered cost is more than conventional.
Assumptions: Conventional energy cost is $600 per year.
Earth sheltering represents 60% savings in energy.

Year	Cash Savings		Difference in Net Assets Accumulated	
	for year	cumulative	for year	cumulative
1	-672	-672	552	552
2	-622	-1,294	749	1,301
3	-560	-1,854	976	2,277
4	-487	-2,341	1,234	3,511
5	-399	-2,730	1,530	5,041
6	-293	-3,023	1,869	6,910
7	-166	-3,189	2,256	9,166
8	-13	-3,202	2,702	11,868
9	170	-3,032	3,213	15,081
10	389	-2,643	3,798	18,879
11	653	-1,990	4,475	23,354
12	971	-1,019	5,254	28,608

3-7: Comparison of Earth Sheltered House to Conventional House

Positive value indicates earth sheltered cost is less than conventional.
Negative value indicates earth sheltered cost is more than conventional.
Assumptions: Conventional energy cost is $500 per year.
Earth sheltering represents 52% savings in energy.

Year	Cash Savings		Difference in Net Assets Accumulated	
	for year	cumulative	for year	cumulative
1	-572	-572	652	652
2	-518	-1,090	853	1,505
3	-453	-1,543	1,083	2,588
4	-379	-1,922	1,342	3,930
5	-292	-2,214	1,637	5,567
6	-190	-2,404	1,972	7,539
7	-70	-2,474	2,352	9,891
8	70	-2,404	2,785	12,676
9	235	-2,163	3,278	15,954
10	428	-1,741	3,963	19,917
11	656	-1,085	4,478	24,395
12	924	-161	5,207	29,602

3-8: Comparison of Earth Sheltered House to Conventional House

Positive value indicates earth sheltered cost is less than conventional.
Negative value indicates earth sheltered cost is more than conventional.
Assumptions: Conventional energy cost is $400 per year.
Earth sheltering represents 40% savings in energy,
10% savings in insurance and $150 +12% annual
savings in maintenance.

year, and cash payback does not occur until the thirteenth year. But the earth sheltered home owner is still ahead in assets from the first year. Cash flow is greater for the earth sheltered house by $56 per month the first year, $47 the third, $33 the fifth, and $14 the seventh.

Figure 3-8 lowers the energy cost to $400 per year and lowers the energy efficiency of the earth sheltered house to 40 percent savings. This example should not be construed to mean that earth sheltered houses are less efficient in milder climates with lower heating bills; rather, it is merely a matter of carrying the example to extremes to see how the cost comparison is affected. In this case, because cash paybacks would not be achieved for quite some time, a 10 percent annual savings in insurance for the earth sheltered home and an additional maintenance cost for the conventional house of $150, with 12 percent annual inflation, were figured into the calculations. All other factors remained the same. Because some of the factors are figured at 12 percent annual inflation, rather than at the 20 percent inflation rate calculated for the energy factor, the cash payback is not achieved for a relatively long period (thirteen years); yet the maximum total cash differential is less than $2,500 (compared to $3,200 in figure 3-7, where no insurance or maintenance savings are included). In this case the cash flow becomes positive in the eighth year. The monthly payments are $48 more for an earth sheltered house than for a conventional house in the first year, $38 more in the third year, $24 more in the fifth year, and $6 more in the seventh year. Again, the difference in assets favors the earth sheltered house from the first year, although the second owner would have to accept a relatively long payback period in order for the first owner to be able to receive the full appreciated value if the house were sold before the cash payback was achieved.

In figure 3-9, effects of changes in other factors are shown graphically, starting with initial cost, which is calculated at both 14 percent and 15 percent annual interest. The vertical scale in all the graphs represents years to cash payback; positive cash flow begins slightly more than halfway through the cash payback period. In evaluating initial cost differences, it is worth considering whether all of the cost difference results from earth sheltering. If site conditions or material availability cause excessive differences in cost, a different earth sheltered design or alternate energy conservation measures such as additional

insulation or more solar heating should be considered.

The second major factor is the interest rate. Figure 3-10 illustrates the effect on the cash payback period of two different relative energy consumptions. Figure 3-11 illustrates cash payback versus energy cost difference, using two different annual energy costs—$800 and $600—for the conventional house. Figure 3-12 shows annual cash payback versus energy inflation rate for energy costs of $600 and $300 for the conventional house and $800 and $240 for the earth sheltered house.

Studies of the length of loan, tax rate, insurance cost differential, and insurance inflation rate found that these factors have only minor effects on the length of time until payback.

Given all of these variables, it is obvious that claims that earth sheltering does or does not pay for itself must be backed up by very careful clarification and calculations for each case. Cost studies must define such terms as "pay for itself," specify what costs and savings were included in the considerations, and note the assumptions made about future costs. In the end the home owner must make some value judgments as to what kinds of paybacks are acceptable, what types of short-term investments are possible, and what his or her long-term goals as a home owner are.

Like the decision to live in a colonial or a contemporary home, the decision to live in a conventional or an earth sheltered house is often an emotional one. Such a decision may reflect an optimistic viewpoint—for

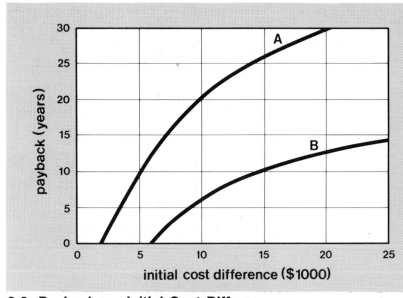

assumptions	base case	alternative
A: initial cost	$60,000	$60,000 + X
interest rate	16%	16%
energy cost	$600	$300
energy inflation	12%	12%
B: initial cost	$60,000	$60,000 + X
interest rate	14%	14%
energy cost	$800	$240
energy inflation	20%	20%

assumptions for all cases:	
term of loan	30 years
tax rate	35%
annual insurance cost	$500
insurance inflation rate	12%

3-9: Payback vs. Initial Cost Difference

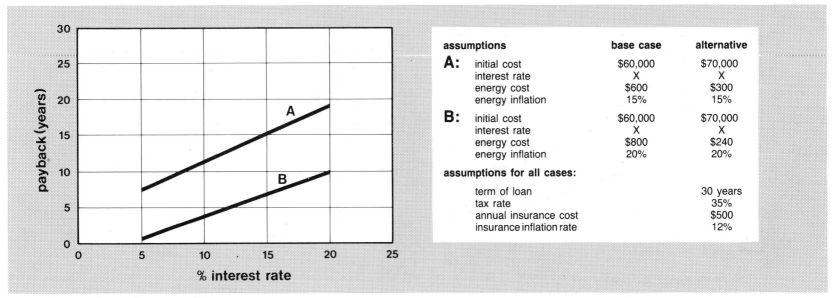

assumptions		base case	alternative
A:	initial cost	$60,000	$70,000
	interest rate	X	X
	energy cost	$600	$300
	energy inflation	15%	15%
B:	initial cost	$60,000	$70,000
	interest rate	X	X
	energy cost	$800	$240
	energy inflation	20%	20%
assumptions for all cases:			
	term of loan		30 years
	tax rate		35%
	annual insurance cost		$500
	insurance inflation rate		12%

3-10: Payback vs. Interest Rate

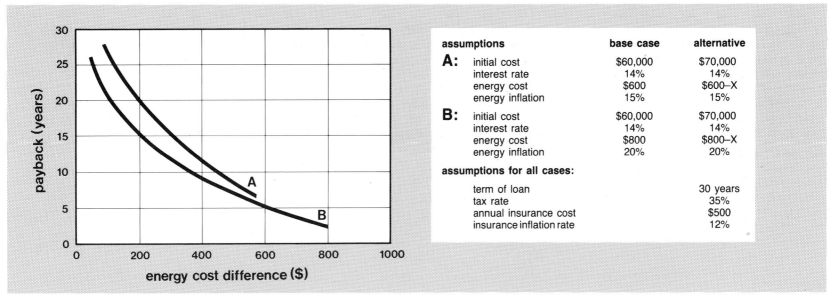

assumptions		base case	alternative
A:	initial cost	$60,000	$70,000
	interest rate	14%	14%
	energy cost	$600	$600–X
	energy inflation	15%	15%
B:	initial cost	$60,000	$70,000
	interest rate	14%	14%
	energy cost	$800	$800–X
	energy inflation	20%	20%
assumptions for all cases:			
	term of loan		30 years
	tax rate		35%
	annual insurance cost		$500
	insurance inflation rate		12%

3-11: Payback vs. Energy Cost Difference

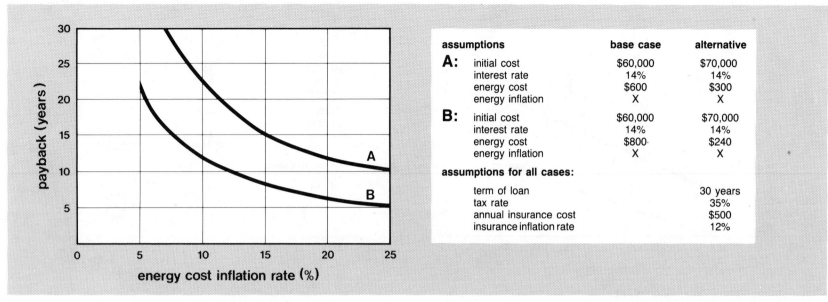

assumptions	base case	alternative
A: initial cost	$60,000	$70,000
interest rate	14%	14%
energy cost	$600	$300
energy inflation	X	X
B: initial cost	$60,000	$70,000
interest rate	14%	14%
energy cost	$800·	$240
energy inflation	X	X
assumptions for all cases:		
term of loan		30 years
tax rate		35%
annual insurance cost		$500
insurance inflation rate		12%

3-12: Payback vs. Energy Cost Inflation Rate

example, that one can in fact obtain a degree of independent self-sufficiency, or that the energy shortages of the last decade will end and permit old life-styles to continue. Or it may be based on a pessimistic view: protection from imminent catastrophe is vital, or nothing can be done to prepare for future disasters.

Regardless of the home buyer's psychological attitudes, there are some factual criteria against which the decision to buy a particular type of home can be measured to check whether the buyer's expectations are realistic and whether emotion is running with or against more objective criteria. The pros and cons of climate with regard to heating, cooling, and severe weather; the response of the structure to fire, nuclear fallout, and

earthquake; the use of the land and environment; aesthetics; and the economics of initial costs are all worthy of careful consideration by the owner, designer, and financer. At the same time, any analysis of housing options that ignores the function of a home as a shelter and refuge for the human spirit and a setting for some of the most important and positive interactions between people will be terribly incomplete.

PART TWO:

DESIGN AND TECHNICAL INFORMATION

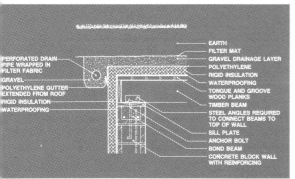

EARTH
FILTER MAT
GRAVEL DRAINAGE LAYER
POLYETHYLENE
RIGID INSULATION
PERFORATED DRAIN PIPE WRAPPED IN FILTER FABRIC
GRAVEL
POLYETHYLENE GUTTER EXTENDED FROM ROOF
RIGID INSULATION
WATERPROOFING
WATERPROOFING
TONGUE AND GROOVE WOOD PLANKS
TIMBER BEAM
STEEL ANGLES REQUIRED TO CONNECT BEAMS TO TOP OF WALL
SILL PLATE
ANCHOR BOLT
BOND BEAM
CONCRETE BLOCK WALL WITH REINFORCING

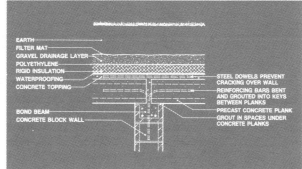

EARTH
FILTER MAT
GRAVEL DRAINAGE LAYER
POLYETHYLENE
RIGID INSULATION
WATERPROOFING
CONCRETE TOPPING
STEEL DOWELS PREVENT CRACKING OVER WALL
REINFORCING BARS BENT AND GROUTED INTO KEYS BETWEEN PLANKS
BOND BEAM
CONCRETE BLOCK WALL
PRECAST CONCRETE PLANK
GROUT IN SPACES UNDER CONCRETE PLANKS

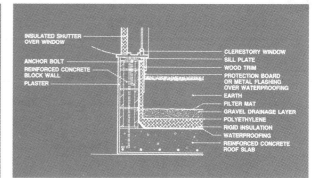

INSULATED SHUTTER OVER WINDOW
ANCHOR BOLT
REINFORCED CONCRETE BLOCK WALL
PLASTER
CLERESTORY WINDOW
SILL PLATE
WOOD TRIM
PROTECTION BOARD OR METAL FLASHING OVER WATERPROOFING
EARTH
FILTER MAT
GRAVEL DRAINAGE LAYER
POLYETHYLENE
RIGID INSULATION
WATERPROOFING
REINFORCED CONCRETE ROOF SLAB

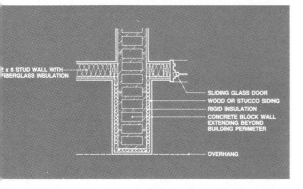

2 x 6 STUD WALL WITH FIBERGLASS INSULATION
SLIDING GLASS DOOR
WOOD OR STUCCO SIDING
RIGID INSULATION
CONCRETE BLOCK WALL EXTENDING BEYOND BUILDING PERIMETER
OVERHANG

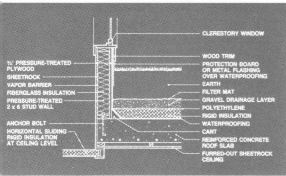

CLERESTORY WINDOW
¾" PRESSURE-TREATED PLYWOOD
SHEETROCK
VAPOR BARRIER
FIBERGLASS INSULATION
PRESSURE-TREATED 2 x 6 STUD WALL
WOOD TRIM
PROTECTION BOARD OR METAL FLASHING OVER WATERPROOFING
EARTH
FILTER MAT
GRAVEL DRAINAGE LAYER
POLYETHYLENE
RIGID INSULATION
WATERPROOFING
CANT
REINFORCED CONCRETE ROOF SLAB
ANCHOR BOLT
HORIZONTAL SLIDING RIGID INSULATION AT CEILING LEVEL
FURRED-OUT SHEETROCK CEILING

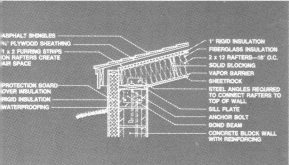

ASPHALT SHINGLES
½" PLYWOOD SHEATHING
1 x 2 FURRING STRIPS ON RAFTERS CREATE AIR SPACE
PROTECTION BOARD OVER INSULATION
RIGID INSULATION
WATERPROOFING
1" RIGID INSULATION
FIBERGLASS INSULATION
2 x 12 RAFTERS—16" O.C.
SOLID BLOCKING
VAPOR BARRIER
SHEETROCK
STEEL ANGLES REQUIRED TO CONNECT RAFTERS TO TOP OF WALL
SILL PLATE
ANCHOR BOLT
BOND BEAM
CONCRETE BLOCK WALL WITH REINFORCING

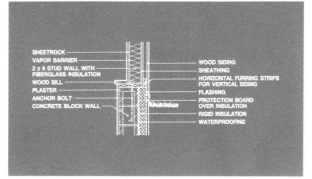

SHEETROCK
VAPOR BARRIER
2 x 6 STUD WALL WITH FIBERGLASS INSULATION
WOOD SILL
PLASTER
ANCHOR BOLT
CONCRETE BLOCK WALL
WOOD SIDING
SHEATHING
HORIZONTAL FURRING STRIPS FOR VERTICAL SIDING
FLASHING
PROTECTION BOARD OVER INSULATION
RIGID INSULATION
WATERPROOFING

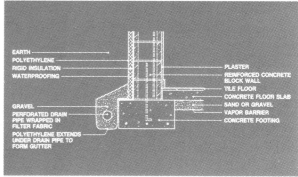

EARTH
POLYETHYLENE
RIGID INSULATION
WATERPROOFING
PLASTER
REINFORCED CONCRETE BLOCK WALL
TILE FLOOR
CONCRETE FLOOR SLAB
SAND OR GRAVEL
VAPOR BARRIER
CONCRETE FOOTING
GRAVEL
PERFORATED DRAIN PIPE WRAPPED IN FILTER FABRIC
POLYETHYLENE EXTENDS UNDER DRAIN PIPE TO FORM GUTTER

CHAPTER 4

SITE DESIGN AND BUILDING FORM

Introduction

The first section of this book assessed
earth sheltering as a housing option,
considering the multitude of possible
reasons for building an earth sheltered
house. The second section, beginning with
this chapter, assumes that the decision
has been made to proceed with an earth
sheltered design and provides the
information necessary to do so. Chapters 5
through 9 examine the specific technical
issues involved in the design process: soil
conditions on the site, structure,
waterproofing, heating, cooling, and
insulation, and plant materials. This chapter
considers some of the more general—but
nonetheless major—factors that must be
addressed at the start of the design
process. Decisions about these issues of
site and building form establish the
framework for making decisions about the
more technical concerns. This study
classifies the generators of building form
into six basic categories: site, function,
structure, energy conservation, daylighting,
and building codes. Following sections on
each of these is a discussion of typical
earth sheltered house configurations, which
are determined to a great extent by the
interrelationships among the six basic form
generators.

Site Design

The site is one of the most important determinants of a successful house design, as it presents both design limitations and opportunities. The site not only serves as a generator of form, but also establishes the character of the house within its surroundings. Even the most well-designed and beautifully detailed house will look awkward if the house appears to be in conflict with its environment. Evaluation of a potential site involves many factors that vary in importance and scope. This section deals with basic site design considerations involved in site evaluation, including integration of the house with its surroundings, orientation of the house, the relationship of the site to winds, site drainage issues, access to the site, and the amount of privacy offered by the site. Of course, site selection is also affected by a number of other issues, such as cost of the site and proximity of the site to jobs, schools, churches, commercial centers, and recreational activities. Because the number of available sites is limited and not all of those sites will be convenient, affordable, or appropriate for earth sheltered housing, careful site selection and design are extremely important.

Integration with Surrounding Landforms and Buildings

The relationship of an earth sheltered building to its surroundings is extremely important. These structures present opportunities for almost complete integration with the natural environment as well as some unique possibilities for new forms in urban settings. The various design approaches should be considered carefully, however, since there are also pitfalls. Each structure should be designed in response to its particular setting. For example, one design response to the physical features of a broad, open, flat site is to blend the house with the natural environment by using a low profile design. The building is set almost completely below grade with only gentle changes in the topography and the native plant materials continuing over the rooftops (fig. 4-1). One drawback to this design is the limited view with a sunken courtyard. Another approach on a flat site in a more urban setting might involve placing the building on grade and building earth berms around it with tiers of retaining walls. This design results in a more geometric appearance with definite boundaries and a scale that is compatible with the built-up surroundings (fig. 4-2). Earth-bermed

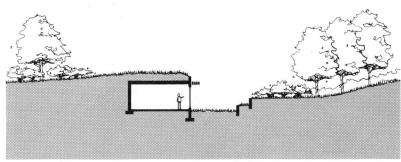

4-1: Recessed Structure on Flat Site

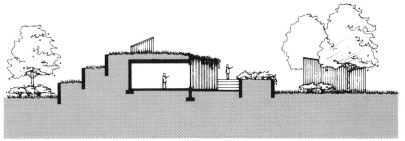

4-2: Bermed and Covered Structure on Flat Site

structures with conventional roofs are even more compatible with above-grade structures. On sloping sites, integrating the building into the landforms is a natural solution without the drawback of limiting the view (fig. 4-3).

Adjacent structures, from freeways to vine-covered cottages, affect form not only in terms of issues such as noise, view, and privacy, but also because they must be considered if a design is to "fit in" with its surroundings. The most successful house designs achieve a harmonious appearance that uses the best features of the area, without resorting to imitation of the less desirable features.

Orientation

In cool climates the ideal site for an earth sheltered house has a south-facing slope. A southern exposure is preferable to an eastern or western exposure in terms of both winter and summer benefits. In the winter the most heat is gained from the more direct rays of the southern sun, rather than from the lower-angled and therefore less intense rays of the morning and evening. In the summer the overhangs that do not shade the winter sun will protect the windows from the unwanted heat of the summer sun. On the east and west, on the other hand, the sun is low in the sky every day; thus the early morning glare and late afternoon heat from the summer sun cannot be blocked by a simple overhang.

In a warm climate, the emphasis is different. Even in warm climates, some heating is required. For example, Houston has temperatures below 50°F 7 percent of the time, and below 68°F 39 percent of the time; the average January temperature

is 52.1°F. Given relatively modest heating requirements, it is not too difficult to design a house for which normal heating requirements are met entirely by the sun, by using the mass of the structure and the earth to store the heat, reduce heat loss, and moderate temperature extremes. In such a case it is more important to minimize summer heat gains. In the southern latitudes, where the summer sun is located almost directly overhead, this can be accomplished rather easily through the use of a relatively small overhang to shade south-facing windows.

When evaluating a potential home site, it is important to consider shading from adjacent buildings and plants and to keep in mind that the December shadows will cover much more territory than the June shade. It is also wise to consider future development to the south. Trees on adjacent property that are no problem when a site is selected will gradually grow taller and eventually may begin to shade solar collection areas. A vacant lot to the south can become a problem if a two-story

building is constructed at the setback line.

In some situations a home owner may choose a site that does not have good solar exposure because the view, the price, or the convenient location are considered to be compensating factors. The conservation possibilities of earth sheltering may become even more important when solar heating is not an option. Such a situation also makes consideration of natural lighting even more important, particularly when the site is very shady.

Relation to Wind

One of the advantages of earth sheltering is the protection from wind that the earth gives, reducing both infiltration through the building and cooling of the building skin by the moving air. A disadvantage of earth sheltering is that a limited window arrangement may limit the cross-ventilation that is often almost automatically designed into a conventional house. Both of these

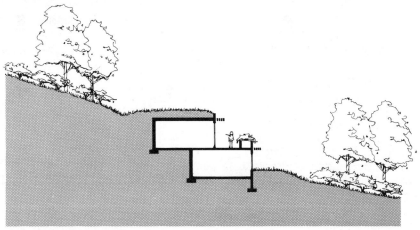

4-3: Two-Level Structure on Sloping Site

features of earth sheltering point up the need to consider wind patterns when evaluating a site.

The topography will affect the feasibility of providing openings for cross-ventilation on the side of the house opposite the major exposure. If such openings are not feasible, some vertical chimney effect may be employed to exhaust unwanted warm air through either a roof opening or an opening high in the exposed wall (see fig. 4-4). The designer should consider how this type of ventilation would be enhanced by or conflict with prevailing winds at the site.

Shelter from prevailing winds is also important for wintertime conservation of heat. The charts in chapter 2 indicate the prevailing wind direction in each region; this factor is, however, subject to many local conditions, such as proximity of the site to hills and valleys or bodies of water. On a smaller scale, nearby buildings or windbreaks of trees may offer partial protection or may be located so that they channel even more wind across the site.

Site Drainage

The fear that their homes will resemble musty, leaky basements is one of the greatest concerns people have about earth sheltering. While water control is an issue that certainly can be handled successfully, it should be considered in the first stages of site selection and planning. A designer should avoid selecting a site that presents serious water control problems and then depending on a magic material that can be smeared on the walls to make those problems disappear. Moisture control involves three lines of defense, none of which can be ignored if the home owner is to feel confident about the ability of the house to withstand moisture. The first defense is proper surface drainage, the second is subsurface drainage, and the last is the waterproofing material applied to the building. The first two of these defense strategies are related to site selection and planning.

In site drainage considerations, the natural contour of the land is the first thing to

evaluate. A natural valley between two hills may be nicely sheltered from the wind, but it may also channel all the rainfall and melting snow from the surrounding hillside directly toward the house. An attractive low area may also act as a ponding area where all of the rainfall collects before it soaks into the ground. The best sites channel surface water away from the area around the house in all directions before much of it has an opportunity to soak in. Although in some instances regrading will help, it may destroy the natural beauty of the site and kill much of the native vegetation that contributes to water control. In other cases, as when the original contours are composed largely of clay and the new fill above them is sandy, some water may continue to run toward the house, but as subsurface water instead of surface drainage.

The second line of defense against water problems, subsurface drainage conditions, is also site related. Water can run through sandy soil relatively easily, whereas clay stops the flow of water to a large degree. In order for water to be carried away safely, the water should have a free-flowing path to the drain tile at the footings. If, however, the remainder of the site is composed of clay and the path to the drain tile is the only drainage path for water, a layer of clay should be placed near the surface to prevent too much water from flowing down by the house. This clay layer will act as a dam so that the capacity of the drain tile is not exceeded. Subsurface conditions, including structural implications, are discussed in greater detail in chapter 5, which deals with soils. A more detailed discussion of drainage and an evaluation of various waterproofing materials appears in chapter 7.

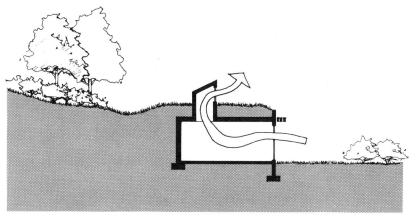

4-4: Ventilation through Roof Opening

Site Access and Privacy

Another major site-related generator of form is the requirement for access, in that the requirements the site imposes must be reconciled with the requirements the project demands. Several kinds of access must be considered: construction access, to enable heavy equipment and materials onto the site in order to build the building; visual access, both from inside and outside the house, for view and privacy; solar access, discussed in the previous section; and physical access, so that the family, guests, services, and cars of the normal household can enter and leave the house in an orderly fashion. Although any house has these same requirements for access, solar orientation, grade changes, and limited exposure (because of earth-berming against the walls) can make a satisfactory resolution of access needs more difficult for an earth sheltered house than for a conventional house.

Access from the south frequently presents

the problem of too much exposure. For many earth sheltered houses that are passively solar heated, the major indoor-outdoor relationship is oriented to the south. If access is also from the south, it generates conflicts with the guests, groceries, and garbage all entering and exiting from the same direction—which is also, presumably, where the private family outdoor living area is located (fig. 4-5). If the street is nearby on the south, southern access can even present privacy problems on the inside of the house, particularly if large areas of the facade are glazed. Of course, during the day, reflections on the glass of the bright outside would assist in preserving privacy, and at night, curtains or movable insulation could provide privacy.

Screening by fences or other building elements, such as a detached garage, are probably better because they do not interfere with ventilation or require manual operation to be effective. Although shrubbery is also a good screen, it may require several years to grow high enough

to be effective. Walls, fences, plantings, and outbuildings can also be used to separate and direct different kinds of traffic to the house by channeling visitors to the most appropriate door without requiring them to cross private patios or play areas.

Access from the north presents different problems (fig. 4-6). Aesthetically, a north access may be too private in an earth sheltered house. In some cases all that is visible is a garage with a walk-in door next to it, set in an apparently vacant lot. Most people prefer to avoid having the garage be the most prominent element of their house, and many like to be able to observe other people approach the house.

A north opening also brings more of the skin of the building into closer contact with the more severe temperatures of the air than does a south entrance. More of the earth around such an opening is near the surface and, hence, subject to colder temperatures and larger temperature swings. In a warm climate, the north entry penetration will also reduce the cooling

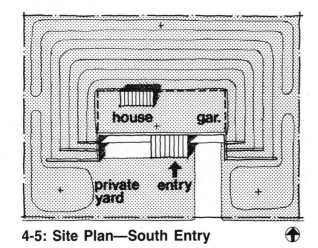

4-5: Site Plan—South Entry

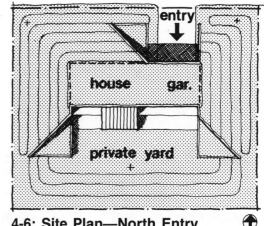

4-6: Site Plan—North Entry

potential somewhat. A north entry may, however, also present opportunities for improved ventilation and for daylighting without solar gain, a benefit in warm climates.

Access from the east or west, when possible, seems to offer many advantages (fig. 4-7). While it may result in some additional exposure of the exterior of the building, it still leaves a much greater proportion of the building and the earth around it further away from surface temperatures than does a northern penetration. It also enables people to enter the building without having to cross the prime area adjacent to southern windows, where privacy and separation of activities may be desired.

All of the previous examples of site organization are based on a building form that is basically rectangular with the majority of the window openings on one side of the structure. Although this is the most common form for earth sheltered houses, another basic configuration is the atrium design. An atrium design presents different opportunities and limitations. For instance, greater privacy can be achieved in the enclosed courtyard; however, solar orientation and views are more limited. This and other alternative building configurations are discussed in more detail later in this chapter.

Automobile access and storage also deserve careful consideration when analyzing the site. In mild climates, where a carport is sufficient, grade changes may present the biggest potential problem. When automobile access is on a higher level than the living areas of the house, people arriving by car must use stairs to enter or leave the house.

In more severe climates, where an enclosed garage is usually desirable, additional factors must be considered. For example, when a house is earth sheltered, the issue of an attached versus detached garage takes on additional importance.

For both conventional and earth sheltered housing, the garage can be used to screen private areas. As shown in figure 4-8, the mass of the garage can help to define and separate public and private spaces for a house that has its major access and exposure on the south side. If it is located close to the street, the garage may be the most visible part of the house to passersby. In such a case, the garage may present a potential aesthetic problem if its high visibility contrasts too greatly with an earth sheltered house that is virtually invisible under its earth cover.

When an attached garage is being considered for an earth sheltered house, the first question that must be answered is whether the garage should also be earth covered. A garage with a conventional roof may offer the opportunity for an attic that can be used for bulk storage, an area usually difficult to provide space for in an earth sheltered house. In addition, it may be hard to justify the additional structural and waterproofing costs of earth sheltering the garage, given the limited benefits it offers.

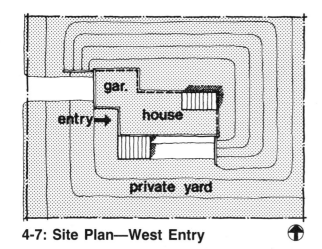

4-7: Site Plan—West Entry

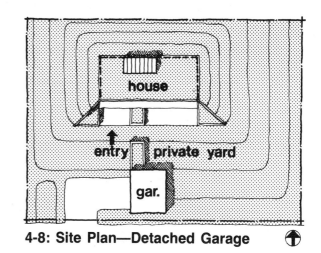

4-8: Site Plan—Detached Garage

Function

When energy efficiency is defined as one of the primary objectives of a residential design and earth sheltering has been selected as the means of meeting that objective, some very powerful form generators—earth, structure, waterproofing, code requirements, and energy-efficient features such as passive solar elements—will automatically be involved in the design process. Even in the design of a conventional house, the influence of function on form may ultimately be subordinated to other concerns. For an earth sheltered house, even more elements are competing with function for consideration in the design. Thus, the designer must carefully define the function of the house in terms of the inhabitants' needs and should not lose sight of that function during the design process. Otherwise, given the importance of the other factors, the designer may unwittingly design a house that works very well thermally, for example, but does not fully serve the residents' basic social, psychological, and utilitarian needs.

In defining the function of a particular house, the designer must consider the number, ages, goals, personalities, and life-styles of the future inhabitants and design accordingly. A wide-open design that helps provide daylighting to a large area of a single-exposure, earth-covered home may fit in with the casual life-style of one family very well but be totally inappropriate for another family's more formal way of living. One family may feel very comfortable with a design that places all of the exterior space that is readily accessible to the house on one side, whereas another family may wish to

separate public entry areas, adults' exterior spaces, children's exterior spaces, and service areas. Families that wish to emphasize common areas will need relatively small private spaces; those that prefer substantial private areas for each member of the family will need only minimal common areas. It is not possible or necessary to discuss in this chapter all the ways that earth sheltering can assist or hinder the functions of a family; however, it is extremely important to consider these functions—as well as the effects of energy, structure, economics, and other factors discussed in this manual—when making the initial decisions that determine the form of the home.

Many of the earth sheltered homes that have been designed and built to date have demonstrated excellent integration of function with the other aspects of earth sheltering. One aspect of function that few such houses have addressed, however, is that functions change over the years. Many families move through the following cyclical life pattern: individual; couple; family with small children, school-age children, and adolescents; couple again; and finally, individual who may be infirm. Societal changes may also bring about changes in house function: for example, in the past twenty-five years, smaller families, two-career families, and families in which adult children remain at home beyond young adulthood have become more common. These types of family and societal patterns affect how a house will be used by a family or a succession of families over the years.

Thus far, it appears that families that choose an earth sheltered house are more

likely to view it as long-term housing, whereas families that expect to move to another house within a relatively short period of time are more likely to choose a conventional house. A house that can accommodate change would seem appropriate for a family that expects to stay in the same house for a long time; however, an earth sheltered house structure, which must resist the forces of the earth, is likely to use materials associated with permanence—reinforced concrete and load-bearing masonry walls. Very few earth sheltered homes include basements that can be finished off into recreation rooms, and increasing space by adding a room to the back or by raising the roof is rarely a practical option. Some earth sheltered houses deliberately use non-load-bearing frame partitions that could be moved to alter room configurations, and some may have an unfinished garage or shop that could later be finished to become a habitable space. But the concept of a starter house that can easily be expanded as a family's size and income increase has yet to be explored.

Structure

The structure of a house is so important in determining the form of a house that it may be overwhelming. For example, the choice between a concrete dome and a rectangular wood-frame structure would fundamentally change every other decision made, not only with regard to the form of the house but also in terms of virtually every detail. The overall structural design and the ultimate form of an earth sheltered house is influenced most significantly by earth loads on the roof. If the roof is earth covered, the loads are many times greater than those on a conventional roof. In most cases, a flat or sloping roof is used, which typically requires a heavy roof structure—a cast-in-place concrete slab, precast concrete planks, or heavy timbers and wood planks. Since it is desirable to minimize roof spans, bearing walls spaced between 12 and 25 feet apart are usually required (fig. 4-9). This can place definite constraints on the plan arrangement unless relatively expensive, longer-span structural elements are used.

One response to the layout and cost limitations placed on a structure by heavy earth loads is the use of a shell structure. These curving structures—including barrel vaults, domes, and other thin shell variations—are capable of spanning longer distances using less material than conventional flat roof systems. Although very efficient structurally, a shell structure also presents constraints and is a very dominant element in the overall form and layout of the building (fig. 4-10).

The earth loads on walls can also affect the form and layout of the building, although less dramatically than the roof. Examples of this influence are the need for shear walls to help resist lateral forces or forming the building to step down a sloping site to minimize loads on deep vertical walls. All of the factors related to the structure of a building are too numerous and complex to discuss here. The key structural issues for earth sheltered houses are presented in chapter 6.

Some designers may be intrigued by a particular structural approach or may find that one approach is more appropriate to their area because of cost, availability, or requirements of the climate or soils in that area. Unless the structural decision is based on requirements that are so strong that they must take precedence over all others, it is important to evaluate the structural decisions in light of the other form-giving issues discussed, rather than choosing a structural system that may require that all other choices be shoehorned into an inappropriate context. The structure, the form, and the aesthetics of a house must all come together to express what that house is. The curve of a dome, the massiveness and strength of a concrete wall, the interrelated network of a wood frame—all are important expressions of the form, the structure, and the art of a house.

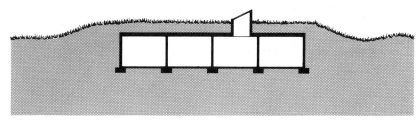

4-9: Bearing Wall Structure

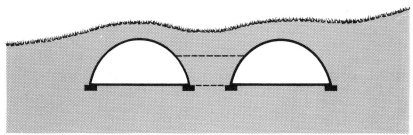

4-10: Shell Structure

Energy Conservation

In a small structure such as a house, the largest component of energy use is space heating. In warmer climates, however, significant amounts of energy may be required for cooling. The amount of heating or cooling required is directly related to the size and shape of the building envelope as well as to the materials that comprise the envelope (insulation, earth, glass, etc.). In addition, features such as solar systems can enhance energy conservation by providing energy from renewable sources. In a number of ways, energy conservation is becoming an increasingly important generator of housing forms. This is particularly true for earth sheltered housing, as energy conservation is one of the reasons typically cited for building such structures. In this section the envelope, degree of earth sheltering, and integration with other energy conservation concepts are discussed with respect to the form of earth sheltered housing.

Building Envelope

The size and shape of any house affect its energy efficiency, in that a greater surface area provides more opportunity for heat gains and for heat losses to the surrounding environment. In hot climates, where summer cooling is the primary objective, the greater the area in contact with the lower temperature of the earth, the greater the cooling effect on the structure. Even in cold regions, increased contact with the earth (which is warmer than the winter air) will help a house that is temporarily without a heat source use the warmth of the earth to slow the

cooling of the house, thus helping tide the house over until heat can be restored. Increased earth contact may also help prevent a freeze-up if a house is left unheated for relatively long periods of time.

When the house is warmer than the soil, however, which is normally the case during a northern winter, a greater surface area will result in greater heat loss. A dome has less surface area (in relation to floor area) than does a cube, a cube less than a rectilinear shape, and a rectilinear shape less than a shape that incorporates alcoves and projecting wings. Although an arch shape could be quite energy efficient, as a practical living space it is likely to be

somewhat narrow. To compensate for the narrowness, either the module would have to be relatively long, or several arched units would have to be combined. Both of these options can increase the surface area of the structure beyond that of a more conventional square or rectangular structure.

The shape of the house is also related to other energy conservation concepts. For example, a long, narrow house that has a greater surface area than a dome shape or cube—and, therefore, greater potential for heat loss—may also have more area for solar heat gain. A house that has projecting wings may offer more opportunity for cross-ventilation.

4-11: Earth-Bermed House

4-12: Earth-Covered House

Degree of Earth Sheltering

Earth sheltering has been defined as the deliberate use of the mass of the earth to modify environmental conditions in a habitable space. This definition of earth sheltering is purposely broad, in order to avoid making arbitrary distinctions among various degrees of earth sheltering (for example, a house that is 30 percent exposed is earth sheltered, whereas a house that is 31 percent exposed is not). Within the broad definition of earth sheltering, however, probably the most significant distinction is between an earth-bermed house and an earth-covered house. The term *earth bermed* refers to a house that is sheltered with earth on some portion of the exterior walls but has a conventional roof that is exposed to the weather (fig. 4-11). An earth-covered house has earth on a significant portion of the roof (fig. 4-12). Presumably, if the roof is earth covered, the walls will be primarily sheltered with earth as well. However, this is not to say that a situation could never occur where a designer would find it more advantageous to leave the walls exposed while using use earth on the roof. Experience has also shown that, although distinctions are useful and even necessary for discussions and explanations, in actual practice they tend to blur; hence, in some cases it may make sense to cover part of the roof on an earth-bermed house or to expose part of the wall on an earth-covered house.

The degree to which earth placement against the walls and on the roof of a structure affects energy use involves many interrelated factors. The generally perceived energy-related benefits of earth sheltered buildings include the following:

- reduced infiltration
- reduced heat loss through the envelope in winter
- increased heat loss through the envelope in summer
- reduced heat gain in summer
- damping of daily temperature fluctuations
- seasonal temperature lag in the ground

Although these benefits present some potentially great opportunities for energy conservation in heating and cooling, they are available in varying degrees depending mainly on the climate and the specific design of the house. Thus, decisions concerning the amount of earth cover on the walls or roof must be based on a variety of conditions and factors. A more detailed discussion of heating and cooling benefits as well as limitations for earth sheltered structures appears in chapter 8.

In discussing the manner in which energy conservation influences the form of an earth sheltered building, it is important to remember that decisions such as whether or not to place earth on the roof are based on a number of other factors. For example, many of the basic characteristics of earth sheltered houses such as protection, low maintenance, and various land-use, environmental and aesthetic benefits are most strongly associated with buildings that have earth-covered roofs. On the other hand, an earth-bermed house with a conventional roof has certain advantages compared to an earth-covered house. The heavy structure is not required to support the earth loads, thus reducing costs. In addition, a structure with a conventional roof is more acceptable to most people and therefore more marketable.

Integration with Other Energy Conservation Strategies

Although the energy-saving techniques of earth sheltering are the primary focus of this study, one of the clearest lessons that has emerged since the need for energy conservation has become an important issue nationally is that no one simple best solution exists for saving energy. It is therefore important to consider some of the other strategies that can be used in conjunction with earth sheltering. It is far beyond the scope of this book to discuss all facets of every energy conservation strategy. Fortunately, numerous excellent reference works on the specifics of each strategy are available. The discussion that follows is limited to an investigation of the strategies as they complement earth sheltering. Each strategy must be evaluated in light of the site selected for the project, during the initial stages of developing the design, rather than after all of the other design decisions have been made.

passive solar systems

The most important concept in terms of its impact on form, as well as the most common energy-conserving strategy employed in earth sheltered houses, is passive solar design. Passive design differs from active solar design in that all or most of the passive design components serve some other function in addition to the heating function and would be present in the building in some form even if solar heating were not being used.

It appears that passive solar heating offers close to an ideal opportunity for energy conservation, although there are a few limitations on its applicability. First, the site must have access to solar radiation. Second, because substantial nighttime heat loss through unprotected glazing can occur, it is important to take steps (such as installation of insulated drapes or shutters) to prevent the night heat loss through unprotected glazing in winter from counteracting the daytime heat gain. Finally, some shading device or other protection is usually necessary to prevent unwanted summertime heat gain.

Passive solar heating is very compatible with earth sheltering. The high-mass structure usually required in earth sheltered houses in order to resist the forces of the earth is also highly suitable for storing solar heat. In addition, depending on the placement of insulation, the additional mass of the earth may be available for heat storage. An earth sheltered design in which most of the principal rooms and glazing are oriented south is ideal for making maximum use of the windows as solar collectors. Furthermore, the efficiency of earth sheltering in minimizing infiltration and heat loss through insulation complements the passive solar gain by making use of the heat that is gained, rather than permitting it to escape.

active solar systems

Active solar systems, which consist of collector panels, storage tanks, and a mechanical system to operate the tanks, can also be used in conjunction with earth sheltered housing; however, their impact on form and layout is not as great as the impact of a passive system. Appropriate uses include situations when passive heating does not provide sufficient heat or where orientation prevents or limits passive heating. The panels for an active system

can be oriented in a different direction than the rest of the house or even located away from the house itself, either on an outbuilding or freestanding. Currently, active solar systems are most economical when used for water heating, because hot water is required year-round and solar gains are higher in the summer.

double-envelope systems

A variation on the passive solar home is the double-envelope home. This type of house is designed with double walls, floor, and ceiling, creating an air passage between the inner and outer surfaces of the house. The south side is a glazed sunspace that absorbs solar heat, which is then circulated by convection around the loop between the inner and outer surfaces. To some degree, excess heat is absorbed, stored, and reclaimed from the mass of earth below the floor. In earth sheltered homes, the double envelope may be accomplished by using furring strips on walls and ceiling and by placing the floor on sleepers over a concrete slab.

Because the double-envelope concept has not been integrated into earth sheltered houses to any great extent, it must be considered more experimental than either the active or passive solar system used in conjunction with earth sheltering. The impact on the form of the house would be similar to that of a passive solar design: most windows would be oriented to the south and somewhat elongated in the east-west direction. For the envelope concept to function effectively, however, there must be a large sunspace on the south side and the shape of the house must be extremely simple.

superinsulated houses

Another approach to energy conservation is the superinsulated house. Rather than obtaining heat from the sun, the superinsulated house contains heat within the structure. An unusually large amount of insulation and minimal window openings are incorporated into the house, and considerable care is taken to close off possible infiltration routes. The concept of superinsulation is very compatible with earth sheltering in a cold climate, regardless of whether earth, manufactured insulation, or a combination of these two elements is used to reduce infiltration and heat flow out of the house. In a warm climate, where the coupling of the structure to the earth actually helps cool the structure, extensive insulation may be counterproductive. Although above-grade superinsulated houses usually employ south-facing windows and a very compact configuration, the concept is adaptable to a variety of forms and window patterns; thus, it is not as powerful a form generator as is a passive solar system, for example.

Each of these energy conservation strategies is appropriate in certain situations, and each has some application in conjunction with earth sheltered housing. It is important not to approach design with the attitude that any one idea will produce the only "right" solution, but rather to evaluate the merits and drawbacks of each strategy in light of the particular situation. Only by doing so will the designer achieve an integrated solution, in which each component is in harmony with the others from both a functional and an aesthetic standpoint.

Daylighting

Dark and damp are the two words that first occur to many people when earth sheltered or underground construction is mentioned. Dampness is a function of drainage, waterproofing, and ventilation, which are discussed elsewhere in this manual. The light that most people expect to miss in an earth sheltered structure is not just any light—it is sunlight. They may associate light in an earth sheltered home with memories of sunlight trying to come through a small, dusty basement window, only to be absorbed in a large, rough, gray room. Those who have seen a well-designed earth sheltered home, especially on a sunny winter day, have often been astonished to discover that carefully planned windows in a house with earth on the roof can bring in more light than the minimal, haphazardly oriented windows typical of many conventional homes.

When considering lighting for an earth sheltered house, the designer must take care to avoid both too little and too much light. Code requirements for minimum window openings are discussed in the section of this chapter on building codes; the related section on egress addresses the issue of providing openings into rooms. Both the code and good design practice also permit rooms to "borrow" light from other rooms if a part of their common wall (e.g., 50 percent) is open. This arrangement presents no problem in areas where privacy is not a problem—between a dining room and living room, for example. In other rooms some degree of openness may be acceptable even when some privacy is also required.

One way of combining privacy and openness is to raise the floor of the room that is further from the windows several steps above the floor of the room nearer the windows and then to add a wall between the two rooms (see fig. 4-13). Provided that the wall is relatively low, people on the upper floor can easily see over it. This technique permits half the wall space to remain open for lighting, while some privacy for the upper room is maintained because the top of the wall shields that room from the view of people on the lower level. Although this strategy may require a higher than normal ceiling over the lower room, it permits more windows, creates a more spacious feeling in the higher space, may provide an opportunity to deal with a site that has some slope without resorting to extensive regrading, and may be simpler than either building clerestories or skylights or forcing all the rooms to face exposed exterior walls.

When emergency egress is not required, skylights and clerestories do present some opportunities to provide daylight to spaces that are not adjacent to exposed walls. But, since these openings often must clear the roof structure and earth cover in order to prevent snow and rain from draining in, they may rise considerably above the ceiling surface. In such a situation, a skylight may create a rather focused vertical flashlight beam of light that shines down on a relatively small area. This effect can be moderated by flaring the sides of the shaft out to an opening that is wider at the ceiling than at the top of the skylight. Reflective surfaces on the sides of the shaft, ranging from gloss white enamels to foil wallcoverings or mirrors, as well as diffusing lenses, will also help diffuse the light. Because the vertical rays coming through the skylight may be more intense than the horizontal

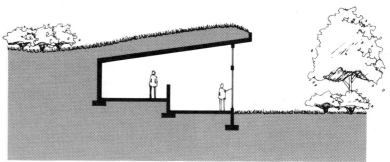

4-13: Section

rays entering a clerestory, the clerestory will normally provide more diffuse light.

One of the most crucial aspects of lighting is the contrast between brighter and darker areas. Our eyes may adjust rather easily to functioning in a relatively dimly lit room or outside on a bright, sunny day, but they have difficulty adjusting to sharp contrasts, such as a bright window in an otherwise dimly lit room. Earth sheltered homes may be bathed in bright, glaring sunshine on one side, while the spaces on the side located away from the windows are much darker. Although glare, like many aspects of lighting, is a very subjective matter, it can be moderated by attacking the problem of too much light, too little light, or both. Shading devices such as trees, roof overhangs, and louvers can reduce excessive light. Because most earth sheltered houses are designed to bring in as much sunlight as possible from the low winter sun in order to obtain the maximum heating benefits, however, it may be counterproductive to limit the sunlight when it is likely to be at its peak, except to the extent of providing a means of controlling the summer sunshine. A more satisfactory solution to daylighting problems is to seek ways to introduce more light into the darker parts of the house, thus reducing the contrast by brightening the dim areas instead of by dimming the bright areas.

A variety of plan arrangements using courtyards and smaller openings in walls and roof can provide opportunities to introduce daylight into multiple areas of a house. It is important to remember that uniform brightness is not necessarily the goal; indeed, some contrast is a useful design element. In the past, the uniform brightness of supermarkets, discount stores, and large offices has tended to create a bland environment. Many of these types of environments are now being altered to create brighter highlights and more softly lighted "mood" areas that provide variation in lighting levels. Even a flashlight beam shaft of light from a skylight may provide the right amount of light to reduce the contrast at the back of a house from a glare-producing situation to a pleasant system that includes brightness near the windows, a more softly lit intermediate area, and a much appreciated highlight at a point well away from the windows.

Designers of large-scale earth sheltered buildings have begun to experiment with bringing daylight deep into earth sheltered and even mined buildings by using systems of lenses and mirrors. Periscopelike arrangements of mirrors can bring view as well as light to areas far from windows. By using a lens to concentrate light, a large amount of light can be brought into a window that has a small area (and, therefore, small heat loss). A focused beam of light can be reflected deep into the building, directed by mirrors to where it is needed, and then diffused by another lens. Even when mirrors are not used, white or light-colored smooth surfaces can distribute and diffuse light within a building. Although much of this technology may not yet be applicable to residential construction, decorators have been using mirrors to create apparent light and space for many years, and the opportunities to introduce them into earth sheltered housing may be limited only by the imagination of the designer.

Like almost every other consideration dealt with in this manual, the need to bring light into an earth sheltered building is accompanied by trade-offs. Skylights and the increased window area (to provide additional natural light) will require shading during the hotter seasons of the year in order to limit unwanted heat gain, as well as protection from cold nights to avoid losing heat gained during the day. Aluminum-curbed skylights require a thermal break in the curb in order to avoid condensation problems during cold weather. Also, a skylight on an accessible roof may require protection for safety, especially if snow or plant material might obscure its location from the view of someone walking on the roof.

The quality of daylighting provided to a space is very important to the occupants' satisfaction in using that space. A room can always be redecorated to make it a more attractive color or more interesting. But the difficulty of adding sunshine later, combined with the importance of contact with the outside environment to a family's enjoyment of a space, make provision of daylight worthy of careful consideration and inventiveness; it should be a high priority when the form of the house begins to take shape.

Building Codes

One of the most basic house form generators is the need to protect the life safety, health, and public welfare of the occupants through applying either standards of good practice or more specific requirements of a building code. A building code becomes law when it is adopted by a local community or state legislature. Several model building codes are prepared for adoption into law; the major codes are the Uniform Building Code (UBC), the Basic Building Code (BBC), the National Building Code (NBC), and the Standard Building Code (SBC). The provisions regarding housing in all of these codes have been combined into a document called the One and Two Family Dwelling Code (FDC).

Although these codes generally apply to specific regions of the country, it is virtually impossible to indicate exactly where each code requirement applies, since every state or local community may choose among and amend the model codes as it sees fit. Some areas, particularly small towns and rural areas, have adopted no building code at all. Because it would be impossible to research all the local code variations, this section deals with code constraints found in the major model building codes. Individual designers will have to determine the extent to which these issues apply to the particular code used in their area.

Another document, the HUD Minimum Property Standards (MPS), is also included in this discussion. Although the HUD Minimum Property Standards do not have the force of law, as do the building codes, they serve as a guidance document for the programs of the Department of Housing and Urban Development. The MPS are used by the Federal Housing Administration (FHA) to determine the acceptability of housing for FHA loans. Therefore, the provisions of these standards will be evaluated as they are for the building code documents.

Many earth sheltered homes have been built to meet the requirements of the various codes. Most code requirements are compatible with the concept of earth sheltering, although the codes are oriented toward more conventional construction. Several areas in the codes deserve special consideration by those designing or evaluating earth sheltered homes because they are major determinants of form and they deal with standards that may present problems for designers who wish to use an unfamiliar or unusual construction technique. The chief areas of concern are fire safety and egress, the effects of grade changes on safety, and provision of natural light and ventilation. Although discussed in general terms in this chapter, a more detailed treatment of code issues appears in *Earth Sheltered Housing: Code, Zoning, and Financing Issues* [4.1].

Building code requirements for structural integrity, waterproofing, and energy use are aimed more at conventional construction and usually do not specifically address issues related to earth sheltered construction. Generally, the physical requirements of earth sheltered construction are as rigorous as the code requirements for conventional housing, if not more so; hence, if the functional requirements have been met, the legal requirements very probably have automatically been met or exceeded. These types of requirements are unlikely to change the form of the building substantially from what the designer would have planned in any case.

Fire Safety and Egress

One of the most fundamental goals of building codes is to protect the inhabitants from fire and provide them with egress in case of fire. All of the codes approach this issue by means of a prescriptive requirement for sleeping rooms in residences [4.1]. Every sleeping room is required to have at least one operable window or exterior door for emergency egress or rescue. When windows are provided, the sill height must be no more than 44 inches above the floor. The codes also set minimum net clear opening height and width dimensions (24 inches and 20 inches, respectively).

These requirements are the same in all of the codes, with a few important exceptions. In addition to the window provision, the NBC and MPS allow for two doors that provide separate paths of escape as an alternative. Although the BBC does not offer specific alternatives, provision 600.2 states that "when strict compliance with provisions of this code is not practical, the building official may accept alternate means of egress which will accomplish the same purpose." [4.2]. One final minor exception is that the NBC allows the egress window sill to be 48 inches off the floor instead of the more common 44 inches.

In many earth sheltered house designs, all the bedrooms have windows that meet these egress requirements. Figure 4-14 illustrates such a house. Other houses do not meet the requirements, however. For example, a compact plan in which window openings are limited to one elevation of the house will usually result in greater energy efficiency and lower construction costs. In attempting to accomplish both goals, it is sometimes easier not to provide windows in every space. Often the bedrooms are strong candidates for windowless spaces because they are used mainly at night. If the designer assumes that the option of a windowless bedroom is desirable in a house design, the important issue then becomes how best to provide adequate alternative methods of fire safety and egress.

The intent of the egress requirement is clear. If a fire should start in any part of the house other than the bedrooms, occupants should have a clear means of escape directly to the outside without having to go through a smoke- or fire-filled part of the house. Further restrictions are placed on the window size and height from the floor so that occupants who may not be young or healthy can escape and so that fire fighters carrying bulky equipment can enter the rooms easily.

It is interesting to note that the provision of an operating window in all sleeping spaces applies to structures up to three stories high. In the case of windows above the first floor, the purpose of the window is not direct egress, but rather access to fresh air and a place where the occupant will be visible for rescue. In sleeping rooms located above the third story, as in hotels and apartment buildings, egress is provided by other means, such as

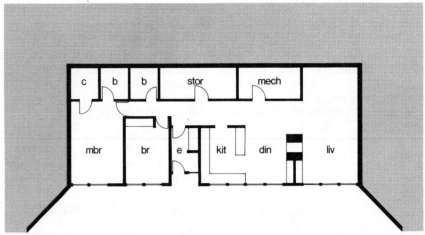

4-14: Floor Plan

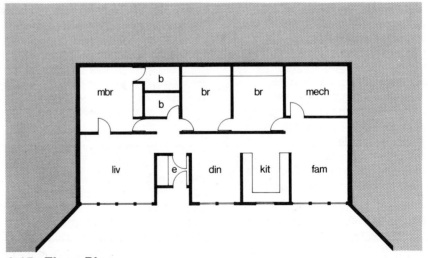

4-15: Floor Plan

stairways designed as smokeproof enclosures. The deaths in the 1980 Las Vegas hotel fires have generated further discussion about whether such buildings should also have sprinkler systems. At any rate, it is not economically feasible to prohibit sleeping rooms above the third floor, and it has not been considered economically feasible to provide alternate smokeproof passage out of sleeping rooms in single-family homes. The many homes, both earth sheltered and conventional, that have been built to conform to fire safety codes make it difficult to argue that direct egress is not practical. Nonetheless, precedent exists for providing alternative methods for fire egress, even though most housing codes are written in a narrow, prescriptive way that requires bedroom windows and allows no alternatives.

In examining the various alternatives to this code provision, one possible solution seems to be to substitute a second means of escape for a window. The NBC permits a second separate means of escape instead of a window; however, because it does not define what constitutes separation, several interpretations of such an alternative are possible. The plan shown in figure 4-15 illustrates one interpretation of the use of two separate means of escape from each bedroom. Each room has two doors that clearly lead to separate paths. Another solution might provide one door from the bedroom leading into a corridor with two clear paths of escape. In both alternatives, however, a fire located almost anywhere in the house could fill the whole house with smoke, as there are no smoke barriers. Such an

occurrence would leave the occupants no choice but to try to escape through the smoke. In addition, these alternatives would provide no means of reaching children, injured occupants, or others in need of assistance except through the smoke. It can be argued that smoke detectors, already required by code, would give adequate warning to escape before the smoke became too hazardous. Conventional houses, however, are required by most codes to have both the alternate escape route and the smoke detectors; the presence of one does not eliminate the need for the other.

Figure 4-16 illustrates a plan that provides an adequate alternate escape route but may be a poor design. Bedroom 1 is the alternate escape route for bedroom 2. Acknowledging that the designer cannot anticipate or be responsible for any action future occupants may take, it is still worth observing that the door from the hallway to bedroom 1 and either of the doors into bedroom 2 would require door closers to prevent accumulation of smoke in the escape route. Yet most occupants would consider automatic door closers in those locations to be a nuisance and would probably render them useless. A door closer activated by fire or smoke would be an alternate, but rather sophisticated and expensive, solution for such a house. The other potential problem is that although bedroom 1 is obviously a useful room and is therefore unlikely to become a blocked storeroom, the doorway to bedroom 2, which serves as the alternate escape route, may present problems because it probably would have no day-to-day function. In a room with an infrequently used door and limited wall space, it is not unusual to place furniture in front of the door.

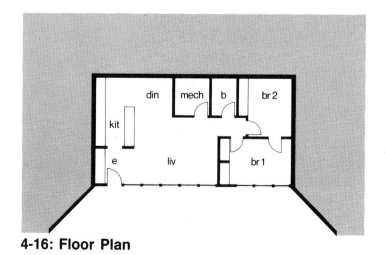

4-16: Floor Plan

Another more costly, but safer, alternative is the use of a separate corridor that leads to a fire exit. This type of exit should include doors and frames with at least a twenty-minute fire rating, automatic door closers, fire dampers, or ¼-inch-thick wire glass in steel frames in any openings, and a one-hour separation from the rest of the house for walls, floors, and ceilings. This arrangement would meet the requirements of the HUD One and Two Family Dwelling Code (FDC). One drawback of this concept is that an escape corridor that is useful only in the event of a fire but is not used on a regular basis as an integrated part of the house is likely to be costly compared to other approaches to the egress problem. Another problem is that such a space probably would not be left empty and idle in a compact house. A readily accessible, out-of-sight space that is not being used for anything else is very likely to become a storage space. Hence, occupants might find their way blocked by accumulated stored goods in the event of an emergency. Required exits are not permitted to pass through storerooms, mechanical rooms, or garages—and for good reason. A secondary escape corridor may be an adequate and cost-effective solution, however, if it is required for other functions in the house such as a connecting corridor to the garage from the kitchen.

Figure 4-17 illustrates another facet of emergency egress. In this plan the secondary exit from all bedrooms is through a covered atrium sunspace or greenhouse. Wire glass and automatic door closers to separate these areas from the primary paths of egress would not be in keeping with the design; however, a door left open or a fire that broke the unprotected glass would permit both paths

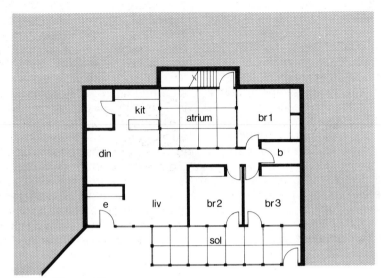

4-17: Floor Plan

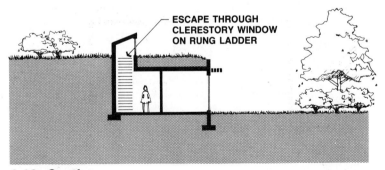

4-18: Section

ESCAPE THROUGH CLERESTORY WINDOW ON RUNG LADDER

of escape to be filled with smoke. One possible solution, which has been accepted by the FDC, is to install an automatic smoke vent in either the primary or secondary escape path. The FDC permits substitution of such an automatic vent in one of the paths of escape for protected openings between the two different paths. Thus, the plan shown in figure 4-17 could substitute a smoke vent for the fire-rated doors with closers for the bedrooms.

Two other solutions that have been suggested for fire safety in windowless bedrooms are the use of sprinkler systems and smoke detectors. A sprinkler system such as those used in commercial structures could be a rather expensive addition to a single-family house, although it would provide a certain degree of protection. A major problem is that sprinklers may not be activated rapidly enough to prevent poisonous gases and smoke from filling the house. Most present codes require smoke detectors in the bedroom area in addition to egress windows. It has been suggested that a smoke detector at the door of each bedroom would provide additional protection. It is questionable whether such a feature would be a sufficiently adequate safety measure to permit it to be substituted for egress windows or a second door.

Another technique for escape from a windowless bedroom is the use of an operable skylight with a rung ladder cast into the wall below it (fig. 4-18). As with many of the other alternatives, a second means of escape is clearly provided. The main reservations expressed about this alternative are the inability of elderly or handicapped people or very young children to effectively use such an escape, and the

danger that rising smoke may fill the openings. Although an individual home owner may not see this as a problem for his or her particular family, the code must consider that it is likely that any property will have a series of owners and therefore must assure the protection of the public in general.

A final code issue concerning egress from bedrooms relates to the maximum windowsill height of 44 inches from the floor. If a wall is substantially earth covered, it may be possible to provide a well to a window near the top of the wall, as is typically done for a basement. It may, however, be more costly and difficult to provide a large, deep well for a window of the lower standard height or for a high clerestory window. The 44-inch maximum height requirement is obviously intended to ensure that most people could climb out of the window or at least be visible to rescuers. A reasonable alternative would be to provide a permanent chest/seat combination or a raised floor built adjacent to the wall under the window so that the windowsill could be raised to within 44 inches of the top of the seat or raised floor. The same minimum window dimensions would still apply.

A number of code officials, architects, builders, and others in the construction industry were contacted about their opinions of these various alternatives. Most of them were quite open to considering changes as long as the primary goal of equivalent safety was met. Most of those contacted expressed definite reservations about the use of a rung ladder and operable skylight. They felt that this alternative was not acceptable because of the difficulty that young children and elderly and handicapped people would

have in managing such an escape route. The construction industry representatives also expressed great reluctance to accept the use of smoke detectors alone as a substitute for a window egress. Sprinkler systems generally seemed to be a more acceptable but unlikely alternative, as they are prohibitively expensive for most houses. Finally, the use of a permanent step-up structure to allow higher windowsill heights seemed to be a very acceptable alternative to the code requirement.

It can be concluded from these reactions, as well as from research into the various codes, that reasonably safe egress can be achieved by alternatives other than bedroom windows. Although the professionals contacted expressed flexible attitudes toward alternatives, many of them asserted that a bedroom egress window still seemed to be the best and most direct solution to fire safety concerns.

Grade Changes

The use of guardrails at the edge of earth-covered roofs and on retaining walls is an important issue in designing an earth sheltered house. A discussion of guardrails requires preliminary clarification of three related issues. The first is the determination of whether or not earth-covered houses that have retaining walls actually represent an unsafe condition and thus require some protective measures. Second, the actual code provisions for guardrails must be analyzed to determine how they affect earth-covered housing. Finally, assuming that some protection is required in some cases, it is necessary to explore various alternatives to guardrails.

Earth sheltered houses typically have a vertical drop of 10 feet or more from the edge of the roof to the ground. The design often includes 4- to 10-foot-high retaining walls adjacent to the structure. The earth-covered roof is usually accessible from the surrounding grade. Although these characteristics seem to represent an unsafe condition, most earth sheltered houses built to date have not provided protective guardrails. One reason for this is that the earth-covered roofs, although available for use, often are not actively used as outdoor space by the owners. Because the plant-covered roof is regarded more as an aesthetic element, a guardrail would not be a pleasing addition. Another reason for the lack of devices to protect against falls from roofs is that most earth-covered houses are located in rural areas where there is little likelihood of someone inadvertently wandering onto the property and accidentally falling.

Although it is obvious that an unsafe condition may exist in some cases, opinions differ with regard to what the building code actually requires and what alternate solutions would be acceptable. The national codes appear to lack clarity rather than to differ in principle about guardrail requirements. The UBC and MPS both include quite specific provisions; the UBC requirement is broader, whereas the MPS requirements permit exceptions in a number of instances applicable specifically to earth sheltered roofs [4.1].

As of this writing, changes that would make the FDC provisions more similar to those in the MPS are under consideration. The concern about handrail provisions for earth sheltered houses is focused mainly on the edge of an earth-covered roof and on other places where large vertical drops

occur, such as retaining walls. Most of the model codes do not directly address earth-covered roofs and retaining walls in their specific guardrail requirements. Only the UBC and the MPS refer specifically to the necessity of guardrails on roofs or roof decks. The FDC requires guardrails for raised floor surfaces, which could be interpreted as an earth-covered roof. Guardrail requirements in the BBC, SBC, and NBC only refer directly to ramps, stairs, and balconies. Minimum standards for the height of the rails also differ. The UBC, MPS, SBC, and BBC allow 36-inch rails for housing; the FDC and NBC standards require 42-inch rails.

Although most of the national codes have no specific provisions for guardrails on top of retaining walls, the BBC and MPS deal with this issue directly. It is interesting to note that both provisions allow alternatives to guardrails, referred to as "other approved protective measures" in the BBC and "other suitable barriers" in the MPS.

The MPS probably address the special case of an earth sheltered roof most specifically, by defining situations where a guardrail is required or may be omitted and by listing alternate acceptable measures. They assume that guardrails may be omitted in certain cases, as when embankments, drop-offs, or loading docks are present and in other situations where protection from a fall is not required, expected, or needed. That is, the code assumes that a person approaching an embankment, for example, realizes that he or she is responsible for taking reasonable safety precautions. Similarly, the code assumes that a person would have to make a conscious effort to pass through a barrier represented by a fence around a rooftop, a retaining wall or steep

embankment that would have to be scaled, a steeply pitched roof, or an 18-inch-high barrier located between 4 and 6 feet from the roof edge; and that, therefore, the responsibility for exercising due caution rests with the person approaching the barrier.

It can certainly be argued that these types of barriers do not necessarily protect those who are unable to exercise judgment, especially very small children. The types of protective measures that people commonly provide around swimming pools, for example, are intended to ensure total protection, for children as well as adults. A small, unsupervised child would not be protected by a railing that has 9-inch openings however. Although such a railing meets many of the code standards, a small child can easily pass through it—and it may even have a special allure as a child-sized jungle gym on which to climb, hang, and swing. The provisions for guardrails in the MPS, then, are based on giving adequate warning to a reasonable, responsible, mature individual rather than on providing a totally impenetrable barrier.

The other issue addressed by the MPS is the proximity of the hazard to people who might be endangered by it. Guardrails are required for any grade change within 5 feet of any sidewalk, driveway, or other paved area such as a patio. The code assumes that a rail is not necessary for changes of less than 6 feet unless the drop-off is near a traveled area. It also assumes that changes between 6 and 12 feet do not require a rail if they are sufficiently removed from public access, specified as a distance of not less than 50 feet from a property line. This requirement translates into a lot size of at least one-third acre. In a more remote setting—100 feet from a property line requiring a 1-acre minimum site—no railing is required for a grade differential of up to 18 feet. Some protective measure is always required for a grade change of 18 or more feet. Thus, rails would more likely be required in an urban area divided into small lots than in a rural setting characterized by large lots.

In addition to allowing substitution of a means of restricting access to a roof edge for a guardrail, the MPS permit substitution of a horizontal protection device that uses the same principle as a safety net. Such a device must be separated from grade by at least 16 inches but not more than 36 inches in order to discourage traffic, must be at least 36 inches wide, and must be capable of preventing a person from collapsing it or falling through it. Thus, a sunscreen could serve a dual function, providing both shade and safety.

Some designers prefer to use a hedge of dense or thorny plant material to limit the movement of people on the roof. The code does not list this as an acceptable barrier for several reasons, one of which is that it would be very difficult to specify how thick or thorny a hedge must be in order to offer sufficient protection. Also, the shrubs may take several years to grow large and thick enough to serve as a barrier. In addition, plants are subject to death, disease, breaking, pruning, and simply failing to thrive. Finally, one of the main reasons for selecting shrubbery as a barrier is aesthetic. The same aesthetic effect could be achieved by combining a guardrail with the plantings to combine an effective barrier with an acceptable appearance.

In some areas the code will require a guardrail where the owner or designer may not believe it to be necessary. The

challenge to the designer in this case is to to create a barrier that is appropriate or to seek either an alternate means of protection or an exemption from that provision of the code, based on the unique circumstances that might justify it. Additional discussion of the guardrail issue and its aesthetic implications appears in chapter 10.

Natural Light and Ventilation

The third code issue that may require the designer to alter the form of the house from the original plans is the requirement for natural light and ventilation. Most codes already permit substitution of a mechanical system of ventilation for natural ventilation, and if the house already has a forced-air heating system, it meets the requirement at no extra cost. Because it is possible to build an earth sheltered house with extremely low infiltration, a mechanical system to introduce outside air into the house may be necessary in order to maintain adequate air quality (see chapter 8 for further discussion of this issue).

Although the issue of windows may be more difficult to deal with than that of ventilation because the inventiveness of the designer may come into play to a greater extent, the code requirements are all fairly clear-cut. All the codes require a glass area equal to either 8 or 10 percent of the floor area in each habitable room. In sleeping rooms this requirement logically combines with egress requirements to argue for a simple window, although the natural light requirement can be met with a skylight or clerestory window when the alternate egress strategies discussed previously are being explored. In rooms other than sleeping rooms, a skylight or

clerestory can meet the requirements of the code without regard for egress provisions, although other factors, previously discussed under *Daylighting*, should also be considered.

A second option offered by the codes is opening various spaces into each other so that they can be considered as one room for code purposes. This strategy permits all spaces to benefit from the window, which may not be in close proximity to some of the spaces. Such a design strategy challenges the designer to find ways to transmit light and view to spaces away from the windows while still maintaining the visual, acoustical, and psychological separation that the different spaces may require. The MPS carry this concept one step further by permitting the lighting requirements to be treated on an aggregate basis; thus, some rooms may be windowless and have only artificial light, provided that the total window area for all habitated rooms exceeds 8 percent of the total floor area of all habitable rooms.

A change under consideration for the FDC addresses another possible problem for required windows. Windows that face into a glazed atrium, sunspace, or greenhouse do not technically meet the code requirements because they actually open into another room, although they may provide as much light as a window in direct contact with the outdoors. The code previously permitted windows to face into covered porches, and the contemplated change would also permit required windows to open into glazed spaces.

Configuration

The actual configuration of an earth sheltered house results from the interaction of all of the form generators discussed in this chapter. Site forces, function, structural systems, energy conservation, daylighting, and building codes, combine to create a form; however, the ultimate configuration also represents many compromises and trade-offs. Generally, maintaining a simple, compact form is desirable because it will be easier and less expensive to construct and will expose less of the exterior envelope to the weather. Many variations in form are possible because the site, building program, and proximities differ on every project. Nevertheless, some basic patterns emerge in configuration that successfully satisfy most of the form-giving criteria. In this section the most common plan configurations for earth sheltered housing are presented in conjunction with a discussion of one- and two-story design considerations.

Typical Plan Arrangements

All houses that are broadly defined as earth sheltered can also be classified according to the basic plan arrangement and pattern of openings. The house forms that can result from these relationships fall into three main categories: elevational, penetrational, and atrium designs. Elevational houses are characterized by continuous exposed walls and continuous earth-covered walls. An elevational house typically is bermed on three sides and has one exposed elevation facing south. If the exposed portions with windows are intermixed with berms on any or all sides of the structure, the plan is referred to as

penetrational. The atrium type of house is oriented toward an interior courtyard that is substantially below grade or completely surrounded by the house. Features characteristic of each of these three basic types can be, and often are, combined to suit a particular program on site. For example, an atrium house may also have an exposed elevation or may include penetrations in the earth at the exterior walls opposite the atrium walls.

elevational

Elevational houses are probably the most common type of earth sheltered house configuration. They are well suited to sloping lots, especially those with southern exposure, which offer the best possible combination of shelter from cold and access to heat. Homes built on northern slopes in a cold climate may need earth protection even more than those built on southern slopes because of the lack of opportunity for solar gain. Northern slopes may, however, be very appropriate in areas where cooling is a greater concern than heating. Sites that slope too much for conventional development can be ideal for elevational earth sheltered homes. Even on less steeply sloped sites, a higher-density development can be achieved with earth sheltered homes working with the slope than with conventional homes, which cannot take full advantage of the slope. If sufficient land is available for berms, elevational homes can also be built on relatively flat sites—for example, by recessing the house somewhat into the ground and including a slightly sunken courtyard on the exposed side. An example of a typical earth-bermed

elevational design is shown in figure 4-19.

An elongated plan provides substantial opportunity for direct solar gain to reach main rooms, as well as a long perimeter that is in contact with the earth's heat sink. A greater perimeter means that more wall area is available for heat loss, which is an advantage in summer but a drawback in winter. The elongated form sometimes generates a plan in which all of the main rooms have windows and are located on one side of a long corridor, while windowless storage and service rooms (for example, bath and laundry) are located on the opposite side of the corridor. This floor plan is very similar to those of high-rise apartments, which back up to the public corridor and face all windows in one direction. The designer's challenge is to make the long, exposed facade interesting and well proportioned while devising a plan that neither uses too much of its valuable floor space for hallways nor includes more windowless rooms than are needed.

A number of strategies can assist the designer in developing an efficient and attractive end product. The most obvious solution may be to avoid having both too many rooms and rooms that are too large. Very large or numerous rooms can result in "plan sprawl"—not only because of the area of the rooms themselves, but also because of the required supporting spaces, such as hallways. A big, efficient house can easily become a contradiction in terms. An open plan incorporating spaces that are shared physically and visually can be used to develop a satisfactory house that need not extend an overly long distance along the hillside.

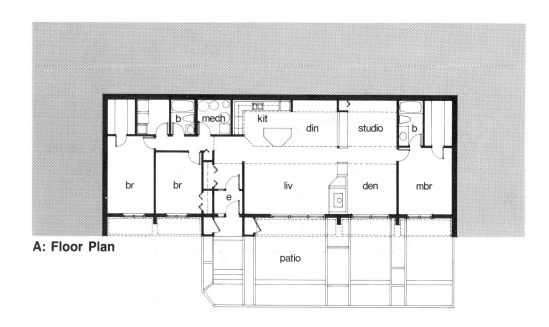

A: Floor Plan

Labels within floor plan: b, mech, kit, din, studio, b, br, br, e, liv, den, mbr, patio

Further variations present more opportunities. Exposing a second side of the house or using an L-shaped, angled, or curved plan can open up many new possibilities for a pleasant, efficient plan that may require a shorter perimeter and less floor area. Of course, the trade-offs between these more complex forms and larger floor areas must be weighed carefully. If the site is suitable, elevational designs can also be adapted to two-story designs, which are often more compact than a single-story design. Advantages and disadvantages of two-story construction are discussed later in this chapter.

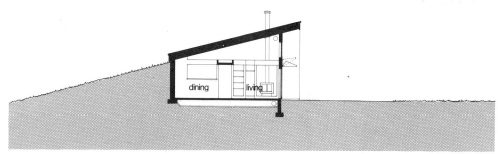

Labels within section: dining, living

B: Section

4-19: Elevational House

Hadley House, Burnsville, Minnesota
Architect: Ellison Design and Construction
Minneapolis, Minnesota

penetrational

In some situations a designer may choose to move from an elevational to a penetrational concept. A penetrational design allows many more possibilities for floor plan development because the plan can accommodate openings in a number of different locations. Elevational plans generally are more rigid, offering only very limited options for openings in the structure. In a penetrational type of design, light, air, and view can enter the structure from several directions, thus aiding ventilation and allowing more means of emergency egress. In addition, the exterior of a penetrational house may have a more harmonious, consistent appearance than does an elevational house, which often features a vast array of glass, entries, and patios on one side while the other side appears to be nothing but an undisturbed grassy field. Figure 4-20 shows a penetrational design for a small house on an urban site.

Some disadvantages counterbalance the advantages of a penetrational earth sheltered house. From an energy standpoint, the penetrations provide a path that brings the weather into the protective berm. In comparison with an elevational design, a much larger percentage of the earth cover is within 2 or 3 feet of the surface and a much smaller percentage is more than 6 or 8 feet from the surface, thus reducing the benefits of earth sheltering. More money is likely to be invested in the additional retaining walls that are likely to be necessitated by a plan that has multiple openings.

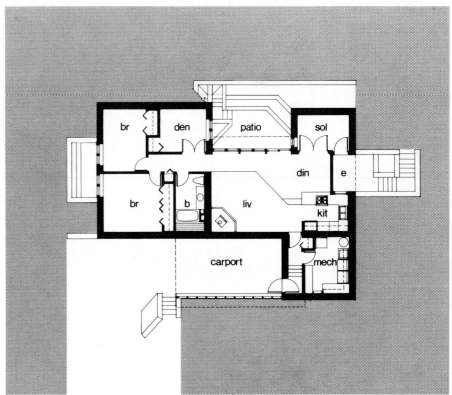

A: Floor Plan

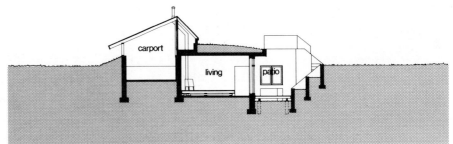

B: Section

4-20: Penetrational House

Sticks and Stones House, Minneapolis, Minnesota
Architect: Froehle, Saphir, Joos
Sticks and Stones Design
Minneapolis, Minnesota

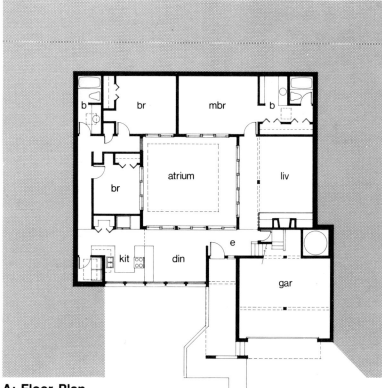

A: Floor Plan

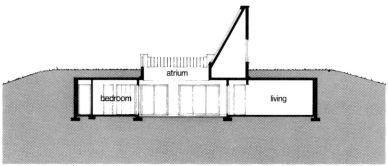

B: Section

4-21: Atrium House

Clark House, Portland, Oregon
Architect: Norm Clark
Portland, Oregon

atrium

The third main type of earth sheltered house is the atrium, in which rooms open off a central courtyard. In some instances the courtyard is the only exposed area; the entrance to the house is through the court, and all other exterior walls are below grade. In other cases, such as when the atrium is used in conjunction with elevational or penetrational plans, the courtyard is a private space accessible only from within the house. An example of this type of design is shown in figure 4-21. An atrium is a useful device for getting light and air to the "back" side of an elevational house. It is somewhat sheltered from the wind and, if the atrium can be glazed over the top, can serve as a passive solar collection sunspace. In warm climates the atrium can function much as the ancient courtyards did, as a passive cooling device in which warm air escapes out the open top of the courtyard while any cool air settles at the bottom. A fountain in the middle of the courtyard can provide not only a pleasant auditory and visual delight, but evaporative cooling as well. Sometimes spaces that are bounded by the house on only three sides—for example, when the fourth side is open or serves as a retaining wall—are also referred to as atriums.

Atriums are particularly appropriate in areas with no attractive view or in densely developed areas where a private outdoor space would otherwise be difficult to obtain. Their inward orientation, which offers the possibility of designing to eliminate all outside windows, makes the atrium design ideal for multiple-family, attached units. Such developments can achieve a relatively high density while still providing private outdoor spaces in the courtyards and common greenspaces on landscaped, earth-covered roofs.

Like each of the other two basic types of earth sheltered houses, atriums have their drawbacks. Because much of the glass on the sides of the atrium designs is in shadow at any given time, solar gain through the glass is limited. This factor is less important in warm climates or if there is elevational or penetrational glass in other areas of the house.

Small atrium homes, in which a few rooms can open directly off the main room and little or no hallway area is required, can be extremely efficient. In homes where more hallway space is necessary (as when there are more rooms), either the hallways tend to become relatively long or the rooms themselves act as hallways. In typical housing design, the most efficient access is from a single point at the center of a building, with large spaces radiating from that point. Access in atrium houses is usually just the reverse: the center point is occupied by the atrium, and the rooms are located on the ring adjacent to the atrium. The outermost ring, which has the greatest circumference, is usually designed as the hallway access to the rooms because, unlike the rooms, it does not need the light provided by the atrium windows. In milder climates this problem is sometimes dealt with by using the atrium as the central access point and having no perimeter corridor or indoor access to some rooms. This is a more efficient use of space, provided that the climate and life-style of the inhabitants do not make such an arrangement impractical.

One-Story and Two-Story Design Considerations

The decision about whether to use a one-story or a two-story design is another important issue in determining house configuration. Perhaps the greatest single determinant of this design aspect is the site. A steep site generally encourages a two-story design that follows the site contours and requires that a smaller area of the site be disturbed, whereas a flatter site may be more conducive to a one-story design. If either choice can be accommodated on the site, other factors come into play.

Many people prefer a one-story design so that they do not have to deal with stairs, which often complicate the access between rooms. Stairs take on considerable importance when the needs of small children or of elderly or handicapped people are involved. A single-story design also usually offers better access to outdoor living areas and a shorter drop-off from the rooftop area than does a two-story design. Structurally, the horizontal forces acting against the earth-covered walls are less on a one-story than on a two-story house. Although some of the forces acting against a two-story wall can be resisted by the intermediate floor, only a stronger, more carefully designed and constructed, and more expensive floor will have a significant effect in counteracting the forces against the wall.

A two-story design also has some distinct advantages, perhaps the most significant of which relate to energy performance. Although the perimeter of the wall surface is greater for a two-story than for a one-story design, the total exterior or surface area of the house is smaller. The smaller roof area is especially important from an energy standpoint, because the roof has a higher heat loss, higher interior temperature, and less earth protection than do the walls. A two-story house can also more easily recapture and recirculate the heat that rises to the top of the house.

The warmer living areas in a two-story design can be located on the upper level, facing the larger, sun-catching windows, while the cooler bedrooms (and smaller windows) can be placed on the lower level. If the floor of the upper level acts as a heat sink—a use that is consistent with its function as a structural brace for two-story walls—any heat lost from the heat sink floor will go into the rooms instead of into the mass of the earth. The energy efficiency of a two-story design is also assisted by the larger percentage of the exterior (in comparison with the one-story design) that is located further away from the surface temperature swings.

The smaller roof area of a two-story design also reduces the amount of waterproofing required, which in turn reduces both the cost and the area in which leaks could develop. In addition, the two-story configuration offers both functional and aesthetic opportunities. Although the stairway somewhat increases the space required for circulation, it is often possible to devise a plan that requires less hallway space than a one-story elevational unit, particularly in a larger house. Such a plan can help alleviate the "railroad car" atmosphere associated with some one-story designs. A slight increase in the size of a stairwell opening can help a small house feel larger by creating a more open feeling.

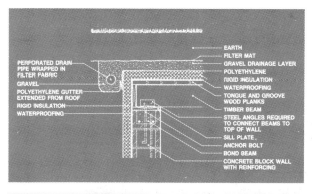

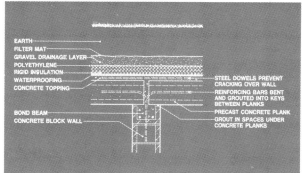

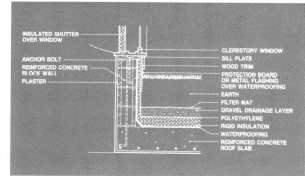

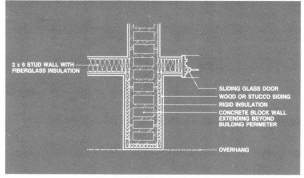

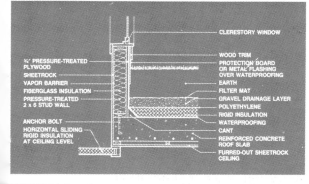

CHAPTER 5

SOILS

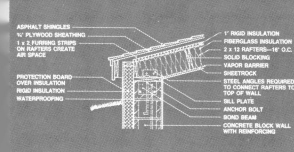

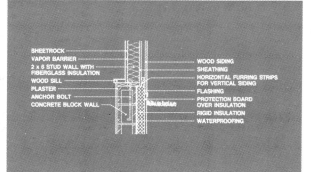

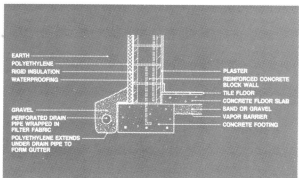

Introduction

A subsoil investigation should be a necessary part of the design process for any substantial dwelling structure. For a building substantially below ground, the site investigation is even more important than for an above-grade structure because of the greater interaction the underground structure will have with the soil. Design foundation loads for earth-covered buildings can range from 6,000 to 12,000 pounds per foot under the walls supporting the earth-covered roof, compared to only 1,500 to 3,000 pounds per foot for a typical one-story conventional house with a basement. Hence, allowable foundation bearing pressures are more critical to the earth-covered design. The walls of an earth sheltered house, which are buried to depths greater than 5 to 6 feet, require competent engineering, and the structural requirements for the walls vary considerably according to the assessment of the type of soil surrounding the structure.

The greater structural requirements and generally higher structural costs of an earth sheltered house underscore the importance of investing in a subsoil investigation. Because soils tests can provide close estimates of the soil parameters used in design, the designer does not have to rely on generalized figures, which are usually conservative and thus can result in costly overdesign (see examples below). The cost of the soil investigation will normally be offset later by the resultant savings in construction costs. Such an investigation may also yield the less tangible benefit of reducing the designer's uncertainty about the soils aspects of the project.

Initial financial savings are only one reason to conduct a subsoil investigation. Poor subsoil conditions that go undetected during the design and construction phase can cause major problems years after the structure is finished. This problem is not limited to earth sheltered houses. The annual cost of repairs to foundations in the United States has been estimated to exceed $2 billion per year [5.1], and damage to buildings as a whole from expansive clays has been estimated at over $8 billion per year [5.2]. For an underground structure, uneven settlement of foundations can cause structural cracking and distress to the waterproofing system. Wall pressures that are higher than anticipated can cause bowing of the wall and possibly even collapse. Because of the time-dependent nature of the settlement or loading, some of these conditions may not show up until well after construction is complete. Other problems may become dramatically apparent while excavation or backfilling is in progress.

It is not necessary to search very hard to find examples of these problems in houses that have already been constructed. A few typical mishaps are briefly discussed below.

- *Earth-covered house, with steel columns carrying the roof; columns supported on individual pad foundations.*

  Steel columns at the centerline of the house were supporting the ends of two rows of precast plank. The foundations were inadequately sized, causing rapid settlement of the foundations when the roof was loaded with earth. The settlement of the center of the roof caused damage to the waterproofing and simultaneously caused water to pond on the roof. The remedy was to remove the earth from the roof, repair the waterproofing, jack the columns to their original position, and underpin all the pad foundations.

- *External retaining wall of an earth sheltered house.*

  An approximately 15-foot-high wall failed in a heavy rainstorm during the construction period. The soft clay soil slumped against the wall during the rain, causing the wall to collapse. The wall had to be entirely rebuilt and strengthened.

- *Earth-covered house with excessive foundation sizes.*

  The 4-foot wide, 4-foot deep, nonengineered foundations were constructed on an excellent bearing soil. Seventy-two cubic yards of concrete were used in the foundations alone. Typical engineered foundations for this site condition would probably have contained only 20 cubic yards of concrete and only half as much steel as was used. The added cost incurred by the foundation overdesign alone was certainly at least several thousand dollars, far more than the cost of a subsoil investigation and professionally engineered foundation design.

- *Earth-covered house with excessive structure.*

  The structural shell costs for this house were $35 per square foot, at 1980 prices. A typical figure would have been $17 to $23 per square foot, also at 1980 prices. Foundations were 7 feet wide and 18 inches thick, even though the soil had a relatively good bearing capacity.

General Considerations

Designing a subsoil investigation to fulfill the requirements of safety and economy outlined above requires a good understanding of the characteristics of soil and rock that are important to the project design. A number of subsoil characteristics are briefly discussed below; actual parameters for design are covered later in this chapter.

Type of Soil and Size Classification

It is assumed that most earth sheltered buildings will be constructed in soil. Soil characteristics and most aspects of soil behavior are primarily determined by the soil type. Soil classification is not an exact science, however, since any particular soil may contain numerous constituent elements and the proportions of these elements do not usually remain constant even over short distances. The most basic classification of soils is by the size of the soil particles (see fig. 5-2 for common terminology for different ranges of particle sizes). The Unified Soil Classification (see fig. 5-1) classifies soils on the basis of gradations, constituent materials, and laboratory testing. The main division in soils behavior occurs between the cohesive soils and the granular, or cohesionless, soils. Granular soils are characterized by more predictable and less time-dependent behavior, generally higher bearing strengths, lower lateral pressures, and higher permeabilities. Cohesive soils are associated with more time-dependent behavior, are less permeable, and when soft, can exhibit low bearing strengths and high lateral pressures.

major divisions			letter symbol	description
coarse grained soils	gravel and gravelly soils	clean gravels (little or no fines)	GW	well-graded gravels, gravel-sand mixtures, little or no fines
	more than 50% of coarse fraction retained on no. 4 sieve		GP	poorly-graded gravels, gravel-sand mixtures, little or no fines
		gravels with fines (appreciable amount of fines)	GM	silty gravels, gravel-sand-silt mixtures
			GC	clayey gravels, gravel-sand-clay mixtures
more than 50% of material is larger than no. 200 sieve size	sand and sandy soils	clean sand (little or no fines)	SW	well-graded sands, gravelly sands, little or no fines
			SP	poorly-graded sands, gravelly sands, little or no fines
	more than 50% of coarse fraction passing no. 4 sieve	sands with fines (appreciable amount of fines)	SM	silty sands, sand-silt mixtures
			SC	clayey sands, sand-clay mixtures
fine grained soils	silts and clays	liquid limit less than 50	ML	inorganic silts and very fine sands, rock flour, silty or clayey fine sands or clayey silts with slight plasticity
			CL	inorganic clays of low to medium plasticity, gravelly clays, sandy clays, silty clays, lean clays
			OL	organic silts and organic silty clays of low plasticity
more than 50% of material is smaller than no. 200 sieve size	silts and clays	liquid limit greater than 50	MH	inorganic silts, micaceous or diatomaceous fine sand or silty soils
			CH	inorganic clays of high plasticity, fat clays
			OH	organic clays of medium to high plasticity, organic silts
highly organic soils			PT	peat, humus, swamp soils with high organic contents

5-1: Soil Classification Chart

At the upper end of the size range, boulders can be quite troublesome when encountered during the excavation and construction process because they are difficult to excavate and remove from the site. Boulders should not be left immediately underneath portions of the foundation because cracking of the foundation can occur over such a hard inclusion in a generally softer foundation soil.

Consistency

The same type of soil, having a similar gradation and composed of similar constituent materials, will exhibit very different engineering behavior based on what can be generally termed *consistency*. The consistency of cohesionless soils primarily relates to the density of the soil or the degree to which the soil is packed. Consistency can be determined by examining the unit weight of the soil, the blow count (explained below under *Investigation Process*), and the void ratio of the soil (the measure of how much space in the soil is occupied by air and water; see *Moisture Content and Water Tables*, below). In general, the denser the material and the lower the void ratio, the better the strength characteristics (bearing capacity) of the soil. These attributes are indicated by a higher blow count when driving the soil sampler.

The consistency of cohesive soils is usually referred to in terms of softness, stiffness, or hardness. The consistency is affected by the mineralogy of the clay or silt, the moisture content, and the degree of compaction or preload. Cohesive soils can also exhibit plastic behavior, in which the clay or silt slowly creeps or distorts

description	particle size	sieve size
boulders	12 in. diameter or larger	
cobbles	3 to 12 in. diameter	
coarse gravel	¾ to 3 in.	
fine gravel	5 mm to ¾ in.	¾ in. to #4
coarse sand	2 mm to 5 mm	#4 to #10
medium sand	.4 mm to 2 mm	#10 to #40
fine sand	.07 mm to .4 mm	#40 to #200
silt	.002 mm to .07 mm	
clay	smaller than .002 mm	

5-2: Particle Size Identification

Cohesive Soils			
consistency	Q_u(psf)	N(bpf)	w(pcf)
very soft	0– 500	0–2	100–110
soft	500–1,000	2–4	105–120
medium stiff	1,000–2,000	4–8	110–125
stiff	2,000–4,000	8–15	115–130
very stiff	4,000–8,000	15–30	120–140
hard	over 8,000	30–100	130–145
very hard	—	over 100	

Granular Soils			
density	w(pcf)	N(bpf)	∅
very loose	70– 90	0–4	25°–30°
loose	80–110	4–10	27°–33°
medium dense	105–125	10–30	32°–36°
dense	115–135	30–50	35°–42°
very dense	130–150	over 50	36°–50°

Q_u: unconfined compressive strength (pounds per square foot)
N: blow count (blows per foot)
w: soil weight (pounds per cubic foot)
∅: angle of internal friction

5-3: Typical Properties of Cohesive and Granular Soils

under load. The consistency of cohesive soils is determined by analyzing the appearance of the clay and the results of some simple field identification tests, together with the blow count and laboratory testing of the unconfined compressive strength of a sample of the soil. Figure 5-3 lists typical properties for both cohesive and granular soils having different consistencies; figure 5-4 is a simple field identification guide to the consistency of cohesive soils.

The moisture content of a clay determines its plasticity. When a sample is mixed with water until it reaches a liquid state and then is allowed to dry, it will first reach a point, called the liquid limit, at which the clay ceases to behave as a liquid and begins to acquire plastic properties. The liquid limit is expressed as a percentage moisture content (the weight of water in the sample divided by the dry weight of the sample, expressed as a percentage). As the soil dries further, it will eventually cease to behave in a plastic fashion and will behave in a brittle manner. The state at which this second changeover occurs is known as the plastic limit. A final limit, the shrinkage limit, is reached when the clay reaches a moisture content at which shrinkage of the sample stops. These three limits are called the Atterberg limits, and the liquid limit and plastic limit combined are used to obtain the plasticity index of the clay. If the liquid limit is substantially different from the plastic limit, the clay will exhibit plastic behavior over much of its range of moisture content. If the two limit figures are close together, then the clay will pass relatively quickly from a liquid state to a firm internal structure when drying. The plasticity index is simply the liquid limit minus the plastic limit; high numbers indicate a high degree of plasticity. The liquid limit varies with the clay or organic content of the soil; in inorganic soils a high liquid limit indicates a high proportion of finely divided material. Certain clays composed of unusually small particles, such as bentonite, have liquid limits as high as 600 percent. A high liquid limit may also indicate high organic content.

Figure 5-5 indicates the plasticity index in relation to the degree of plasticity of the clay or silt. The plasticity index cannot be used on its own but must be considered in conjunction with the liquid limit and other parameters of the cohesive soil.

Consistency	Field Identification	Q_u (psf)
very soft	easily penetrated several inches by fist	0–500
soft	easily penetrated several inches by thumb	500–1,000
medium	can be penetrated several inches by thumb with moderate effort	1,000–2,000
stiff	readily indented by thumb but penetrated only with great effort	2,000–4,000
very stiff	readily indented by thumbnail	4,000–8,000
hard	indented with difficulty by thumbnail	over 8,000

5-4: Field Identification of Cohesive Soils

Degree of Plasticity	Plasticity Index (PI)
none to slight	0–4
slight	5–10
medium	11–30
high to very high	over 30

5-5: Plasticity of Clays

Moisture Content and Water Table

Under normal field conditions, soil consists of soil particles, air, and water. The spaces occupied by air and water are considered the voids in the soil; the extent to which these voids exist is quantified as the void ratio of the soil. Most subsoils contain upper layers of soil that can become relatively dry during periods when there is little rainfall and, hence, considerable evaporation of water from the soil. Beneath these layers is a zone that is moist but not saturated and, finally, a level at which the soil voids are completely filled with water. This bottom level is termed the groundwater table. Above this level the ground moisture results from downward percolation of rainfall; the pores of a fine soil can also be fed by capillary rise. The capillary rise, which is caused by the pull of the surface tension of the water in the narrow pore spaces, is greater in fine clays than in coarser silts. Because moisture is present even above the water table, the air in the void spaces of such soil is normally saturated with water vapor. If temperatures within an earth sheltered structure are not sufficiently elevated, the high vapor pressure within the soil will cause moisture to move against the temperature gradient, thereby raising the interior humidity within the building. For this reason a vapor barrier or some zone for release of the high ground humidities is needed between a damp soil and the building, even when the structure is well drained and located above the water table.

Frost Heave

Capillary rise is also primarily responsible for frost heave. Moisture near the ground surface freezes and thus expands in volume. After this moisture freezes, the cycle may be repeated if more water can be drawn from deeper in the ground by capillary action. The ice lenses formed by this process can cause substantial movement in the ground.

Frost heave is worse in silts than in clays. Although the height of capillary rise is greater in clays than in silts, clay has very low permeability (ability to transmit moisture); hence, the transport of water to the freezing zone occurs very slowly. In silts, the combination of capillary rise and higher permeability causes more concern for frost heave. Techniques to reduce frost heave and its associated damage usually include:

- placing important foundations below the freezing zone,
- replacing frost-sensitive soils with granular material within the freezing zone,
- interrupting the capillary draw of moisture from below by introducing a drainage layer composed of a material coarser than the existing soil,
- insulating the ground surface around shallow footings, rather than extending the footing below the frost line. This technique holds particular promise for earth sheltered houses, as it will simultaneously reduce heat losses and material costs.

Percolation/Drainage

Percolation and drainage are both related to the permeability of soil. The term *percolation* is generally used when dissipation of water into the ground is the primary concern, as for the drain field of a septic tank. In such a case, the ability of the natural ground to drain away a certain flow rate of water must be assessed. The term *drainage* also refers to the removal of water; however, in this case the principal reason for removing the water is to divert it from a structure or from a particular area. In addition to referring to surface drainage paths, drainage often implies providing granular backfills to promote drainage around structures. Figure 5-6 indicates the range of permeabilities to be expected from different types of soil. A soil with a permeability rate of over 4 inches per hour is generally considered to provide good drainage; a rate of less than 2 inches per hour generally indicates poor drainage. Percolation rates are measured in minutes per inch of fall of water in a percolation test pit. A rate of under 5 minutes per inch is considered fast; a rate of over 200 minutes per inch is very slow. Acceptance criteria for drainfields are often in the range of 60 minutes per inch.

Shrink/Swell Potential

Certain types of clays have a mineralogy and a particle structure that cause the clay to undergo volume changes as the moisture content changes. The best-known of these clays is montmorillonite. A relatively pure, sodium-substituted montmorillonite clay can have a free-swell capacity of approximately twenty-two times its dry volume. The pressures required to fully restrain this swelling range from

Soil	Permeability (field rate)	Relative Permeability
fine to coarse, clean gravel	23 ft./min.	100,000,000
uniform, fine gravel	11 ft./min.	50,000,000
uniform, very coarse, clean sand	6.9 ft./min.	30,000,000
uniform, coarse sand	1.0 ft./min.	4,000,000
uniform, medium sand	14 ft./hr.	1,000,000
clean, well-graded sand and gravel	1.4 ft./hr.	100,000
uniform, fine sand	13 ft./day	40,000
well-graded, silty sand and gravel	1.3 ft./day	4,000
silty sand	9.8 ft./month	1,000
sandy clay	5 ft./month	500
silty clay	1.2 in./month	10
clay	.12 in./month	1

5-6: Permeability

approximately 2 to 3 tons per square foot. Other clays that can exhibit swelling characteristics to a lesser extent are illite, attapulgite, and kaolinite.

Although the swelling and squeezing behavior of bentonite clay is used to advantage in waterproofing structures, in most circumstances swelling clays should be avoided if possible. In many areas of the country, such as Colorado, Oklahoma, and Texas, however, where such clays are quite common, techniques to prevent damage to the structure caused by swelling or shrinkage of the surrounding clay often must be employed.

Since designing the structure to resist the swelling pressures is not economical, two main techniques are used to prevent damage. One technique is to isolate the structure from the ground, by using a suspended floor on a pile foundation, for example. The other means of preventing damage to the structure involves attempting to maintain the original level of moisture in the ground. If the moisture content of the soil is stable, there will be no drawing force to cause a change in volume. Changes in moisture content can result from:

- changes in ground cover
- the removal or addition of trees or other large vegetation
- loss of heat from a structure, causing moisture migration away from the building
- drainage backfills or utility trenches
- an increase or decrease in moisture content in the clay while it is exposed during construction
- leaks from utility systems

When a swelling clay is present on the site, the site investigation should examine the factors listed above to determine whether moisture changes in the clay are to be expected.

Shrinking of the clay can be as big a problem as swelling, because it will cause settlement of foundations (usually unequal) and will open cracks around the earth-covered walls, where water can penetrate during the next rainfall.

Settlement Characteristics

Changes in loading on soils (resulting, for example, from foundation pressures) force an adjustment of the stresses within the soil matrix. In dry, granular soils, the stresses are carried through the soil by contact stresses between the soil particles. Increasing the load on these soils will cause an almost immediate increase in these stresses and, hence, a rapid settlement from particle readjustment, particle strain, and local crushing. In soils below the water table, part of the load at any level within the soil is carried by the water pressure between the particles, and a lower effective stress exists between the soil particles. When the loading is changed under these conditions, the pressure will change not only between the particles but in the water itself. The local change in water pressure will cause water to flow through the soil to remove the unequal water pressures. In granular soils this water movement can occur quickly; thus, these settlements also will be rapid. In the finer-grained soils, particularly clays, this is not the case. In clay soils changes in loading are, again, initially carried by the water in the soil as well as by the soil particles. Because of the low permeability

of the clay, however, the increase in local pressure cannot be dissipated quickly, as it can be in granular soils. As the excess water pressure in the clay slowly dissipates, more of the load will gradually be transferred to the soil particles. Thus, settlement in the clay itself will take place slowly—sometimes over a period of many years. Laboratory tests and calculation procedures have been devised to estimate the rate of this type of settlement for different soils.

Techniques for reducing settlement include:

- preloading the soil before construction. In cohesive soils, preloading is usually coupled with increased drainage to promote dissipation of the local water pressure.

- increasing the area of the foundations in order to lower the increased stress placed on the soil.

- excavating the soil and replacing it with an underground section of the building. Since the building volume is much lighter than the soil that has been removed, it is possible to "float" a building with little net change in pressure on the soils beneath the foundation. This technique is used primarily with raft foundations, in which the whole building floor is designed as a single foundation.

Almost all foundations placed on soil will settle a measurable amount after the building is loaded. Settlements of ¼ to ½ inch do not usually cause problems if the settlements are uniform. Differential settlements between individual foundations of the building must be more severely limited, however, to prevent distress to the structural shell of the building. Uniform settlements are achieved by correctly proportioning each foundation to its expected load.

Compaction/Backfilling Characteristics

Usually the soil from the site of an earth sheltered building must be not only excavated, but also used as backfill around or over the completed structure. The important characteristics that a fill or backfill should have are ease of compaction, in order to prevent settlement from occurring later, and ease of placement. Settlement around the walls of the structure can alter drainage patterns on the surface and abrade or drag down insulation and/or waterproofing on the walls. As a general rule, granular soils, which are easily compacted, make good backfills; cohesive soils must be compacted carefully in order to perform satisfactorily. Moisture content is a very important factor in the degree of compaction of cohesive soils. If there is too much water in the soil, most of the compaction stresses are carried in the water rather than by compressing the soil; if there is too little water, the soil lumps or particles will not redistribute into a more compact form.

The effectiveness of compaction and the optimum moisture content for compaction are measured by a Proctor test. This laboratory test establishes the density possible, given a certain (high) energy level of compaction. To establish the optimum moisture content, several tests are run at different moisture contents, using the same level of compaction energy. The moisture content that should produce the greatest density for a specific soil can be determined by comparing the tests. The compaction of field soil is specified as a certain percentage of the Proctor maximum density; higher percentages indicate higher levels of compaction.

Erosion Potential

Fine-grained soils can be susceptible to both water and wind erosion. The potential for erosion is increased when the ground surface is exposed, that is, when no artificial or natural ground cover is present. The potential for wind erosion is reduced in damp soils, strongly cohesive soils, and soils composed predominantly of large-sized particles. Water erosion is particularly bad in fine soils on steep slopes where no surface protection is provided against surface water and no organic matter or root system binds the soil particles together. Junctions between artificial structures and the soil that follow the fall of the slope can often provide a channel for erosion to start unless surface water is directed away from such areas.

pH Value

The pH value of a soil indicates its acidity or alkalinity. The acidity or alkalinity of a soil affects the ability of the soil to support different types of vegetation, as well as the degree to which it will corrode concrete or steel placed underground. A pH value of 7.0 indicates a neutral soil; numbers less than 7.0 indicate increasingly acidic soils, and soils assigned pH numbers over 7.0 are increasingly alkaline.

Corrosivity

Although the pH value of the soil has a significant effect on the degree to which concrete and steel will corrode when placed underground, other factors also can contribute to corrosion. The degree of corrosion of concrete varies with the type of salt in the soil. A high sulphate content in the soil can be particularly detrimental to concrete unless special cements are used or the concrete is isolated from the ground environment by a waterproofing that is not susceptible to deterioration caused by the ground conditions. The corrosion of steel underground may be affected by any stray underground electrical currents, as well as by connection of the steel with materials that have a different electric potential. Groundwater, particularly when acidic, lowers the electrical resistance to currents, thereby aiding corrosion. Protection from corrosion can be provided by attempting to isolate the steel from the soil environment, by electrically connecting the steel to a material that will corrode before the steel (such a material is referred to as a sacrificial anode), or by passing an electrical current through the steel to alter its electric potential with respect to the ground (a technique termed cathodic protection). Galvanizing involves protecting the steel with a zinc coating that provides isolation with a degree of sacrificial protection.

Organic Content

When the organic content of a soil is high—when more than 10 percent of the soil is composed of organic matter—the soil is generally considered to be a poor material on which to build a foundation because highly organic soils (such as peat) are very compressible and will hold large quantities of water. Organic matter can help reduce the potential for erosion of a soil. The organic content of a soil also is considered in conjunction with the soil pH value and percentage of clay in determining appropriate plant materials.

Bedrock

Bedrock usually provides a good bearing stratum for building foundations, although the presence of surface weathering or a large number of joints can cause allowable bearing pressures to be considerably less than they are in solid rock. Because excavation in bedrock can be expensive, especially on small sites, it should be minimized. It is also important to avoid designing some building foundations that bear on bedrock while others bear on soil, because the amount of settlement of the two foundations will differ unless special provisions are made (piers to bedrock under the soil foundations).

When carrying out the soil investigation, it is important to distinguish boulders just above the bedrock or a loose, weathered layer of bedrock from the sound rock below. Borings are therefore often specified to be continued to a certain depth into the apparent bedrock. The depth specified will depend on both the expected load on the foundations and the severity of the problems that could occur if the foundation design would have to be altered after the foundation was eventually exposed.

Soil Profile

Since soils often contain alternating strong and weak zones, it should not be assumed that, just because the soil at the foundation depth has a good bearing capacity, the foundation will be satisfactory. If a weak zone underlies a stress zone of better bearing material, the weak zone may be overstressed by the foundation and allow damaging settlement. Consequently, soil borings are continued several feet below the anticipated level of the foundations. As a rule of thumb, this additional depth is twice the width of the individual foundations and, for houses, at least 10 feet. Several methods of analysis can be used to determine the behavior of layered soils. The simplest rule of thumb assumes a one-to-two horizontal-to-vertical load spread through the soil from the foundation; the bearing strength at any level can be checked against the reduced foundation pressure resulting from the larger area over which load is distributed.

Slope Stability

When building on hillsides, carrying out significant excavations, or using steep berms around a building, it is important to know how stable the existing slope is and what angles are safe to use for excavation slopes and for permanent slopes. Slopes may fail because of surface sloughing or flow or because of more deep-rooted failures in which slip occurs along weak zones within the soil or in approximately circular areas under the toe of the slope. Normally stable slopes may become unstable during heavy rainfalls or seismic activity. Steeper angles are generally used for construction slopes, as opposed to permanent slopes, because the chance of failure is not as great and consequences of failure are normally less severe during the short construction period. Figure 5-7 indicates typical maximum slope angles for construction in cohesionless soils and the angles of internal friction for different soil densities.

Soil	Range	Typical	Slope (vertical to horizontal)
sand and gravel	32–50°	32–36°	1 on 1.5
well-graded sand	30°–46°	30°–34°	1 on 1.6
uniform, fine to medium sand	26°–36°	26°–30°	1 on 1.8
silt (nonplastic)	26°–34°	26°–30°	1 on 2

5-7: Angle of Internal Friction for Granular Soils

Values in this table from reference 5.4.

Thermal Characteristics

Thermal characteristics of the soil have not usually been considered in traditional soil investigations, probably because they are somewhat less important for conventional than for earth sheltered buildings. The thermal conductivity of soil is more affected by the moisture content of the soil than by the type of soil: for example, the conductivity of a wet soil may be seven times higher than that of very dry soil. The important parameters to be aware of for earth sheltered building design are the average temperature of the soil at depth in the specific region, the moisture content of the soil near the building, and the likely fluctuation in moisture content throughout the year. This information, in combination with information about the soil type, can be used to establish the thermal conductivity and thermal diffusivity based on published tables [5.3] and, hence, the heat transfer through the ground.

Major Design Parameters

Although all the considerations discussed above can be important in the design of an earth sheltered house, two quantitative soil properties normally comprise the main soils information used in determining the structural design: the allowable bearing pressure, and the suggested lateral pressures to be used for the design of earth-covered building walls and freestanding retaining walls.

Figure 5-8 summarizes some of the general characteristics of soils according to the Unified Soil Classification and indicates typical bearing capacities for each type of soil. Given the range of bearing capacities within each soil type, it is not wise to use an average value and it will probably not be economical to use a conservative value. The soil testing firm should be asked to recommend a value to be used for the soil being tested.

group symbols	typical names	drainage characteristic	frost heave potential	volume change	backfill potential	typical bearing capacity	range (psf)	general suitability
GW	well-graded gravels & gravel-sand mixtures, little or no fines	excellent	low	low	best	8000 psf	1500 psf to 20 tons/ft²	good
GP	poorly graded gravels & gravel-sand mixtures, little or no fines	excellent	low	low	excellent	6000 psf	1500 psf to 20 tons/ft²	good
GM	silty gravels, gravel-sand silt mixtures	good	medium	low	good	4000 psf	1500 psf to 20 tons/ft²	good
GC	clayey gravels, gravel-sand-clay mixtures	fair	medium	low	good	3500 psf	1500 psf to 10 tons/ft²	good
SW	well-graded sands & gravelly sands, little or no fines	good	low	low	good	5000 psf	1500 psf to 15 tons/ft²	good
SP	poorly graded sand & gravelly sands, little or no fines	good	low	low	good	4000 psf	1500 psf to 10 tons/ft²	good
SM	silty sands, sand-silt mixtures	good	medium	low	fair	3500 psf	1500 psf to 5 tons/ft²	good
SC	clayey sands, sand-clay mixtures	fair	medium	low	fair	3000 psf	1000 psf to 8000 psf	good
ML	inorganic silts, very fine sands, rock flour, silty or clayey fine sands	fair	high	low	fair	2000 psf	1000 psf to 8000 psf	fair
CL	inorganic clays of low to medium plasticity, gravelly clays, sandy clays, silty clays, lean clays	fair	medium	medium	fair	2000 psf	500 psf to 5000 psf	fair
MH	inorganic silts, micaceous or diatomaceous fine sands or silts, elastic silts	poor	high	high	poor	1500 psf	500 psf to 4000 psf	poor
CH	inorganic clays of medium to high plasticity	poor	medium	high	bad	1500 psf	500 psf to 4000 psf	poor
OL	organic silts and organic silty clays of low plasticity	poor	medium	medium	poor	400 psf or remove	generally remove soil	poor
OH	organic clays of medium to high plasticity	no good	medium	high	no good	remove	—	poor
PT	peat, muck and other highly organic soils	no good	—	high	no good	remove	—	poor

5-8: General Characteristics and Typical Bearing Capacities of Soils

The lateral pressure of soils against retaining walls is a complicated subject that is still being researched. Several design theories are practical to use, however, and have yielded good results over a long period of time. The principal design method assumes slip lines that correspond to the angles of internal friction within the soil. The pressure on a retaining wall then depends on whether or not the wall deflects significantly when it is pressured by the ground. If the top of the wall can deflect with the ground pressure, then the internal friction of the soil is mobilized to help resist the tendency to fail, thus reducing the necessary design pressure for the wall. This "active pressure" condition is used for designing simple external retaining walls in cases where these assumptions are appropriate (see fig. 5-9). The main walls of an earth sheltered house, however, are usually quite rigidly supported by the floor, roof, and any intermediate floors of the structure. Under these conditions it appears more reasonable to calculate wall design on the basis of "at rest" lateral pressures in which no resistance of the soil is mobilized. Pressures on walls designed on the assumption of "at rest" lateral pressures have correlated well with measured wall pressures on instrumented buildings [5.6]. A third pressure condition, involving "passive pressure," occurs when a surface is being pushed against the soil and mobilizes the internal friction of the soil to resist this movement. These pressures are used to check whether the toe of a retaining wall, for example, will move as a result of the active lateral pressure (see fig. 5-9). Typical values for these three types of pressures are given in figure 5-10. The term "equivalent fluid pressure" is used because the pressure increases linearly with depth, as it does in a fluid.

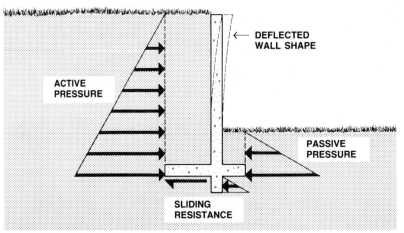

A: External Retaining Wall

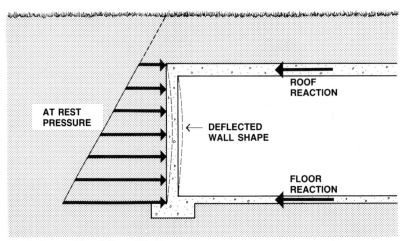

B: Exterior Building Wall

5-9: Types of Ground Pressures

Classification	Friction Angle (degrees)	Density or Consistency	Unit Soil Weight (pcf)	Equivalent Fluid Pressure (psf/ft. depth)		
				Active	At Rest	Passive
coarse sand or sand and gravel	45	compact	140	24	41	820
	38	firm	120	29	46	510
	32	loose	90	28	42	290
medium sand	40	compact	130	28	46	600
	34	firm	110	31	48	390
	30	loose	90	30	45	270
fine sand	34	compact	130	37	57	460
	30	firm	100	33	50	300
	28	loose	85	31	41	280
fine, silty sand or sandy silt	32	compact	130	40	61	420
	30	firm	100	33	50	300
	28	loose	85	31	45	280
fine, uniform sand	30	compact	135	45	68	400
	28	firm	110	38	58	300
	26	loose	85	33	48	220
clay silt	20	medium	120	59	79	245
		soft	90	44	59	183
silty clay	15	medium	120	71	89	204
		soft	90	53	67	153
clay	10	medium	120	84	99	170
		soft	90	63	74	153
clay	0	medium	120	120	120	120
		soft	90	90	90	90

5-10: Typical Values of Unit Weights and Equivalent Fluid Pressures

Values in this table from reference 5.4.

The Investigation Process

The subsoil investigation not only plays an essential part in the design of an earth sheltered building, but also should be used in making the site purchase decision for such a building, since poor soil conditions on a site will very likely increase construction costs.

In many cases a substantial amount of data about the site can be gathered prior to a physical investigation of the site. Figure 5-11 lists items that should be considered and potential sources of information. An often overlooked information source is the U.S. Department of Agriculture's Soil Conservation Service, which has offices in all regions of the country. Figure 5-12 is a sample of one of the agency's information sheets. This information, although only applicable to shallow depths, can offer valuable preliminary information about the site and can help in planning the detailed investigation. In most cases soil borings taken at the site will still be necessary. Typical instructions for the soil-testing firm that will carry out the borings are given in figure 5-13.

When a soil test is taken, an auger or other rotary bit is used to advance the bore hole to the depth to be sampled. The drill hole has a diameter of 4 to 8 inches. Samples are customarily taken with a split barrel sampler at 2½-foot intervals to a depth of 10 to 15 feet, and then at 5-foot intervals as the boring extends deeper into the soil. The samples are obtained from undisturbed soil just below the bottom of the bore hole after it has been advanced to each sampling depth. After a sample is obtained, the bore hole is drilled to the next sampling interval.

Most soil-boring investigations call for a blow count reading when each sample is taken. The standard penetration test measures the number of blows required to drive the sample into the soil using a 140-pound weight dropped from a distance of 30 inches. The sample is obtained with a split tube attached to a drive cone that serves as the cutting head. The tube has a 1⅜-inch inside diameter and a 2-inch outside diameter. After the split tube sampler has been driven 6 inches into the soil, the number of blows required to drive the device down another 12 inches is counted and recorded on log sheets. These numbers on the log sheets, termed "blow count" numbers, are represented as N. The results of the standard penetration tests, which indicate the relative density and comparative consistency of the soils, can help in estimating the bearing capacity and the compressibility of the soil being sampled. Logs of all borings should always be included in the appendix of the soils

---

Typical Information to be Gathered

- original plat/survey information
- easements (horizontal and vertical extent)
- mineral rights (together with any agreements as to access from the property)
- existing topographic information
- existing utility and building information
- records of seismic activity or zone clarifications for seismic design
- existing surficial and bedrock geologic information
- existing information on groundwater conditions and surface drainage
- soil temperature

Typical Sources of Site Information

- local city or county engineer's office
- city or county records department
- aerial survey companies
- state geological survey information
- U.S.G.S. maps and reports
- U.S. dept. of agricultural soils information (usually shallow only)
- previous records from nearby construction
- well-drilling records
- drilling records of public agencies
- technical papers on local geology, microclimate, soil conditions, etc. (in nearest university library)
- experienced local soil-testing firms and consultants (as paid service)
- government agency responsible for adjacent roads
- local weather-reporting agency

5-11: Site Investigation Information

Information in this figure from reference 5.7.

SOIL INTERPRETATIONS RECORD

MN0060
MLRA(S): 103
REV. ELB, 5-77
TYPIC HAPLUDALFS, FINE-LOAMY, MIXED, MESIC

HAYDEN SERIES

THE HAYDEN SERIES CONSISTS OF DEEP WELL DRAINED SOILS FORMED IN GLACIAL TILL UNDER DECIDUOUS FOREST ON GROUND AND TERMINAL MORAINES. TYPICALLY THEY HAVE VERY DARK-GRAY LOAM SURFACE LAYERS 2 INCHES THICK; DARK GRAYISH BROWN LOAM SUBSURFACE LAYERS 7 INCHES THICK; BROWN AND YELLOWISH-BROWN LOAM AND CLAY LOAM SUBSOILS 34 INCHES THICK; AND LIGHT OLIVE-BROWN LOAM UNDERLYING MATERIAL. SLOPES RANGE FROM 2 TO 35 PERCENT SLOPES. MOST GENTLY SLOPING AREAS ARE CROPPED; OTHER AREAS USED FOR PASTURE AND FOREST.

ESTIMATED SOIL PROPERTIES (A)

DEPTH (IN.)	USDA TEXTURE	UNIFIED	AASHTO	FRACT >3 IN (PCT)	4	10	40	200	LIQUID LIMIT	PLAS- TICITY INDEX
0-9	L, SIL	ML, CL-ML, CL	A-4	0	100	98-100	85-98	50-80	20-36	4-10
0-9	FIL, L	SM, SM-SC, SC	A-4	0	100	95-100	65-85	35-50	20-30	NP-8
9-43	CL, L	CL	A-7, A-6	0	95-100	90-98	80-95	55-75	30-50	15-26
43-60	L, SL, FSL	CL, SC	A-6, A-4	0-5	95-100	90-98	75-90	35-70	20-35	8-15

DEPTH (IN.)	CLAY (PCT <2MM)	MOIST BULK DENSITY (G/CM3)	PERMEA- BILITY (IN/HR)	AVAILABLE WATER CAPACITY (IN/IN)	SOIL REACTION (PH)	SALINITY (MMHOS/CM)	SHRINK- SWELL POTENTIAL	EROSION FACTORS K T	WIND ERO. GROUP	ORGANIC MATTER (PCT)	CORROSIVITY STEEL	CONCRETE
0-9	10-28	1.40-1.60	0.6-2.0	0.20-0.22	5.6-7.3	–	LOW	.32 5		4-6	.5-1	LOW	MODERATE
0-9	8-15	1.45-1.70	2.0-6.0	0.14-0.18	5.6-7.3	–	LOW	.32 5	3	.5-1		
9-43	18-35	1.50-1.65	0.6-2.0	0.15-0.19	5.1-7.3	–	MODERATE	.32				
43-60	15-27	1.65-1.80	0.6-2.0	0.14-0.19	7.4-8.4	–	LOW	.32				

FLOODING			HIGH WATER TABLE			CEMENTED PAN		BEDROCK		SUBSIDENCE		HYD GRP	PCTNT'L FROST ACTION
FREQUENCY	DURATION	MONTHS	DEPTH (FT)	KIND	MONTHS	DEPTH (IN)	HARDNESS	DEPTH (IN)	HARDNESS	INIT. (IN)	TOTAL (IN)		
NONE			>6.0			–		>60		–	–	B	MODERATE

SANITARY FACILITIES

SEPTIC TANK ABSORPTION FIELDS	2-8%: MODERATE-PERCS SLOWLY 8-15%: MODERATE-PERCS SLOWLY,SLOPE 15+%: SEVERE-SLOPE
SEWAGE LAGOON AREAS	2-7%: MODERATE-SLOPE,SEEPAGE 7+%: SEVERE-SLOPE
SANITARY LANDFILL (TRENCH)	2-15%: MODERATE-TOO CLAYEY 15-25%: MODERATE-SLOPE,TOO CLAYEY 25+%: SEVERE-SLOPE
SANITARY LANDFILL (AREA)	2-8%: SLIGHT 8-15%: MODERATE-SLOPE 15+%: SEVERE-SLOPE
DAILY COVER FOR LANDFILL	2-8%: FAIR-TOO CLAYEY 8-15%: FAIR-TOO CLAYEY,SLOPE 15+%: POOR-SLOPE

CONSTRUCTION MATERIAL

ROADFILL	2-25%: POOR-LOW STRENGTH 25+%: POOR-SLOPE,LOW STRENGTH
SAND	UNSUITED-EXCESS FINES
GRAVEL	UNSUITED-EXCESS FINES
TOPSOIL	2-8%: FAIR-THIN LAYER 8-15%: FAIR-SLOPE,THIN LAYER 15+%: POOR-SLOPE

WATER MANAGEMENT

POND RESERVOIR AREA	2-6%: SEEPAGE 6+%: SLOPE,SEEPAGE
EMBANKMENTS DIKES AND LEVEES	FAVORABLE
EXCAVATED PONDS AQUIFER FED	NO WATER
DRAINAGE	NOT NEEDED
IRRIGATION	2-6% L,SIL: FAVORABLE 6+% L,SIL: SLOPE 2-6% FSL,SL: SOIL BLOWING 6+% FSL,SL: SLOPE,SOIL BLOWING
TERRACES AND DIVERSIONS	2-12% L,SIL: FAVORABLE 12+% L,SIL: SLOPE 2-12% FSL,SL: SOIL BLOWING 12+% FSL,SL: SLOPE,SOIL BLOWING
GRASSED WATERWAYS	2-8%: FAVORABLE 8+%: SLOPE

BUILDING SITE DEVELOPMENT

SHALLOW EXCAVATIONS	2-8%: SLIGHT 8-15%: MODERATE-SLOPE 15+%: SEVERE-SLOPE
DWELLINGS WITHOUT BASEMENTS	2-8%: MODERATE-SHRINK-SWELL,LOW STRENGTH 8-15%: MODERATE-SLOPE,SHRINK-SWELL, LOW STRENGTH 15+%: SEVERE-SLOPE
DWELLINGS WITH BASEMENTS	2-8%: MODERATE-SHRINK-SWELL,LOW STRENGTH 8-15%: MODERATE-SLOPE,SHRINK-SWELL, LOW STRENGTH 15+%: SEVERE-SLOPE
SMALL COMMERCIAL BUILDINGS	2-4%: MODERATE-SHRINK-SWELL,LOW STRENGTH 4-8%: MODERATE-SLOPE,SHRINK-SWELL, LOW STRENGTH 8+%: SEVERE-SLOPE
LOCAL ROADS AND STREETS	2-15%: SEVERE-LOW STRENGTH 15+%: SEVERE-SLOPE,LOW STRENGTH
LAWNS, LANDSCAPING AND GOLF FAIRWAYS	2-8%: SLIGHT 8-15%: MODERATE-SLOPE 15+%: SEVERE-SLOPE

REGIONAL INTERPRETATIONS

| PASTURE AND HAYLAND | 0-18%: GROUP 1
18-25%: GROUP 2
25+%: GROUP 8 |

HAYDEN SERIES
MN0060

RECREATIONAL DEVELOPMENT

| CAMP AREAS | 2-8%: SLIGHT
8-15%: MODERATE-SLOPE
15+%: SEVERE-SLOPE | PLAYGROUNDS | 2-6%: MODERATE-SLOPE
6+%: SEVERE-SLOPE |
| PICNIC AREAS | 2-8%: SLIGHT
8-15%: MODERATE-SLOPE
15+%: SEVERE-SLOPE | PATHS AND TRAILS | 2-15%: SLIGHT
15-25%: MODERATE-SLOPE
25+%: SEVERE-SLOPE |

CAPABILITY AND YIELDS PER ACRE OF CROPS AND PASTURE (HIGH LEVEL MANAGEMENT)

CLASS- DETERMINING PHASE	CAPA- BILITY	CORN (BU) NIRR IRR	SOYBEANS (BU) NIRR IRR	OATS (BU) NIRR IRR	GRASS- LEGUME HAY (TONS) NIRR IRR	BROMEGRASS- ALFALFA (AUM) NIRR IRR	KENTUCKY BLUEGRASS (AUM) NIRR IRR
2-6%	2E	100	30	75	4.5	6.5	3.5
6-12%	3E	85	26	70	4.5	6.5	3.5
12-18%	4E	65	22	60	4.0	6.0	3.0
18-25%	6E	–	–	–	3.0	4.5	3.0
25-35%	7E	–	–	–	–	–	1.5

WOODLAND SUITABILITY

CLASS- DETERMINING PHASE	ORD SYM	EROSION HAZARD	EQUIP. LIMIT	SEEDLING MORT'Y	WINDTH. HAZARD	PLANT COMPET	COMMON TREES	SITE INDX	TREES TO PLANT
2-12%	2O	SLIGHT	SLIGHT	SLIGHT	SLIGHT	SLIGHT	NORTHERN RED OAK		BLACK WALNUT
12+%	2R	MODERATE	MODERATE	SLIGHT	SLIGHT	SLIGHT	AMERICAN BASSWOOD	65	NORTHERN RED OAK
							SUGAR MAPLE		AMERICAN BASSWOOD
							BLACK WALNUT	62	SILVER MAPLE
							EASTERN WHITE PINE	64	WHITE OAK
							WHITE OAK	62	

WINDBREAKS (B)

CLASS-DETERMINING PHASE	SPECIES	HT	SPECIES	HT	SPECIES	HT	SPECIES	HT
2-12%	EASTERN WHITE PINE	28	GREEN ASH	35	COMMON HACKBERRY	34	EASTERN COTTONWOOD	60
	PONDEROSA PINE	26	SIBERIAN CRABAPPLE	18	AMUR MAPLE	23	GRAY DOGWOOD	12
	TATARIAN HONEYSUCKLE	12	LILAC	11	NORTHERN WHITE-CEDAR	20	WHITE SPRUCE	22

WILDLIFE HABITAT SUITABILITY

CLASS- DETERMINING PHASE	GRAIN & SEED	GRASS & LEGUME	WILD HERB.	HARDWD TREES	CONIFER PLANTS	SHRUBS	WETLAND PLANTS	SHALLOW WATER	OPENLD WILDLF	WOODLD WILDLF	WETLAND WILDLF	RANGELD WILDLF
2-6%	GOOD	GOOD	GOOD	GOOD	GOOD	–	V. POOR	V. POOR	GOOD	GOOD	V. POOR	–
6-18%	FAIR	GOOD	GOOD	GOOD	GOOD	–	V. POOR	V. POOR	GOOD	GOOD	V. POOR	–
18+%	POOR	FAIR	GOOD	GOOD	GOOD	–	V. POOR	V. POOR	FAIR	GOOD	V. POOR	–

POTENTIAL NATIVE PLANT COMMUNITY (RANGELAND OR FOREST UNDERSTORY VEGETATION)

COMMON PLANT NAME	PLANT SYMBOL (M.SPN)	PERCENTAGE COMPOSITION (DRY WEIGHT) BY CLASS DETERMINING PHASE

POTENTIAL PRODUCTION (LBS./AC. DRY WT):
FAVORABLE YEARS
NORMAL YEARS
UNFAVORABLE YEARS

FOOTNOTES

A   BASED ON TEST DATA OF 7 PEDONS.
B   0-12% WINDBREAK GROUP-1; 12+% WINDBREAK GROUP-3; TOO STEEP FOR WINDBREAKS

I. General

1. Prior to undertaking the project, the soils engineers shall furnish the owners with information regarding the estimated cost of furnishing the services described below and when these services may be performed.

2. Test borings and a detailed engineering report shall be made by or coordinated through a Registered Professional Engineer skilled in soils and foundation engineering.

3. The owner will accurately describe the location of the project site. The Engineer should contact the owner, however, if any questions arise during the work, including changes in the test boring program and/or unusual site conditions.

II. Field Testing.

1. Soil sampling shall be performed in accordance with ASTM standard D1586 and D1452. Although a minimum of two test borings is suggested, the Engineer should indicate if one boring is adequate or if more are necessary. The test borings should terminate 10+ ft. below the planned footing elevation, or as determined by the Engineer.

2. Description of the soils shall be in accordance with ASTM S2487 (Unified Soil Classification System).

3. Water level measurements shall be made upon completion of each test boring and, again, prior to filling the test holes.

III. Engineering Report.

1. The detailed report shall contain a discussion of both the soil and groundwater conditions at the site. Recommendations addressing foundation type, soil bearing pressure, safe values for lateral soil pressure, and a soil friction value for developing resistance against the lateral pressure shall be included.

2. Attached to the report shall be the test boring logs, complete with water-level measurement data, soil type and USCS symbol, depth of soil layers, and ground surface elevation of each test boring. The "N" values, per the ASTM D1586 test, should be clearly shown for the depth at which each test was taken.

3. A sketch showing boring locations (properly dimensioned) and information regarding the benchmark used in determining boring elevations at the site shall be included.

5-13: Instructions to Soils Engineers

report. All soil strata encountered are described in the logs, usually using the Unified Soil Classification system. Sampling information, pertinent field data, and field observations are recorded in addition to the blow count readings.

Sometimes soil-testing firms will do grain-size distribution tests (sieve analysis) and determine soil moisture contents to aid in classifying soils. Tests other than the standard penetration test can be performed. Unconfined compressive strength and pocket penetrometer tests, for example, can be used to help determine the strength of cohesive soil and bearing capacities.

Soil boring logs often use descriptive terms to indicate the relative proportions of the different constitutents of the soil. Figure 5-14 is a guide to the proportions commonly associated with these terms.

Description	Percent
trace	1-10
little	11-20
some	21-35
with	36-50

5-14: Relative Proportions

Design Recommendations from Soil Borings

For the designer the design recommendations are probably the most important part of the soils report. The report should include information related to the following concerns:

location of the groundwater table

In most cases the groundwater table is not of major concern, assuming the structure is located at least 3 feet above it. In soils containing swelling clays, however, the groundwater table is of major concern. When swelling clays exist on-site, it is important to build drainage systems to local code requirements and to analyze wall, footing, and piling loads for uplift.

bearing capacity

Recommendations for bearing capacities of major soil layers are generally given in the soils report. The report will also state which, if any, layers should be removed and what kind of fill should be used to replace them.

selection of footings

Whenever possible, continuous footings, rather than spread footings, should be designed, because continuous footings allow an earth sheltered structure to settle more uniformly. As a general rule, spread footings will also settle more than will continuous footings, given the same load per square foot. Frost footing requirements are usually established by local or state code. All elevational-type earth sheltered homes must have frost footings on the exposed sides.

lateral pressure

Designers of earth sheltered houses should be aware that many design assumptions for wood foundation and block masonry basements tend to be unconservative when applied to walls buried at greater depths. For example, it is unrealistic to assume lateral pressures of 25 to 30 pounds per square foot of depth for most backfills against building walls. In general, lateral pressures affect the design of retaining walls for earth sheltered houses in one of two ways. In the first case, the wall is unrestrained at the top and, hence, can deflect away from the soil pressure. If the wall is allowed to deflect, the design can be based on the values for "active" lateral pressures. Active values seem adequate for the design of retaining walls and may be suitable for cases in which a conventional roof is attached to an earth-bermed house. In the second case, the retaining wall is restrained from movement at its top, center, or both by stiff supports in the form of a roof or intermediate floor. In this case, it should not be assumed that soil pressures will be reduced by movement of the wall; hence, "at rest" lateral pressure values should be used in these design calculations.

settlement predictions

The amount of settlement that will occur when the structure is placed in soil is probably one of the most difficult parameters to estimate in a soils report. Line loads on footings are far greater for most earth sheltered homes than for conventional houses; however, if the footings are properly sized, the settlement will probably be limited to ½ to 1 inch. This amount of settlement should not cause any problems, provided that the footings are sized properly.

potential problems with adjacent property

When excavating close to another building in soil, it is important not to disturb the footings of the adjacent buildings. In addition, the berms against the side walls of an earth sheltered home should not be so steep as to divert water directly onto neighboring property. A three-to-one slope ratio is normally considered the maximum slope for such berms. The designer also must take care to contain the berms within the property line.

percolation, drainage, backfilling, and compaction

Free-draining granular soil backfills not only can significantly lower lateral pressures, but can also divert water from the structure. It is recommended that the soil used for backfilling side walls be compacted to within an approximate density range of 88 to 90 percent of the Standard Proctor maximum density. The soil should be compacted only enough to ensure that no major settlements occur; overcompaction of the soil around the side walls can induce additional lateral stress. The backfill should be placed in 8- to 12-inch lifts and compacted with a jumping jack or tamper. Tamping the backfill with approximately six passes should be adequate. Although water may be added if the backfill is very dry, adding too much water will not permit good compaction. If backfilling takes place in the winter and sandy soils are not available, the clay soils must be carefully applied. Large chunks of frozen clay should not be allowed in the backfill area, as frozen clay boulders tend to damage waterproofing and cause excessive settlement of the backfill when they melt in the spring.

Fill required beneath floor slabs should have a low plasticity index (i.e., below 15) and should be compacted to a dry density of at least 95 percent of the Standard Proctor maximum dry density. Compaction of this fill should be accomplished by placing the fill in 6- to 8-inch-thick lifts. Soil under footings and slabs on grade is compacted more heavily than that adjacent to the walls because the lateral pressures induced are not a concern in the former situation.

Soil placed on the roof should be only moderately compacted. Vegetation on the roof will play an important role in how the soil will behave over time. Soil loads on the roof should be estimated at 110 to 130 pounds per cubic foot. Estimates of live loads on the roof should include additional weight for cases when the soil will be saturated with water: 24 pounds per square foot of water weight per foot of depth of soil can be assumed. This means that, for 18 inches of soil, a live load of 36 pounds per square foot should be added to the estimate of the weight of the soil.

potential problems with frost and swelling clays

Most of these kinds of problems can be reduced if silts are avoided as a backfill material. State and local codes also require a minimum depth for footings to help assure that no frost uplift occurs under footings.

Expansive material at the site is subject to volumetric change with fluctuations in the soil moisture content. Unless extensive testing is performed, estimates of anticipated structural movement resulting from expansion can only be based on experience with materials of similar geological origin. Expansion can cause movement and distress to lightly loaded footings, floor slabs, and foundation walls. Experience has shown that the most severe problems caused by expansion occur when the material in its natural state has low moisture content or is allowed to dry during construction. Wetting—either by groundwater movement or by capillary action after construction is completed—causes the soil moisture content to increase and the material to swell. The resulting vertical or lateral movement, on the order of 2 to 3 inches or more, is not considered to be a one-time occurrence. Consequently, it is desirable to avoid constructing lightly loaded footings or floor slabs within or immediately above expansive material. If structures must be constructed in such material, however, initial design measures can be taken to reduce future problems.

The swell potential of a soil depends upon the magnitude of the surcharge. Vertical heaving of structural elements can be reduced by applying a high surcharge to the material. Generally, it is necessary to proportion footings for a minimum dead load foundation pressure of 2,000 to 2,500 pounds per square foot to resist the swell pressure and thereby reduce the amount of structural movement. If this magnitude of sustained load cannot be generated, it may be necessary to over-excavate and to place a minimum of 3 feet of cohesive, nonexpansive soil beneath the footing. While this technique applies additional surcharge to resist the swell pressures, it primarily tends to reduce moisture content fluctuation within the underlying material. Expansive material, whether natural or backfill, should not be located within 2 to 3 feet of the exterior foundation walls.

Pavement, sidewalks, and slab-on-grade floor systems are typically very lightly loaded and provide little resistance to expansion. The most effective technique to reduce the possibility of slab damage is to suspend the slab above the expansive material. This technique allows the expansive material to expand without coming in contact with the floor system. Suspended slabs are, however, often considered economically unfeasible when initial construction costs are evaluated. An alternate—but less effective—method for reducing the amount of movement is to over-excavate at least 3 feet below the bottom of the slab and replace that material with nonexpansive cohesive soil that has been compacted to a minimum of 95 percent of its maximum Standard Proctor dry density. The expansive material should not be allowed to dry excessively before the fill is placed.

Structures may also be designed to minimize damage caused by expansive material. Walls that extend more than 4 feet into expansive zones should be additionally reinforced to resist lateral swell pressures. Waffle and post-tensioned slabs have been used as a means of minimizing swelling soil problems.

Gravel backfill utility trenches and other potential water-collecting facilities should be designed to preclude water accumulation within the building area. The exposed subgrade should be observed during excavation and construction in order to further evaluate the extent and significance of expansive materials on the site.

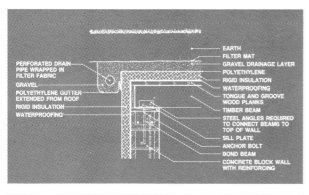

PERFORATED DRAIN PIPE WRAPPED IN FILTER FABRIC
GRAVEL
POLYETHYLENE GUTTER EXTENDED FROM ROOF
RIGID INSULATION
WATERPROOFING

EARTH
FILTER MAT
GRAVEL DRAINAGE LAYER
POLYETHYLENE
RIGID INSULATION
WATERPROOFING
TONGUE AND GROOVE WOOD PLANKS
TIMBER BEAM
STEEL ANGLES REQUIRED TO CONNECT BEAMS TO TOP OF WALL
SILL PLATE
ANCHOR BOLT
BOND BEAM
CONCRETE BLOCK WALL WITH REINFORCING

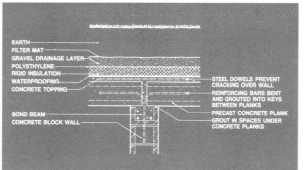

EARTH
FILTER MAT
GRAVEL DRAINAGE LAYER
POLYETHYLENE
RIGID INSULATION
WATERPROOFING
CONCRETE TOPPING

BOND BEAM
CONCRETE BLOCK WALL

STEEL DOWELS PREVENT CRACKING OVER WALL
REINFORCING BARS BENT AND GROUTED INTO KEYS BETWEEN PLANKS
PRECAST CONCRETE PLANK
GROUT IN SPACES UNDER CONCRETE PLANKS

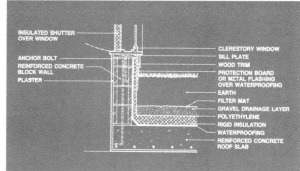

INSULATED SHUTTER OVER WINDOW

ANCHOR BOLT
REINFORCED CONCRETE BLOCK WALL
PLASTER

CLERESTORY WINDOW
SILL PLATE
WOOD TRIM
PROTECTION BOARD OR METAL FLASHING OVER WATERPROOFING
EARTH
FILTER MAT
GRAVEL DRAINAGE LAYER
POLYETHYLENE
RIGID INSULATION
WATERPROOFING
REINFORCED CONCRETE ROOF SLAB

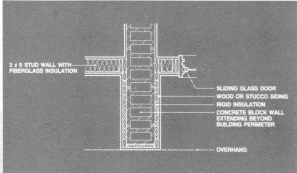

2 x 6 STUD WALL WITH FIBERGLASS INSULATION

SLIDING GLASS DOOR
WOOD OR STUCCO SIDING
RIGID INSULATION
CONCRETE BLOCK WALL EXTENDING BEYOND BUILDING PERIMETER

OVERHANG

CHAPTER 6

STRUCTURAL SYSTEMS

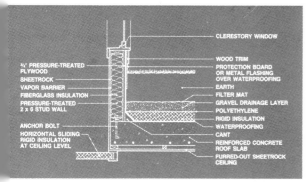

CLERESTORY WINDOW

¾" PRESSURE-TREATED PLYWOOD
SHEETROCK
VAPOR BARRIER
FIBERGLASS INSULATION
PRESSURE-TREATED 2 x 6 STUD WALL

ANCHOR BOLT
HORIZONTAL SLIDING RIGID INSULATION AT CEILING LEVEL

WOOD TRIM
PROTECTION BOARD OR METAL FLASHING OVER WATERPROOFING
EARTH
FILTER MAT
GRAVEL DRAINAGE LAYER
POLYETHYLENE
RIGID INSULATION
WATERPROOFING
CANT
REINFORCED CONCRETE ROOF SLAB
FURRED-OUT SHEETROCK CEILING

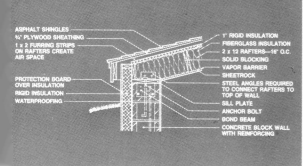

ASPHALT SHINGLES
½" PLYWOOD SHEATHING
1 x 2 FURRING STRIPS ON RAFTERS CREATE AIR SPACE
PROTECTION BOARD OVER INSULATION
RIGID INSULATION
WATERPROOFING

1" RIGID INSULATION
FIBERGLASS INSULATION
2 x 12 RAFTERS—16" O.C.
SOLID BLOCKING
VAPOR BARRIER
SHEETROCK
STEEL ANGLES REQUIRED TO CONNECT RAFTERS TO TOP OF WALL
SILL PLATE
ANCHOR BOLT
BOND BEAM
CONCRETE BLOCK WALL WITH REINFORCING

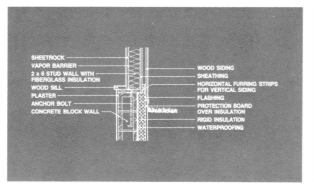

SHEETROCK
VAPOR BARRIER
2 x 6 STUD WALL WITH FIBERGLASS INSULATION
WOOD SILL
PLASTER
ANCHOR BOLT
CONCRETE BLOCK WALL

WOOD SIDING
SHEATHING
HORIZONTAL FURRING STRIPS FOR VERTICAL SIDING
FLASHING
PROTECTION BOARD OVER INSULATION
RIGID INSULATION
WATERPROOFING

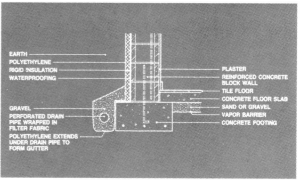

EARTH
POLYETHYLENE
RIGID INSULATION
WATERPROOFING

GRAVEL
PERFORATED DRAIN PIPE WRAPPED IN FILTER FABRIC
POLYETHYLENE EXTENDS UNDER DRAIN PIPE TO FORM GUTTER

PLASTER
REINFORCED CONCRETE BLOCK WALL
TILE FLOOR
CONCRETE FLOOR SLAB
SAND OR GRAVEL
VAPOR BARRIER
CONCRETE FOOTING

Introduction

Chapter 4 dealt with the determination of a structural form in a general sense. This chapter discusses how the structural needs of the building will affect its detailed design. Although this chapter should not be considered a handbook for detailed design, it can be used as a guide to methods of minimizing building costs by considering structural needs in the remainder of the design process. It can also be used by regulatory or financial officials to help determine whether designs presented for review have addressed the structural issues of design and whether member sizes and reinforcement are reasonable for the depth of structure burial.

The engineering design of earth sheltered structures is relatively standard engineering practice and, as such, should not present a problem to a qualified engineer. The four basic stages involved in the design of any structure are:

- Determining the form and layout of the structure
- Determining the potential loading on the structure
- Analyzing the structure to determine the worst combination of loading conditions for each portion of the structure
- Comparing the stresses within the structure against the strength of the structure or permissible stresses for the structural material at each critical location

This process is usually cyclical; for example, a preliminary analysis of one structural layout may suggest the need for a different structural system, which in turn must be analyzed. In order to achieve a cost-effective design, the building design process should be cycled until the structural needs of the building are met as effectively as possible within the framework determined by the other design constraints—aesthetics, the availability of structural materials and skilled labor, and the building program. A safety factor is built into the design process, either through determining the applied loads or by assessing permissible stresses. In the first method, higher-than-anticipated loadings are evaluated against the ultimate load resistance of the structure. In the second case, actual anticipated loads are used to determine expected maximum stresses, which then are examined to determine whether they fall within safe limits.

The following section of this chapter discusses design loadings on an earth sheltered structure. Subsequent sections deal with each of the typical components of an earth sheltered structure—roof, walls, floors—with respect to the major issues involved in their design, typical materials used, and some specialized construction techniques.

Design Loads

Because many structures use loads on one part of a structure to balance the loading on another portion and because many structural materials respond differently to long-term and short-term loads, structural loads are usually divided into two main categories: dead loads and live loads. Dead loads refer to any load on the structure that may be considered permanent—such as the weight of the structural components (a concrete or wood roof, steel beams, etc.), waterproofing, finish plaster, and permanent equipment. Although soil loads are normally considered dead loads because they are long-term loads, the effects of possible later partial excavation of the earth on the roof or adjacent to the walls of an earth sheltered building must be considered in design. Soil pressures are depended on to resist lateral loading of an earth sheltered structure and to balance lateral earth pressures when the opposite walls of the structure are buried. Unequal excavation or backfilling around the structure can call these assumptions into question, however. The likelihood of maintaining a permanent soil load must be considered in designing an earth sheltered building, particularly if it is a post-tensioned structure.

Live loads are transient: they are likely to change in magnitude, location, and/or point of application over the life of the building. They include snow, rain, wind, people, cars, backfilling equipment, partitions, and furniture. It is important to assess how many of these possible loadings can occur simultaneously and to design for a reasonable likelihood of such combinations of circumstances occurring. In roof or floor designs, an average live load (calculated in pounds per square foot) is usually assessed to cover almost all eventualities. Examples of typical live-loading assumptions are given under each category of loading discussed below.

Roof Loads

The most dominant roof loading condition is the presence or absence of soil on the roof. Normal soils can vary in weight from 90 pounds per cubic foot to 135 pounds per cubic foot, although it is possible to design lighter soil mixes by including a lightweight filler material. Even though a fully saturated soil may well weigh more than 135 pounds per cubic foot, if the roof is well drained, the water loading can be considered a live-load condition. The soil density most commonly assumed in design is 120 pounds per cubic foot, which equals 10 pounds per square foot of loading for each 1 inch of soil depth. Thus, a 2-foot soil depth would yield a loading of 240 pounds per square foot on the roof structure.

For roofs that have reasonable spans and are carrying heavy loads, the weight of the structure itself can also be important. A 12-inch prestressed concrete plank will weigh approximately 80 pounds per square foot and a 12-inch poured concrete slab approximately 150 pounds per square foot. Figure 6-1 lists typical weights for different roof structures; figure 6-2 provides

Component	Weight (psf)
8 inch prestressed concrete plank	55
10 inch prestressed concrete plank	65
12 inch prestressed concrete plank	80
2 inch concrete topping on plank	25
8 inch poured concrete deck	100
10 inch poured concrete deck	125
12 inch poured concrete deck	150
wood plank and beam system	20
conventional wood truss roof	10

6-1: Typical Roof Loads

Case A:

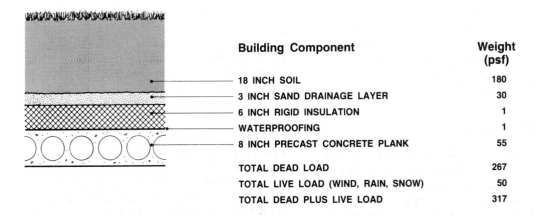

Building Component	Weight (psf)
18 INCH SOIL	180
3 INCH SAND DRAINAGE LAYER	30
6 INCH RIGID INSULATION	1
WATERPROOFING	1
8 INCH PRECAST CONCRETE PLANK	55
TOTAL DEAD LOAD	267
TOTAL LIVE LOAD (WIND, RAIN, SNOW)	50
TOTAL DEAD PLUS LIVE LOAD	317

Case B:

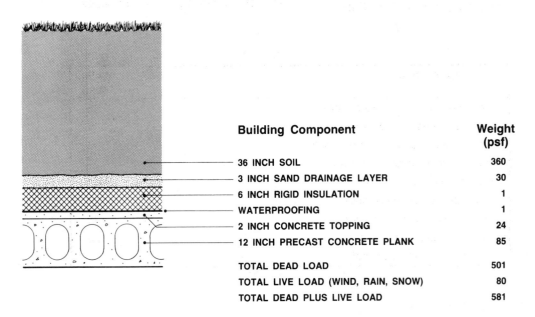

Building Component	Weight (psf)
36 INCH SOIL	360
3 INCH SAND DRAINAGE LAYER	30
6 INCH RIGID INSULATION	1
WATERPROOFING	1
2 INCH CONCRETE TOPPING	24
12 INCH PRECAST CONCRETE PLANK	85
TOTAL DEAD LOAD	501
TOTAL LIVE LOAD (WIND, RAIN, SNOW)	80
TOTAL DEAD PLUS LIVE LOAD	581

6-2: Roof Load Comparison

examples of complete roof loadings for different design configurations.

Live-load allowances for earth-covered roofs usually range from 50 pounds per square foot to 100 pounds per square foot. These figures include an allowance for snow load, any vehicular traffic expected on the roof, and rain-saturated soil. When heavy snow is typical and extensive drifting of snow on the roof can occur or when large vehicles can drive onto the roof, the design must allow for these possibilities. Although wind uplift is not a problem for earth-covered roofs, it must be considered in the design of exposed roofs. Live loads for inaccessible conventional roofs in areas where snow seldom falls may be as little as 10 pounds per square foot, which allows for occasional maintenance. Large landscaping elements, such as trees, will require special consideration of their dead weight and the transfer of wind loading to the structure.

Wall Loads

Walls in an earth sheltered structure must resist lateral earth pressures if they are placed against the earth; if they are exposed, they must resist wind loadings. The walls also act as components of the structure, transferring forces from the roof and other walls to the foundations. This section examines only the external applied loads.

The soils report in chapter 5 should provide guidelines for the lateral pressure that the soil or backfill material will exert (fig. 5-10 lists typical pressures for different types of soil). As explained in chapter 5, lateral soil pressures will vary considerably, depending on whether the wall is able to deflect away from the load (active pressure), is held rigid (at-rest pressure), or is actually forced towards the soil (passive pressure). Although the actual soil pressure conditions are greatly affected by backfilling procedures and building geometry, at-rest pressures should generally be used in the design of the earth retaining walls of a fairly rigid structure such as a concrete wall, roof, and floor system; active pressures can be used for external cantilever retaining walls.

Figure 6-3 illustrates the differences in the magnitude of the loading caused by different building and berm arrangements. Stepped walls reduce lateral pressures against the lower wall section but also increase the surface area of the building. Berms that slope down and away from the building will also reduce lateral pressures to a degree. Figure 6-3 also illustrates the typical triangular loading assumption for two different soil pressures that correspond roughly to active (the lower value) and at-rest pressure conditions, respectively. The

deeper the structure, the more important an accurate assessment of the lateral loading becomes.

When the lateral pressure exerted by a backfill material is used in design, it is important that other soil materials that would exert a higher pressure on the wall be placed outside the zone in which they could influence the wall. A rule of thumb is to assume that this zone lies within a line drawn at 30 degrees from the vertical, extending out from the base of the wall (also illustrated in fig. 6-3).

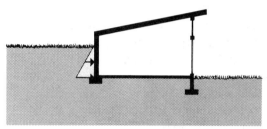

A: One Story Partially Bermed

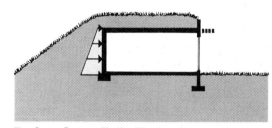

B: One Story Fully Bermed

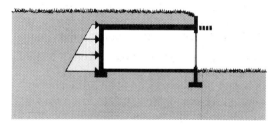

C: One Story Below Grade

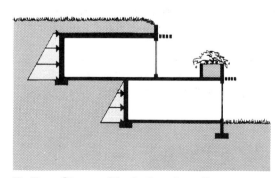

E: Two Story with Active Loading
6-3: Various Exterior Wall Loading Conditions

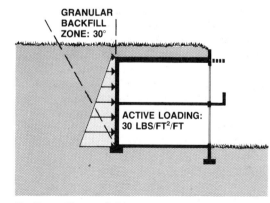

GRANULAR BACKFILL ZONE: 30°

ACTIVE LOADING: 30 LBS/FT^2/FT

D: Two Story Offset

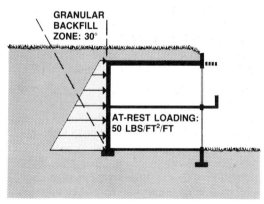

GRANULAR BACKFILL ZONE: 30°

AT-REST LOADING: 50 LBS/FT^2/FT

F: Two Story with At-Rest Loading

Other loads that must be considered in wall design are:

- *Saturated soil conditions*: Water pressure can add significantly to the wall loading. The pressure exerted by water increases with depth at a rate of 62.4 pounds per square foot, per foot of depth. A granular backfill, which provides good drainage in addition to lowering normal lateral pressures, is generally used for backfill whenever it is available. When gravel backfills and drainage tile are used, the wall is normally designed for unsaturated conditions.

- *Swelling pressures/frost pressures*: As discussed in chapter 5, these pressures must be considered in design whenever soil conditions are potentially hazardous.

- *Surcharge loads/live loads*: These are heavy loads placed on the surface of the soil adjacent to a retaining wall. The vertical pressure from the load causes a corresponding increase in the horizontal pressure on the wall. If any live loads are considered in retaining wall design, they are usually treated as a surcharge load. A major live-load item will be the surcharge load from any heavy vehicle that may be driven on the surface adjacent to the top of the retaining wall. Fire-fighting equipment access should be considered in calculating these loads.

- *Backfilling pressures*: Overcompaction of backfill as a result of using heavy equipment can place a higher load on a retaining wall than the wall might have to withstand in the course of normal service. Backfilling procedures should be specified to avoid this problem (see the discussion of backfilling in chapter 5).

Floor and Foundation Loads

Interior floor loadings are usually treated as a uniform load; design loads for different types of residential occupancy are specified in the building code. Values for a single-family residence are normally 30 pounds per square foot for sleeping areas and 40 pounds per square foot for other rooms [6.1]. Floor loadings for slabs cast directly on the ground are assumed to be carried directly by the ground below. All other floor loadings must be carried by the floor system to beams or wall supports. Exterior loads on floors and foundations can arise from groundwater pressures, swelling clay, frost-heave pressures, or earthquake forces. Distributed loads from other portions of the structure can result from providing horizontal support to the base of an exterior retaining wall, resisting shear and sliding forces from retaining walls and shear walls, or transferring the vertical load of the building to the ground through the foundations.

Curvilinear Structures

Not all structures can be neatly divided into roof, wall, and floor components. Curved structures below ground normally support a soil pressure perpendicular to the surface of the structure with a magnitude of an equivalent fluid pressure, which increases with the depth below ground. Relatively flat shell structures essentially must carry the full weight of the soil across the span. Flexible structures that have a more complete arch and smaller radius of curvature are often designed using empirical coefficients to adjust the design pressure from the pressure at the top of the arch [6.2]. Thin-shell structures, which are usually flexible, will deform relatively easily under soil loading; this phenomenon tends to equalize pressures over areas where the radius of curvature is constant.

Checklist of Loading Conditions

The following conditions should be considered in calculating the potential loading on the structure:

- self-weight of structure and finishes
- vertical soil loading on roof
- snow loads
- loads from landscaping elements
- rain saturation of roof and wall backfill
- groundwater pressures
- construction equipment loading on roof and adjacent to walls
- service vehicle access to roof and adjacent to walls
- swelling clay conditions
- frost-heave pressures
- earthquake forces
- wind loading on exposed portions of the structure
- live loading on interior floor structures
- mechanical equipment on roof or on intermediate floors
- soil/structure interaction (for flexible structures such as thin shells)
- slope stability (for structures on hillsides)

Materials

The common structural materials for earth sheltered housing are concrete, steel, and wood. In this section, these materials are subdivided into major categories of use; advantages and disadvantages are listed for each category. Following this section are a description of more specialized uses of structural materials and a discussion of the basic materials with reference to each structural component.

Reinforced and Plain Cast-in-place Concrete

Reinforced and plain cast-in-place concrete are the most common materials for earth sheltered structures. They are used for floors on grade, self-supporting floors and roofs, bearing walls, retaining walls, shear walls, columns, beams, and footings. Plain, unreinforced concrete is usually restricted to noncritical structural elements such as floors on grade, exterior building walls that have less than 6 feet of earth cover, and mass concrete foundations. Concrete can also be used for curved structures in beams, columns, or thin membranes.

Advantages of concrete are its durability, fire resistance, and high compressive and shear strength, which can be tailored to the required strength for specific applications. Concrete can be placed in large or complex shapes. Well-designed concrete mixes that are carefully placed, vibrated, and reinforced can be quite watertight because the reinforcing limits the width of any shrinkage or settlement cracks. The heavy weight of concrete resists uplift and sliding pressures.

A disadvantage of concrete is that some cracking will usually occur as a result of shrinkage, temperature, movement, and settlement. These cracks can allow some water seepage under pressure; hence, a waterproofing membrane is required for habitable building applications. In addition, the heavy weight of concrete increases the size of foundations required. Poured concrete is usually not a very rapid building system and concrete curing can delay construction unless high-early-strength concretes are used. Cold-weather concrete work requires special provisions to prevent the fresh concrete from freezing. The residual moisture load in concrete can also cause high humidities in a building for several months after construction.

Reinforced or Prestressed Precast Concrete

Precast concrete is used to simplify the forming process of concrete by casting the concrete at an on-site location or in a remote factory or casting yard. The uses for precast concrete are similar to those for cast-in-place concrete, except that precast concrete works best in simple or repeatable shapes.

Although many of the advantages of precast are also similar to those of cast-in-place concrete, precast offers the special advantages of rapid construction on site (because there are no cure time delays) and prefabrication of the building components. Factory precasting can use mass-production techniques that reduce costs, and factory-controlled conditions can produce a high-quality concrete and finish. The concrete sections themselves are usually quite watertight, and if the components have not been produced immediately before placement, there will be less moisture load in the building following construction.

Special disadvantages of precast concrete include the need to tie the structure together carefully with well-designed joints and the difficulty of sealing these joints against water penetration. The price of precast units depends on the distance required for transporting the units. Simple, standard units must usually be used in order to obtain the lowest cost. Although specialized shapes can be produced for large projects, their production usually requires a substantial lead time.

Prestressed Concrete

Prestressed concrete was included above as a form of precast concrete because it is always used in a precast form. The advantage of prestressing is that it allows higher-strength steels to be used; hence, smaller steel areas are required. If these higher-strength steels were not prestressed, the concrete sections would deflect excessively before the steel was strained sufficiently to reach its capacity. Wires are stretched in a casting bed to tensions close to the yield point of the steel (as much as 180,000 psi). The concrete is cast around the steel. When it has hardened, the wires are cut at the ends of the section, thereby causing the steel to contract and place the concrete in compression. This compressive force in the concrete limits cracking of the sections. Factory precasting generally ensures good quality control.

The steel in simple concrete sections is usually at the bottom of the plank or beam. When this steel contracts, the eccentric force induces a tension on the upper side of the beam, thus creating an upward curvature in the beam. The prestressing force is designed so that the beam will not be overstressed in tension at the top surface before any load is applied and so that the downward deflection of the beam when it is loaded will approximately equal the initial upward camber. Prestressed beams must be carefully handled during erection in order to avoid damaging them: lifting a prestressed beam only at its center, for example, would almost certainly cause failure of the beam. The uneven deflection of adjacent planks must also be considered in waterproofing design and the design of interior partitions that are non-load-bearing. Simply prestressed planks should only be used in simple span situations, when there are no intermediate supports.

Post-tensioned Concrete

Post-tensioned concrete is actually a variation of prestressed concrete in which the steel is not tensioned until after the concrete has hardened. It can be used in precast or cast-in-place concrete construction. Instead of casting the reinforcing bars directly into the concrete, sleeves are used so that the bars or wires can be stressed with jacks after the concrete hardens. Conical wedges or nuts and threads are used to lock the stress

into the steel after the bars have been stretched. Usually the sleeve is then grouted to protect the steel against corrosion. The advantage of the post-tensioned format is its adaptability to site-cast concrete and the possibility of carrying out the tensioning in stages so that it can balance permanent loads on the structure (this level of tensioning could cause tension failure on the upper surface if it were done with no load). The main disadvantage of post-tensioned concrete is that it requires specially trained crews on the site and is a more exacting method of construction not usually contemplated on single-family housing construction. Post-tensioning can be used for both the walls and roof of an earth sheltered structure.

Reinforced and Unreinforced Masonry

Unreinforced masonry is used for exterior building walls that have significant vertical loads from earth cover. These vertical loads create compression stress to offset flexural tension due to lateral earth pressure loads. Unreinforced masonry walls generally do not depend upon steel reinforcement to resist loads; however, a nominal amount of horizontal joint reinforcement (16 to 24 inches o.c.) is normally used for crack control. Reinforced masonry is employed where significant tension stress occurs. Tension is resisted by steel bars placed in the cores of masonry and bonded by concrete grout to the units.

The special advantage of masonry over cast-in-place concrete is that, because formwork is not required and the elements are mass-produced, unit costs are

relatively low. In areas where concrete block is commonly used for basements and commercial buildings, plants are usually well distributed and trucking costs are low. Blocks can be assembled into large and relatively complex shapes. In addition, there is less residual moisture in masonry than in poured concrete.

The disadvantages are that a structure constructed of unreinforced or reinforced masonry units contains voids within the blocks that provide water transmission paths for any water leakage, and that cold-weather work requires special provisions [6.3]. Concrete mortar requires cure time in order to gain sufficient strength to withstand the subsequent applied loading.

Steel

Steel is rarely used for the primary structural envelope in an earth sheltered building. Exceptions include corrugated highway culvert sections used to form a thin-shell structure, and extruded metal decking used in roof structures either as the roof element itself or as a permanent formwork/reinforcing to a concrete roof. Steel is present in most earth sheltered structures, however, as an integral structural material used in beams, bar joists, columns, concrete reinforcing, and special formwork systems.

Advantages of steel include its very high strength in both tension and compression. Also, it can be formed into efficient structural configurations such as I-beams, tubular columns, or the curved corrugated plates that are used to construct thin-shell structures. Because individual steel sections are completely watertight, the joints between sections of exposed steel are the only areas of concern for water leakage. Construction with steel can be continued without undue difficulty in cold weather. Also, connections are easily and inexpensively made with welds.

The primary disadvantage of steel is that it requires corrosion protection when exposed to exterior or groundwater conditions, and fire protection is required to preserve the structural integrity. Because steel also has a high unit price, it must be used efficiently to be economical as a structural material.

Wood

Wood is the one material that is almost certain to be used in any house constructed in the United States. It is used extensively both for interior finish work and, structurally, for floors, roofs, and exterior and interior walls of earth sheltered houses. Depths of burial of wood-framed walls that must resist lateral pressure are usually restricted to one story because of the rapid increase in wall costs beyond this depth of embedment.

Advantages of timber as a structural material are its high strength/weight ratio and similar strengths in tension and compression. Its light weight reduces foundation sizes and eases construction handling. Timber framing can be constructed rapidly by standard house-building carpenter crews, and constuction is relatively unaffected by weather conditions. Finally, producing timber as a structural material requires only a low level of embodied energy.

The most obvious disadvantage of timber is that it requires chemical treatment to prevent decomposition under moist conditions or in situations where the possibility of undetected water seepage exists. There are some lingering concerns about the possible toxicity of these preservative treatments. Also, in certain areas of the country, the timber must be protected against termite attack. Nailed timber structures are more likely to distort with time than more rigidly connected materials, and timber members themselves can develop substantial deflections over the long term. An earth sheltered structure built with wood requires good drainage because its light weight does not resist sliding and uplift pressures well. High shear strength and diaphragm action in walls and floors are difficult to develop without considerable nailing and gluing of components to help the wood transfer the stress.

Shotcrete/Gunite

Shotcrete and Gunite are both terms for concrete that is pneumatically sprayed onto surfaces where it will harden to form a structural member. Shotcrete uses larger-sized aggregate, similar to normal concrete; Gunite is sprayed concrete composed of smaller, sand-sized aggregate. Because mixes of these materials can be designed so that the concrete will stick to overhead as well as vertical and horizontal surfaces, they can be used to form concrete shells when they are sprayed on a preformed reinforcing mesh. In one patented system, after an air-inflated mold is erected, urethane foam and then Gunite are sprayed on the inside of the dome surface to form a concrete exterior-insulated shell (see *Shell Structures*, below) [6.4]. Shotcrete, which is commonly used in rock excavation work, is also often used for swimming pool construction and water canals. Advantages of shotcrete and Gunite are that their application requires no conventional formwork and that they can be used to create curved surfaces easily. The disadvantages are that specialized equipment and experience are necessary for successful application and that the spraying process involves substantial waste of concrete.

Analysis and Design of Structural Components

The variety of structural systems available for earth sheltered housing can be divided into two general categories. The first group includes the more conventional systems, for example, those that incorporate concrete walls with precast or poured concrete roof structures, as well as steel and wood post-and-beam systems. These most commonly used systems create houses that have vertical side walls and flat or sloped roofs. The second group comprises a variety of more unconventional structural systems, including concrete and steel arch and dome shapes, which offer unique potential for earth sheltered structures. Because the conventional systems are not only the most likely to be used, but also have a number of general structural characteristics in common, most of the major structural components discussed in this section pertain to the first group. A brief discussion of the more unconventional systems is included at the end of the section.

Roof

Most buildings are designed beginning with the roof because the roof span and its loading will significantly influence the sizing of the walls, columns, and foundation. The primary function of the roof is to support the vertical loads above it (soil, snow, vegetation). In flat-roof systems (which need not necessarily be completely horizontal), support is primarily accomplished by bending (see fig. 6-4). Because bending is a relatively inefficient load transfer method, sufficient vertical supports must be provided to produce an economical structural system. Bending moments in the roof are proportional to the vertical load imposed as well as to the square of the length of span. It is important therefore to maintain reasonable spans in flat roof buildings. Intermediate supports can be provided by bearing walls, beams, and columns.

Most roof systems will be designed to span in only one direction and will use simply supported slabs or beams. An exception is a poured concrete roof design, which can span in two directions if the ratio of the sides of the slab is less than one and one-half to one and can be designed to transfer moments at the connection of the roof and walls. Although designing some fixity (moment capacity) at the end of the beam increases the overall carrying capacity of the roof slab, it necessitates proper connection detailing and wall design to withstand this moment transfer.

Deflection and drainage are other important criteria in roof design. The inevitable deflection of a perfectly flat roof slab will cause ponding of water on the roof, which in turn will lead to additional deflection and an increased likelihood of water drainage problems. When precast components are used, the differential deflection between individual planks that can occur if they are not fastened or keyed together can rupture the waterproofing system. A concrete topping, which will help distribute loads to even out the deflection, can be tapered to improve drainage. A minimum slope of at least 1 percent is recommended for all roof designs that do not incorporate internal drains. Tapered insulation can be used to provide a roof slope, but this reverses the sequence of waterproofing

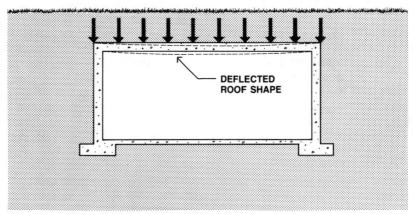

6-4: Roof Loading and Deflected Shape for Simply Supported Condition

and insulation. Precast planks that have different spans should not be used adjacent to each other because they have different deflection characteristics. For a house that has an earth-covered roof, non-load-bearing interior partitions should allow for deflection of the roof structure, both immediately upon loading and as a result of long-term creep deflections.

The secondary function of the roof is usually to provide support to the walls of the structure that are retaining an earth pressure. The compressive or diaphragm forces in the roof structure that this support involves must be considered in the roof design. For reinforced cast-in-place concrete and precast concrete roofs, providing support should not have great design implications for the roof except when large openings through the roof are located close to the wall being supported. For a timber roof, it is difficult to provide sufficient diaphragm action and compressive strength perpendicular to the

beams when the lateral earth loads are high. These design issues are discussed further in the section below on intermediate floors; they should not be overlooked in designing the roofs of earth-bermed structures that have conventional roofs. Figure 6-5 illustrates how the lateral earth pressures are distributed through the structure.

Characteristics of the wide variety of components for an earth-covered roof system are discussed below.

concrete roof systems

One of the most common concrete systems, used for both roofs and floors, incorporates flat slabs that have a minimal structural depth. This minimal slab depth reduces the total height of the structure and, hence, lateral earth pressures for an earth-covered structure. Flat slabs are not efficient for long spans; spans should typically be less than 20 to 25 feet for

earth-covered roofs. Flat slabs can easily be designed to span in one or in two directions.

Beam-and-slab construction uses a thinner concrete slab than does the flat slab system. Because of the depth of the beams, however, this type of system requires a greater depth within the structure in order to support the roof. Either integral or separate beams can be used to support the slab.

Waffle slabs are similar to flat slabs except that they replace the structurally ineffective portions of flat slabs with voids that are open on the underside of the slab. Although this type of slab reduces both the amount of concrete required and the self-weight of the roof structure, the formwork costs are higher. Waffle slabs are usually used for two-way roof spans. They are generally considered to have a positive effect on the interior appearance of the structure.

Post-tensioned slabs have been discussed above under Materials. Less steel reinforcement is used and smaller stuctural depths are usually possible with this type of slab than with conventional reinforced slabs. Although the steel can also be more widely spaced in the slab, it must be of higher strength. Construction involving post-tensioned slabs requires skilled crews.

Prestressed concrete planks were also discussed under Materials. They are readily available in well-populated areas. Planks usually come in standard widths of 2 feet, 3 feet 4 inches, 4 feet, and 8 feet. Because the plank supplier will not necessarily be known until after construction bids are received, it is wise to design the structure to fit a standard 2-foot module. Engineering for the roof system is

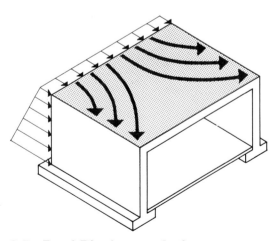

6-5: Roof Diaphragm Action

usually supplied by the plank manufacturers. Economical spans are generally in the 15- to 25-foot range, although occasionally planks can be used in spans of more than 30 feet, with low levels of earth cover. A concrete topping is normally used over the plank to provide additional strength and a smooth surface for waterproofing. To enhance the bond between the plank and the topping, the top surface of the plank can often be specified as "rough." Hollow cores of the plank are sometimes used for utilities and air handling. Some planks are shaped so that a space between adjacent planks may be filled with concrete, thus keying the planks together to avoid differential displacements.

Single-T or double-T beams are similar in many respects to precast planks except that they are optimized for long, lightly loaded spans and have great structural depth. It is possible, however, to use the depth of these beams for building services.

timber roof systems

Heavy timber beams and wood decking can provide a decorative interior appearance if exposed to the interior and need not be preservative treated if there are no concealed areas in which moisture could collect. Bentonite waterproofing should not be installed next to nontreated decking because it is moist when activated. Rough sawing of lumber maintains a larger structural cross-section for the beams. Less expensive green lumber can be used if the drying shrinkage movement and deflection of the wood is anticipated and allowed for in the design.

Glue-laminated beams or microlaminated lumber can also be used with wood

decking for an earth-covered roof. Glue-laminated beams are usually manufactured for specific projects that require ¾- to 1½-inch-thick laminations. Microlaminated lumber uses thinner laminations (approximately $\frac{1}{10}$ to $\frac{1}{8}$ inches thick) and is purchased more as standard lumber is. It is available in standard sizes from 2½ to 24 inches deep and up to 80 feet long. The primary advantage of laminated beams is that the quality of lumber can be varied in the laminations, so that the best quality is provided only where needed. In addition, because individual flaws in the wood do not affect the strength of more than one lamination, allowable stresses are higher for laminated beams than for sawn lumber. The lamination process provides warp-free lumber that is easy to use.

Manufactured configurations of lumber, such as box beams and I-beams, are also available. Here again, the intent is to use the lumber more efficiently for structural purposes. The cost of fabrication suggests, however, that these configurations should be used primarily for larger structural sections, where significant savings of material can be realized. These configurations are usually not as suitable as timber beams or glue-laminated beams for an exposed interior finish.

Wood decking with steel joists is an alternative to an all-wood system. It should be used with a false ceiling for living spaces; however, services can be run through the ceiling area if open web joists are used.

Exterior Building Walls Retaining Earth

Unlike the roof, which is loaded from above, external building walls that retain earth are essentially slabs loaded from the side. Support for the wall is provided either by the roof and floor slabs (fig. 6-6) or by designing the wall to be self-supporting, as is a typical exterior retaining wall. It is generally less expensive to design the structural components to work together than to ignore this available support in the design of the wall. Loading pressures are assumed to be triangular in form (see discussions under *Loads* and in chapter 5). During the design process, it is necessary to decide on the end restraint conditions of the wall at the roof, at intermediate floors, and at the foundations. In design practice it is normally assumed that the connection of the wall at the foundation and the roof will not transfer a bending moment, that is, a pinned condition, except when cast-in-place concrete is to be used. The condition at an intermediate floor will depend on whether or not the wall system is continuous through that section. In reinforced cast-in-place wall systems, partial or full fixity at the foundation or roof can be used to lower the maximum moments in the wall; however, this is only possible if the connections, roof slab, and foundation are designed appropriately.

Retaining walls that are part of a building are usually designed as vertical strips spanning from roof to floor. Although horizontal or two-way spanning of the wall can lessen the vertical moments to be resisted, they will only be effective if vertical wall supports—such as pilasters or shear walls—provide support to the wall at

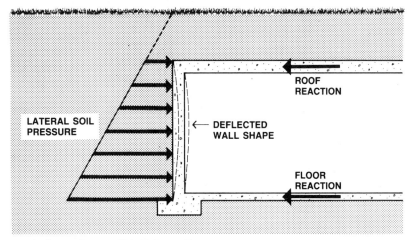

6-6: One Story Wall Loading

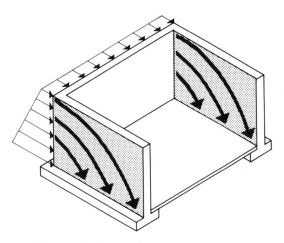

6-7: Exterior Shear Wall Action

intervals of less than one-and-one-half times the vertical span of the wall.

Exterior building walls may also carry the direct compression loads created by their support of the roof structure. Other exterior walls will be essentially nonbearing in the vertical direction. Almost all building walls will be required to act as a shear wall or diaphragm to a lesser or greater extent, as shown in figure 6-7.

In determining wall heights and burial depths for earth sheltered structures, it should be remembered that the maximum moment in a fully buried wall increases as the cube of the wall height. Therefore, in order to achieve low structural costs, the height of walls adjacent to the earth should be kept to a minimum. Also, when floors or roofs are designed as supports to the wall, they must be installed prior to backfilling the wall.

The major wall systems of concrete, concrete block, and pressure-treated wood have been discussed under *Materials*. Additional design information on these systems is presented below. A number of less common systems that can be and have been used for earth sheltered structures are also briefly described.

unreinforced block walls

Lateral earth pressures on unreinforced block walls are stabilized by vertical compression stress or tensile strength of the wall or a combination of vertical load and tension strength. The tensile strength of masonry in the vertical direction is limited. According to model building codes on basement construction, 12-inch basement walls should not be backfilled more than 7 feet, without an offsetting compression load. Lateral earth pressures

111

may span horizontally in running bond walls, in which case the tensile strength is twice that of the vertical direction. However, in the horizontal span there is no vertical load to offset flexural tension.

reinforced block walls

The reinforcing in the block wall provides the tensile resistance in bending. After the reinforcing bars have been placed in the cores of the wall, the cores containing reinforcing are grouted solid. Design parameters for this type of wall are the size and spacing of the reinforcing bars and the compressive strength of the concrete blocks. Reinforced concrete block can be used for both one- and two-story earth retaining walls provided that the intermediate floor can provide sufficient reaction. Requirements for minimum reinforcement, reinforcement spacing, and allowable ratios of unsupported height or length to the thickness of the wall may be found in the American Concrete Institute publication A.C.I. 531 [6.5].

surface bonding of concrete block

In this system, after concrete blocks have been dry stacked to form the wall, a thin fiber-reinforced coating is applied to both sides of the wall in order to provide the necessary tensile strength to resist bending moments. The coating, which is also resistant to water penetration, is intended to function as the waterproofing. Although dry-stacking the blocks without worrying about concrete bedding or reinforcing steel permits very rapid erection of the wall, the absence of mortar bedding makes it difficult to keep the wall level and perfectly flat unless the blocks are manufactured with a high degree of dimensional accuracy.

It is imperative that the wall be designed to resist lateral loads, such as from earth pressure; in many instances, reinforcing steel may be necessary in addition to the flexural strength provided by the glass fibers. Design criteria is furnished by surface bonding material manufacturers.

rammed earth and adobe

These techniques involve using earth as the primary wall construction material. Wall strength is achieved by compacting the soil by force (rammed earth) or by puddling the soil with an organic reinforcing such as straw (adobe). It is relatively easy to build thick walls at low material cost with these systems, and when hardened, both have good resistance to occasional rain. Although the techniques were developed in hot, arid regions where the earth walls will remain predominantly dry, it may be possible to adapt them to wetter regions if proper water protection is provided. Overall, the solutions that these techniques offer are low cost in terms of materials but are also labor intensive. Although structures using these systems may provide savings to the owner-builder, they will probably be substantially more expensive than conventional systems if they are constructed commercially in areas typified by high labor costs.

plain cast-in-place concrete

Use of plain concrete basement walls should be limited to less than a full-story embedment. The minimum thickness for such a wall is usually 8 inches. Concrete that is intended to be watertight should have a maximum water/cement ratio of 0.48. A stronger and more waterproof concrete is obtained when a low water/cement ratio is used and adequate

vibration of the concrete occurs during placement. When sulphates are present in the ground in high concentrations, sulphate-resisting cements should be used.

When pipes are embedded in concrete (as for radiant heating), the temperature of the contents should not exceed 150°F and pressures should not exceed 200 psi. Aluminum pipes should not be embedded in concrete. Pipes should not exceed 4 percent of the stress area of a structural slab unless special analysis has been done. Pipes that are to be embedded should be tested at 150 psi for four hours before concreting. This test requirement does not apply to drainpipes or to pipes used for pressures of less than 1 psi above atmospheric pressure. The shear wall capacity of a poured concrete wall usually presents no design problems.

reinforced cast-in-place concrete

Reinforced concrete can be used for both one- and two-story construction, as the reinforcement can be easily varied to suit the varying stress conditions within the wall. Eight-inch-thick walls should be sufficient for most house construction unless the intermediate floor cannot provide the necessary reaction. Costs associated with reinforced concrete walls rise very slowly with increasing depths of embedment in the soil because only the cost of the reinforcing steel increases significantly. The minimum concrete cover for reinforcement exposed to earth or weather is 2 inches for bars that have a $\frac{3}{4}$-inch or larger diameter and $1\frac{1}{2}$ inch for bars that have a diameter of $\frac{5}{8}$ inch or less. The minimum concrete cover for reinforcement when concrete is cast directly against the earth is 3 inches.

precast concrete

Precast concrete planks can be used for one- and two-story construction. The cost of the planks rises very little with increasing wall height: although the material costs rise, bigger units are handled, thus reducing the handling costs per square foot of wall. Precast units usually have good quality control and an excellent finish. In many cases it is possible to spray-texture walls and ceilings directly and thus save on finishing costs.

Structural design involving precast planks is usually done by the supplier. The supplier should be PCI (Precast Concrete Institute) Plant Certified, have a registered civil or structural engineer on the staff, or obtain the stamped approval of the plans from a registered engineer. Generally, the more precast concrete sections used on a job from one supplier, the cheaper the cost per square foot of installed plank. If the travel distance to the job is significant, erection teams are usually charged to the job for a full day, even though installation time may only be a matter of only two or three hours. Hence, installation of additional planks may increase only the material and transport costs.

Normal plank widths vary from 2 to 8 feet. The narrower planks are not usually recommended for wall construction because of the higher costs of erecting and tying together the larger number of elements required for a wall system. Precast wall panels (as opposed to planks) are also available; they are generally designed for one-story embedment. Precast concrete shear walls are designed using a shear friction approach, which should present few problems unless the shear wall is very short.

integral forming and insulation techniques

For several available products, hollow blocks of insulation serve as the concrete formwork. The insulation remains in place to provide the insulation for the structure. Most of these systems provide for horizontal and vertical steel in the wall, although both the thickness of the concrete section and positioning of reinforcing bars are quite limited. When the limited strength of readily available sections is adequate for the wall under design, this technique can be a fast and inexpensive way to construct an underground wall. For passive solar houses, this system has the disadvantage of providing insulation inside the mass of the concrete in the wall, thereby limiting the ability of the mass to diffuse heat. Other mass within the structure may be able to compensate for this situation, however.

tilt-up walls

This technique reduces the formwork required for wall construction and simplifies the placement of the wet concrete for the wall. The wall is cast in a horizontal position on the ground adjacent to its final position; a bond breaker is used to separate the wall from the ground surface. When the slab has hardened, it is tilted into position by a crane and held in an upright position until supporting walls and the roof are installed. No formwork is needed for the major surfaces of the wall, however, and the concrete is easy to place and finish. This technique does require lifting equipment on-site, and the walls must be designed to resist the handling stresses. The system is not as easy to use on a confined site as on an open site, and the construction cycle will probably take longer than the cycle for a conventional poured system due to curing time before tilting. As with any precast system, the connection details must tie the structure together to form a coherent unit.

trenched walls

This technique can be used in certain soil conditions where trenches for vertical walls will stand for a considerable period of time [6.6]. In this system, narrow, vertical-sided trenches are excavated with a backhoe or trenching machine at the locations where the walls will be placed. A reinforcing cage is then lowered into each trench, and the concrete is poured to create the walls, using the earth sides of the trenches as formwork. The roof can be poured at the same time as a slab on grade. When the concrete has hardened, the earth is dug out from underneath the slab between the walls. This digging out is done in a careful pattern so that strips of the floor can be poured to brace the walls against the side earth pressures. Columns and footings might also be placed at specific locations before digging out completely. This type of structure has an unusual foundation arrangement: the vertical loads are carried by wing slabs at the roof level because it is not possible to pour conventional footings using this technique. The trenched wall system is similar to slurry wall design except that the bentonite slurry is not required to support the trench walls. Slurry techniques are usually too cumbersome to use on a single-family residence.

reinforced earth

Reinforced earth is a patented retaining system using steel straps laid horizontally in a vertical grid pattern in a prepared backfill. The straps act as tension reinforcement in the fill, thus forming a stable gravity earth wall to resist pressures in the earth behind the backfill. The wall itself becomes merely a facing to hold the earth between the straps in place. Water protection is provided primarily by using a free-draining material for the backfill, as the attachment of the straps to the wall makes external waterproofing difficult to apply. Because corrosion of the straps is probably the most serious concern with this system, the straps must be galvanized. The reinforced earth technique has been used on a number of large-scale earth sheltered housing developments built on steep slopes in Europe.

pressure-treated wood

Widely available lumber sizes can be used for one-story wood foundation walls. For earth burial deeper than one story, member sizes increase rapidly. Although wood can appear to be economical in first costs for conventional basement embedment depths, it quickly becomes uneconomical for embedment deeper than one story.

Shear wall action can be a problem when the reactions from the floors are considerable. Design nail spacing decreases rapidly as higher shear loads are carried. Again, wood walls will normally be strong enough for one-story structures that have a small amount of earth cover.

Because of potential problems with connection details, wood walls are most practical when used with a wood roof

system. When cuts in the pressure-treated lumber are made on site, a concentrated preservative solution should be painted on the cut end. Creosote and pentachlorophenol preservatives are not permitted for wood foundations of dwellings. CCA and ACA treatments are the only waterborne preservatives permitted for this use.

Pressure-treated wood suppliers recommend that a dampproofing and drainage system be used with the wood foundation. Stainless steel nails or staples are recommended except under very dry conditions, when hot-dip-galvanized nails are a possible alternative.

prefabricated fiberglass-coated wood panels

This system uses a fiberglass coating on the exterior of prefabricated plywood sheathing and wood-beam panels [6.7]. The panels are then bolted together to act as the walls and roof of an earth sheltered structure. The fiberglass, which is essentially impervious to water (provided that the sections contain no cracks), is intended to protect the wood and provide water resistance for the structure. Weak points in the system are the joints between the panels (which are caulked), along with the potential dangers of the fiberglass coating cracking under deflection and uneven settlement of the panels.

Load-Bearing Interior Walls

Interior walls in an earth sheltered house may be required to resist vertical loads from the roof in compression and transfer lateral earth pressures from the outside walls to the floor and footings by acting as shear walls. The direct compression loads on an interior bearing wall can be substantial, often twice those on an exterior bearing wall. But, because interior load-bearing walls are not subject to bending forces caused by lateral earth pressures, they are simpler to design and less costly than exterior walls retaining earth. If shear wall design proves to be critical, the most common solution is to add another shear wall between the existing shear walls, perhaps in place of a nonstructural partition (fig. 6-8).

Materials for interior walls are basically the same as those for exterior walls—predominantly concrete or masonry. A wood-frame wall may be used if the loads are not too great. Because the interior walls carry no lateral loads, concrete and masonry interior walls have far less need for reinforcing. Similarly, reinforcing is generally not required for concrete and masonry walls to resist the direct compressive loads on load-bearing walls. Resisting shear stresses should be no problem for reinforced or unreinforced cast-in-place concrete walls. There should be few problems in providing masonry walls with adequate resistance to shear unless such a wall is very short (less than 10 feet) or the total width of openings in the wall is large. Precast concrete shear walls are designed using a shear friction approach that should present few problems unless the shear wall is very short. Shear wall action can be a problem in wood structures, however, when the reactions

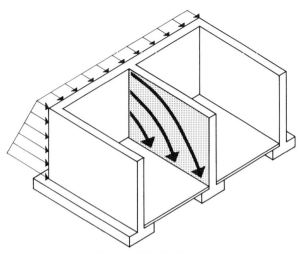

6-8: Interior Shear Wall Action

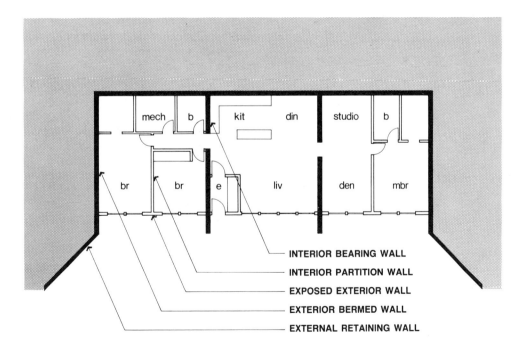

INTERIOR BEARING WALL
INTERIOR PARTITION WALL
EXPOSED EXTERIOR WALL
EXTERIOR BERMED WALL
EXTERNAL RETAINING WALL

6-9: Various Types of Walls

from the floors are considerable. Nail spacing must be decreased considerably so that wood walls can carry higher shear loads.

Non-Load-Bearing Interior Walls

Interior walls that are non-load-bearing pose no special restrictions on design. Non-load-bearing walls should not be constructed tight against the earth-covered roof slabs because the deflection of the slab can damage the partition finishes. A typical detail for this condition is illustrated in chapter 10. Wood studs are normally acceptable for non-load-bearing walls, unless insurance provisions require that steel studs be used to obtain the fireproof rating given to the rest of a concrete structure. Interior walls should be designed to allow the maximum number of building services to be placed within the non-load-bearing partitions because it is easier to run services within such partitions.

Exposed Exterior Walls

These walls may carry a vertical load from the roof, or they may only be required to provide protection against wind and inclement weather. Because window openings in an earth sheltered house will tend to be massed on any exposed wall, that wall will not have the same kind of continuous load-bearing capability as other exterior walls. When the wall does support vertical loads, steel or reinforced concrete beams will usually be required above any openings. Even when the wall does not continuously support vertical loads (fig. 6-9), columns may have to be incorporated into the wall to support cross-beams. The question of whether these walls should be designed to carry substantial loads must be considered in conjunction with the roof design and the extent of the proposed openings in the wall. If the exposed wall is nonbearing, it may have to be designed with a gap at the top of the wall that is sealed with a compressible sealant to allow for deflection of the roof structure. As for interior walls, the effect on fire rating of using combustible materials should be checked with an insurance underwriter.

Parapet walls

Parapet walls are sometimes used at the exposed edges of earth-covered roofs. A parapet acts as a small retaining wall for the typically small thickness of earth cover on the roof (fig. 6-10). In urban or suburban areas, parapets also usually serve as the base for guardrail systems installed to provide structural safety. The main concerns in designing parapets are to provide structural continuity with the remainder of the structure and to resist soil pressure, repeated freeze/thaw action, and any guardrail forces. Parapets cast integrally with the roof slab will induce torsional stresses that should be considered in their design. Typical materials for parapets are concrete, masonry, or wood. Concrete and masonry are usually reinforced to resist deterioration from freeze/thaw action and any external applied forces, such as those from a guardrail. A number of schematic solutions for dealing with frost pressure and soil pressure problems are illustrated in chapter 10.

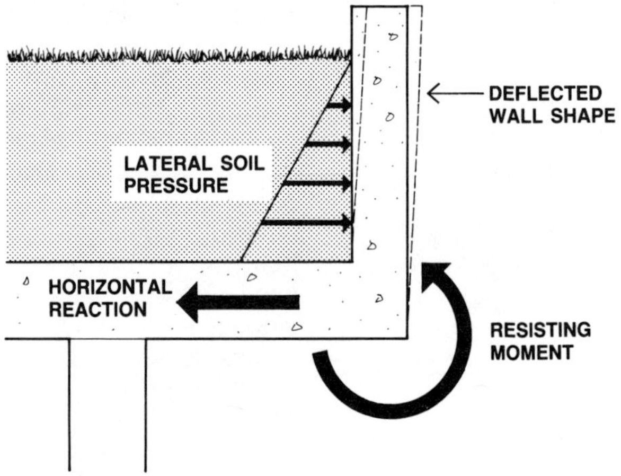

6-10: Parapet Loading

DEFLECTED WALL SHAPE

LATERAL SOIL PRESSURE

HORIZONTAL REACTION

RESISTING MOMENT

Retaining Walls Outside Building

Exterior retaining walls are usually designed to be self-supporting: they do not derive support from other elements of the building in the same fashion as do building walls supporting earth loads. The types of stresses to be designed for in exterior retaining walls depend to a great extent on the type of retaining wall selected (discussed below). Although massive walls that depend on gravity for their resistance generate low stresses within the wall, they will be large in size and their construction will require large quantities of material. Many retaining walls are cantilever-type walls, with bending stresses that increase downward from the top of the wall to the point of embedment. The bending moment at the bottom of the wall is resisted either by a foundation or by an additional depth of embedment for the wall itself. Bending stresses are greater for a cantilever wall than for a wall supported at both top and bottom by the building.

Although exterior retaining walls can derive some support from the building structure adjacent to the building, relying on such support can cause thermal isolation problems for the retaining wall. Because retaining walls can add significantly to the cost of an earth sheltered structure, their use should be minimized through careful site design and grading. The integration of building form with exterior retaining walls is explored further in chapter 10.

Some common techniques for retaining earth are illustrated in figure 6-11 and discussed below.

Gravity wall: The mass of wall resists overturning and sliding. Because the wall is usually designed to induce no tension within the wall, plain concrete or loose-laid stones may be used.

Cantilever wall: Earth pressures are resisted by bending moments in the wall. The placement of the footing relative to the wall affects both the stability of the wall with regard to overturning and sliding and the amount of extra excavation required. Although any structural material capable of resisting the bending stresses may be used, it must also be capable of developing the moment resistance at its connection to the footing (with the exception of the pile retaining wall). Reinforced concrete is the most commonly used material for cantilever walls.

Tiebacks: These are tension members connected to ground anchors in the soil. Although tiebacks can be used with the exterior walls of the building, they are unlikely to be used in situations where an intermediate floor can limit the vertical wall span to 8 feet. Steel cables protected against corrosion are used for large concrete retaining walls. Timber tiebacks as shown in figure 6-11 can be used for residential-scale retaining walls.

Reinforced earth: In this earth-retaining technique, reinforcing strips laid in the soil at frequent spacings resist any tensile forces that develop in the soil near the face of the wall. The soil transfers the load to the reinforcement in shear, and the reinforcement will be in tension. The nonstructural facing provides resistance to erosion. Reinforced earth is most effective for high retaining walls where great shear stresses can be transferred to the strips because of the vertical pressure. The strips are galvanized steel, and the backfill is carefully specified to provide drainage and minimize corrosion.

Cribbing: Cribbing involves containing the earth to form a steep but stable embankment. Concrete shapes, railroad ties, wire mesh baskets, rubber tires, etc., can be used for cribbing. Cribbed retaining walls usually have a slightly backward slope when their height is substantial.

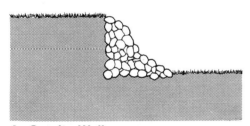

A: Gravity Wall

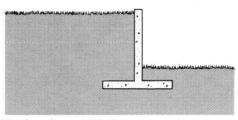

B: Cantilever Wall

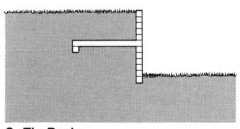

C: Tie Backs

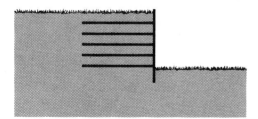

D: Reinforced Earth

6-11: Types of Retaining Walls

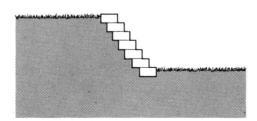

E: Cribbing

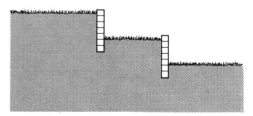

F: Stepped Walls

Stepping the cribbing provides an excellent opportunity for landscape planting that can soften the appearance of the wall.

Stepped retaining walls: The basic types of retaining wall described above can also be used in smaller segments as a stepped retaining wall. Although the change in grade cannot be as abrupt, maximum bending moments in a cantilever wall decrease with the cube of the wall height. Often lower-quality structural material can be used for each segment of the wall than would be needed for a single wall. To take full advantage of this technique, the angle of a line through the footings of the individual walls must not be greater than the stable slope angle for the soil.

Some techniques for reducing wall costs are listed below. (See chapter 10 for illustrations of some of these alternatives).

- wrapping the earth around the front of the retaining wall to reduce unsupported wall heights
- stepping the retaining wall horizontally to stiffen the structure and reduce the foundation reaction
- curving the retaining wall to induce membrane stresses rather than bending stresses
- using tiebacks or deadmen (described above)
- using rock or boulder slopes when available and appropriate to the design
- exposing small portions of side walls to lower necessary retaining wall heights

Intermediate Floors

Intermediate floors include the upper-level floor of a two-story design as well as any lower floor that is designed as a suspended floor system. A suspended ground floor system may be used either to isolate the floor from movement—as when a house is built in soils that contain swelling clays—or in an underfloor plenum system that distributes air and routes other building services beneath the suspended floor. Intermediate floors must support the floor loadings in bending and transfer any necessary forces in diaphragm action (see figs. 6-12 and 6-13).

Compared to the roof and lower floor slab, the intermediate floor in a two-level design must provide a greater horizontal reaction to a wall supporting earth pressures unless this requirement is specifically eliminated by designing the wall to span two stories from floor to roof. Therefore, the floor design should avoid large openings in the floor adjacent to an exterior building wall that is resisting an earth load. Floor sections adjacent to the wall should be wide enough to enable them to support the wall as a beam on its side. Because the wall reactions on the intermediate floor are so great, typical wood floor construction is not suitable when the floor must act as a diaphragm unless frequent shear walls are used to limit the shear buildup.

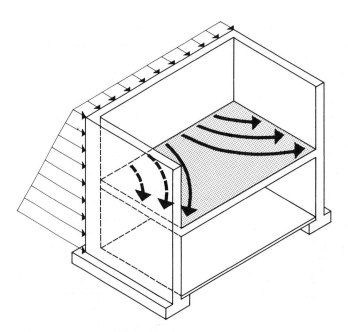

6-12: Intermediate Floor Diaphragm Action

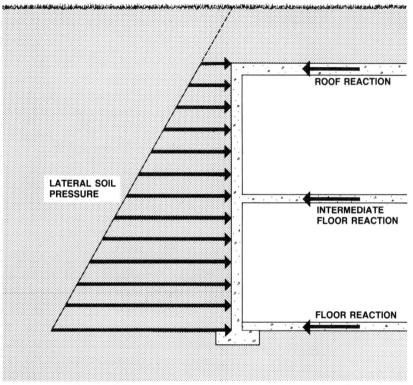

6-13: Two Story Wall Loading

The figure is labeled with: LATERAL SOIL PRESSURE, ROOF REACTION, INTERMEDIATE FLOOR REACTION, FLOOR REACTION

Slab-on-grade Floor

This is generally the simplest floor system because the concrete slab is poured directly on the ground. Required building services are placed in trenches beneath the level of the floor. If any fill is required beneath the floor slab, fill that has a low Plasticity Index—less than 15—should be used, compacted in 6- to 8-inch lifts to 95 percent of Standard Proctor Density (see chapter 5 for more detailed information about fills and soil ratings).

Unless underfloor pressures are expected from sources such as groundwater or swelling clays, the floor is poured at a nominal thickness of 3½ to 4 inches. The floor is usually lightly reinforced with a reinforcing mesh. The manner in which a slab-on-grade floor and the building foundations share the lateral forces from the building walls and transfer them to the soil is not easy to analyze. Normally, the slab will have adequate strength to provide diaphragm action (fig. 6-12); however, a sliding analysis should be carried out for light one-story construction or for two-story construction.

Slabs subjected to underfloor water pressures must be much thicker; the floor will transfer loads to walls and interior supports in much the same way that the roof does. When the design water pressures are substantial, a more continuous construction is substituted for the conventional footing-and-slab construction.

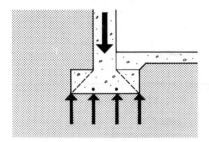

A: Conventional Footing

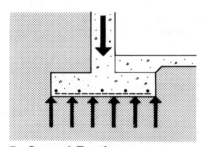

B: Spread Footing

6-14: Foundation Loading

Footings

Foundation design is a relatively simple matter to deal with after the soils engineer has determined an allowable bearing pressure. The load per foot length of wall is divided by the allowable bearing pressure to determine the necessary width of the foundation. For example, a 10,000-pound-per-foot load on a soil that has a bearing capacity of 2,500 pounds per square foot will require a 4-foot-wide foundation. On medium-to-poor bearing soils, the foundations of walls carrying earth loads from the roof will be substantially larger than the foundations of conventional houses. When some wall loads are heavier than others, it is not wise to design all the foundations to be equally wide, as this not only wastes materials but may cause uneven settlement problems.

When the base of the footing extends beyond a 45-degree spread from the edges of the wall (fig. 6-14), the footing must be reinforced to spread the load from the wall across the entire width of the footing. Although the actual pressures on the underside of the footing are seldom uniform, they are assumed to be so in design unless the footing has a moment transferred to it from the wall. Footings are usually made of concrete. In a wood foundation system, the footings may be a combination of pressure-treated wood and gravel. The wood bearing-plate and gravel foundation is not recommended for walls carrying roof earth loads; a concrete footing could be substituted. Typical details for both concrete and wood foundations are shown in chapter 10.

Shell Structures

A shell structure is relatively thin in comparison to its clear span and resists the imposed loads primarily in compression. In nature, the equivalent of such a structure is the eggshell, which is extremely strong under a uniform applied pressure but may be broken relatively easily by applying large point loads. Curved shell forms can be used for the entire structure or only for the roof elements carrying high vertical loads (figs. 6-15 and 6-16).

Shell structures are well suited to earth loadings for house-sized structures because the magnitude of the loading is less important than the uniformity of loading obtained. The use of exposed shell structures is hampered by the need to design for eccentric loadings and the stresses induced by temperature fluctuations. Both of these conditions are less problematic when the shell is placed underground.

The materials used for earth-covered shell structures are usually concrete and steel. Concrete shells may be poured, placed, shotcreted, gunited, or made from ferro-cement—a high-strength concrete of fine aggregate that is troweled over a thin reinforcing mesh. Steel shells are usually restricted to corrugated steel plate culvert sections such as those used for highway drainage structures.

The major advantage of shell structures is that the heavy earth loads are carried more efficiently by the structure, thus allowing thinner sections—and, hence, considerably less structural material—to be used than are required for a rectangular wall and roof system. Also, much longer

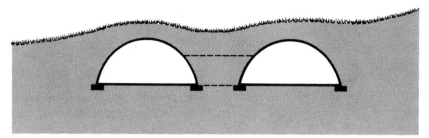

6-15: Shell Structure Forming Roof and Walls

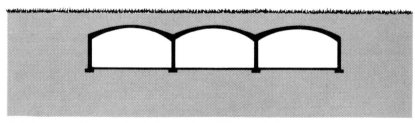

6-16: Shell Structure Forming Roof Only

open spans are possible, allowing more flexibility in arranging interior spaces. Disadvantages are related to the marketability and desirability of a curved interior boundary, the additional design time usually required for structural analysis and detailing, and the greater labor cost of erecting and forming the curved structural shape. Openings through shell structures, which interfere with the continuity of the load transfer and can thus defeat the advantage of this type of structure, should be minimized and carefully designed. In addition, the support points for shells must be capable of resisting both the horizontal and vertical components of the force within the shell structure. Relatively flat shells, which are subject to great horizontal forces, or structural ties or special foundations will be required.

Not all of these disadvantages apply to all shell systems or in all locations; for example, in areas where labor is cheap and structural materials expensive, a shell structure should make considerable sense. Using repeatable forming systems for shell construction will greatly reduce both design costs and labor costs per structure. Several systems are available for constructing shells without designing and forming the system as a one-time-only job. Applications of several types of shell systems are briefly discussed below.

corrugated steel plate culvert sections

Curved corrugated steel plate culvert sections are available in spans of up to 40 feet. The structure is erected by bolting sections of the curved corrugated plate together to form the arch. Generally, these structures can easily withstand several feet of earth cover; in fact, they may not be stable if sufficient earth cover is not provided. Thin-wall structures such as these are most effective when uniform pressures are exerted on the arch. Because interruptions in the continuous profile generally introduce local bending stresses, they should be avoided if possible. Design criteria for steel culverts can be found in the American Association of State Highway and Transportation Officials' (AASHTO) book, *Standard Specification for Bridges.* The following three major concerns should be addressed when these structures are used for a dwelling.

- The plate arches are usually used for drainage and for highway structures, where the structure can easily be inspected from the inside and can be relatively easily replaced if problems occur. Because a poor structural performance will have much greater consequences for a dwelling, design safety factors for a house should reflect greater concern for providing a stable, safe structure.

- Corrosion is always a problem with steel structures underground. Again, when such a structure is intended for use as a residence, greater attention should be paid to ensuring a long-life structure than is necessary in designing for the normal uses of the plate arches.

- Even and careful backfilling is important in working with these flexible structures.

barrel vault structures

Poured concrete shell stuctures are easily constructed using barrel vault reusable forms. The cost of the formwork decreases with the number of reuses of the specially constructed forms; however, more than one form may be required to allow rapid construction. A more recent application of a patented system is the use of curved, perforated steel plates (originally developed for tunneling) as a base for the application of shotcrete, in order to form a rigid barrel vault [6.8].

air-formed shotcrete concrete domes

In this patented system, a flexible membrane is anchored to the ground on the site and then inflated [6.4]. The profile of the shell to be created is controlled by the shaping and seaming of the flexible membrane. An air-lock door is included in the membrane so that the dome can be entered after it is inflated. Then, using spray equipment and applicator protection from the toxic chemicals, a layer of urethane foam is built up on the inside of the membrane. Although this layer will insulate the final shell, it serves primarily to stiffen the membrane so that the shotcrete can be applied to the inside of the foam after the foam has hardened. Shells that have spans greater than 100 feet can be constructed using this system.

concrete shell module

In this system reusable formwork has been designed to construct shell modules that are square in plan, with vertical side walls and a dome roof [6.9]. A variety of house plans can be achieved by using different numbers and arrangements of the modules. Half modules can be poured to create open facades. This technique introduces a flexibility into the use of shell structures that is typically not possible with repeatable whole-shell forming methods.

earth-formed concrete shells

When the soil conditions are suitable and the excavating and labor costs are reasonable, the ground surface can be shaped to act as the bed on which the concrete shell is poured. When the concrete has gained sufficient strength, the earth beneath the shell is excavated, leaving a clear-span structure. Structures that have very large spans—clear spans greater than 300 feet—have been constructed using this technique, as have small, house-scale structures such as those constructed by architect Paolo Soleri.

Typical Sizing for Primary Roof and Wall Structural Elements

Because one of the purposes of this manual is to provide guidance to non-engineers in evaluating buildings for the soundness of their design, a few typical sizes for the primary structural elements are included in figure 6-17. It is not possible within the scope of this manual to include design tables for all structural elements because of the many potential variables that affect their design. However, the sizings given in figure 6-17 can be used to provide a rough comparison with a design under review, in order to help prevent unengineered, grossly underdesigned structures from passing final code or planning reviews.

It must be stressed that these figures should not be considered "safe" values to use, but rather are typical *for the design conditions specified*. They should not be used in lieu of an engineered design, but may indicate that further clarification of the engineering design should be requested (e.g., a registered engineer's stamp of approval on the plans, if it has not already been submitted).

Structural Element	Span (feet)	Material	Thickness or Size	Details
Roof (one way spanning)	24	reinforced cast-in-place concrete	12 in. thick	concrete strength: 4000 psi main steel: #8 bars at 12 in. o.c. transverse steel: #6 bars at 18 in. o.c.
	24	prestressed concrete plank	10 in. thick	2 inch concrete topping included
	16	timber gluelam beam	6 in. wide 14 in. deep	beams placed at 4 ft. o.c. 2 inch wood decking permissible bending stress: 2400 psi
Wall (spanning vertically not fixed in rotation at roof or floor)	9	reinforced cast-in-place concrete	8 in. thick	concrete strength: 4000 psi main steel: #5 bars at 18 in. o.c. transverse steel: #4 bars at 18 in. o.c.
	9	reinforced concrete masonry	8 in. thick	masonry strength: 1500 psi main steel: #7 bars at 24 in o.c. transverse steel: joint reinf. 16 in o.c.
	9	pressure-treated wood	2 in. wide 12 in. deep (nominal)	vertical framing members at 12 in. o.c. shear at the bottom of the wall may require additional reinforcement

6-17: Typical Sizes for Common Roof and Wall Systems

Note: These figures are for general comparative purposes and are not to be used for design. Figures are based on 18 inch earth cover on roof and 40 psf/foot lateral pressure from soil.

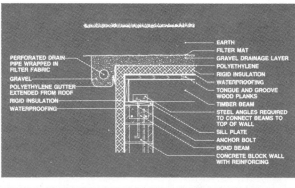

EARTH
FILTER MAT
GRAVEL DRAINAGE LAYER
POLYETHYLENE
RIGID INSULATION
WATERPROOFING
TONGUE AND GROOVE
WOOD PLANKS
TIMBER BEAM
STEEL ANGLES REQUIRED
TO CONNECT BEAMS TO
TOP OF WALL
SILL PLATE
ANCHOR BOLT
BOND BEAM
CONCRETE BLOCK WALL
WITH REINFORCING

PERFORATED DRAIN
PIPE WRAPPED IN
FILTER FABRIC
GRAVEL
POLYETHYLENE GUTTER
EXTENDED FROM ROOF
RIGID INSULATION
WATERPROOFING

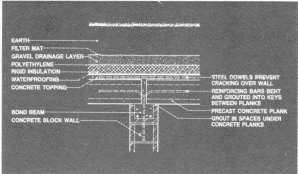

EARTH
FILTER MAT
GRAVEL DRAINAGE LAYER
POLYETHYLENE
RIGID INSULATION
WATERPROOFING
CONCRETE TOPPING

BOND BEAM
CONCRETE BLOCK WALL

STEEL DOWELS PREVENT
CRACKING OVER WALL
REINFORCING BARS BENT
AND GROUTED INTO KEYS
BETWEEN PLANKS
PRECAST CONCRETE PLANK
GROUT IN SPACES UNDER
CONCRETE PLANKS

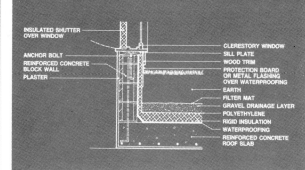

INSULATED SHUTTER
OVER WINDOW

ANCHOR BOLT
REINFORCED CONCRETE
BLOCK WALL
PLASTER

CLERESTORY WINDOW
SILL PLATE
WOOD TRIM
PROTECTION BOARD
OR METAL FLASHING
OVER WATERPROOFING
EARTH
FILTER MAT
GRAVEL DRAINAGE LAYER
POLYETHYLENE
RIGID INSULATION
WATERPROOFING
REINFORCED CONCRETE
ROOF SLAB

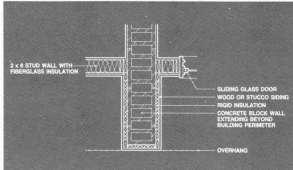

2 x 6 STUD WALL WITH
FIBERGLASS INSULATION

SLIDING GLASS DOOR
WOOD OR STUCCO SIDING
RIGID INSULATION
CONCRETE BLOCK WALL
EXTENDING BEYOND
BUILDING PERIMETER

OVERHANG

CHAPTER 7

WATERPROOFING

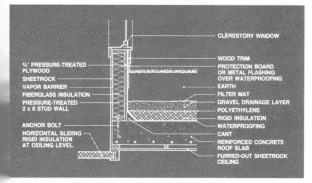

CLERESTORY WINDOW

WOOD TRIM
PROTECTION BOARD
OR METAL FLASHING
OVER WATERPROOFING
EARTH
FILTER MAT
GRAVEL DRAINAGE LAYER
POLYETHYLENE
RIGID INSULATION
WATERPROOFING
CANT
REINFORCED CONCRETE
ROOF SLAB
FURRED-OUT SHEETROCK
CEILING

¾" PRESSURE-TREATED
PLYWOOD
SHEETROCK
VAPOR BARRIER
FIBERGLASS INSULATION
PRESSURE-TREATED
2 x 6 STUD WALL

ANCHOR BOLT
HORIZONTAL SLIDING
RIGID INSULATION
AT CEILING LEVEL

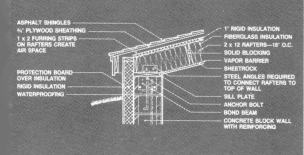

ASPHALT SHINGLES
¾" PLYWOOD SHEATHING
1 x 2 FURRING STRIPS
ON RAFTERS CREATE
AIR SPACE

PROTECTION BOARD
OVER INSULATION
RIGID INSULATION
WATERPROOFING

1" RIGID INSULATION
FIBERGLASS INSULATION
2 x 12 RAFTERS—16" O.C.
SOLID BLOCKING
VAPOR BARRIER
SHEETROCK
STEEL ANGLES REQUIRED
TO CONNECT RAFTERS TO
TOP OF WALL
SILL PLATE
ANCHOR BOLT
BOND BEAM
CONCRETE BLOCK WALL
WITH REINFORCING

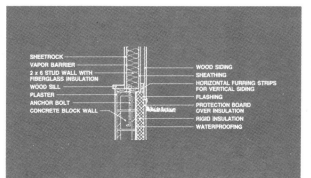

SHEETROCK
VAPOR BARRIER
2 x 6 STUD WALL WITH
FIBERGLASS INSULATION
WOOD SILL
PLASTER
ANCHOR BOLT
CONCRETE BLOCK WALL

WOOD SIDING
SHEATHING
HORIZONTAL FURRING STRIPS
FOR VERTICAL SIDING
FLASHING
PROTECTION BOARD
OVER INSULATION
RIGID INSULATION
WATERPROOFING

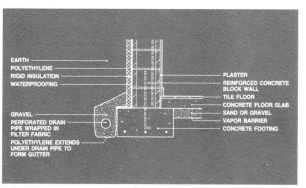

EARTH
POLYETHYLENE
RIGID INSULATION
WATERPROOFING

GRAVEL
PERFORATED DRAIN
PIPE WRAPPED IN
FILTER FABRIC
POLYETHYLENE EXTENDS
UNDER DRAIN PIPE TO
FORM GUTTER

PLASTER
REINFORCED CONCRETE
BLOCK WALL
TILE FLOOR
CONCRETE FLOOR SLAB
SAND OR GRAVEL
VAPOR BARRIER
CONCRETE FOOTING

Introduction

Adequate waterproofing of earth sheltered structures is one of the major concerns of architects, contractors, and clients. Usually, concerns about potential water leakage in earth sheltered structures are based largely on experiences with wet or damp basements in conventional aboveground houses. Most basements have been built with little or no attention to preventing moisture problems, however. In fact, the use of adequate waterproofing to ensure dryness in earth sheltered houses is one of the primary factors (along with sufficient heat and light) that distinguishes the comfortable, fully functional space characteristic of such houses from the typically "secondary" quality of most basements.

Although some people remain skeptical about whether it is possible to provide a completely waterproof structure, competent waterproofing systems are available. But successful waterproofing involves more than simply selecting and installing a reputable product. It requires a comprehensive approach to keeping water out of the building, based on an understanding of all possible sources of moisture. The basic sources of moisture are:

- surface runoff
- water table below grade
- temporary water pressure below grade
- vapor pressure
- capillary draw

Waterproofing is referred to as a system because maintaining dryness in an earth sheltered structure depends on a combination of layered elements and techniques, rather than on a single shell material. Each layer of the system is intended to deflect moisture at a point nearest its source and furthest from the interior of the structure. Successful waterproofing systems comprise three interdependent lines of defense against moisture. The first involves careful site planning and landscaping in order to limit or control the sources of water. The second component of the system is designed to reduce the amount of unavoidable moisture by means of backfilling and drainage techniques. The last line of defense against moisture problems consists of a protected waterproofing skin system.

Each of the basic sources of moisture is dealt with by one or more of these three lines of defense. Surface runoff must be handled by proper site planning and landscaping. Since building below the water table is a very poor condition for construction, the first objective in site selection and planning should be to avoid the water table. A house that must be built partially below the water table will require either extensive drainage in order to permanently depress the water table, or a structure that is completely waterproof and designed to withstand the pressures in both walls and floor. Temporary water pressure against below-grade walls is caused by excessive rains that cannot be adequately handled by surface or subsurface drainage systems. Although the frequency of occurrence and the magnitude of these temporary pressures can be reduced by site planning and drainage techniques, they are unlikely to be completely eliminated.

The final two sources of moisture problems, vapor pressure and capillary draw, are primarily handled by placing the waterproofing skin against the structure of the building. Reducing the moisture content of the soil through drainage can also help minimize these problems. Depending on the relative humidity and temperature conditions of the soil and the interior air of the house, differential vapor pressures can occasionally cause water vapor to flow from the soil into the house. When this occurs, the waterproofing on the outside of the wall can alleviate the moisture problem. In reality, vapor pressure from the soil into the interior space is not as great a problem as the vapor that flows from the warm space to the colder ground. The condensation problems caused by humidity from the inside of the space are not a result of inadequate waterproofing. Capillary draw, another moisture transport mechanism, which can occur through concrete walls in contact with moist soil, is usually handled by an impervious waterproofing or dampproofing system. It can also be eliminated by creating an air gap between the earth and the wall.

This chapter provides information about the techniques and products required for successful waterproofing of earth sheltered structures. It must be emphasized, however, that no perfect method exists and that selecting appropriate methods often depends on specific site and building design conditions.

The chapter is divided into five sections. The first section deals with the first two lines of defense—site planning and drainage techniques. The last four sections—design considerations affecting the waterproofing system, construction and application considerations, criteria for system selection, and evaluation of the various systems—deal primarily with the waterproofing skin.

Site Planning and Drainage Techniques

Site Selection

The first steps in waterproofing a house should be taken in conjunction with site selection and consideration of preliminary layouts and landscaping. At this stage, the main aim is to avoid as many water problems as possible, so that the house will not have to be designed to cope with them later. The first decision is obviously connected with the choice of site. A perfect site with regard to waterproofing will rarely be found and is not, in fact, necessary. But, a good site (opposed to a bad one) will save money and reduce the number and probably the severity of potential problems.

If possible, low areas, gullies, and flood plains should be avoided for any type of housing. The exposure of an earth sheltered house to undesirable surfaces and subsurface water problems depends very much on its design. An earth sheltered house that is built above grade and covered and surrounded by berms will not be in any more danger from flooding than a conventional house would be and it would be far less likely to suffer serious structural damage. On the other hand, the risk of flooding for an atrium design located completely below grade in a low-lying area is much greater. Implications for waterproofing for most other types of earth sheltered designs lie between these two extreme cases. If a low-lying area is being considered as a potential site, the contours of the surrounding area should be studied closely to determine the low spots, where water will tend to collect during heavy rains or snow melt.

A high water table, like a low-lying site, should be avoided if possible, although if a site that has a high water table is selected for other, overriding considerations, this problem can usually be overcome. For example, a simple drainage system can be used to draw down the water table around the structure. If a high water table exists in very permeable soil, a drainage system may not be able to drain the area fast enough; in this case, a substantial waterproofing system must be applied to the entire structure.

Once a site has been selected and a building form appropriate to the site determined, a more detailed system of surface and subsurface drainage must be designed. The remainder of this section discusses some of the most common situations and their detailed solutions.

Drainage Design for Sunken Courtyards

On relatively flat sites, particularly those with little view or solar exposure, a design centering around a sunken courtyard is an appropriate solution for an earth sheltered house. Careful design and detailing is required to prevent water problems since the open courtyard and floor of the house are often lower in elevation than any point on the site. As much as possible, the surrounding ground should slope away from the structure on all sides (see fig. 7-1). A subsurface drain pipe at the perimeter of the roof edge can help to collect and remove the water that accumulates on the earth-covered roof of the structure. Additional drain pipes should be installed along the foundation.

Provision for rapid drainage of the sunken courtyard is essential. If the topography of the site permits, the water can be collected from the courtyard as well as from the foundation drain pipes and flow by gravity to an outfall on the site. Because this technique often cannot be implemented, however, pumping may be required. If building codes permit, water may be pumped into storm sewer systems; otherwise, it will have to be pumped to a drainage area away from the house. In

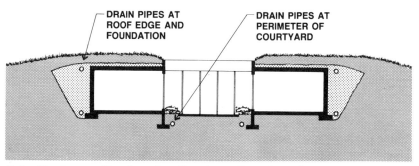

7-1: Drainage Design for Sunken Courtyard

order to ensure that the capacity of the drainage system is not exceeded, a catch basin beneath the center of the courtyard is a good solution for holding the water until it can be drained or pumped away at a more moderate rate.

Drainage Design for Earth Berms

On sites where an earth-covered house is surrounded by berms sloping away from the structure, two key potential drainage problems must be resolved. First, there must be provision for subsurface drainage of the water that is collected on the earth-covered roof unless soils are extremely porous. The placement of an interceptor drain at the crest of the berm along the edge of the rooftop is recommended. The water from the gravel drainage layer of the roof can be collected and the interceptor drain pipe can be connected with the foundation drain system (see fig. 7-2a).

The second drainage concern with berms is control of the surface runoff from the rooftop and berm areas so that they do not collect and pond around the structure. A related concern is potential runoff from the berms onto any adjacent property—a situation that is unacceptable. An appropriate design solution is to shape the land form so that it distributes the water to interceptor drains for collection. An interceptor would be located at the base of the hill to collect the runoff from the surface of the berm (see fig. 7-2a). That runoff, which is accelerated by the steepness of the slope, is less likely to run down the surface as rapidly if the berm is planted with shrubs or vines, rather than sod. When slopes must have a greater than 2 to 1 ratio in order to meet

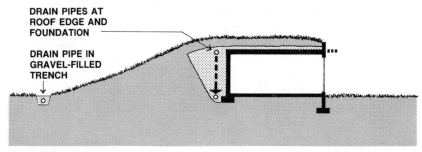

A: Section

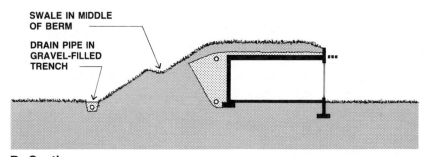

B: Section

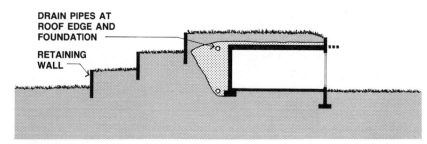

C: Section

7-2: Drainage Design for Earth Berms

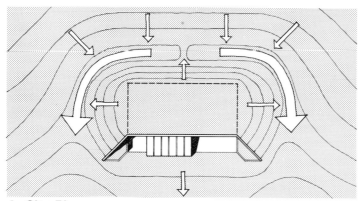

A: Site Plan

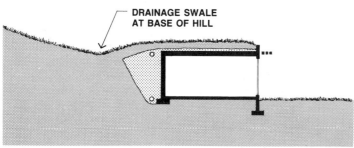

B: Section

7-3: Drainage Swale at Base of Hill

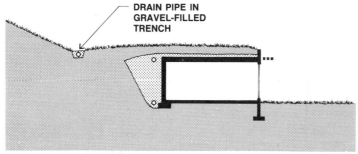

7-4: Interceptor Drain at Base of Hill

the lot lines or other restrictions, the berm should be graded differently from a more gradually sloped berm. Such a berm should be terraced, with a swale midway down the hill and an interceptor drainage system at the toe (see fig. 7-2b). A series of retaining walls may be used instead, provided that there is adequate drainage for the retaining walls (see fig. 7-2c). The need for interceptor drains is most crucial in unstable soil conditions, such as expansive clays; it is less critical in sandier soils.

Drainage Design for Sloping Sites

Earth sheltered and energy-efficient structures are often built into hillsides for solar advantage, visual aesthetics, and ease of berming. Although construction on a hillside may well be a desirable option, it also requires that special consideration be given to problems of surface runoff from uphill and subsurface water percolation. Neglecting to plan for such conditions may lead to occasional leakage to the interior of the structure. When a house is built into the middle or base of a slope, water can be diverted away from the structure by two methods: a drainage swale or gully can be formed to divert water around the house (see fig. 7-3), or a gravel-filled trench with a drain tile leading to an outfall can be installed at the base of the slope (see fig. 7-4).

129

Roofs

Proper backfill and drainage techniques for earth-covered roofs are essential to the overall success of the waterproofing system. Although such considerations are easily neglected, they have the potential to create serious problems. For example, a 1-inch rainfall deposits 1,000 gallons (8,000 lbs.) of water on the roof of a modest-sized (1,600-sq.-ft.) structure. Since it is not desirable for excess water to accumulate on the roof, that water must first flow horizontally across the roof before it can be collected or dissipated. To hasten such drainage, a porous backfill material above the final waterproofing layers and beneath the topsoil is critical. Filter fabric placed beneath the topsoil can help prevent clogging of the porous granular fill (see fig. 7-5). To discourage ponding, roof structures should have at least a slight slope (1 to 8 percent) but not so much that soil slumping, waterproofing displacement, or topsoil erosion will occur. It is important to consider that too much emphasis on fast drainage of the roof will affect the available moisture for the plant materials. The drainage system, type of soil, and plant materials must be designed in an integrated manner. For more information about these concerns, see chapter 9.

The rather large amounts of water that can accumulate on the roof must, of course, go somewhere after they are drained off. When the typical granular backfill and foundation drain pipes are used, all of this water runs down the wall to the drain, thus placing additional demands on the waterproofing skin and the capacity of the drainage system. It can also be argued that forcing additional quantities of water past the walls is disadvantageous thermally because the water accelerates the conduction of heat away from the structure. An excellent alternative, especially when soils are not completely free-draining, is to place an additional drain tile along the roof edge, as shown in figure 7-5. The roof should be covered by a layer of polyethylene that extends off the roof and under the drain pipe, forming a gutter. To prevent clogging of the system with soil, wrapping the perforated drain pipe with filter fabric is recommended. Compaction of the backfill is important so that the drain tile does not move. A tuck is placed in the polyethylene to allow some movement without tearing.

Walls

To counteract potential moisture problems on earth-covered walls, drainage pipes work in conjunction with construction-placed soil, which is compacted between the building and the surrounding soil to capture and remove temporary water pressures from the structure. The intent of these techniques is to intercept, divert, and drain unavoidable subsurface moisture in order to eliminate or reduce the frequency, duration, and intensity of moisture conditions that actually test the final waterproofing layers. Proper backfilling and drainage not only help in waterproofing the structure, but can also reduce structural requirements and costs, since they eliminate the need to design the walls to resist fully saturated soil conditions.

Except for a capping layer of less permeable soil, backfill should consist of a porous granular material (coarse sand, pearock, or gravel). Properly sized materials also act as a filter in preventing the surrounding soil from settling and from clogging foundation drain pipes [7.1]. The available soil on site will be suitably porous in some cases, but in other cases material may have to be brought on-site.

The cost of bringing backfill on-site varies according to local availability. If the cost is excessive for a smaller structure such as a house, it is possible to use the existing soil on-site. It is essential, however, that some porous material at least be placed around the foundation drain pipe and that the perforated pipes are wrapped in filter fabric to prevent clogging (see fig. 7-6).

To give even better performance, a commercially available drainage mat which provides a drainage path down the wall may be used. Such systems not only provide a clear drainage path but include a filter fabric cover that wraps around the drain pipe at the base. As discussed in the previous section, it is very desirable in any case to include a second drain tile at the upper edge of the wall to intercept any water from the earth-covered roof. Backfill should be compacted in 9- to 12-inch layers. This layered compaction not only requires less force than compaction of overly thick layers, but also offers superior results. Insufficient compaction may cause surface slumping and, possibly, displacement of insulation and waterproofing membranes.

An outlet must be provided for water from surface runoff and saturated soils that accumulate in the perforated plastic or clay drain tile placed around the perimeter of the footings. On a sloping site, drains should be placed so that water will flow naturally to an exposed surface outlet. In situations where subsurface drains are exposed, the ends should be screened to prevent entry of rodents or other small animals. When this is impractical, drains

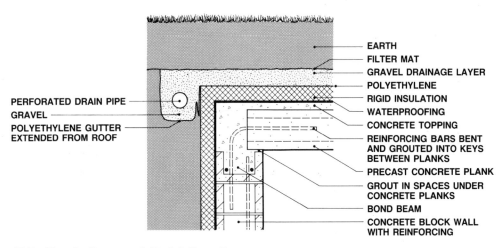

7-5: Earth-Covered Roof Detail

Labels (left): PERFORATED DRAIN PIPE, GRAVEL, POLYETHYLENE GUTTER EXTENDED FROM ROOF

Labels (right): EARTH, FILTER MAT, GRAVEL DRAINAGE LAYER, POLYETHYLENE, RIGID INSULATION, WATERPROOFING, CONCRETE TOPPING, REINFORCING BARS BENT AND GROUTED INTO KEYS BETWEEN PLANKS, PRECAST CONCRETE PLANK, GROUT IN SPACES UNDER CONCRETE PLANKS, BOND BEAM, CONCRETE BLOCK WALL WITH REINFORCING

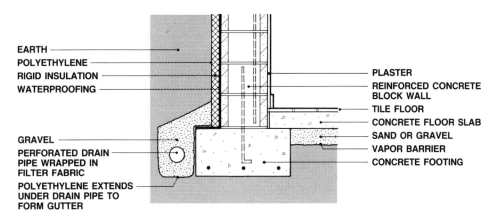

7-6: Foundation Detail

Labels (left): EARTH, POLYETHYLENE, RIGID INSULATION, WATERPROOFING, GRAVEL, PERFORATED DRAIN PIPE WRAPPED IN FILTER FABRIC, POLYETHYLENE EXTENDS UNDER DRAIN PIPE TO FORM GUTTER

Labels (right): PLASTER, REINFORCED CONCRETE BLOCK WALL, TILE FLOOR, CONCRETE FLOOR SLAB, SAND OR GRAVEL, VAPOR BARRIER, CONCRETE FOOTING

can be routed to a storm sewer or to a sump that can be pumped out when necessary. The design of the structure should provide for access to foundation drains for clean-out operations. If severe soil moisture is anticipated or relatively impermeable backfills must be used, the air-gap type of drain material or matting mentioned above can be applied to the wall for positive vertical drainage and as a capillary break. In relatively impervious soils, it may be advisable to cover the wall with polyethylene and extend it beneath the drain tile to prevent water from saturating the soil beneath the footing and floor and direct the water to the drain tile.

Floors and Foundations

Generally, it is recommended that concrete floors be poured over a plastic vapor barrier with a layer of sand placed over the plastic to help in the curing of the concrete and to protect the plastic sheet during pouring (see fig. 7-6). This helps to prevent moisture migration problems and occasional water leakage through the floor. In cases where underfloor water problems are definitely anticipated, several inches of porous fill are recommended beneath the plastic layer. This underlying porous fill should drain to the perimeter drain pipes in order to remove any accumulated soil moisture. If the structure is built into the water table, the drainage system may be designed to constantly draw down the water table to a level below the floor. In such cases a series of drain pipes topped by a granular layer may be required and it is also usually necessary to completely waterproof under the floor and design the floor and footings to withstand the water pressure from below.

131

Design and Detail Considerations

General Design Issues

Although basic design decisions about an earth sheltered structure, such as the shape of the building and the structural materials used, are made for a variety of reasons, facilitating the method of waterproofing is usually not a major consideration in design. Nevertheless, these basic characteristics directly affect the difficulty and cost of waterproofing a building, as well as limit the number of systems that are appropriate. It is useful to recognize the implications of these design decisions so that the waterproofing system can be designed as an integral part of the building rather than applied as an afterthought, when it is more difficult to make changes.

The design decision to build a completely underground structure with an earth-covered roof, as opposed to an earth-bermed structure with a conventional roof, obviously affects the waterproofing design. Similarly, if an earth-covered roof is included in the design, the slope of the roof will affect the choice and the detailing of the waterproofing system. Waterproofing requirements for horizontal roof surfaces and vertical wall surfaces differ. Walls are generally easier to deal with because the water can be drained away more quickly by using proper backfilling and drainage techniques. Roofs, on the other hand, must be designed to resist leakage from standing water.

The shape of the structure, as well as the placement of openings and projections in the walls and roof, can greatly influence the waterproofing system. The simplest configuration, a basic rectangular box, has a minimum number of corners and no awkward shapes. Many types of waterproofing products would be suitable for such a simple shape. On the other hand, only a few types of products may be applicable to more complicated shapes and surfaces—for example, on a structure that has an unusual plan arrangement, a curvilinear structure such as a barrel shell, or an irregular surface such as corrugated steel.

In addition to being affected by the basic shape of the structure, waterproofing can be made far more complex by the placement of openings and projections, particularly on the roof. Skylights, flues, and vents usually require seams and patches in sheet membranes. Greater strains will occur in these areas in any system—liquid, sheet, or troweled-on products—because movement caused by structural deflections and thermal expansion can occur. The transition from below-grade to above-grade materials requires especially careful flashing (see the discussion of flashing details, below). Generally, the areas around roof openings and projections are a major source of leaks. The best strategy is to avoid numerous scattered penetrations in the waterproofing by bringing them through on the open side of the structure if possible or by consolidating them in one or two larger projections (see figs. 7-7 and 7-8).

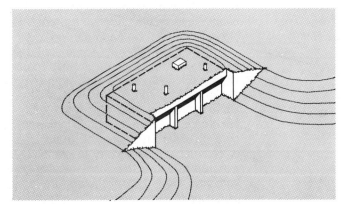

7-7: Scattered Roof Penetrations

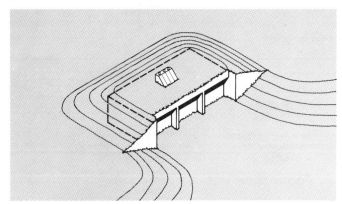

7-8: Consolidated Roof Penetrations

A final major design decision that affects the waterproofing is the choice of materials. Various forms of wood, concrete, or masonry can be used for underground walls and roofs. The degree of compatibility of the surface material with the various types of waterproofing may limit choices: certain waterproofing methods are only appropriate for one material, whereas others are effective on almost any surface.

Location of Waterproofing on Structure

Current thought and practice in regard to the placement of waterproofing materials on roofs and walls of earth sheltered structures (see fig. 7-9) suggest a sequence of materials similar to the Protected Membrane Roof (PMR) system currently used on many conventional above-grade, flat-roof structures. In the PMR system, the waterproofing material is placed directly on the roof deck, followed by insulation. The system is usually capped with a thin layer of gravel and asphalt that weighs down the insulation and protects it from wind updrafts and inclement weather. This top layer of gravel and asphalt is not necessary in below-grade waterproofing applications because the weight of the earth holds the system in place.

The PMR waterproofing system is a reversal of the older, conventional built-up roof systems, in which the insulation is placed on the roof deck first. A multi-ply layer of asphalt or pitch and felts are then placed over the insulation and topped with a thin layer of gravel for weight and protection. Thus, the waterproofing membrane in the conventional system is exposed to the temperature and climate

extremes. The membrane must be able to handle thermal cycles ranging from well below freezing to 180° to 190°F. This thermal stress results in cracking, tearing, and checking of the membrane, which in turn necessitates continual roof maintenance. Such roof maintenance is not possible on an earth sheltered structure.

Although waterproofing membranes used underground will not undergo the extremes of thermal cycling common to aboveground roof membranes, a membrane under 2 feet of soil cover can still be subject to thermal cycles that span a 50°F temperature range. This temperature range can be reduced by placing the waterproofing material under the insulation and next to the structural substrate. The roof insulation will also serve as a protective covering for

the waterproofing membrane, as it insulates the underlying waterproofing material from damaging thermal shock, protects the waterproofing during backfilling, deflects some incidental water problems, and protects the waterproofing materials from damage caused by roots, digging, and some soil chemicals. It is common practice to overlap sheets of polyethylene on the exterior of the foam board in order to promote drainage. In cases when no insulation is specified by the design, some other form of protection must be used such as 15-pound building felt, heavy-gauge PVC or polyethylene sheeting (6 mil.), thin fiberboards, or a 4-inch layer of sand on the roof.

Two major reasons underlying the development of the PMR system were the

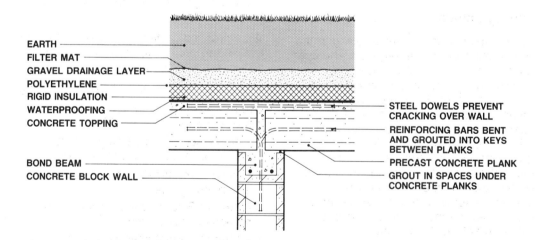

7-9: Earth-Covered Roof Detail

EARTH
FILTER MAT
GRAVEL DRAINAGE LAYER
POLYETHYLENE
RIGID INSULATION
WATERPROOFING
CONCRETE TOPPING

BOND BEAM
CONCRETE BLOCK WALL

STEEL DOWELS PREVENT CRACKING OVER WALL
REINFORCING BARS BENT AND GROUTED INTO KEYS BETWEEN PLANKS
PRECAST CONCRETE PLANK
GROUT IN SPACES UNDER CONCRETE PLANKS

frequent leaks and repairs necessary for built-up roofs, and the development of waterproof membrane and foam insulations that could perform adequately in this inverted configuration. Some of the same materials developed for PMR flat roofs made possible the modified PMR systems suggested for below-grade application. In many ways below-grade conditions are less harsh than those associated with exposed roofs. Many insulation and membrane materials that work well on exposed roofs may, however, prove unacceptable in the underground environment. Special caution must be exercised in determining which above-grade materials and techniques can successfully adapt to below-grade applications.

Critical Details in Waterproofing

flashing details

Special attention to careful detailing in the waterproofing system is required wherever a transition from a below-grade surface to an above-grade surface or an edge occurs. Such transitions are common around skylights, vents, and other projections, as well as at parapet walls and other edge conditions. In these areas movement resulting from structural deflections or freeze-thaw cycles causes greater strain on the waterproofing material. In some cases this strain must be absorbed by the weakest part of the system, which might well be the waterproofing seam. In addition, waterproofing in these locations is directly exposed to surface runoff, sun, snow, and a wider range of temperatures. Many waterproofing products that are suitable

below grade simply cannot be exposed to these above-grade conditions.

Usually, problems can be avoided by extending the waterproofing material above grade (never simply ending it at the grade line), and then covering it with a second flashing material, as shown in fig. 7-10. Aluminum or galvanized metal often are used to cover the waterproofing material above grade and are extended a few inches below grade as well. However, if the appearance of shiny metal is not desirable, other materials can be used (see list below). Another reason for providing flashing at the grade line is that it is usually necessary to extend the insulation over the above-grade as well as the below-grade portions of the wall. Although the insulation can also serve as a soft cushion to protect the waterproofing, most insulation products should not be left directly exposed to the exterior environment. In such cases a cement or proprietary plaster can be applied directly to the insulation.

Waterproofing protection materials that can be used to protect waterproofing exposed above grade include:

- galvanized metal and aluminum flashing
- heavy-gauge (45-mil.) PVC plastic sheet, below grade
- thin (1/8-inch) fiberboards, such as masonite, above and below grade
- 1/8-inch cement-asbestos board, above and below grade
- a strip of EPDM rubber at the grade portions of the house
- a fiberglass-reinforced cement coating applied directly over rigid insulation board that runs continuously from below grade into the above-grade wall finish.

Depending on the type of waterproofing product used, special items may be available for use in certain common flashing situations—for example, a specially shaped piece of waterproof membrane material that fits around a typical plumbing vent. Unfortunately, simply providing a good but inelastic seal around a plumbing vent or other projection will not be enough. Leaks can occur if the roof structure deflects significantly (over 1/4-inch deflection on an earth-covered roof is common) while the vent pipe remains stationary. To help prevent such occurrences, the earth should be placed on the roof so that most of the deflection occurs before the complete plumbing assembly is fixed into place. Also, a number of details, such as flexible boots and expansion joints or bends in the pipes, can allow for movement. A variety of flashing conditions at parapet walls, bermed walls, and roof penetrations are shown and discussed in chapter 10.

cants

Sharp corners or bends can cause problems for most waterproofing products, particularly membranes and roll goods, by creating additional stress in the waterproofing material. Another problem is that water does not drain away easily from corners. The common solution is to place a cant to provide a more gradual bend and promote better drainage (see fig.7-10).

footings

Waterproofing generally is not placed under the floor of an earth sheltered structure, except in the more unusual case of a structure that is built into a water table. Waterproofing is, however, usually applied on the walls. It is important to

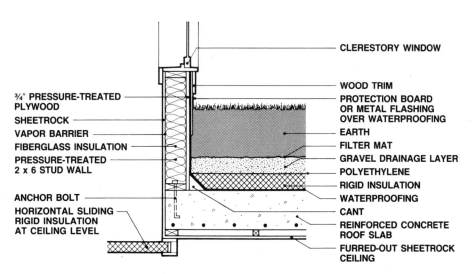

¾" PRESSURE-TREATED PLYWOOD
SHEETROCK
VAPOR BARRIER
FIBERGLASS INSULATION
PRESSURE-TREATED 2 x 6 STUD WALL

ANCHOR BOLT
HORIZONTAL SLIDING RIGID INSULATION AT CEILING LEVEL

CLERESTORY WINDOW

WOOD TRIM
PROTECTION BOARD OR METAL FLASHING OVER WATERPROOFING
EARTH
FILTER MAT
GRAVEL DRAINAGE LAYER
POLYETHYLENE
RIGID INSULATION
WATERPROOFING
CANT
REINFORCED CONCRETE ROOF SLAB
FURRED-OUT SHEETROCK CEILING

7-10: Earth-Covered Roof Detail at Clerestory Window Opening

extend this waterproofing as far down as possible in order to cover the footing (see fig. 7-6). When the waterproofing extends well below the floor level, water that accumulates during a heavy rain is prevented from entering the structure before it drains away.

construction and expansion joints

A number of joints typically occur in underground structures—between footings and walls, walls and roofs, building walls and retaining walls, roofs and parapet walls, as well as within the walls and roofs themselves. All of these joints have the potential for some movement and subsequent cracking and leaking. If movement is limited to a relatively small amount, leakage can be prevented by

many waterproofing products that either stretch over or expand to fill the crack.

In some cases waterstops are used to reduce leakage at cold joints and other construction joints in concrete. In the joints where the most leakage occurs—in poured concrete walls, floors, etc.—a waterstop simply provides a much longer leakage path for the water. However, water may travel laterally along the waterstops, and leakage can occur at places remote from the original source of water unless the joints between waterstop sections are perfect. Waterstops are therefore not recommended when a full waterproofing system is used on the outside of the wall. Additionally, if water gets through the main membrane, the waterstop can mask the true location of the leak, thus making it

extremely difficult to find. Waterstops are most commonly used when reduction in the amount of water leakage, rather than elimination of all leaks, is of major importance. If it is determined that extra protection is necessary at a joint, a chemical waterstop may be more suitable, provided that it can expand to fill the crack and will localize leaks when properly applied.

In larger structures (more than a few hundred feet in either dimension), expansion joints are often required so that any building movement occurs at the joint instead of causing cracking of and damage to materials. If an expansion joint is required on an earth sheltered roof or wall, a membrane type of flashing could be placed over the joint and bonded to both sides of the structure. Excess material should be left so that the joint can widen without breaking the bond or the material. The regular waterproofing material—whether sheet, roll, sprayed- or troweled-on—can then be placed over or connected to this expansion material, depending on the specific product requirements. Although expansion joints are usually not required on smaller structures, similar details might be appropriate at joints where movement is anticipated, such as between two sections of a concrete roof that are divided by a thermal break or between a below-grade wall of a structure and an exterior retaining wall (see figs. 10-3 and 10-26 in chapter 10 for illustrations of these details).

Construction and Application Considerations

Waterproofing systems and materials are only as good as their application. In general, underground waterproofing and design details should be done only by an experienced, professional waterproofing subcontractor, although a do-it-yourself system or installation by a general contractor is occasionally acceptable. Some products and systems require highly technical skills, while others can be done by relatively inexperienced laborers. Improper application of waterproofing materials is one of the major reasons for waterproofing material failures. No material, regardless of cost or quality, will work unless it is applied properly. Material specifications must be carefully followed; and application must take place under the right conditions. Field supervision during waterproofing application by the architect, manufacturer, or general contractor is essential.

Construction Schedule

The construction schedule affects the choice of waterproofing materials in several ways. Because many products are quite sensitive to the temperature and humidity conditions under which they are applied, scheduling during the proper weather conditions is often critical. Several products also require that particular parts of the construction sequence either precede or follow the waterproofing application. For example, preparation of the surfaces often must precede application. After application, some products require immediate backfilling or protection, whereas others must be exposed for curing. Meeting the correct weather conditions and sequence of construction requirements demands

scheduling that is often more exacting than is usually the case for residential construction. The necessary materials and labor crews must be available on time, and the activities of various trades must be carefully coordinated. Given the importance of proper application, the availability of materials and labor as well as the complexity of the construction sequence for a particular product may be deciding factors in system selection.

Surface and Weather Conditions

Concrete surfaces can be quite rough because of bumps, pits, and other flaws, and they may be covered with formwork release agents or other substances. The bond between the substrate and the waterproofing material is a critical element of most systems. Most waterproofing materials require full adherence to the structural surface, either to maintain their own integrity or to localize leaks. Usually, release agents, oils, solvents, grease, and water must be removed from the surface before application of the waterproofing begins. For many materials it is necessary to smooth the concrete surface, grind projections, fill depressions, patch flaws, and clean the surface before applying waterproofing. It is important to remember that the requirements are different for each product.

Most waterproofing systems require a moisture-free structural surface in a specified temperature range for proper adhesion. For example, the specifications may require that the surface temperature of the substrate be above 40°F. Problems

can arise, however, because an air temperature of 50°F does not necessarily mean that the structural surface of the wall or roof will also be above 50°F. If the substrate surface is cooler and below the dew point, invisible condensation that may be present will affect the adhesion of the waterproofing materials. In cases when the air temperature is near the specified limit, attention should be paid to the surface temperature, as well as to whether the air temperature is rising or falling.

Chemical Compatibility and Dangers

Not only must the proper surface and weather conditions exist to ensure successful application of the waterproofing, but a chemical compatibility also must exist between the various elements. For example, adhesives and seam sealers must not only be appropriate for the particular materials and surfaces on which they are to be used, but also must not destroy the insulation materials placed on top of the waterproofing. The chemicals contained in some waterproofing products, as well as some of the chemicals in bonding materials, pose two dangers. First, they can cause problems of toxicity for the applicators. Second, where some compounds are combined, their reaction with waterproofing materials can destroy the waterproofing. Therefore, great care should be exercised in the selection and use of dangerous or incompatible materials.

Flood Testing

Whenever possible, it is advisable to test waterproofing products for leakage before backfilling. On horizontal surfaces this is done by flooding the area and then inspecting it for leaks. On larger structures the waterproofing is flooded in sections so that any leaks can be located more easily. Of course, neither roofs that slope significantly nor vertical surfaces can be tested in this manner. Flood testing is possible with all materials except bentonite-based products, which must remain dry until they are backfilled. Bentonite only works effectively when it is held in place under pressure by the soil.

Backfilling Procedures

If not done carefully and properly, backfilling against the walls and on the roof of an earth sheltered structure can cause problems with the waterproofing system. All waterproofing materials should be protected from the soil during backfilling. Sharp aggregates, debris, and high friction induced during the backfilling can tear and damage the material. In many cases the external insulation placed over the waterproofing material will offer some protection. If rigid insulation is glued to the waterproofing membrane, however, any shear forces induced during backfilling on the insulation may be transferred to the waterproofing. As the weight of the backfill slides downward on the walls, the insulation can be dragged across the waterproofing, causing it to tear or unbond from the structure. Similar shear forces can also be transferred through the insulation to the waterproofing if settling occurs. It is therefore essential to compact the soil during backfilling. Where no insulation board is used over the waterproofing, another form of protection board must be used. Often, a separate, unfastened protective covering over the insulation or waterproofing is used so that some potential for slippage is provided. Such protective materials include cement asbestos board, heavy-gauge PVC sheets, building felt, and even thin plywood. All waterproofing materials should be regarded as vulnerable with respect to stresses induced during backfilling.

Backfilling on an earth-covered roof must also be done carefully to avoid damage to the waterproofing and displacement of the insulation. Insulation usually is placed over the waterproofing, and a layer of gravel is installed over the insulation for drainage. Most earth sheltered structures are designed so that only lightweight earth-moving equipment can be supported by the roof. Dirt cannot be pushed around as forcefully as it would be under normal circumstances without inducing stresses on the insulation and waterproofing layers. In some cases the earth is lifted to the roof and placed in small piles by a front end loader, backhoe, or crane, depending on the size of the job. The earth is then spread by driving on top of the soil to cushion and distribute its weight. The light-weight equipment should be driven to the edge of the soil line, where the earth load can be dropped and the top surface of the earth can be graded back instead of pushing it forward. Pushing the soil forward transmits greater shear stress through the soil than does pulling it over earth that has been packed by the weight of the equipment.

Timing of Backfill

The various waterproofing materials have different requirements for the scheduling of the backfilling operations. These requirements are usually related to the curing time required for a concrete structure to reach design strength as well as to potential unfortunate consequences if the waterproofing materials are exposed to sun, rain, wind, or air-temperature extremes. If the waterproofing material to be used cannot be exposed to the elements for a long period of time, the concrete structure should be allowed to cure until it reaches design strength before the waterproofing is applied. After it has been applied, backfilling should occur as soon as possible. The opposite is true for some liquid-applied waterproofing products, however: there can be negative consequences if the product is backfilled before it has had adequate time to cure. In this case, the waterproofing can be applied immediately after the concrete structure is complete and both can cure simultaneously. In fact, the curing of the concrete is aided by the waterproof cover, which prevents it from drying out too quickly. This arrangement will not work, however, if proper adhesion of the waterproofing is prevented by the moisture in the concrete.

Criteria for Selecting Waterproofing Systems

Summarized below are the most important criteria to be considered in selecting a waterproofing system for an earth sheltered structure. These criteria are applied to each of the generic systems evaluated in the following section.

Durability and Stability Underground

Although durability and stability underground appear to be obvious requirements for any waterproofing material, some products do not meet these criteria, at least under certain conditions. For example, emulsified asphalt coatings, which are commonly applied as dampproofing below grade, can re-emulsify in groundwater and become ineffective over time. The product selected should be compatible with the soils on the site with respect to alkalinity and other chemical characteristics. Information on the site soil conditions can be obtained from a soils-testing firm, as discussed in chapter 5. Waterproofing products should be chemically compatible not only with the soil, but also with other construction materials.

Most waterproofing products are bonded to the structure in some manner. It is important to select a product in which the bond, as well as the waterproofing material itself, will last for the lifetime of the structure. Moisture vapor often permeates from the inside of a house through the wall and roof (especially as concrete cures), thus coming in contact with the underside of the waterproofing material. This moisture can affect the bond.

The strength and integrity of seams is another consideration in assessing the long-term durability and stability of products under subsurface conditions. As a general rule, the fewer seams necessary with sheet and roll membrane waterproofing products, the better. Where seams are necessary, the designer must consider whether the field-bonded seam is as strong and chemically stable as the sheet material itself, as well as whether the quality control in making proper field seams is adequate. It is also important to know how much shrinkage of the sheet material will occur and how shrinkage will affect the stress on and performance of the seam. The unrestrained shrinkage of a black membrane exposed to the sun during application and then buried in the cooler ground environment may be as much as two inches in a 50-foot length. If this condition is not avoided or enough slack provided to accommodate the movement, the membranes can easily rupture at the field seams. A related concern is that the shrinkage of waterproofing materials not only can affect the stress on the seams, but may also affect the bond to the structure. In products that require curing, such as some liquid-applied materials, shrinkage can result in cracking or checking of the material or breaking of the bond.

Ability to Withstand Movement and Cracks

Earth sheltered structures are very vulnerable to the dynamic forces created by the earth, such as differential settling and freeze-thaw cycles. Their structural

systems even when properly designed, will settle, rotate, and shift slightly under the changing soil loading conditions. The same dynamic flexibility is also required of the waterproofing material, which is placed directly adjacent to the structural material.

The waterproofing material must be able to give and respond to the movements of the structural components. The greatest movement usually occurs at the joints between the different structural system components: joints at footings, walls, roof edges, parapet walls, cold joints, skylights, and other roof projections.

The cracking and shifting that result from these forces generally do not occur until after the soil loading; by then, the waterproofing has already been placed. In order to deal with these problems of movement, a waterproofing system must have either the ability to stretch over cracks or to expand and reseal itself.

Ability to Minimize Leaks and Facilitate Repair

Some initial leaks in any waterproofing system should be regarded as at least a possibility, if not a probability. Because the difficulty of locating leaks and the cost of repair underground can pose significant problems, opportunities for potential repair and replacement should also be considered when choosing the waterproofing material. To ease these problems, a waterproofing system should have two basic characteristics. First, it should not allow any water that penetrates the waterproofing to travel and emerge on the inside of the structure in a location remote from the original source of the leak. Second, once a leak is found, it should be easily repairable, preferably from the inside so that excavation is unnecessary.

Appropriate Use

The suitability of a waterproofing system is related to various characteristics of the building design and structural surfaces to which it can be applied. The first limiting factor is the type of surface materials to which a waterproofing material can be applied. Another important determinant of suitability is whether a waterproofing system is appropriate for horizontal surfaces, vertical surfaces, or both types of surface. Along with the suitability of the material on horizontal surfaces, it is important to know whether a minimum slope for the surface is recommended. Finally, the usefulness of a product can be limited by the geometric shape and detailing of the structure to which it is applied. For example, complex geometric shapes, curving surfaces, and numerous projections, penetrations, and flashing details present virtually no additional problems for some products. For others, however, they can make application far more difficult, resulting in diminished effectiveness for the system.

Application Considerations

Product selection may also be based partially on various considerations and limitations related to application. The need for highly skilled versus relatively unskilled labor can affect the cost and, sometimes, the availability of qualified applicators.

Some of the most important considerations with regard to the application of waterproofing products are the physical condition of the structural surface that is required and the limitations imposed by weather. The degree to which surfaces must be clean, smooth, dry, and within certain temperature and humidity ranges can affect costs and scheduling. Products that have very little tolerance for these somewhat uncontrollable weather and surface conditions should be regarded with caution because they carry a greater risk of failure. A final characteristic worth considering is the extent to which the product can be damaged after application. If products are easily damaged and extensive protection is required during backfill, the possibility of failure is increased.

Costs

The cost of competent waterproofing systems is often quite substantial, compared to the lower-cost dampproofing products with which most residential contractors and home owners are familiar. Because repair costs can be significant, waterproofing is no place to economize. Nonetheless, comparative costs can become a key criterion in product selection, provided that the other basic performance criteria are met. While the cost of labor exceeds the cost of materials for some waterproofing products, the material accounts for the greatest part of the total cost of many of the highest-quality products. In addition, costs will vary from location to location depending on the availability of materials and qualified applicators.

Guarantees

In some cases a final criterion for selecting a waterproofing system may be the type of product guarantee that is offered. Most waterproofing manufacturers offer a limited guarantee. The terms of the guarantees vary widely; however, they generally offer only to repair or replace any portion of the waterproofing material found to be defective. This means that the owner is usually responsible for finding the source of the leak, removing the soil and materials to facilitate repair, replacing the soil backfill and landscaping, repairing all consequent damage to contents inside the structure, and paying costs resulting from loss of use of the building. Most of these items are not covered by standard insurance policies.

Because a guarantee against material failure does not ensure the home owner of reimbursement for the total cost of repair, and because inadequate application is not always included in a guarantee and is difficult to prove in any case, guarantees should not be a primary criterion for product selection unless the guarantee is unconditional against any cause of a waterproofing leak.

Since guarantees can vary depending on the manufacturer, the contractor, and the specific circumstances of the project, it is not possible to provide reliable information for an entire generic category of waterproofing products. Thus, an assessment of guarantees is not included in the waterproofing system evaluations in the following section.

Evaluation of Waterproofing Systems

Selecting the proper waterproofing for an earth sheltered structure may be a difficult task, not only because many waterproofing systems have similar characteristics, but also because new products or new formulations of existing products are constantly appearing on the market with claims of improved performance over existing systems. In this section, a wide range of waterproofing methods that could be applied to underground structures are described and evaluated, based on the typical characteristics of seven types of generic waterproofing products. Specific products must be carefully examined to determine to what extent they may differ from these general classifications. The generic categories are:

- dampproofing techniques
- asphalt and pitch built-up membranes
- cementitious materials
- liquid-applied systems
- modified bitumens
- sheet membranes
- bentonite clay products

The product evaluations are based on the criteria discussed in the preceding section of this chapter. The following characteristics are discussed for each category of products.

- durability and stability underground
- ability to withstand movement and cracking
- ability to minimize leaks and facilitate repair
- appropriate use
- application considerations
- relative costs

Other criteria for evaluation and comparison, such as type of guarantee, exact cost, and availability of materials and applicators are not discussed because they are too dependent on the specific product used and specific location of the job. In some cases, of course, these factors could be overriding criteria for product selection.

Even after a designer or home owner has compiled a considerable amount of technical information and has held numerous discussions with experienced contractors, product representatives, architects, and engineers, it is not always easy to say that one product is better than another. Some categories of these products, notably dampproofing techniques, definitely cannot be recommended as providing competent waterproofing. But products in the other categories have characteristics that not only affect their performance in major or minor ways, but also affect the conditions under which they should be used. More than most other products selected in building construction, waterproofing systems must be selected on the basis of a thorough understanding of both their typical characteristics and their appropriateness for a specific building design and site.

Dampproofing Products

This group of products includes concrete admixtures, polyethylene sheets, and a variety of surface treatments such as epoxy and acrylic paints, simple asphalt and pitch coatings, and cement pargeting that can be applied to concrete and masonry walls. Although commonly used for foundations and basements, these products should not be considered complete and adequate waterproofing systems. The term *dampproofing* actually connotes the prevention of dampness but not full protection from water that may enter the structure. It is important to distinguish between these relatively inexpensive, easily applied products and other systems that use some of the same materials in different ways to yield products with different characteristics and, in some cases, improved effectiveness (see the sections below on cementitious materials, built-up membranes, and modified bitumens).

stability and durability

The effectiveness of two of the most commonly used dampproofing products—asphalt and pitch coatings—is questionable when they are used underground for two reasons. First, asphalt emulsions can tend to re-emulsify in the presence of groundwater over a long period of time and eventually become ineffective. Second, the quality of both asphalt and pitch has deteriorated in recent years. Improvements in the oil refining process have resulted in poorer chemical properties in the asphalt by-product. Similarly, as health standards have caused some of the more volatile substances to be removed from coal tar pitch, a more brittle, less effective product has resulted. It should be pointed out, however, that a great variety of asphalt and pitch products, with potential differences in properties, is available. Naturally occurring asphalts, for example, would not suffer from most of the disadvantages mentioned above.

Because polyethylene is manufactured at a consistent quality, it can serve as a good vapor barrier if it is carefully applied and seams are overlapped. Although clear polyethylene is subject to degradation if it is exposed to the ultraviolet rays of the sun, this is no problem in underground applications. The main reasons that polyethylene is totally inadequate as a waterproofing system are that it is not sufficiently strong or puncture resistant and that it is difficult, if not impossible, to make watertight seams in the field.

Epoxy and acrylic coatings can be tough and adhere well to concrete surfaces. Using concrete admixtures and pargeting with a dense cement plaster can greatly reduce the permeability of concrete. Although some of these dampproofing products can be effective in preventing water from entering the structure and are also relatively stable underground, they nonetheless do not represent a long-term solution to waterproofing because of the drawbacks discussed below.

ability to withstand movement and cracking

Dampproofing products may be integral with the concrete structure (admixtures), very brittle (cement pargeting), or applied in a relatively thin layer bonded to the surface (epoxy paints, asphalt and pitch coatings). In none of these cases does the product have any real ability to respond to movement in the structure or to bridge cracks. Although asphalt and pitch have some softness and flexibility in exposed locations in summertime, they are usually more brittle and subject to cracking when used at consistently low temperatures underground. Since cracks and movement are virtually inevitable in concrete structures, this is the greatest shortcoming of these coatings. Polyethylene, on the other hand, has some ability to bridge cracks and adjust to movement without failing because it is a sheet rather than a coating. In this regard, the clear polyethylene is superior to black polyethylene for underground applications, where it is not exposed to sunlight.

ability to minimize leaks and facilitate repair

Dampproofing products basically have no ability to reseal any punctures, tears, or breaks in the coating. In a soft and flexible state, asphalt and pitch have a limited ability to reseal; however, this quality is irrelevant in the presence of cooler, below-grade temperatures where these materials can become brittle. Most of the products are integral with the concrete or bonded to the surface. Because any leaks that do occur cannot travel extensively under the coating (as they could with a sheet or membrane), they are easier to locate. Water can, however, travel through the structural cracks and voids, which can be extensive in block walls. The problem of localizing a leak is considerably worse with polyethylene, as water can travel easily behind the loose-laid sheet. If the sheet is bonded to the surface, the tendency for water to travel is reduced.

appropriate use

These products are not recommended for any underground application where a complete waterproofing job is desired. They are only appropriate for secondary spaces in which some moisture and dampness can be tolerated or as a vapor barrier.

application considerations

The various coatings can be applied by unskilled labor and are either sprayed, troweled, or brushed on. Specifications for temperature, humidity, and surface conditions vary with the different products. Polyethylene sheets should be overlapped generously to act as an effective vapor barrier.

relative costs

Most of these dampproofing products have relatively low labor and material costs, compared to costs of first-class waterproofing systems.

Built-up Asphalt and Pitch Membranes

This type of membrane, which consists of layers of hot-mopped asphalt or pitch alternated with felt or fabric reinforcing that is bonded to the structure, is a very familiar and commonly used product in waterproofing above-grade roofs. Although this system has been used with some success in various underground applications, there are some basic questions concerning its long-term durability below grade, as well as its ability to perform in the same manner that it does under above-grade conditions. Long-term performance is more critical underground because the waterproofing is not easily accessible for the continued program of repair and eventual replacement that is characteristic of built-up membranes above grade.

stability and durability

As stated in the previous section on asphalt and pitch dampproofing coatings, the long-term stability of many such products underground is not reliable. Although the basic built-up membrane is relatively impervious to water and water vapor when first installed, continual exposure to water—which is common underground—can cause deterioration of the asphalt. With respect to the fabric reinforcing, organic felts will eventually rot with constant exposure to water, whereas glass-reinforced fabrics will last much longer.

The normal formulations of asphalt and pitch products suggest that considerable caution should be exercised in using these materials underground. Improvements in oil refining processes in the last twenty years have resulted in a deterioration of some of the asphalt properties that are most important for waterproofing use; hence, asphalt simply is not as high quality a product now as it once was. Good-quality pitch, which is derived from coal tars, is generally a superior, longer-lasting product than manufactured asphalt. Health regulations now require that many of the most

volatile substances in pitch be removed to protect the applicators, however. Removal of these substances has reduced the quality and effectiveness of the pitch by making it brittle at underground temperatures.

ability to withstand movement and cracking

Built-up membranes have mechanical strength that simple asphalt or pitch coatings do not have. Nevertheless, because membranes are relatively brittle and inflexible at the cooler below-grade temperatures, they cannot absorb movement or bridge cracks in the concrete structure.

ability to minimize leaks and facilitate repair

Built-up roofs used on the roofs of above-grade structures are noted for some ability to reseal punctures, primarily because they become soft and flexible when heated by the sun. In the cooler below-grade environment, however, they remain too brittle and inflexible to have very good resealing ability. If a leak does occur, the built-up membrane does not always adhere to the structural surface as well as other waterproofing products that are chemically bonded. Thus, water that penetrates the membrane may be able to travel behind it to some degree, making leaks difficult to locate. Any repairs to the membrane must be made from the outside.

appropriate use

Built-up membranes can be applied to all types of surfaces, including wood, masonry, and precast or poured concrete. Because poured concrete is likely to have fewer cracks than other types of surfaces, it is the best surface for application of built-up membranes, which are unable to absorb movement and bridge cracks. Horizontal surfaces that have a slight slope for drainage are the most typical and best applications for built-up membranes. Although they can be applied to vertical surfaces, such

application is more difficult (particularly when the membranes are applied hot) and requires a very smooth surface. Because these membranes are not continuous flat sheets or roll goods, but rather are built up from smaller pieces in layers, they are better suited to more complex forms than are other sheet goods. The waterproofing can be formed on complicated shapes, curving surfaces, and flashings around penetrations as an integral part of the built-up membrane.

application considerations

Although the basic work of mopping on the hot asphalt can be done by relatively unskilled labor, knowledge, experienced supervision, and proper equipment are necessary to ensure that an adequate job is done. The conditions required for successful application are not as stringent as for many other products. The surface must be relatively clean, dry, and smooth, but some leeway for irregularities exists. The membranes can be applied in a wider range of temperature and humidity conditions as well. Because the membrane may be relatively soft after application, it should be carefully protected from punctures or damage during the backfilling process.

relative costs

Material and labor costs for built-up membranes are moderate compared to costs for other waterproofing products. One advantage of these materials is that, because they are quite familiar and there are numerous applicators, more competitive bidding may be possible.

Cementitious Materials

The various cementitious waterproofing materials, which are sprayed, brushed, or troweled onto concrete surfaces, consist of portland cement and certain organic or inorganic additives. When this mixture is placed on a concrete surface, it comes in contact with moisture and unhydrated cement, causing the formation of crystals in the voids of the concrete. The size of the crystals is such that water molecules cannot pass through, while air and water vapor can. Thus, the concrete can cure properly while maintaining a waterproof surface.

durability and stability

Most cementitious materials are stable underground and compatible with most soil chemicals and conditions. These alkaline materials (pH of approximately 9.0 to 9.5) will resist pH levels between 3.5 and 11—a range that includes most soil conditions. Products that use sodium-based additives to react with the cement in the concrete may be less desirable because sodium is water soluble and could leach out of the concrete over time. In general, however, cementitious products themselves have a long life span.

ability to withstand movement and cracking

The major disadvantage of cementitious waterproofing materials is that they have very little ability to bridge any cracks in the concrete caused by settling, thermal expansion, or other movements. Although very small hairline cracks can be bridged, any larger cracks—which are common in most concrete structures—represent a break in the waterproofing system. Buildings that incorporate precast elements, cold joints, or masonry walls are generally more likely to crack than are monolithically poured concrete structures. Post-tensioned structures in particular resist cracking because the concrete is held in constant compression. Thus, a post-tensioned structure represents the best possibility for successful waterproofing with a cementitious product.

ability to minimize leaks and facilitate repair

As stated above, any leaks that occur with cementitious waterproofings are likely to result from cracks in the concrete structure. Since the waterproofing is integrated within the concrete, water cannot travel behind the waterproof layer as it can when an attached membrane material is used. It can, however, travel within and along any cracks, thereby increasing the difficulty of finding the major source of the leak. Although cementitious materials have no resealing capabilities, they have one advantage if a leaky structure requires repair: these materials can be applied from the inside of a structure, even against hydrostatic pressure. Presumably, application could be done after major cracks were carefully resealed from the inside, although this can merely cause the entry point of water to shift to a new location by migration of water along unsealed portions of the crack.

appropriate use

Cementitious products are limited to use on concrete and masonry surfaces. Basically, a product that can be sprayed or troweled on and actually penetrates into the concrete appears to have certain advantages. It can be applied to complex geometries and curving forms, for example. Also, it can be applied to vertical or horizontal surfaces. Unfortunately, this apparently wide range of applications must be carefully limited to situations in which cracks are unlikely to appear or to result in leaks.

application considerations

Unlike most waterproofing systems, cementitious materials can be applied by relatively unskilled or moderately skilled labor. Another advantage is that they cannot be easily damaged during the backfilling process. The major concerns with regard to successful application of cementitious materials are the condition of the concrete surface, the moisture content of the concrete, and the temperature. Although the concrete surface should not have any major defects (honeycombing, rock pockets, or faulty construction joints), small irregularities are acceptable. In fact, a surface that is extremely smooth may be undesirable because the waterproofing material must be able to penetrate into the open capillary system of the concrete. Surfaces must also be clean and free from concrete form oil, curing compounds that seal the concrete pores, or other foreign matter that could inhibit penetration. Light sandblasting or water blasting may be necessary. Modified cementitious materials that can be applied on concrete block walls are available. Additional surface preparation is usually required for block walls in order to cover cracks and render the surface smooth.

Because moisture is required to form the crystals, newly poured concrete that is damp throughout is the ideal application condition. Under other conditions some prewatering may be required. It is important that the surface be moist, but if it is wet, it will dilute the penetrating material. Cementitious materials should not be applied at temperatures below 40°F. Proper curing depends on the temperature and the reaction of the materials with water. Most cementitious waterproofing materials require air for curing and must be sprayed regularly over a period of two to three days with a misty spray. Therefore, the materials should not be covered immediately by polyethylene. During curing, however, they must be protected from excessive wind, sun, rain, and frost.

relative costs

Because a number of cementitious materials are available, costs can vary widely. In general, however, material costs can be considered moderate and labor costs low to moderate in comparison with other waterproofing systems.

Liquid-Applied Waterproofing Systems

This group of products includes a variety of urethanes, elastomers, rubbers, and other synthetic compounds that are applied in a liquid form. They typically cure in forty-eight to seventy-two hours to form a single, seamless, membranelike coating that is bonded to the surface of the structure. In general, they can be applied in thicknesses of 15 to 100 mils. (1 mil. = 1/1000 inch); 60 mils. is generally the minimum thickness desirable for underground application. These products are applied in one or more coats by spray, trowel, roller, or brush. The liquid-applied systems included in this category are:

- urethane
- polyisobutylene (butyl)
- polychloroprene (neoprene)
- chloronated polyethylene (Hypalon)
- polyvinyl chloride
- polysulfide
- silicone
- acrylic latex

Because of the large number of products and the almost infinite variations possible with some of them, it is somewhat difficult to generalize about their characteristics. This discussion will emphasize the polyurethanes because they are the most common and most likely to be used underground. The basic properties of the rubbers—butyl, neoprene and Hypalon—are discussed in greater detail in the section below on vulcanized sheets, which is their more common application. Although the specific chemical properties of these liquid-applied materials can vary considerably, they can be evaluated as a group because most of the general characteristics—the ability to withstand movement, and design and application considerations—are quite similar.

stability and durability

The properties that affect the stability and durability of products within this classification of waterproofing systems can vary widely; hence, these characteristics must be carefully examined. Some products can be prepared to suit a particular application, so that they are especially resistant to certain chemicals, to sunlight, or to abrasion, for example. With respect to underground applications, only the polyurethanes have a reasonable history of use. Although a discussion of the chemical makeup of these products is beyond the scope of this evaluation, some basic points can be made. One-component polyurethane systems are relatively inexpensive and easy to apply but can become brittle and lose adhesion. They are not recommended for use underground in important applications. Two-component systems, although more costly, perform much better. Products based on esters and ethers are also not recommended for underground waterproofing because they were developed to resist abrasion above grade but will become brittle over time.

One characteristic of liquid-applied membranes that would appear to be an advantage over factory-produced membrane sheets is that they are seamless (seams are usually the weak point of loose-laid membranes and roll goods). Attaining the same levels of stability and durability characteristic of factory-produced materials in a liquid that is cured in the field may, however, be a significant problem. The rather exacting conditions required to produce a plastic or synthetic rubber are difficult to duplicate in the field, given the variations in surface conditions, temperature, humidity, and manner of application. Although these requirements are discussed in detail under *application considerations*, a few key examples are given below in order to illustrate some potential problems with stability and durability in liquid-applied waterproofing.

One concern with the liquid systems is that the use of spray-on applications can seriously weaken the membrane by entrapping air

bubbles. Thicker products that can be troweled on are generally more desirable. Some liquids are intended to be applied in a "self-leveling" form. Since it is nearly impossible to build a completely flat, smooth surface, the self-leveled membrane will be thicker in some areas than others. Sections of the membrane that are too thick can blister, adhere poorly, and cure improperly. A final example of application problems affecting product performance is the need for proper curing time. Although polyurethanes should react and cure slowly, when the time required for curing is incompatible with construction schedules, additives are sometimes included to speed up the curing process. The drawback to this technique is that the decrease in curing time results in a product that may be more brittle.

As noted above, most of the remarks in this section apply specifically to polyurethanes, although many of the general problems are common to all liquid systems. The more specific properties of the synthetic rubbers are discussed in the section below on vulcanized sheets. Acrylic latex-based products are not recommended below grade because the groundwater can cause the latex to re-emulsify and migrate from the wall. Polysulfides are composed of synthetic rubber that is quite impermeable to water and resistant to chemical attack. They are quite costly and excessively soft; they are not currently manufactured in the United States. Liquid-applied waterproofing systems based on silicone are relatively new and have little history of application. Because of their poor adhesion to concrete and other properties, silicones seem better suited to above-grade, rather than below-grade, applications.

ability to withstand movement and cracking

Liquid-applied waterproofing systems are fully bonded to the structure; therefore, any strain caused by movement and cracking must be taken up by the material lying immediately over the crack. Although these materials have some of the properties exhibited by factory-made membranes—toughness, tensile and shear strength—the capacity of relatively thin, fully bonded materials to bridge cracks is quite limited. Thus, these products are not recommended for precast concrete roofs, which have great potential for movement and cracking, but rather may be more suited to reinforced and post-tensioned poured slabs, in which cracks are minimized.

ability to minimize leaks and facilitate repair

Like most membrane and sheet materials, liquid-applied systems have no ability to reseal punctures or tears. They do have two advantages over sheet goods in minimizing leaks, in that they are seamless and are fully bonded to the structure. Provided that the material has good adhesion, leaks cannot travel under the membrane, making it far easier to locate the source and facilitate repair. But if improper application has resulted in both a leak and loss of adhesion in the membrane, the leak problem can be compounded. After the leak is located, it cannot be easily repaired from the inside with a similar material, because the liquids must be exposed to the air for curing. Punctures and tears can be patched from the outside, however.

appropriate use

Liquid-applied systems will bond to a wide range of structural and insulation materials if the product is correctly formulated to do so. The limitations on the appropriate type of surface are based not on the ability of the products to bond, but rather on their inability to bridge large cracks that may occur during the life of the structure. Therefore, direct application is not advisable on precast roof decks, masonry surfaces, wood decks, or other surfaces that have great potential for movement and cracking. These products are best applied to reinforced and post-tensioned poured concrete slabs, in which cracks are minimized. In

general, the liquid-applied systems are best suited to horizontal surfaces that have a slight slope, although the self-leveling products require a completely flat surface. Some liquid products are formulated to be applied to vertical surfaces, usually in several coats.

Compared to flat sheet membranes and roll goods, materials with good adhesion that can be troweled or sprayed on are more suitable for designs that incorporate complex geometries and curving surfaces. Some question remains, however, as to whether or not the controlled, uniform thickness required for proper curing and the performance of some liquid products can be easily achieved on a complicated shape.

application considerations

Although the actual brushing or troweling on of these liquid-applied materials does not require highly skilled labor, it is very important to use experienced applicators in order to ensure proper surface preparation, control of the application, and adequate curing time. Some products require a primer or masonry condition, which can raise labor and material costs. If the materials are not applied in an even thickness, problems can result. Bubbles can form as gases are released during curing, and adhesion can be lost in areas where the membrane is too thick. Improper application can result in irregularities in the coating, especially in corners and around vent pipes. For best results, two coats are often desirable, whereas on vertical surfaces several coats may be required, along with embedment of the fibers into the first coat. One important consideration is that because many of these products release toxic fumes during application and curing, respirators—and in confined areas, good ventilation—are required.

The most critical aspects related to the application of these materials are the preparation of the surface, the air temperature, and the humidity conditions. More than any other type of waterproofing product, the liquid-applied systems require a very clean, smooth, dry surface. All oils must be removed, voids

filled, and any imperfections in the surface smoothed. The concrete structure should be allowed to cure the full twenty-eight days before the waterproofing is applied, to ensure that most of the moisture is gone from the surface. Some manufacturers do not recommend that their products be applied in situations where moisture must evaporate from the concrete surface underneath, because it will cause the waterproofing to blister and lose adhesion. These situations include lightweight concrete decks, which release large quantities of moisture, and concrete over steel decking, where the moisture cannot escape downward from the slab.

Under the best temperature and humidity conditions, curing of a typical membrane may take forty-eight to seventy-two hours, depending on the specific product. Curing of waterproofing that is applied in temperatures below 40°F would take several weeks, whereas application in above 80°F may result in too rapid curing, which can cause brittleness in the membrane. Similarly, if the relative humidity is below 30 percent, the membrane would cure too slowly; above 85 percent humidity, it cures too fast.

After application, the material should be inspected to make sure no voids or bubbles are left in the membrane. Insulation should not be placed over the waterproofing too quickly since some volatile substances given off during curing can attack polystyrene insulation. Like most waterproofing products, the fully cured liquid-applied material should be protected from damage during backfilling.

relative costs

Labor costs are moderate for the application of this group of products. Material costs can vary considerably because of the many types of liquid-applied systems. Generally, material costs range from moderate to high for the best-quality products in comparison to costs of other waterproofing systems.

Modified Bitumens

These materials, often referred to as rubberized asphalt, consist of asphalt combined with a small amount of synthetic rubber, applied to a polyethylene sheet. In some cases, a second polyethylene sheet is placed between two layers of the rubberized asphalt. The material comes in rolls ranging from 3 to 4 feet wide. The strips of rubberized asphalt adhere to the structural surface and are overlapped to adhere to each other.

durability and stability

Since modified bitumens come in factory-produced rolls, they have uniform thickness and quality, although the quality of the asphalt itself can vary. The rubberized asphalt has good resistance to most chemicals found in the soil. Polyethylene also has good stability in underground conditions, where it is not exposed to the ultraviolet rays of the sun. Generally, these materials will not rot or mildew.

Deterioration of asphalt in contact with groundwater is reduced considerably with this system because the polyethylene prevents moisture from coming in contact with the asphalt. In addition, the polyethylene acts as a good vapor barrier. The addition of rubber to the asphalt gives the product tensile strength and stability. The rubber makes the asphalt softer and may reduce its tendency to deteriorate with time. The rubberized asphalt products can last a relatively long time if they are carefully installed in an appropriate situation.

ability to withstand movement and cracks

The tensile strength of the polyethylene and the rubber in modified bitumen materials make them effective in bridging over cracks up to ¼-inch wide. The softness and flexibility of the rubberized asphalt allow for some movement to occur without stressing the product to the point of failure. The ability of the material to bridge cracks without leaking depends on very good adhesion at the seams, as movement usually creates extra stress in these areas. It is probably best not to place seams directly over points where cracking is likely to occur, such as at cold joints or other structural connections.

ability to minimize leaks and facilitate repair

Modified bitumens are intended to be used with a primer that helps bond the product to the structure. Along the overlapping seams, the rubberized asphalt bonds quite well to the polyethylene. Ideally, the material will be completely bonded to the structure, thus preventing any water that penetrates the membrane from migrating. This means that the source of a leak will be easier to find, because the water is prevented from traveling behind the membrane. Completely bonding the material to the structure may be almost impossible under most field conditions, however. Because loss of adhesion can occur for a variety of reasons, modified bitumen products must be very carefully applied (see *application considerations*, below).

appropriate use

Modified bitumen products are versatile in that they can be used on concrete, masonry, or wood surfaces. They are well suited to applications on vertical surfaces where there is no continuous head of water; however, they must be used with more discretion on horizontal surfaces. Because these products have numerous overlapping seams, it is not advisable to use them on flat horizontal surfaces where they could be exposed to ponding. If a modified bitumen product is to be used on a horizontal surface, the surface should be sloped slightly to provide drainage and the seams must be overlapped in a manner similar to shingles on a conventional roof.

application considerations

Successful application of modified bitumens depends on great care in the preparation of the surface and application only under the proper temperature and humidity conditions. Experienced, skilled labor is usually required for successful application. A smooth, clean, dry surface is necessary for good adhesion of the product to the surface. Mechanical grinding may be required on concrete surfaces, but slight irregularities are acceptable. The waterproofing material should be applied only when the surface temperature is above 40°F, because colder temperatures reduce the quality of both the bonding and the seams. Space heaters should never be used to warm the surface or the rubberized asphalt because they add moisture, which can cause condensation that may loosen the bond.

Modified bitumens are incompatible with pitch and certain solvents and sealants. Because membranes are combustible, they should not be exposed to flames, sparks, or temperatures over 100°F. Modified bitumens, like most elastomeric materials, have a high degree of memory, a tendency to return to the original sheet or roll configuration. Therefore, if any wrinkles or voids are created during application and then rolled out, the material will tend to return to the wrinkled state.

During the backfilling process, the waterproofing products should be protected from damage. Insulation can serve this purpose; on uninsulated roofs a layer of sand can be used, whereas some form of protection board is necessary on uninsulated walls. The backfilling operation should occur relatively soon after the waterproofing is installed so that the polyethylene is not exposed to ultraviolet degradation from the sun.

relative costs

Compared to costs of other waterproofing products, the cost of modified bitumen products can be considered moderate or average.

Vulcanized and Plastic Sheets

This classification of waterproofing materials includes various natural and synthetic rubber compounds and plastic that are formed into sheet membranes by vulcanization or other processes. The generic names and chemical compositions of the six major types of sheet membranes are:

- isobutylene isoprene (butyl)
- ethylene propylene diene monomer (EPDM)
- polychloroprene (neoprene)
- chlorosulfonated polyethylene (Hypalon)
- chloronated polyethylene (CPE)
- polyvinyl chloride (PVC)

Most of these materials are available in roll stock or sheets in sizes up to 50 feet wide and 200 feet long, depending on the product. Flexible sheets of PVC are available in sizes up to 80 feet wide and 700 feet long. Thickness ranges from $\frac{1}{32}$ to $\frac{1}{8}$ inches in the vulcanized products and typically between 10 and 45 mils. for CPE and PVC. They can be seamed at the site, using special cements or solvents, or in the factory to form a single membrane that will cover the entire structure. The membranes can be loose laid or partially or fully bonded to the structure. Some are used for above-grade conventional applications as well as below grade. Some of the products, EPDM and neoprene in particular, are used as flashing materials and are available on rolls as narrow as 12 inches for this purpose. Most of the generic types of sheets are also available in a liquid form that has the same basic chemical composition. Although most of the characteristics of stability and durability are similar for these liquids, the other criteria—such as the ability to withstand movement or facilitate repair and the application considerations—are quite different. For this reason the liquid forms of these products are discussed in the section on liquid-applied systems.

stability and durability

With the possible exception of PVC sheets, the stability of this group is quite good. In addition, the products in this group have among the longest life spans of all the waterproofing products. The high quality control in the manufacture of the sheets results in very consistent products. Generally, these membranes are moderately tough, puncture resistant, and resistant to most chemicals. Soft and flexible, most of these products can be elastic in temperatures ranging from 40°F to 200°F. The vulcanization process helps prevent the stress cracking that can occur when sheet membranes are used on sudden, sharp bends.

Although the membranes themselves have excellent characteristics for underground applications, the presence of seams is always a concern. The vulcanization process gives butyl, EPDM, and neoprene great strength and resistance to permanent deformation under long-term loading. Unfortunately, seams that are made in the field with cold-applied solvents or cements do not have these same inherent characteristics. They can be sufficient, however, if they are not located in areas with great potential for movement or stress from other forces. For best results the number of seams should be minimized and application should be done with extreme care by professionals. The sheets can be seamed in the factory into one custom-fit membrane. Although this process guarantees a good bond, the resulting rather large, heavy membrane may be difficult to work with.

Because the six major types of membranes, although similar in many of their general characteristics, also differ in some ways, the key characteristics of each type are briefly discussed below.

Butyl membranes are lightly vulcanized, resulting in high strength, flexibility, and softness. They can be reinforced with nylon and have a high resistance to heat and ozone. Although they are resistant to bacteria, fungi, and most soil chemicals, they should not be exposed to acids, oils, or solvents. The very low permeability of butyl rubber to gas makes it a good vapor barrier.

EPDM is a synthetic rubber that is quite similar to butyl in most respects. It is even more resistant to weathering, chemicals, and the ultraviolet rays of the sun. Like butyl rubber, it can be reinforced with nylon. The sulfur included in its composition provides EPDM with high strength.

Neoprene is a synthetic rubber that has good resistance to chemicals, oils, solvents, high temperatures, and abrasion. It is more sensitive to degradation caused by exposure to the sun than are the other vulcanized membranes, and it can be permeated by water vapor to a greater degree. Generally, neoprene membranes are not used in underground applications as often as are butyl membranes or EPDM. Neoprene is commonly used for flashings because it can be formed into complex shapes in the field when heat is applied to it. Rolls of neoprene flashing material are available in cured or uncured form.

Hypalon is distinguished from the other sheet membranes in a number of ways. Its chemical composition gives it some unique characteristics. Because Hypalon is highly resistant to the ultraviolet rays of the sun, ozone, and high temperatures, it is suitable for exposure above grade. Unlike the other membranes, it can be manufactured in a variety of colors. Perhaps the most important characteristic of Hypalon is its relatively high rate of water absorption—an undesirable condition if it is constantly exposed to water. Thus, it is generally not recommended for use underground.

CPE, which is also quite durable and stable underground, is available as a 20-mil. sheet laminated to a polyester backing that can be fully bonded to the structure. Seams can be made on site by welding the sheets with solvents, cements, or adhesives, and in the factory by means of an electrothermal process.

If properly done, the seams can have the same characteristics as the sheet itself. This is one of the assets of CPE that distinguishes it from some of the other sheet membranes.

PVC is a well-known plastic. As a raw material, it is hard and brittle. As a flexible sheet material, it is strong, resists tears and punctures, and has resistance to ultraviolet degradation and soil chemicals. A drawback of PVC sheets, however, is that shrinkage can occur. They also can become brittle as plasticizers leach out of the material over time. Some products have additives that slow this process.

ability to withstand movement and cracking

Basically, vulcanized and plastic sheet membranes have excellent properties for bridging any cracks that occur in the structure. They are flexible under a wide range of conditions and have great tensile and sheet strength. Their ability to bridge cracks is affected by the manner in which the membrane is bonded to the structure. Total bonding of the membrane reduces the flexibility of the material over cracks and concentrates the stresses in the small portion of membrane lying directly over the crack. A loosely laid or partially bonded membrane allows for this stress to be dissipated over a greater area, thus reducing the strain on the material. At points where movement is expected, such as at an expansion joint or near seams, it is desirable to leave some extra material to take up any stress that occurs.

ability to minimize leaks and facilitate repair

A vulcanized or plastic membrane has no ability to reseal itself once punctured. Membranes can be repaired with patches from the outside of the structure that are bonded in the same manner as seams, with cold-applied cements. The major drawback of sheet membranes when loose laid is the inability to locate leaks,

because water can travel behind the membrane and enter the structure at a point remote from the original source. This is one of the main reasons why membranes are bonded to the structure. Assuming that an excellent job is done, completely gluing down the sheet can prevent water from traveling behind the membrane; however, this technique is costly and reduces the ability of the membrane to bridge cracks. A compromise solution that is often used is a partial bonding of the membrane in a regular grid pattern so that any leaks will be localized in one section of the grid.

appropriate use

Sheet membranes can be applied over both precast and poured concrete surfaces, as well as on masonry and wood. These large, heavy membranes are best suited to horizontal surfaces, which can be completely flat. No slope is required because the membranes can hold standing water indefinitely. Although the material can easily resist water on vertical surfaces as well, application is quite difficult because of the tendency of the heavy sheets to stretch from their own weight, especially in the heat.

Application of a large, flat membrane over complex shapes is not easy. Flat surfaces and simple shapes are the best applications for sheet membranes. Minimizing projections and penetrations through the membrane simplifies the application by reducing the number of seams, flashings, and other field-bonded details, which are always the potential weak points of the system. Of course, if projections and penetrations are required, they can be waterproofed by using flashing materials and specially formed boots, corners, and other accessories.

application considerations

The application of vulcanized or plastic sheet membranes, particularly the seaming and bonding, is quite exacting work and requires experienced, skilled professionals. If the

membrane is factory seamed, installation requires experience because the material is so heavy and difficult to adjust. Clean, dry, smooth surfaces that are free of oil and grease are required if the membrane is to be bonded. Because the membranes are tough, the surface can be somewhat irregular without causing damage, although sharp edges and foreign objects should be removed. The membrane materials remain flexible over a wide range of temperatures, but applying vulcanized membranes in extremely cold or hot temperatures is inadvisable. Heat can cause the membrane to expand considerably; when placed in the cooler underground environment, it will contract, causing stresses in the membrane and at the seams.

Before bonding or seaming takes place, vulcanized membrane sheets should be laid out and allowed to relax and return to their original size. If they are stretched during application, greater stresses will result. One advantage of the solvents and cements used with these products is that they are cold-applied—no hot mastic is required. The adhesives can be moderately toxic. After installation but before backfilling, the system should be water-tested for leaks. Field inspection and water-testing are advised to ensure watertight seams; however, pinhole punctures can sometimes occur in the manufacturing process. Although the materials are relatively tough, insulation or other protective materials should be used to protect them from punctures by sharp objects during backfilling.

relative costs

The cost of vulcanized and plastic membranes is higher than that of any other category of waterproofing materials. This high cost is largely attributable to the cost of a very high quality, durable material, although skilled labor is also required. The cost can be affected by the complexity of the job and by the number of seams and flashings required. The cost of labor for a membrane that is fully bonded to the structure is significantly higher than for a loose-laid application.

Bentonite Clay Products

Bentonite (montmorillonite) clay is used in several forms to provide waterproofing on underground structures. This highly plastic clay, which is mined in the western United States, has the unique property of swelling from ten to twenty times its original size when saturated with water. As it dries, it returns to its original volume. This process of expanding and contracting can continue indefinitely without wearing out the material. The bentonite material is applied in a thin layer confined between the structure and the soil. As the clay material comes in contact with water, expansion of the material is restrained, resulting in a gel- or paste-like barrier characterized by a high density and impermeability.

The many types and grades of bentonite clays have different characteristics. The major types of these products use specific clays and are available in the following forms:

- raw bentonite
- bentonite mixed with asphalt
- bentonite contained in cardboard panels
- bentonite mixed with binding agent in a trowel- and spray-grade product
- bentonite mixed with polymers in a spray-grade product
- bentonite mixed with polymers for caulking joints

The materials most commonly used on underground buildings are the spray-on and trowel-on mixtures and the cardboard panels.

durability and stability

The fact that bentonite is inorganic and will not deteriorate means that bentonite-based products in general are characterized by long-term stability and flexibility. They should not be used in highly salinated soils, however, because salt diminishes the swelling action of the bentonite clay. Another concern is that, if bentonite is allowed to dry out completely and then is saturated with water, there will be a slight delay before the clay is activated and expands to seal all leaks. Thus, it may not be advisable to use bentonite in a hot, arid climate subject to sudden downpours. Although bentonite products function effectively when exposed to a continuous head of water, they should not be exposed to running water that could cause the clay to wash off the surface.

Raw bentonite in its dry, granular form is often used for well casings and sealing the bottoms of reservoirs. Although it can be used to waterproof buildings, this use is generally not recommended because the bentonite does not adhere as well with other applications, its application is difficult to control, and it will not work on vertical surfaces. It is a mistake to mix raw bentonite with water so that it can be applied in a pastelike form. After expanding during application, it will dry out later, shrink to its original size and, thus, allow water to leak through because the amount of material is inadequate. Bentonite mixed with asphalt is also unsatisfactory and is not recommended. Although this product has been successfully applied, the asphalt tends to coat the clay particles, thus reducing their activity.

Application of bentonite contained in the voids of cardboard panels results in a very consistent thickness of the raw material. The panels must be very carefully handled during transport and application in order to prevent damage. The biodegradable cardboard is intended to deteriorate as a result of the bacteria in the soil. Problems can occur if the backfill soil does not contain sufficient organic matter to cause this deterioraton. For example, water may penetrate past the bentonite and run behind the cardboard and along the seams between the panels.

The effectiveness of the trowel-on and spray-on mixtures of bentonite is dependent on good quality control in product formulation and application. Trowel-on applications do not require the high skill level and exacting tolerances needed for applying other waterproofing products. Two types of spray-on products are currently available. The first, which is similar to the trowel-on product, is applied in a pastelike form and must be covered with polyethylene to help cure and protect it. It is partially activated and remains in a gel-like state that can be maintained at 50 percent relative humidity. A serious disadvantage of certain gel formulations is their tendency to separate upon moisture activation causing a leakage of the binder through cracks in the structure and possible further moisture leakage. The second type of spray bentonite is a relatively new product that dries immediately on application. A polyethylene cover sheet is recommended on the second type of spray to contain the bentonite, even though it is not needed for curing.

ability to withstand movement and cracks

Bentonite clay products have excellent ability to respond to movement and cracks in the structure that occur after installation. Because it can expand to many times its original volume, bentonite can bridge cracks up to $1/4$-inch wide and fill voids created by movement, provided that these cracks or voids do not provide a large enough path to transmit bentonite particles and wash them through the crack to an interior void. Extra protection can be applied to cold joints or other points where cracking is anticipated by means of bentonite-based caulking or tubes of bentonite that decompose in a manner similar to the cardboard panels.

ability to minimize leaks and facilitate repair

The same expansion capability that allows bentonite to bridge cracks also permits it to reseal any punctures or holes that may be present in the waterproofing. Another important advantage is that if any leaks should occur, they will enter the structure near the source of the leak, thereby making it easier to locate. This benefit results from the full adhesion possible with the trowel-on and spray-on products; the adhesion prevents water from traveling away from the source of the leak, as it can when a loose-laid membrane is used. Water can travel somewhat behind cardboard panels unless they are embedded in a gel that is applied to the surface.

If a leak does occur and is located inside of the structure, it can also be repaired from the inside by injecting bentonite through a small hole in the area of the leak. This type of repair has considerable cost advantages over having to excavate in order to locate and repair a leak from the outside. One drawback of bentonite is that, if waterproofing problems occur, options for future repair or replacement by other products may be limited because the bentonite is difficult and messy to remove.

appropriate use

Generally, bentonite products, particularly in the spray-on and trowel-on forms, are quite versatile in comparison with most other waterproofing systems. They can be applied to virtually all types of surfaces, including poured or precast concrete, masonry, and wood (provided that it is pressure-treated). Both vertical and horizontal surfaces can be waterproofed with these products; there are no special requirements for a sloping surface or fast-draining soil. In fact, these bentonite clay products can perform effectively against a constant head of water. Trowel-on and spray-on systems are well suited to complex geometries. Bentonite can be applied to curving forms, complex penetrations, and on very rough, irregular surfaces such as stone, blocks, or corrugated metal. An important design detail is that because bentonite cannot be exposed above the grade line, it must be covered or protected by a flashing that extends over the material.

The cardboard panels containing bentonite have more limitations than do the spray-on and trowel-on products. They are not recommended for use on block walls unless they are first covered with a cement plaster coat. Generally, there is more concern over their effectiveness on horizontal (as opposed to vertical) surfaces.

Problems with the cardboard not deteriorating as expected seem to occur more often on horizontal surfaces. If the panels are used on horizontal surfaces, a slope is desirable. Finally, the large, flat panels are not well suited for situations involving complex geometries, curving forms, irregular surfaces, or numerous penetrations.

application considerations

Application of each type of bentonite product requires a different level of skill and experience. The trowel-on product can be applied by relatively unskilled labor and is one of the only waterproofing products that could possibly be applied adequately by an amateur. The cardboard panels require a moderate level of skill and experience in order to avoid pitfalls. The spray-on application requires an experienced applicator who has invested in the proper equipment for this application. Because bentonite is a relatively new product, the number of qualified applicators is limited.

Very little surface preparation is required for the spray-on and trowel-on products. Rough, irregular, surfaces such as those of spalled or honeycombed concrete are acceptable. The cardboard panels require a smoother surface unless they are applied with a gel. One of the major advantages of bentonite products is that they can be applied in virtually any temperature and humidity. In addition, they are nontoxic.

A critical element in the successful application of the trowel-on and spray-on products is that an even thickness of material must be achieved. For the spray-on product, a $\frac{3}{16}$- to $\frac{3}{8}$-inch thickness is acceptable depending on which system is used; the trowel-on product requires a thickness of $\frac{3}{16}$ inch, with greater thicknesses at corners and construction joints. The application of these products can be interrupted without leaving any seams or joints that could weaken the material. Because bentonite should not be sprayed over 8 feet high without using scaffolding, it may be necessary to backfill before spraying higher; thus, application of spray-on waterproofing

products may require more than one stage. In the second stage of the application process, it is important not to leave spillage of bentonite on top of the first layer of backfill, so that it cannot interfere with the free-draining of the soil.

Polyethylene and insulation are usually placed over spray-on or trowel-on bentonite. Because the bentonite will reseal around any punctures, nails can be used to hold insulation in place. One of the most important application concerns is to prevent the bentonite from getting wet before backfill takes place. Thus, backfilling must be scheduled as soon as possible after the material has been applied and has had time to cure. Curing time for both the trowel-on product and the most common type of spray-on product ranges from four to thirty hours, depending on temperature and humidity conditions. The polyethylene keeps the material from completely drying out during the curing process. The material is too soft to walk on without damaging it before it is cured; however, a newer type of spray-on product dries immediately and can be walked on and backfilled immediately. Backfilling can also be done immediately when cardboard panels filled with bentonite are used.

During the backfilling process, it is important to protect the bentonite from damage. One concern with bentonite applications is that settling of the earth can drag the insulation down the wall and scrape the waterproofing layer off. Because nails can exacerbate this problem, they are not recommended unless absolutely necessary. Although the polyethylene helps reduce friction, it is most important that the backfill be compacted to minimize settling.

relative costs

The cost of the bentonite products is low to moderate in comparison with the other general types of waterproofing systems. One of the key factors influencing costs with the spray-on product is simply the availability of a qualified applicator.

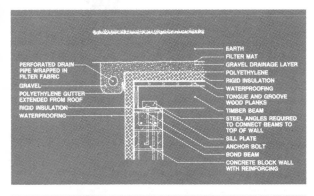

EARTH
FILTER MAT
GRAVEL DRAINAGE LAYER
POLYETHYLENE
RIGID INSULATION
WATERPROOFING
TONGUE AND GROOVE WOOD PLANKS
TIMBER BEAM
STEEL ANGLES REQUIRED TO CONNECT BEAMS TO TOP OF WALL
SILL PLATE
ANCHOR BOLT
BOND BEAM
CONCRETE BLOCK WALL WITH REINFORCING

PERFORATED DRAIN PIPE WRAPPED IN FILTER FABRIC
GRAVEL
POLYETHYLENE GUTTER EXTENDED FROM ROOF
RIGID INSULATION
WATERPROOFING

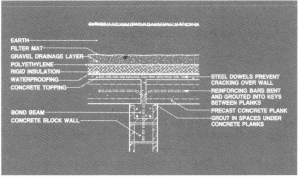

EARTH
FILTER MAT
GRAVEL DRAINAGE LAYER
POLYETHYLENE
RIGID INSULATION
WATERPROOFING
CONCRETE TOPPING

BOND BEAM
CONCRETE BLOCK WALL

STEEL DOWELS PREVENT CRACKING OVER WALL
REINFORCING BARS BENT AND GROUTED INTO KEYS BETWEEN PLANKS
PRECAST CONCRETE PLANK
GROUT IN SPACES UNDER CONCRETE PLANKS

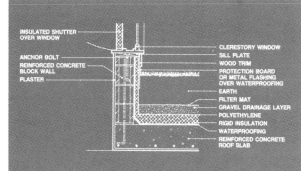

INSULATED SHUTTER OVER WINDOW

ANCHOR BOLT
REINFORCED CONCRETE BLOCK WALL
PLASTER

CLERESTORY WINDOW
SILL PLATE
WOOD TRIM
PROTECTION BOARD OR METAL FLASHING OVER WATERPROOFING
EARTH
FILTER MAT
GRAVEL DRAINAGE LAYER
POLYETHYLENE
RIGID INSULATION
WATERPROOFING
REINFORCED CONCRETE ROOF SLAB

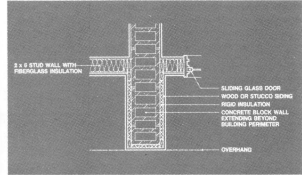

2 x 6 STUD WALL WITH FIBERGLASS INSULATION

SLIDING GLASS DOOR
WOOD OR STUCCO SIDING
RIGID INSULATION
CONCRETE BLOCK WALL EXTENDING BEYOND BUILDING PERIMETER

OVERHANG

CHAPTER 8

HEATING, COOLING, AND INSULATION

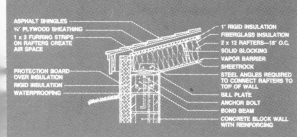

CLERESTORY WINDOW

WOOD TRIM
PROTECTION BOARD OR METAL FLASHING OVER WATERPROOFING
EARTH
FILTER MAT
GRAVEL DRAINAGE LAYER
POLYETHYLENE
RIGID INSULATION
WATERPROOFING
CANT
REINFORCED CONCRETE ROOF SLAB
FURRED-OUT SHEETROCK CEILING

¾" PRESSURE-TREATED PLYWOOD
SHEETROCK
VAPOR BARRIER
FIBERGLASS INSULATION
PRESSURE-TREATED 2 x 6 STUD WALL

ANCHOR BOLT
HORIZONTAL SLIDING RIGID INSULATION AT CEILING LEVEL

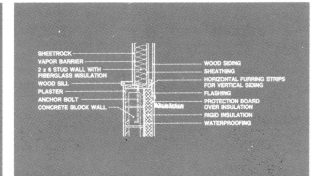

ASPHALT SHINGLES
½" PLYWOOD SHEATHING
1 x 2 FURRING STRIPS ON RAFTERS CREATE AIR SPACE

PROTECTION BOARD OVER INSULATION
RIGID INSULATION
WATERPROOFING

1" RIGID INSULATION
FIBERGLASS INSULATION
2 x 12 RAFTERS—16" O.C.
SOLID BLOCKING
VAPOR BARRIER
SHEETROCK
STEEL ANGLES REQUIRED TO CONNECT RAFTERS TO TOP OF WALL
SILL PLATE
ANCHOR BOLT
BOND BEAM
CONCRETE BLOCK WALL WITH REINFORCING

SHEETROCK
VAPOR BARRIER
2 x 6 STUD WALL WITH FIBERGLASS INSULATION
WOOD SILL
PLASTER
ANCHOR BOLT
CONCRETE BLOCK WALL

WOOD SIDING
SHEATHING
HORIZONTAL FURRING STRIPS FOR VERTICAL SIDING
FLASHING
PROTECTION BOARD OVER INSULATION
RIGID INSULATION
WATERPROOFING

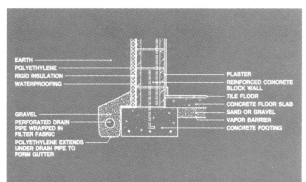

EARTH
POLYETHYLENE
RIGID INSULATION
WATERPROOFING

GRAVEL
PERFORATED DRAIN PIPE WRAPPED IN FILTER FABRIC
POLYETHYLENE EXTENDS UNDER DRAIN PIPE TO FORM GUTTER

PLASTER
REINFORCED CONCRETE BLOCK WALL
TILE FLOOR
CONCRETE FLOOR SLAB
SAND OR GRAVEL
VAPOR BARRIER
CONCRETE FOOTING

Introduction

In some cases energy conservation in heating and cooling is one of the major reasons for building an earth sheltered house. In other cases an earth sheltered house may be built for a combination of aesthetic, environmental, security, and other personal or site-related reasons. Whatever the situation, it is desirable to design the house in response to the climate so that any energy-related benefits of building into the earth can be maximized and any drawbacks can be minimized. Accomplishing these aims requires an understanding of both general concepts of heat transfer and specific details concerning insulation and the design of heating and cooling systems.

The first two sections of this chapter present the background material required for understanding the energy use of earth sheltered buildings in relation to conventional buildings. Included in the first section is a discussion of heating and cooling loads and general strategies used in energy conservation. The potential benefits and limitations of earth sheltered structures with respect to heating and cooling are discussed in the second section. In the final three sections of the chapter, more specific and detailed information about below-grade heat transfer and insulation principles, insulation materials, and mechanical systems is presented.

Although it would be ideal to give detailed recommendations for insulation placement and thicknesses in a variety of climates, it is simply not possible to do so at this time. The below-grade environment is more complex than above-grade conditions, and research in this area is still at an early stage. The current state of the art of heat transfer analysis for buildings in contact with the earth has not yet yielded specific design guidelines; however, much is known in terms of general principles. The purpose of this chapter is to present reliable general information so that differences between earth sheltered and conventional buildings are understood. In addition, rules of thumb and specific information on insulation placement and thicknesses are given whenever possible and appropriate.

Heating and Cooling Loads

In order to discuss the potential benefits and drawbacks associated with earth sheltered structures, it is useful to first examine the nature of heating and cooling loads and the general strategies that can be used either to reduce the loads or to reduce the requirement for conventional fuels by substituting renewable sources of energy. Because this is a vast subject area that cannot be treated in detail here, only the major concepts are presented.

Heating

Basically, human comfort in buildings is based on maintaining temperature and humidity conditions within an acceptable range (see chapter 2 for a discussion of comfort zones). To maintain comfort in a building, conventional heating is required to some extent when the outdoor temperature conditions are below the acceptable range. The amount of heat required is based on the rate at which heat is transferred from the warmer indoor space to the colder outside environment. Heat is transferred by three means: conduction, convection, and radiation. Conduction is the transfer of heat directly through a material such as the wall materials in a house. Convection is the transfer of heat resulting from the movement of fluids, e.g., the rising of warm air through a chimney. Radiation is the transfer of heat from warm bodies to cold bodies by electromagnetic waves, independent of the temperature of the medium between them—for example, the sun radiating heat to the earth or the warmth radiated from a fire.

In calculating heating requirements for houses, these rather complex phenomena are simplified. The calculations are based on the amount of heat lost in two major ways: (1) transmission through the building envelope, and (2) infiltration through cracks and openings in the envelope. Basically, heat loss resulting from transmission varies according to the size of the area being considered, the thermal resistance of the materials that make up the building envelope, and the temperature differential between the inside and outside of the building. Infiltration varies according to the tightness of the house and the wind speed and direction, which create a pressure differential, thus forcing outside air through the house.

The heat losses in a house are offset to some degree by internal sources of heat such as people, lights, and appliances, as well as by radiant heat (when available) from the sun. Any heat losses that cannot be offset by these sources must be offset by heat generated from conventional fuel sources such as oil, gas, coal, electricity, or wood. (Wood, and electricity generated by wind, solar energy, or hydropower, are considered renewable rather than exhaustible sources of energy.)

An important aspect of providing heat within a comfortable range is the effect of radiation from warmer surfaces to cooler ones. Heat that is transferred by electromagnetic radiation is a component of the conventional concept of heating by raising the air temperature within the space. A person can feel comfortable at air temperatures below the comfort zone if his or her body is absorbing radiant heat.

For example, it is far more comfortable in the sun than in the shade on a cold winter day. Exploiting this radiant effect can enhance efficient use of available heat for housing. A floor mass that absorbs solar heat during the day can radiate heat to the occupants to keep them comfortable even at temperatures below the standard range. Also, reflective surfaces are often used as components of insulation products in order to reduce radiant heat losses. Of course, the radiant effects can also be detrimental, as when the surrounding surfaces in winter are colder than the air temperature or a space is overheated by too much radiant energy.

Many design strategies are used to reduce the amount of fuel required for space heating. They fall into the five general categories discussed below.

reduction of transmission losses

Keeping the heat in by means of increasing the resistance to heat loss is probably the most basic design strategy. Techniques in this category include increasing the amount of insulation and minimizing the surface area of the house. Windows, which have the poorest resistance to heat flow of all the typical building envelope components, can be reduced in total area, double or triple glazed, and covered with insulated shades or shutters at night.

reduction of infiltration losses

Infiltration, which can account for 25 to 40 percent of all losses in older houses, can be reduced by weatherstripping and caulking to seal cracks, carefully installing complete vapor barriers, incorporating air-lock vestibules in the house plan, and using trees or other barriers to reduce exposure to the wind. If the house is sufficiently tight, outside ventilation air will be required for health reasons. Heat exchange devices (discussed in the section on mechanical systems, below) will reduce the heat loss that results from ventilation.

increased use of solar heat

Solar heat can be collected, stored, and distributed in a number of ways. An active system, which employs collector panels, a heat transfer fluid, and storage mediums, is basically an addition that is separate from the structure itself. Compared to active systems, passive solar systems are not as dependent on mechanical equipment; however, they must be more closely integrated with the design of the building itself. Approaches include the use of thermal storage walls, floors, and roofs as well as sunspaces or greenhouses in which to collect the radiation. A very common passive solar technique is the direct gain approach, in which the house itself acts as the collector. To achieve maximum benefits from this method, the skylights, clerestories, and windows must be oriented and sized properly and the storage mass—consisting of elements of the structure of the house itself—must be appropriately sized and located.

increased use of mass

Mass within a structure is useful for absorbing heat when it is available and releasing it to the space when it is needed. Mass should not be considered invariably good or necesssary, however, and its effectiveness is affected by its size and surface area in relation to the amount of heat to be absorbed and the time lag required between absorption and release of heat. Mass is particularly useful when used in conjunction with an intermittent source of heat such as the sun (or perhaps a wood-burning furnace), or in climates characterized by significant daily temperature fluctuations. Under these conditions the mass can "dampen" or delay the heating demands, resulting in lower overall energy requirements, lower peak demands, and more flexibility in the times when heat is supplied. On the other hand, because massive structures do not respond quickly, they are not as useful in situations where energy can be saved by adjusting the interior conditions quickly, for example, through the use of thermostat setbacks. Given the proper conditions, the thermal characteristics of mass can be used with a moderate amount of insulation to reduce energy consumption for heating. In other cases, however, a structure that is extremely well insulated and sealed loses heat at a very slow rate and thus may not require a great deal of mass to carry it through periods of intermittent heat input.

increased efficiency in heat generation and distribution systems

In addition to the heat lost through transmission and infiltration in a structure, there are losses that are associated with the generation or combustion process in furnaces for conventional fuels, as well as losses through the ducts or pipes that make up a conventional distribution system. Strategies to combat these losses include well-adjusted, clean, efficient furnaces, efficient duct layout, with insulation in appropriate places, and devices that recover and recirculate heat from flues or exhausts.

Cooling

Like heating needs, cooling requirements for housing are based on the difference between existing climatic conditions and the conditions of temperature and humidity considered to be within the range of human comfort. When the outside air temperature is higher than the desired indoor temperature, heat is gained based on conduction through the envelope of the structure. The amount of gain varies, depending on the resistance of the envelope materials (R-factor) and the temperature differential. Heat gain also occurs via infiltration of warmer air into the house. During the cooling season, heat gain in houses is increased by two other very significant factors: the radiant heat from the sun, especially as it passes through windows, and the internal heat generated in the house from lights, appliances, and people.

Providing comfort during the cooling season is generally regarded as more complex than providing heat because humidity plays a more significant role in cooling. Because the energy required to condense water vapor or evaporate water is very significant in the cooling cycle, cooling loads are divided into two components—the sensible heat load, which represents the energy required to reduce the air temperature, and the latent heat load, which represents the energy required to extract moisture from the air. Comfort conditions can be achieved by various combinations of temperature and humidity conditions. Generally, one can feel more comfortable at higher temperatures when the humidity is relatively low, because the body's evaporative cooling system can work efficiently. At higher levels of humidity, lower air temperatures are required in order to feel comfortable. The movement of air across the skin can help to maintain comfort, as it assists the evaporative cooling system.

A low Mean Radiant Temperature (MRT) of building surfaces surrounding a person can also make a significant contribution to personal comfort. The body loses heat to the building surfaces by radiation and if the MRT is lower than the air temperature in the room, equivalent comfort can be achieved at a higher air temperature. Earth sheltered structures tend to maintain wall temperatures below internal air temperatures. This phenomenon is a significant component of earth contact cooling.

Typically, cooling is provided by electrically powered air-conditioning units that cool the air while extracting moisture from it. A wide range of strategies, referred to as passive cooling techniques, can be applied to reduce the requirements for conventional mechanical cooling. These techniques must be applied selectively so that they both correspond to local climate conditions and are mutually reinforcing: for example, the strategies of using surfaces in contact with the earth and ventilating the house to promote comfort may conflict at times. The various cooling strategies are discussed below.

shading

Heat gain can be reduced considerably by preventing the sun's radiant heat from striking and entering the structure. Vegetation and the shading from other buildings are most effective in completely preventing sunlight from striking the house. Overhangs, trellises, walls, and other shading devices can be used to protect walls and windows. In most regions the placement of vegetation, the use of deciduous trees, and the sizing of overhangs must be based on the dual aims of preventing heat gain in summer and enhancing heat gain in winter.

increased insulation and reduction of infiltration

Heat gain through transmission and infiltration can be reduced by increasing the thermal resistance of the building envelope and sealing cracks.

reduce internal gains

Reduced lighting levels and less use of heat-generating appliances also help reduce cooling loads. Natural lighting can offset the need for artificial light to some extent.

increased use of mass

In many cases the use of mass can be very effective during the cooling season because the most intense periods of heat gain occur only during the day. A massive structure that responds slowly to temperature change can dampen high demands for cooling energy.

ventilation

Comfort can be provided by air movement across the skin. Ventilation is especially important in areas characterized by high humidity and constantly high temperatures, where some other strategies are less effective. To enhance natural ventilation (but not significantly above skin temperature), openings in the house must be properly oriented and sized. Comfort can also be enhanced by mechanical ventilation within the space.

evaporative cooling

In hot, dry climates, it is possible to provide comfort by the addition of water to the air: the water evaporates and, by removing the latent heat of evaporation from the air, lowers the air temperature. Rooftop ponds and spraying are examples of this technique.

night sky radiation

Heat transfer occurs when a warm object is exposed to the cooler clear night sky. The most notable example of this cooling technique is the use of rooftop water ponds that absorb heat from the inside of the house during the day and release it to the sky at night.

radiation to cooler surfaces

Cooling can also be provided from the body when a space is surrounded by surfaces that are cooler than the outside air temperature. This type of radiant cooling occurs when walls, floors, and roofs are in direct contact with the cooler earth temperatures.

Potential Benefits and Limitations of Earth Sheltered Buildings

Structures that are in contact with the earth have unique characteristics that result in some potential benefits—as well as some limitations—with respect to energy conservation for heating and cooling. Many—if not all—of the energy conservation strategies discussed in the previous section are intrinsic to or can be applied to earth sheltered structures. Their drawbacks must also be understood, however, if earth sheltered structures are to be built appropriately in various climate regions and designed to respond to potential benefits while minimizing the effects of these drawbacks. In this section the potential energy-related benefits and limitations of earth sheltered buildings are discussed in general terms; subsequent sections deal with some of these issues in more detail. The word "potential" must be emphasized for two reasons: some of the benefits are not yet easily quantified, and the degree to which energy is conserved can vary greatly depending on the individual design and the climate.

Potential Benefits

Most of the benefits listed below relate to the direct contact of the structure with the earth. Generally, the greater the percentage of surface area in contact with the earth and the deeper the structure penetrates into the earth, the more the structure will benefit from these effects in terms of energy conservation. In reality, a house cannot be a deep, windowless chamber: access to grade and window openings are required for a variety of

psychological, physiological, and safety reasons that are reflected in building codes. Thus, the energy-related benefits are tempered by the requirement for openings, as well as by the structural costs of supporting extensive earth loads at greater depths. Nevertheless, many of the benefits are achievable to some

degree in buildings near the surface that are only partially in contact with the earth. In fact, as noted in connection with the final benefit listed below, earth sheltered structures are compatible with other conservation strategies and systems that require openings and exposure to the surface.

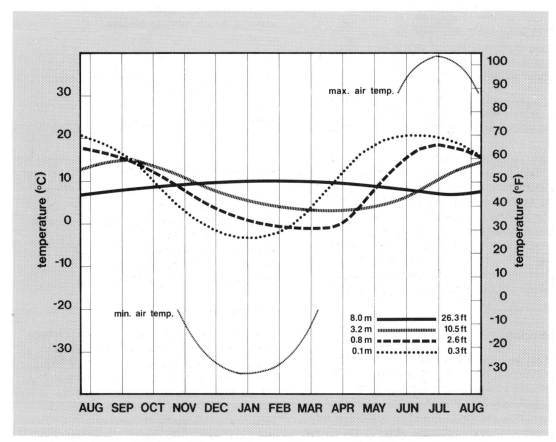

8-1: Annual Temperature Fluctuations—Minneapolis, Minnesota

This chart based on information from reference 8.1.

reduced infiltration

By placing earth against walls and on top of the roof, infiltration through those surfaces is completely eliminated, resulting in both heating and cooling load reduction. In addition, if the exposed surfaces of the structure are located away from the prevailing winter winds, the berms can divert wind over and around the structure to reduce infiltration through these areas.

reduced heat loss through envelope in winter

It is generally assumed that heat loss resulting from conduction will be minimized through surfaces that are in contact with the earth at a reasonable depth below grade. This assumption is based on the fact that temperatures are more moderate below grade than the extremes of above-grade air temperatures, and that below-grade temperatures reach reasonable stability at depths greater than 10 feet (see fig. 8-1 for temperatures for the Minneapolis area). Ground temperatures will generally approximate the annual average air temperature in warm climates and be a few degrees warmer than the annual average temperature in areas with significant winter snow cover. Urban areas also will raise local ground temperatures. Ground temperatures for various climates are given in chapter 2.

Although the R-value per unit thickness of earth is not great compared to the R-value of typical insulation materials, the large mass of earth results in a significant reduction and delay in heat exchange with the surface, which in turn results in a net benefit during extremely cold periods. It is important to note that in most climates these temperature moderation effects are more significant at depths greater than 4 to 6 feet. Areas of the structure with smaller amounts of earth cover may need supplemental insulation (see next section).

increased earth cooling potential in summer

For most climates in the United States, ground temperatures at depths from 2 to 10 feet are lower than the temperatures required for comfort in summer. Thus, when air temperatures within the space of the building exceed the ground temperatures, heat is transferred from the space to the surrounding ground. This phenomenon occurs both by conduction through the envelope and radiation from warmer objects in the space to cooler wall and floor surfaces. Insulation, which separates the interior space from the earth, reduces this cooling effect.

reduced heat gain

Earth-covered roofs and earth-bermed walls reduce radiant heat gain from the sun. The massive earth has the capacity to absorb a considerable amount of radiation before it reaches the envelope. In climates with cool summer nights, the earth may release the heat to the cooler air by conduction and to the night sky by radiation. A very important component in reducing heat gain by radiation is the use of plant materials. In the process of evapotranspiration, plants can effectively cancel out most if not all of the incoming radiation from the sun. This process requires a sufficient level of moisture in the ground to enable the plants to grow.

dampened daily temperature fluctuations

The large mass of the earth surrounding the structure delays and dampens the effect of rapid fluctuations in temperature and typical day-night temperature swings. In addition, because many earth sheltered structures are constructed primarily of concrete and are insulated on the outside, the resultant large mass inside the insulated envelope further stabilizes inside temperature fluctuations. The most significant effect of this phenomenon is that peak loads are reduced, thus resulting in smaller requirements for heating and cooling equipment. Total energy consumption is also reduced to some degree, depending on the exact climate characteristics and on whether the house is in the heating or the cooling season. A final effect associated with reduced temperature fluctuations is that temperatures may remain relatively stable for many days with no heat input. This phenomenon can be a great benefit during a power outage, especially for a house situated in a remote location.

seasonal temperature lag in ground

As indicated in the chart of ground temperatures (fig. 8-1), at greater depths the temperature fluctuations on a seasonal basis are not only dampened but are also delayed. This phenomenon presents the potential for saving heating energy because the warmer ground temperatures from summer are carried into the fall and winter, thus reducing heating needs during the early months of the heating season. Conversely, the cooler ground temperatures of the winter, which are carried into the spring and summer, reduce cooling loads.

compatibility with other conservation strategies

The general concept of a structure benefiting from contact with the earth allows for many variations in utilization and degrees of earth contact. A well-designed earth sheltered house always employs a wide variety of other energy conservation strategies as well. One benefit of earth sheltered structures is their compatibility with passive solar concepts. Direct gain is particularly applicable because there is often a large concrete mass within the insulated envelope of the house that can store solar heat. Exposed portions of earth sheltered houses are likely to be superinsulated. In the summer, ventilation can be provided in even the most enclosed earth sheltered design through proper placement of a few key openings. Operable skylights can effectively ventilate locations or designs where no cross-ventilation exists.

techniques related to earth contact

Most of the benefits discussed here are considered in the context of houses in which the floor, some walls, and sometimes the roof are in direct contact with the earth. The moderating influence of the earth can be tapped in other ways as well to reduce heating and cooling energy requirements. These techniques include the use of tubes in the earth that provide cooler ventilation air in the summer and warmer ventilation air in the winter. Similarly, heat pumps can be connected to the below-grade environment to operate more efficiently; in some cases they can use the very constant temperatures found in deep groundwater to reduce heating and cooling costs. Other possible uses of the ground environment include its use as a

storage medium for solar systems or other intermittent sources of heat and cooling. Ground underneath houses has been used in this manner, and berms surrounding structures could also be considered for this purpose. Any of these concepts could be used in conjunction with houses that are in direct contact with the earth, as well as in more conventional above-grade houses.

Potential Limitations

In addition to energy-related benefits, earth sheltered buildings have potential limitations (listed below). Although the energy-related limitations of earth sheltered buildings represent a possible reduction in the overall benefits of these structures, they need not negate the benefits entirely. First, neither benefits nor limitations are quantified here, and both can exist to varying degrees. Second, the effect of the potential limitations depends on specific climate conditions as well as on the individual design of the structure. After the potential limitations are identified, it may be possible to design the structure to minimize the effects of the drawbacks while maintaining the positive benefits.

structural and economic limitations

The relatively great weight of earth on flat roofs, combined with the lateral earth pressures on buried walls (these pressures increase with depth), require heavier and more expensive structures. This economic limitation is one major reason why most earth sheltered housing structures are not placed more deeply or extensively into the underground environment. Much of the envelope of the structure is within the first few feet of the surface and therefore does not benefit as dramatically from the ground

temperatures and earth mass as do the portions of the envelope that are at greater depths. This limitation has given rise to two methods of combatting the problem. The first is the use of earth-bermed walls and a conventional roof, which is less expensive than a more heavily structured earth-covered roof. The other approach uses structures such as shells and domes, which can support the heavier loads much more efficiently, resulting in lower costs and larger amounts of earth placed over the structure. In spite of the potential cost advantages of these alternatives, many, if not most, earth sheltered houses built thus far have flat earth-covered roofs.

requirements for openings

As indicated in the introduction to this section, a windowless chamber buried in the earth is unsuitable for housing. The various requirements for access, window openings, and other exposed portions of the building envelope diminish the area of the envelope in contact with the ground, as well as the depth of the structure. Access must occur from grade; and windows, courtyards, and other openings are most easily designed in structures that are only partially set into the earth. Numerous openings on various sides of a structure break the continuity of the earth mass surrounding the house, thereby diminishing the energy-conserving benefits related to structure-earth contact.

slow response

Although the mass of the concrete structure within the envelope and the surrounding earth mass are assets in many ways, they result in a structure that cannot respond rapidly to changed conditions. This means that some energy-conserving strategies, such as night thermostat setback, may not work effectively or may work only with an unsatisfactory time-lag. Also, problems may occur in adjusting quickly to unusual or extreme loads such as overheating at a crowded party or meeting.

lack of useful ground temperatures

Ground temperatures are related to the annual climate conditions. During both heating and cooling seasons, a lack of useful ground temperatures can diminish the benefits of a structure's contact with the earth. The parts of the country requiring the most heat have the lowest ground temperatures, and the regions with the greatest cooling requirements have the highest ground temperatures. Because the moderating influence of the ground temperature is useful during periods of extreme temperature fluctuations, the most significant benefits are likely to accrue to houses in climates that have the greatest daily and seasonal temperature fluctuations. Enhanced heat gain reduction due to contact with and protection from the earth can nevertheless be substantial in a variety of climates.

change of ground temperatures caused by structure

The relatively constant ground temperatures that reflect the moderating influence of the earth mass are normally presented for undisturbed ground. After a structure has been placed into the ground and heat has flowed from the structure to the ground over a period of time, the ground temperatures change. Generally, the temperature of the earth immediately

adjacent to the building warms up to a level close to the inside temperature of the building and then gradually diminishes over a distance of more than 10 feet away from the building. This warming of the earth is gradual; computer simulations have indicated that a range of a few months to three years are required before the ground warms to a more or less steady-state condition (depending on the size of the building). This characteristic is included here because it represents a modification and potential limitation of the usually oversimplified discussion of the benefits of constant ground temperatures. In fact, the warmer earth near the building may be a benefit during the heating season more than it is a drawback during the cooling season and the potential for condensation will be reduced—depending, of course, on the local climate. One thing is clear: it is likely that more energy will be required for heating in the initial period of ground warming than in subsequent years.

drawbacks of seasonal time lag in temperatures

Although ground temperatures are often more favorable than the outside temperatures throughout the year, they can also be less favorable at certain points in the seasonal cycle. For example, in a cold climate, the ground at a depth of 10 feet reaches its lowest temperature in spring. Although this time lag is beneficial in the summer, it is detrimental in the spring because the air temperatures, which are warming faster than the ground, would result in a lower heating requirement for the building if it were above grade. In a warm climate, benefits from cooler fall air temperatures are greater than those from

the ground, which has been warmed to its peak by the end of summer and early fall. Two mitigating circumstances may diminish the negative effects of these phenomena. First, because the ground around the structure is not at the same temperature as natural undisturbed ground, these effects may not be as important in a more constant and usually warmer zone of ground temperatures. Second, strategies can be employed to counteract the potential negative effects of the seasonal time lag: for example, solar gain in the spring or ventilation in the fall may offset the limitations of the time lag while maintaining its benefits.

heating/cooling compromises

Although the below-grade ground environment offers potential benefits in both the heating and cooling seasons, maximizing these benefits requires insulation in the heating season but direct earth contact with no insulation in the cooling season. In many cases the necessary compromise prevents optimizing for either condition alone.

condensation

Because the surrounding earth is almost always cooler than the indoor air temperature, condensation on interior surfaces may occur, especially in summer. For condensation to occur, wall temperatures must be below the dew point temperature. In such cases, it is likely that dehumidification would be desirable to provide comfort. This potential problem is mitigated by a number of factors. As the earth and walls adjacent to the building warm up, the temperature difference between indoor air and walls is not very great. This effect of raising wall temperatures is enhanced by insulation on the outside of the walls—sometimes placed there mainly to prevent condensation. Abruptly stopping the insulation halfway down the wall, however, can cause worse condensation problems than would occur on a completely uninsulated wall, as the accelerated heat flow at the point where the insulation stops results in a colder spot and increased potential for condensation [8.2]. Problems with condensation are, of course, dependent on the local climate as well as on the manner in and degree to which outside air is introduced into the house.

lack of moisture for evapotranspiration

Evapotranspiration, the process by which plant materials dissipate incoming solar radiation so that it never warms the ground or the structure, depends on the availability of moisture. In hot, dry climates, the full benefit of this effect from an earth-covered roof may be difficult or costly to realize because water may have to be supplied to the plants by irrigation. The effect could be very dramatic, however, since cooling by evaporation from the soil would be enhanced by the increased capacity of hot, dry air to take on moisture. It should be noted that cooling benefits can be attributed to a massive roof even without the additional benefits from the plant materials.

limited thermal storage capacity of earth

This limitation relates primarily to techniques such as earth tubes, which attempt to benefit from moderate ground temperatures in order to warm or cool

incoming air for the house. These can be direct air-supply earth tubes or an indirect system using a liquid as the heat-transfer medium. As heat exchange occurs in the tube, the ground temperature around the tube changes until the temperature differential is no longer great enough to be useful. At this point the effective heat storage capacity of the earth surrounding the tube has been reached. This situation, however, can be modified or corrected. First, the surface area—circumference times length of the tube—can be increased so that the available heat storage better corresponds to the necessary heating or cooling requirements. This strategy may, however, result in a solution that is not cost-effective. A second solution involves intermittent use of the tube, thereby allowing the ground temperature adequate time to return to its former level. In cooling applications this recharging of the ground could be accelerated by moisture draining through the soil and conducting heat away from the tube more rapidly. This drainage could be accomplished by diverting natural runoff or by mechanically pumping water through the area [8.3]. Another variation for air tubes involves the use of two separate tubes that are used alternately for intake and exhaust.

difficulty in calculating and predicting performance

Because of the complexity of heat flow through the earth, reliable calculations of heating and cooling performance are quite difficult to obtain. Performance cannot be calculated accurately as a simple, steady-state problem because the ground temperatures change over time; similarly, the rates of heat flow change in a manner that is not instantaneously related to

current outdoor conditions. In addition, the heat flow is different at different points in the structure. Performance calculations are further complicated by the fact that heat transfer is affected significantly by a number of largely uncontrollable and complex variables such as soil moisture content, soil type, vegetation, and presence of snow. Although the state of the art of calculation procedures has advanced rapidly in recent years, it is unlikely that any of the present methods—and particularly the simpler hand calculation methods—are completely reliable. Performance calculation variables are discussed in the following section.

indoor air quality

The extremely well-sealed exterior envelope of an earth sheltered house can result in an air exchange rate that is less than desirable for health and comfort. In addition to odors, there is concern over exposure to a wide range of detrimental pollutants, including radon. This problem can be solved, however, without sacrificing the energy saving benefit of low infiltration by the use of efficient heat exchanging ventilation equipment. Additional information on the sources of pollution and the strategies to reduce pollutants is included in the last section of this chapter.

Below-Grade Heat Transfer and Insulation Principles

In order to benefit from the advantages of placing a building below grade and to insulate it properly to avoid any disadvantages, it is necessary to understand some of the basic characteristics of heat transfer underground. Generally, bodies at different temperatures tend to seek a state of equilibrium: thus, heat flows from warm areas to cold areas by the path of least resistance. The rate of flow increases in proportion to the temperature difference between the warm and cold bodies but is impeded by the resistance of the materials placed in the path of flow. Heat flow in an above-grade structure is fairly simple to calculate and understand because the envelope is relatively thin, consistent in its construction and the thermal resistance values of its materials, and the temperature difference between all points inside and outside the envelope can be assumed to be the same. Below grade, however, there is no consistency in the thickness and resistivity of the materials. In addition, the behavior of heat flow through a large mass of material is more complex, changing in a manner that does not directly and instantaneously correspond to outside temperature, as it does above grade. Finally, numerous uncontrolled variables—such as soil moisture content, and snow and vegetation on the surface—can affect heat transfer significantly.

In figure 8-2, heat transfer through the ground from an uninsulated, below-grade chamber is shown in its simplest form. This is the condition that would exist in midwinter in a cold climate when a significant temperature difference between the inside and the outside air exists over a relatively long period of time. The solid lines indicate heat flow; closer spacing of these lines corresponds to a greater heat flow. The dashed lines indicate lines of constant temperature. In this uninsulated condition, the greatest heat loss clearly occurs through the roof and upper walls, where the path to the surface is short. Heat loss gradually diminishes at greater depths on the walls; the least heat loss occurs in the center of the floor, where the path through the ground to the surface is the longest. Although soil has quite a low actual R-value per unit thickness in comparison with most insulating materials, it can reduce heat loss considerably when heat must pass through a large amount of soil, as in the case of the floor and lower portions of the walls.

It must be emphasized that this relatively simple picture of heat flow illustrates only one point in time. During other periods of the climatic cycle, heat flow patterns may appear quite different. In the summer, for example, the greatest temperature differential may exist between the underground space and the deeper, cool ground temperatures, rather than between the space and the surface. In this case heat loss will be directed in a different pattern, similar to the illustration in figure 8-3. Many possible variations involving different patterns can occur between these two extremes, depending on the local climate and other factors. Heat flow analysis is further complicated by the fact that the ground itself is gradually warmed as it retains some of the heat that flows through it over time. This factor can affect

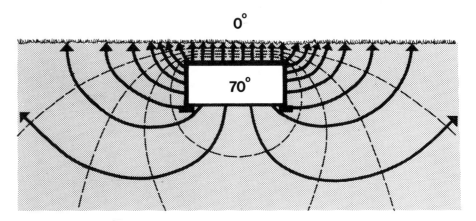

8-2: Schematic Heat Flow in Earth from Below-Grade Structure in Winter

161

the heat flow by changing temperature differentials between the interior space and the surrounding earth.

This pattern of multi-dimensional heat flow, which varies over time, can be calculated using computer techniques although the many variables that affect the analysis are difficult to predict accurately. For example, vegetation on the roof can reduce heat gain in summer considerably by absorbing incoming solar radiation through the process of evapotranspiration, which prevents the radiation from being transferred to the building. The effectiveness of this process varies because it depends on the presence of moisture in the soil. In the winter, vegetation can add somewhat to the insulating value of the soil. The most effective plant materials in terms of insulation would have a thick growth and a dense network of roots so that as much still air could be trapped as possible. A

thick layer of mulch over the soil, which is recommended for most plant materials, would also trap air and add to the insulating capacity of the roof (see chapter 9).

Snow is another variable that can add to the insulating properties of an earth-covered roof although the amount and duration of the snow cover naturally varies, not only in different climates, but also from year to year in the same climate. Also, the type of snow has an important effect on its insulating value. Wet, closely packed snow will conduct heat more easily than drier, fluffy new snow. One foot of fluffy new snow can add an additional R-value of 10 to 15 to the roof and the snow cover will also retard heat loss upwards from the walls. On a conventional roof that is vented with cooler air underneath, snow cover is not as direct a component of the building envelope as it is for an earth-covered roof.

Like the conditions at the interface between the outside environment and the ground, the conditions between the interior space of the building and the surrounding earth are subject to many variables that offset the overall heat transfer. The properties and arrangement of the materials comprising the structure of the envelope, as well as any insulation and interior finishes, affect the heat flow in terms of conductive and radiant transfer in addition to affecting condensation. The remainder of this section deals with these issues in greater detail.

An important aspect of heat flow below grade concerns the properties of the soil medium itself. Because soils are usually not homogenous, the properties of soil resistance and heat capacity vary. Perhaps the most important property of the soil is its ability to hold moisture. The presence of moisture in the ground can increase the conductivity of the soil considerably (as much as seven to eight times), thus increasing heat loss. Although heat transfer will undoubtedly increase when the ground adjacent to a building is wet, the effect may be diminished when certain conditions are present. As the conductivity of the ground increases with the presence of moisture, the zone of warmed earth around the building will spread further out. Although conductivity through the ground will be higher, the longer heat flow path will reduce the effect of the increased conductivity on the heat loss [8.4]. It should also be noted that portions of the structure close to the surface are usually the most heavily insulated areas. Given a substantial amount of insulation on the structure, the R-value of the earth is only a small component of the heat loss for these areas with little earth cover. The

8-3: Schematic Heat Flow in Earth from Below-Grade Structure in Summer

principal value of the earth under these conditions is to moderate temperatures.

Seasonal changes in ground moisture content can provide an energy advantage in some climates. In northern climates ground freezing and winter snow cover, combined with heat loss from the building, will tend to dry out the ground adjacent to the building, thereby lowering the heat loss. In other climates, however, this situation could be reversed. For example, areas in which the heaviest rainfall occurs in winter experience the wettest soil conditions during the heating season, when wet soil is least desirable. Wherever very moist ground is adjacent to a building during the heating season, additional insulation should be considered. Of course, this option must be balanced against the likely reduction in summer cooling benefits.

General Insulation Concepts

Because of the relatively complex characteristics of heat transfer below grade and the limited availability of precise calculation methods, definitive cost-benefit analyses of various insulation placements in various climates are beyond the current state of the art. Ongoing research projects at the University of Minnesota are, however, expected to yield relatively reliable calculation methods that will result in guidelines for insulation placement. In the meantime, insulation placement and thicknesses for below-grade structures are mainly based on general conceptual responses and oversimplified peak-load calculations. This is not to say that these responses are incorrect. They are correct in a general sense; only the specific details remain unknown. In most cases value judgments have been made in

selecting an insulation scheme that will meet individual priorities.

The basic insulation concepts for underground structures are based on a few simple ideas. First, in climates where there is a substantial heating load, the ground is always somewhat colder than the desired comfort conditions in the building. Thus, if the goal is to optimize insulation placement in order to minimize energy expended to heat the building, it is necessary to insulate around the entire building envelope (fig. 8-4). Greater amounts of insulation should be placed on the portions of the building near the surface, where the heat transfer is greatest. Second, in climates where there is a significant cooling load and ground temperatures generally remain lower than the comfort level, it is desirable to lose heat to the cooler ground environment. If the goal is to optimize insulation placement in order to minimize energy expended for cooling, then no insulation should be applied in this circumstance, as insulation would interfere with the desirable transfer of heat from the building to the ground.

This case seldom exists, however. Sometimes where there is a substantial cooling load, ground temperatures at shallow depths are equal to or higher than comfort conditions. In such a case, insulation between the space and the warmer ground temperatures is required. One typical configuration might include installation on the roof only, to reduce heat gain from the warmest soil in the first few feet near the surface while leaving the walls and floor in direct contact with the ground to take advantage of generally cooler temperatures at greater depths (fig. 8-5).

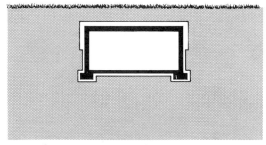

8-4: Optimal Insulation Placement for Winter Heating Season

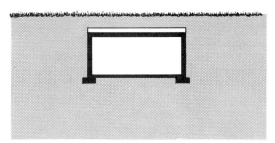

8-5: Optimal Insulation Placement for Summer Cooling Season

Extreme cases similar to those described above, in which concern centers exclusively on either heating or cooling, are not representative of most climates. Usually, the insulation placement must reflect a compromise between heating and cooling needs. In practice, because both heating and cooling needs are often important, but not equally so, insulation placement can take a variety of forms, depending on which needs are emphasized. One typical compromise, shown in figure 8-6, combines the two concepts explained above. Here, the portion of the building nearest the surface is well insulated because it is the zone of greatest heat loss in winter and least cooling benefit in summer. The remaining portion of the building, which is more remote from the surface, is left uninsulated to take advantage of any cooling benefits because it is the zone of least heat loss in winter.

Insulation placement based on some experimental concepts attempts to increase the cooling benefits while not increasing winter heat loss substantially. In the first example, shown in figure 8-7, insulation is extended out from the walls of the structure and placed in the earth mass. Cooling should be enhanced by the greater contact with the structure. Theoretically, the heat loss in winter should be resisted by the insulation because it interrupts or extends the heat loss path through the earth to the surface. Preliminary simulations of this condition indicate that while the summer cooling is enhanced somewhat, the winter heat loss does increase [8.5]. Further research and testing are required to determine the magnitude of these effects so that the effectiveness of this strategy can be assessed.

A similar approach is illustrated in figure 8-8, in which a shell structure is shown. In this case the placement of insulation away from the structure allows for even greater earth mass within the insulated envelope than is provided in the previous example because there is earth between the insulation and the structure on the roof as well. This approach could also solve the problems associated with insulating a curving surface with typically flat insulation materials. It should be emphasized that both these approaches are somewhat experimental, and that, while they enhance cooling benefits, there is some penalty (presently undetermined) in the heating season. Also, the practical construction problems in providing a secure continuous insulating shield that these approaches may pose must be carefully resolved.

In addition to examining the overall location of insulation on the structure, it is important to consider the impact of placing the insulation inside or outside the structural envelope of the building. Assuming the structure is massive concrete or masonry, placement outside allows the mass to be more useful in dampening daily temperature fluctuations and storing solar gain. This is not as great a concern with less massive wood structures. There may be an actual reduction in the effectiveness of the insulation when placed outside the concrete structure, because unless the entire envelope is totally enclosed by insulation, there is the possibility of the concrete conducting heat to the points of least resistance, resulting in a greater rate of loss overall. Further research is required to assess the magnitude of this effect so that the total costs and benefits of differing placements can be determined. Placement of insulation on inside or outside the structure also

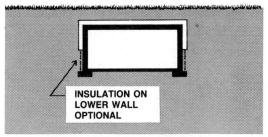

8-6: Compromise Insulation Placement – Winter and Summer

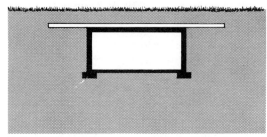

8-7: Alternative Insulation Placement

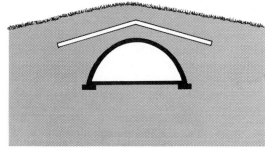

8-8: Detached Insulation Placement for Shell Structure

affects the type, and therefore the cost, of insulation that can be used. Further information on placement and types of insulation materials is included in the next section of this chapter.

Although the general concepts presented in this section seem simple enough, it is important to remember they are only two-dimensional representations of a completely underground chamber. The insulation patterns become more complex in a real three-dimensional structure that has a variety of openings and differing relationships to the surface. In addition, successful energy-conserving performance of the building is related to a number of detailed concerns such as the treatment of interior surfaces and elimination of thermal short circuits. In order to explain these various concerns in greater detail and make general recommendations on insulation thicknesses and placement, the remainder of this section is divided into considerations for roofs, walls, floors, and critical details in earth sheltered houses.

Roof

The roof is the simplest of the three basic components of an earth sheltered house to analyze. If a flat roof is to be covered with earth, it is usually not economical to place more than 3 feet of soil on it. In many cases the minimum to support vegetation (12 to 24 inches) is used. This amount of earth is effective in dampening daily temperature fluctuations but lacks the seasonal stability of deeper ground temperatures. During the winter the heat will flow from the building directly through the shallow earth layer to the colder outside air above it. Generally, this can be considered to be a one-dimensional pattern of flow in which the same loss will occur at any point on the roof, given a uniform soil depth. The heat loss through a given point in the earth-covered roof is usually not greatly affected by its location, whether at the center, the edge, or near a skylight opening.

In the winter the greatest heat loss by far occurs through the roof. Because a depth of 1 to 3 feet of earth does not offer very significant resistance to heat flow by itself, the roof should be insulated to levels that are equal to or slightly less than those recommended for roofs of conventional houses. Some additional benefits will accrue to a house that has an earth-covered roof if snow accumulation on the roof can provide insulating value, together with the vegetation and root layer of the plants. Because most earth-covered roofs are concrete structures that are insulated on the outside, this heavy mass dampens indoor temperature fluctuations; thus, the roof mass is an asset to any intermittent heat sources, such as passive solar gain, where rising heat within the building is absorbed by the ceiling and reradiated.

The benefits attributed to earth-covered roofs are generally considered to be greater during the cooling season than in the heating season. The tendency of the earth mass to dampen daily temperature fluctuations has some energy-conserving value during periods characterized by warm days and cooler nights. Perhaps most important in terms of energy conservation is the reduction in incoming solar radiation that is associated primarily with the presence of vegetation.

As discussed in chapter 4, many houses that are bermed with earth on the walls have a conventional roof because it is less expensive to build and offers similar energy-conserving benefits in the winter. These conventional roofs are often insulated very heavily, to levels referred to as superinsulated (R-40 to R-60, depending on the climate). During the winter heating season, the loss through this type of roof can be extremely low. This loss couples well with the relatively low losses that occur through properly insulated floors and walls in contact with the earth.

The analysis of heat flow and conclusions about rooftop insulation are somewhat different if a shell structure, which can support larger earth loads more efficiently, is used. First, the heat flow is no longer one-dimensional and constant over the entire roof since the depth of earth on the roof usually varies. Second, if there is a greater depth of earth (more than 4 feet), then the ground temperatures become more moderate and a number of the benefits discussed in the previous section are present. As a result, less insulation may be required to achieve the same energy use as that of a structure with a shallower layer of earth.

Walls

Vertical walls below grade are the most complex component of an earth sheltered structure, in terms of both analysis and insulation configuration. Walls generally extend from the surface or near the surface to a depth anywhere from 8 to 20 feet below grade (the latter figure would apply to a two-level house). Because the rate of heat flow varies significantly at different depths on the wall, differing amounts of insulation are most economical.

Although the rate of loss changes gradually with depth, below-grade walls are usually considered as divided into two zones in order to simplify insulation placement. The upper zone comprises the first 6 to 8 feet below the surface, in which the greatest exchange with the surface takes place during periods of cold outside temperatures. This is also the area in which the ground temperatures do not maintain the same stability that they do further below the surface. In this respect, this upper portion of below-grade walls is very similar to the roof and thus is usually insulated in the same manner. That is, if heating is the predominant concern, the upper portion of any below-grade wall should be insulated to the same value as a conventional above-grade wall. Even if cooling is of equal or greater concern than heating, the upper portion of the wall can still be insulated, since cooling can be provided by the lower walls and floor more effectively.

The remaining portion of the below-grade walls (more than 6 to 8 feet beneath the surface) does not have the same type of exchange with the outside air temperatures and is in a more stable ground environment. This is particularly true for two-story structures that may be 20 feet deep, where ground temperatures are virtually constant. It is with regard to this zone that the greatest controversy over the placement and amount of insulation exists. The problem is that the inherent conflict between optimizing for the heating season and the cooling season is further complicated by the possibility of using insulation to prevent condensation. If the goal is to reduce the amount of energy for space heating, then the entire surface of the wall should be insulated to a greater or lesser degree, because the ground temperature is always somewhat colder than the indoor air temperature. It is not necessary, however, to insulate the lower wall to the same extent that the upper portion is insulated in order to achieve optimal placement. For example, it would be better to place insulation in varying thicknesses that increase toward the surface (fig. 8-10) than to place the same total amount on the entire wall, as shown in figure 8-9. Of course, in practice, it is easier to place it with as few variations in thickness as possible.

If the goal is to optimize the cooling effect from direct contact with the cooler ground, then placing insulation on the lower part of the wall is undesirable, as doing so will diminish this effect. A related concern is the condensation that may result from the warm indoor air temperatures meeting the cooler surfaces of the lower wall that are in contact with the ground. In this case it is often recommended that insulation be placed outside the wall in minimal thicknesses in order to keep the wall temperature warmer and avoid an abrupt switch from the relatively heavy insulation on the upper half of the wall to no insulation on the lower half. The accelerated heat flow at the transition point

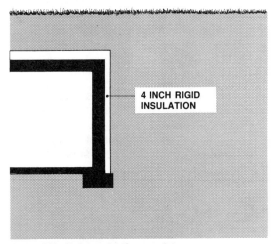

8-9: Wall Insulation with Constant Thickness

4 INCH RIGID INSULATION

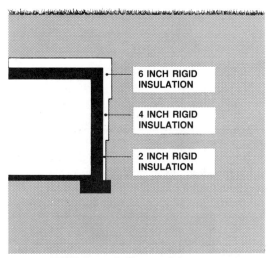

8-10: Wall Insulation with Varying Thickness

6 INCH RIGID INSULATION

4 INCH RIGID INSULATION

2 INCH RIGID INSULATION

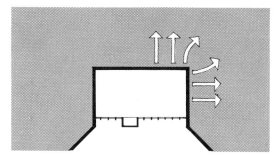

8-11: Increased Heat Transfer at Corner (Plan)

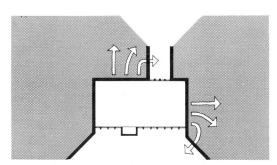

8-12: Increased Heat Transfer Near Openings (Plan)

in the wall that such an abrupt change in insulation causes can result in increased condensation at that point [8.2].

Thus, the decision of whether and to what extent the lower portion of the wall is to be insulated must be based on priorities determined by the local climate and personal value judgments. If heating is the only concern, the lower wall should be insulated. If condensation is a major concern, it could receive at least a minimal layer of insulation (R-5). If cooling is at least as important as heating, however, it is best not to insulate the lower wall. Condensation may be controlled by other techniques if necessary. Sometimes a decision may be shifted in favor of insulating the lower half of the wall for other reasons, such as the value of insulation in protecting the waterproofing layer and cushioning the wall during backfill.

The preceding discussion of heat flow through below-grade walls is again basically a two-dimensional analysis because the rate of flow varies dramatically with depth. Heat flow through walls can also vary along the length of a wall, however, assuming a constant wall depth. These three-dimensional effects further complicate the analysis of heat loss and optimal insulation placement. The main variations in heat flow along the wall occur at corners and near transitions from below- to above-grade walls. Because there is more adjacent earth per unit length of wall at an outside corner, the heat transfer is accelerated at this point (fig. 8-11). Conversely, an interior corner has less earth per unit length of wall, resulting in reduced heat transfer with the ground. To avoid uneven heat loss, it is theoretically advisable to slightly increase insulation at

the corners of walls.

At the transition from a below-grade wall to an exposed wall, which normally occurs at the window and door openings of earth sheltered buildings, there is a great increase in heat transfer between the wall near the opening and the outside air (fig. 8-12). Such openings create a situation similar to that which exists at the upper part of the wall, which is located near the surface. Because there is such a short path to the outside, heat flow is accelerated and ground temperatures will fluctuate more than they would in a continuous, uninterrupted earth berm. In these areas it is important to increase the insulation to the same amount used on the upper zone of the wall. Insulation should extend laterally at least 4 feet from the opening and cover the entire height of the wall.

The overall contribution of the wall surfaces of an earth sheltered house to the heating or cooling load depends on many factors. Assuming that the conduction through the exterior envelope is one of the major sources of energy use for heating and cooling, the area of the walls in relation to the volume of the house will be an important variable. Amounts of wall surface can vary widely among houses that have the same volume and floor area. If heating is the predominant concern, then layouts that use simple, compact geometries will be most efficient. If the cooling effects of earth-contact walls are to be maximized, however, then increasing the wall area by using skin-dominated plan geometries is desirable.

Floors

Because the floor of a below-grade structure is usually more isolated from the surface temperatures than the walls or the roof, it requires the least amount of insulation. But the analysis of heat flow through floors in contact with the earth and insulation recommendations for floors are not as simple as might be expected. Conflicts over optimizing for heating or cooling usually must be resolved, together with concerns about condensation and effective storage of any direct solar radiation. In addition, unlike the situation on an earth-covered roof, the heat transfer with the surface varies at different points along the floor. These variations in heat flow are greatly affected by the presence of exposed wall areas.

As it is for the other components of an earth sheltered house, the heat flow through the floor is affected mainly by the distance to the surface and the ground temperatures at the depth of the floor. Generally, more insulation is required in the areas where there is the greatest rate of heat exchange with the surface. In a typical underground chamber located one level below grade, greater heat flow would occur at the edges of the floor, rather than in the center, as shown in figure 8-13. For a larger floor area, the center of the floor is even more remote from the surface and, hence, the difference in heat loss between the center and edge of the floor would be greater than in the previous example. This analysis implies that, given two floors of equal area, less heat loss would occur through the floor that approximates a circle or square than through the floor of a long rectangular shape in which the center is closer to the edges. It also implies that, if

insulation is to be placed under the floor at all, the edges should be the first concern and the optimal pattern would result in greater thicknesses at the edges than in the center. Since the rate of heat exchange with the surface is also a function of depth, the floor of a two-level chamber would have significantly lower heat loss rates than the floor of a one-level structure.

The most dramatic variations in heat transfer through the floor occur near the exposed portions of the walls, which, in effect, place the floor in close proximity to the surface (fig. 8-14). The resulting ground temperatures fluctuate more and have less of a moderating influence on the structure. In this regard, the heat flow characteristics through the edge of the floor are similar to those of an earth-covered roof or an upper wall, where substantial insulation is mandatory if heat loss is a major concern. In the case of a fully exposed wall, as shown in figure 8-15, insulation should be placed vertically at least down to the frost level or, alternatively, under the floor slab, to at least the same distance horizontally. Because the distance from the interior space to the surface is similar to the distance from the surface to the upper portion of an earth-covered wall or roof, the same levels of insulation are recommended.

In addition to concerns about insulating these areas of great loss through the floor near openings, a basic conflict exists regarding whether or not to insulate the more remote areas of the floor at all. The issue is similar to that which concerns the portions of below-grade walls more than 6 feet below the surface. The conflict again centers on whether to optimize insulation

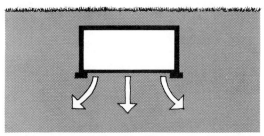

8-13: Heat Transfer through Floor

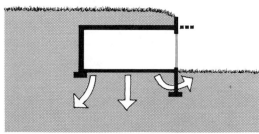

8-14: Increased Heat Transfer Near Exposed Walls

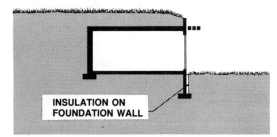

INSULATION ON FOUNDATION WALL

8-15: Insulation Placement Near Exposed Walls

placement to minimize heat loss in winter or to take advantage of direct contact with the cooler earth temperatures in summer. The floor is often left uninsulated because it is the area of least heat loss and most potential benefit for cooling purposes.

Several mitigating circumstances may, however, result in a decision to insulate under the floor slab. First, condensation can be a problem on surfaces in direct contact with the earth, and insulation can assist in raising the temperature of the slab to that of the inside air. It can be argued, however, that the temperature of an uninsulated slab will be raised to very near the room temperature in any case (provided interior temperatures are fairly constant throughout the year). Ignoring condensation concerns, it can also be argued that cold floors are uncomfortable and insulation is necessary to keep them warmer. Actually, it is the high-conductivity concrete and ceramic tile that make floors made of these materials feel colder to the touch than those with wood or carpeting. Unfortunately, floor coverings such as carpeting have a high insulating value themselves and thus will interfere with maximizing the cooling potential of direct earth contact.

A final concern is the use of the floor as a storage medium for solar heat, particularly from a direct gain application in which the floor areas receive direct sunlight. Insulation may be desirable to retard the flow of heat from the warmer slab into the colder ground so that it can be released into the space at a later time during the daily cycle. On the other hand, by not placing insulation under the slab, the solar heat can be transmitted directly to the ground. This creates a larger heat sink, which can produce more limited

benefits over a longer time cycle. Generally, if a decision is made to insulate under the more remote areas of the floor, insulation thicknesses should be no more than R-5 to R-10 in American climate regions.

Detailed Concerns

The effectiveness of proper placement of insulation in appropriate thicknesses to reduce energy consumption can be enhanced or diminished by a number of critical details. Details must reflect overall design strategies and are closely related to the type of structure that is used. Massive, highly conductive concrete presents different problems and opportunities than does a less massive wood structure. The type of structure influences the possible locations of insulation in the building envelope and, therefore, the type of insulation materials suitable for that application. For example, the mass of a concrete or masonry structure presents greater opportunities for storage of solar heat and dampening temperature fluctuations than does a wood structure, but its conductive properties present problems requiring careful attention to thermal breaks. The details discussed in this section are divided into two groups—thermal breaks and interior surface treatments. The following section discusses the location of insulation in the building envelope—an issue that is very closely related to various critical details.

interior surface treatments

Two of the important potential benefits of earth sheltered buildings are the cooling effect that results from direct earth contact and the advantages of a massive structure

in storing solar heat and dampening daily temperature fluctuations. In both cases the ability of the structure to make the most of these benefits is influenced by the interior surface treatments. For a highly conductive, massive concrete or masonry structure, interior surface treatments should be selected that will not impede the transfer of heat from the room interior to the wall and floor masses and the surrounding earth. This need to permit heat transfer from the house interior to the ground to occur renders many of the most typical finishes undesirable for this type of structure. Carpeted floors and furred-out walls with drywall or paneling, for example, insulate the concrete surface from the space instead of permitting the desired heat transfer to occur.

Recommended wall treatments are exposed concrete or block (perhaps with a texture, stain, integral color, or paint for aesthetic reasons), brick, tile, plaster, stucco, or drywall applied directly to the surface (with no air space). Recommended floor treatments include tile, brick, and exposed concrete (which can be colored or textured by grinding it smooth to expose the aggregate pattern). For collecting direct solar radiation, darker-colored and unglazed (nonreflective) surfaces will have the highest absorption capacities. When a concrete roof structure is used, benefits from the roof mass will be enhanced by finishes such as paint or plaster applied directly to the surface, rather than by furred-out treatments.

thermal breaks

A thermal break refers to the placement of insulation at locations where a high-conductivity material (usually concrete) is in contact with both inside and outside conditions. Although these sections of the structure are usually relatively small in area, they can contribute significantly to the heat loss in buildings that are otherwise well insulated and well sealed. Even if the heat loss is not significant, these paths of conduction can create cold spots on interior surfaces, resulting in frost or condensation problems. One of the most typical situations requiring a thermal break occurs when a concrete roof slab extends beyond an exposed wall to form an overhang. A number of solutions can prevent this conductive loss, ranging from a small thickness of insulation placed in the concrete to the elimination of the parapet and overhang entirely.

A similar situation occurs when a concrete wall extends from the interior to the exterior of a building to form a retaining wall or support for an overhang. One solution is to use another material—a wood retaining wall, for example—to break the path of conduction. Two of the most common solutions to reduce heat transfer through these extending walls are shown in the adjacent illustrations. In figure 8-16, insulation is placed around the entire projecting masonry wall, while in figure 8-17 a smaller amount of insulation is placed in a break in the wall, which thermally separates the inside and outside sections. Another common location for a thermal break is at the base of an exposed wall, to protect the floor slab and foundation from exposure to the outside conditions. For further discussion of these critical details and examples of alternative solutions, see chapter 10.

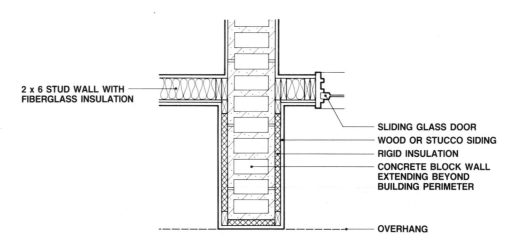

2 x 6 STUD WALL WITH
FIBERGLASS INSULATION

SLIDING GLASS DOOR
WOOD OR STUCCO SIDING
RIGID INSULATION
CONCRETE BLOCK WALL
EXTENDING BEYOND
BUILDING PERIMETER

OVERHANG

8-16: Detail at Extended Bearing Wall (Plan)

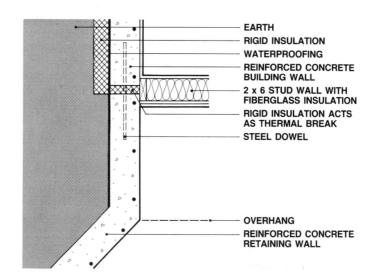

EARTH
RIGID INSULATION
WATERPROOFING
REINFORCED CONCRETE
BUILDING WALL
2 x 6 STUD WALL WITH
FIBERGLASS INSULATION
RIGID INSULATION ACTS
AS THERMAL BREAK
STEEL DOWEL

OVERHANG
REINFORCED CONCRETE
RETAINING WALL

8-17: Detail at Building Corner (Plan)

Insulation Materials

Selection Criteria

Many types of insulation products, with a wide range of characteristics, are available. No one product can be considered the best choice under all circumstances. In selecting an insulation material for application to below-grade roofs and walls, some very special and, in most cases, stringent criteria must be met. The criteria on which to base product selection depend on the specific conditions of the design, as well as on some value judgments concerning costs. Perhaps the most important determinant in the selection process is the specific location of the insulation in the building envelope. In the areas of the envelope that are to be insulated, there are basically four locations for the insulation material: within or inside the structure; outside the structure but inside the waterproofing; outside the structure and the waterproofing; and within the soil mass, detached from the building. The location of the insulation affects a number of important factors related to heating and cooling performance, as well as other concerns such as the suitability of various types of waterproofing and insulation products. The characteristics of each of the four insulation locations are discussed below, along with the major criteria for selecting insulation products.

insulation within or inside structure

Insulation within the building envelope is typically used on a conventional wood-frame structure (which can be built underground with treated wood). Fiberglass batts typically are used for such structures, as shown in figure 8-18. In a concrete or masonry structure, the insulation can be placed on the inside face of the structure (see fig. 8-19). Various types of rigid board insulation are commonly used for these types of structures. Although fiberglass could be used within a wood-frame wall built inside the concrete structure, it is uneconomical to build a second wood wall inside the concrete wall since a greater thickness is required due to the lower insulating value per inch of fiberglass.

One advantage of locating insulation within or inside the structure is that less expensive insulation materials can be used than those required for insulating outside the structure, because the materials located inside do not have to withstand earth pressures and moisture conditions in the ground. In addition, inside insulation should be safer from possible rodent damage and can retain a higher percentage of its original R-value with less exposure to moisture and degradation.

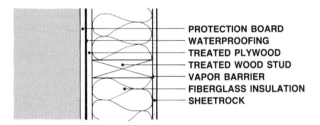

8-18: Insulation Within Wall

PROTECTION BOARD
WATERPROOFING
TREATED PLYWOOD
TREATED WOOD STUD
VAPOR BARRIER
FIBERGLASS INSULATION
SHEETROCK

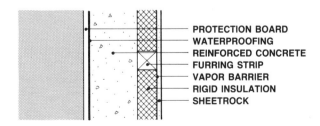

8-19: Insulation Inside Structure

PROTECTION BOARD
WATERPROOFING
REINFORCED CONCRETE
FURRING STRIP
VAPOR BARRIER
RIGID INSULATION
SHEETROCK

Finally, this type of insulation placement is relatively simple, and heat loss through the concrete structure (control of which requires thermal breaks and complicated details) is less of a concern than it is with insulation placed outside the structure.

A major disadvantage of this type of insulation placement is that it reduces the effectiveness of a massive structure in storing solar heat gain, dampening temperature fluctuations, and assisting in passive cooling. Because a wood-frame house has far less mass than a concrete or masonry structure, however, this disadvantage is somewhat irrelevant for that case. Another disadvantage of insulating inside is that freezing temperatures may occur within the wall; this situation can cause structural damage over a number of freeze-thaw cycles if moisture is present. A vapor barrier should be installed on the warm side of the insulation to prevent moisture from condensing within the insulation, which will reduce the thermal resistance of most products.

Because the insulation in this application is not exposed to soil pressures and moisture, the same criteria used in considering conventional insulation can be applied. Important general considerations are low cost, good availability, easy installation, and good dimensional and R-value stability over a long period of time. In addition, products applied on the inside must be safe with regard to the release of toxic fumes, both during a fire and under normal conditions. An insulation product that has been covered with drywall is usually considered safe for an adequate period of time in the event of fire.

insulation outside the structure but inside the waterproofing

If insulation is placed outside the structure, the thermal mass of the concrete or masonry structure is available to work with the passive heating and cooling systems (fig. 8-20). Insulation located inside the waterproofing does not have to withstand the moisture conditions of the ground and will retain a higher percentage of its original R-value by remaining dry. It is necessary to place a vapor barrier on the warm side of the structure or use an insulation product that serves as a vapor barrier itself to prevent condensation within the insulation. Although insulation located outside the structure does have to withstand the ground pressures, it has the advantage of cushioning the structure against frost pressures. Locating the insulation on the outside of a concrete structure requires careful attention, including the use of thermal breaks, to prevent thermal short circuits. A major disadvantage of this arrangement relates to potential waterproofing failures. It is best to apply waterproofing directly to the structure because it is more stable than insulation.

This type of application represents an attempt to gain some of the benefits of insulating outside the structure while protecting the insulation from the soil moisture by placing the waterproofing on the outside. Although it creates opportunities to use some insulation products in a more favorable environment, it is generally not recommended because it creates other problems. Not only is it considered far less desirable to place the waterproofing on the insulation, but moisture can be trapped within the insulation from an undetected leak in the moisture barrier on either side of the

insulation. Thus, this is an unlikely application. Nevertheless, if this arrangement is used, insulation products must meet the typical criteria of low cost, good availability, easy installation, and a stable R-value over time. In addition, the insulation must have a good compressive strength to resist soil pressures.

insulation outside the structure and waterproofing

In many ways this arrangement in which the insulation is placed outside both the structure and the waterproofing (fig. 8-21) is similar to the previous case. For example, the thermal mass of the concrete is available for use in passive heating and cooling. As in the above case, the insulation must withstand ground pressures but also acts as a cushion against frost pressure. Also, the insulation must be installed carefully and completely to prevent heat loss through thermal short circuits because concrete is highly conductive. There are some very important differences, however, between insulation located on the outside, rather than on the inside, of the waterproofing. Placing insulation outermost means that the waterproofing can be applied directly to the structure and will remain at a more stable temperature. No additional vapor barrier is required, and the insulation can serve as a protection board for the waterproofing. Finally, virtually any thickness of insulation can be added without requiring any additional structure.

The disadvantage of this arrangement is that the insulation material is exposed to a harsher environment than it is in the two previous cases. It may be attacked by insects and rodents, but most importantly, it is exposed to the moisture in the

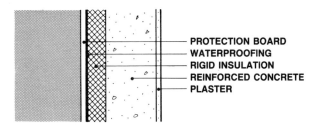

8-20: Insulation Outside Structure but Inside Waterproofing

- PROTECTION BOARD
- WATERPROOFING
- RIGID INSULATION
- REINFORCED CONCRETE
- PLASTER

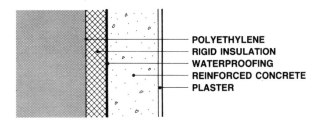

8-21: Insulation Outside Structure and Waterproofing

- POLYETHYLENE
- RIGID INSULATION
- WATERPROOFING
- REINFORCED CONCRETE
- PLASTER

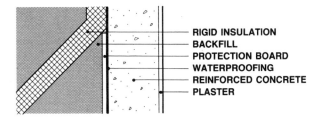

8-22: Insulation in Soil Mass Detached from Building

- RIGID INSULATION
- BACKFILL
- PROTECTION BOARD
- WATERPROOFING
- REINFORCED CONCRETE
- PLASTER

ground, which not only can degrade some products but also can reduce their insulating value considerably. If this insulation arrangement is selected, it is essential to use more expensive insulation products that are best suited to perform under these potentially more harmful conditions.

Although criteria for insulation products are much more stringent for this insulation arrangement than for other applications, this is by far the most common and generally recommended arrangement for earth sheltered structures. The most important characteristics of insulation materials that are in contact with the earth are: a high resistance to water absorption so that the R-value is not greatly reduced over time, high compressive strength, and good resistance to soil chemicals. Assuming these criteria are met, it is also desirable to select the product that has the lowest relative cost, best availability, and easiest installation.

insulation within the soil mass, detached from the building

In all of the three insulation locations discussed above, the direct coupling of the interior of the space to the surrounding earth for cooling purposes is inhibited. Insulation should usually be placed in the areas of greatest wintertime loss near the surface, and no insulation should be placed in the deeper areas, where the greatest cooling benefit occurs. One relatively untested solution suggests placing the insulation within the soil mass, detached from the building, as shown in figure 8-22. The intent is to enhance the cooling benefits by enclosing a larger mass within the insulated envelope while still placing insulation between the building and the surface to limit heat loss in winter. Preliminary calculations have indicated that cooling benefits can be had, but at a cost of increased winter heat loss that could range from slight to very substantial. This application could be suited to unusual situations, such as for insulating curvilinear shell structures (which are hard to insulate with flat materials) or for retrofitting existing basements.

Like insulation applied to the outside of the wall, insulation products in the soil mass must be capable of resisting the ground moisture conditions and attack by insects and rodents. Achieving an adequately high level of resistance generally requires some of the more expensive insulation products. This location arrangement may present some additional drawbacks. Movement in the soil because of settlement and even slight movement during backfilling could damage even the best products, resulting in breaks, gaps, and thermal short circuits. Good backfill compaction under the insulation and careful backfill above are necesary for any success with this approach.

Of the four basic configurations, this is the most experimental and least tested approach. Aside from the heat transfer questions, one of the greatest concerns with this arrangement is the ability of any insulation product to resist pressures from backfilling and settlement. Assuming that these problems can be overcome, the criteria for selecting an insulation product are the same as those given for insulation outside the structure and waterproofing.

Characteristics of Typical Insulation Materials

Figure 8-23 shows the basic characteristics of the major types of insulation that are typically considered for below-grade use. One of the most important criteria for selecting insulation to be used on the outside of the structure below grade is the stability of the R-value over time. Conclusive and objective results can be somewhat difficult to obtain, and the confusion is compounded by the wide range of products with differing performances that may fall under a single category, such as expanded polystyrene. A range of R-values is given according to the variation in available test results [8.6, 8.7, 8.8]. The major types of insulation listed on the chart are discussed below.

extruded polystyrene

This type of insulation is the most highly recommended for below-grade applications where the insulation is exposed to the soil. It has a good resistance to moisture absorption and retains a high percentage of its initial R-value for at least ten years. It is also resistant to soil chemicals and has a relatively high compressive strength. There appears to be little significant difference between the performance of products from the two major manufacturers of extruded polystyrene. The only real drawback of this product is its relatively high cost in comparison to insulation suited for inside use only, such as fiberglass or lower-density expanded polystyrene. Thus, it would not be the recommended choice for inside applications for which the performance criteria are not as demanding. If used in interior applications, it should not be left exposed but should be covered by drywall or other fire-protective material approved by thc building code.

expanded polystyrene

Unlike extruded polystyrene, which basically is manufactured by two well-known producers, expanded polystyrene products are made and sold by approximately one hundred different companies. The density and quality of the material can vary considerably among the various products. Generally, expanded polystyrene products lack the compressive strength of extruded polystyrene and absorb moisture more readily, thus reducing their insulating value in wet ground conditions. The advantage of expanded polystyrene over the extruded product is its lower cost, which makes it worth considering, provided that it can be kept dry and that it is strong enough to withstand the loads placed on it. A higher-density product will have greater compressive strength and be better suited for below-grade application. The higher the density is, however, the higher the cost. In general, the lower-density expanded polystyrene is not recommended in an exposed, below-grade situation; the higher-density (1.5 pounds per cubic foot or more) products are better but still questionable. If expanded polystyrene is used on the exterior, a polyethylene sheet should be placed on the outside to provide at least minimum protection from ground moisture. For inside applications or in conditions where dryness can be assured, expanded polystyrene is recommended as a lower-cost alternative to the extruded product.

product	density (lbs/cf)	initial R-value per inch	probable R-value per inch with time[1]	cost per board ft. (dollars)	R-value per dollar[2]	recommendation for below grade use directly exposed to ground
low density expanded polystyrene (white)	1.0	3.8	2.8-3.0	.13	21.5-23.0	not recommended—based on condition of recovered samples
high density expanded polystyrene (white)	1.5	4.5	no data published	.23	not applicable	insufficient information for recommendation
extruded polystyrene (blue)	2.0	5.0	4.5-4.9	.30	15.0-16.3	yes
extruded polystyrene (pink)	1.7	5.0	no data published[3]	.26	not applicable	yes
urethane foam	2.0	6.2-7.2	3.0-5.2	.36[4]	8.3-14.4	not recommended—based on moisture gain in laboratory and field tests
fiberglass	not applicable	3.2	not applicable	.05	not applicable	not recommended—not intended for this application

8-23: Characteristics of Various Insulation Materials

1. Probable R-value per inch with time refers to situation where insulation is under adverse moisture conditions as it would be if exposed below grade. Figures in the chart for R-value per inch with time are based on testing of previously buried samples [8.6], controlled laboratory testing under a vapor pressure differential across the sample [8.7], and recent test data from an underground building installation [8.8].

2. R-value per dollar figures are based on R-value with time.

3. Although there is no published data on this relatively new product, early tests indicate performance will be similar to the blue extruded polystyrene.

4. Cost of urethane foam varies with R-value and type of facing.

outdoor atmosphere. In addition, with adequate design, installation, and maintenance of ventilation equipment, indoor pollutant levels need not be so high as to rule out the use of combustion in an earth sheltered house. In a study headed by Moschandres, energy-efficient houses were monitored for fourteen days. With no gas cooking or heating, outdoor levels of nitric oxide almost always exceeded indoor levels. With a gas furnace and electric cooking, nitric oxide levels were higher inside than outside most of the time. With gas for both heating and cooking, indoor nitric oxide levels almost always exceeded outdoor levels, with peaks corresponding to cooking times [8.9, 8.10].

Carbon monoxide is not the only pollutant produced by combustion of wood. A high level of polycyclic organic matter, including a benzopyrene and other known or suspected carcinogens, were emitted from two wood-burning stoves and a fireplace monitored by Monsanto Research. It has also been suggested that the warm, humid environment of rock beds used for storage in solar heating systems are a source of potential growth of organic matter, although good long-term experiences with the air quality from rockbeds are regularly reported. Potential pollution hazards associated with electric heat move the discussion of environmental effects of coal and nuclear energy to a more remote level that has broader societal implications. The point is not that any of these heat sources is necessarily a health hazard—many houses use one or more of them with no apparent ill effects to the inhabitants. Rather, the point is that because various pollutants come from a wide variety of sources, the issue is less one of picking a "clean" source of energy than one of

dealing effectively with potential pollution problems associated with the energy source selected.

The selection of a heat source for a conventional house usually includes the requirements that it be readily available at any time and that it be automatic, so that it will operate if the owner is too busy or too ill to tend it or is gone for a long period of time. While these criteria are also desirable for an earth sheltered house and may be very important because of the life-styles of the occupants, in some cases the options for an earth sheltered house may be less restrictive. Because most earth sheltered homes are characterized by generally low heat loss and high thermal mass, they can maintain a reasonable temperature over a relatively long time. A heat source that operates only periodically is a possibility for such houses, because heat can be stored in the mass of the building when the heat source is operating and will radiate out to warm the space when the other heat source is not operating. Thus, a wood fire, even if it dies down while the residents are sleeping or absent, or solar heat, which is unusable at night or when there is heavy cloud cover, can be a practical, major heat source for an earth sheltered home.

An earth-covered residence in Shakopee, Minnesota, was monitored for a two-and-a-half month period without heat, when outside temperatures fell as low as $-15°F$. It took one full month for the temperature to fall from an initial temperature of $68°F$ to $40°F$. For the remainder of the test period, the temperature stayed within $5°F$ of this figure [8.11]. Of course, as a rule, because house designs and weather conditions vary, houses should not be left unattended for long periods unless

precautions have been taken to prevent damage from frozen pipes.

Off-peak electrical energy is another strategy for using energy that might not be suitable for most conventional houses. In order to make more efficient use of their generating capacity, some utility companies will charge less for electricity used during nighttime hours, when demand is lower. If a house is served by a utility with that rate structure, electric heating could be run primarily at night, when the electricity rates are lower. Usually the need for heat is greater at night, when temperatures are frequently lower and there is no solar gain. Heat stored in the mass of the building will help keep it comfortable with little or no electricity during the day, when the higher daytime power rates are in effect. Although off-peak rates are not available in all areas, they are likely to become more widely available as power companies explore alternatives to constructing more generators. Even if off-peak rates are not regularly available, a power company might be willing to offer them on a test basis to a few residences to study how they affect costs and consumption. The lower rates might also affect other patterns of electricity usage, for example, users might tend to run dishwashing machines, clothes washers and dryers, and even ovens more during off-peak hours, rather than during regular daytime hours. Of course all restrictions on electricity usage should be considered when potential savings are being evaluated.

A frequently suggested energy conservation measure for conventional houses is to set the thermostat down to a lower temperature at night or whenever the house is unoccupied for substantial periods during the day. This operation may be automated relatively easily through the use of a clock thermostat that automatically raises or lowers the temperatures at preset times. Thus, the house can be warmed up when the occupants get up in the morning or return from activities away from home without maintaining these higher temperatures when they are not needed.

In a low heat loss, high thermal mass structure such as a typical earth sheltered home, more factors affect the usefulness of this strategy. Because less heat loss occurs in such a home, less can be gained by lowering the house temperature for periods of a few hours. In addition, because the large mass causes both cooling off and warming up of the structure to occur very slowly, the times that the temperature of a room are low or high do not necessarily coincide directly with the times when the temperature on the thermostat are set lower or higher. Thus, an automatic thermostat would have to be set to lower the temperature a rather long time before the lower temperature was actually desired; conversely, it would have to be set to start raising the temperature again well before the warmth was needed. Although these adjustments can be made, it may be very difficult to assess accurately the impact of all the factors involved in achieving maximum efficiency with a set-back system (the amount of thermal mass in the house, the amount of heat stored in it, and the time required to cool off and warm up the mass under various conditions). Because the gains to be had from such a system are already relatively small for an earth sheltered structure, less than optimum operation of the system may reduce its usefulness below the point at which it is worth including in the house.

A house that uses a fluctuating heat source must be designed to limit overheating as much as possible. When a house is kept at a constant low temperature, the inhabitants learn to dress accordingly and adjust to the usual temperature so that they are comfortable at a lower temperature than might be expected. If solar heat or a crackling fire makes all or part of the interior space very warm during certain times of day or night, however, the occupants will adjust to the higher temperature and may come to desire that temperature for comfort. In such a case, the residents will probably either feel cold in lower temperatures that would be acceptable if they were kept at a constant level, or they will push the thermostat higher to keep the temperatures at the higher level all the time. This situation can reduce the anticipated cost savings associated with some types of fluctuating heat sources; it can also significantly increase the amount of supplemental energy necessary for the occupants to feel comfortable in a house that by calculation should be energy self-sufficient. Such physiological and psychological factors can overshadow numerical calculations of Btu's gained or lost. The habits and patterns of the occupants in their daily activities—door and window opening, cooking, and setting of the thermostat—can greatly affect energy consumption regardless of building design. This variable often accounts for the difference in calculated and actual performance.

heat distribution systems

Many of the considerations in the distribution of heating and cooling are the same for an earth sheltered as for a conventional house, except that the quality of the air may take on more importance and the temperature less importance for the earth sheltered house. A room that has relatively constant temperatures and low infiltration may need fresh air more often than it needs heating or cooling, or it may require that water vapor be added or removed. Although hot water heat provides quiet, economical heat that is easy to control for individual rooms, it does not deal with air quality and requires operating temperatures that may be too high to couple efficiently with some alternate energy sources, such as solar heating. Radiant heating systems can often integrate well with the mass of the structure; prestressed concrete plank cores can even be used as part of the system. Because a uniform surface temperature is achievable with these systems, the occupants can remain comfortable at relatively low air temperatures. This system cannot, however, accommodate air purification needs. Gravity systems, which are low in cost and independent in the event of power failures, may not work well with some house configurations (for example, a long, one-story elevational house).

A forced-air system works well for heating, cooling, air purification, humidification, and dehumidification; can reduce vertical stratification of air; works with low temperatures that integrate well with alternate energy systems; presents no danger of water leaks; and may provide desirable background noise in a quiet environment. In a conventional house, because the ductwork for a forced-air system often passes through conditioned space—in the walls or ceilings of rooms, the basement, or an insulated crawl space—heat lost from the duct is lost to habitable space rather than being wasted. In an earth sheltered house, it is more likely that at least some ductwork will be located below grade. It is not unusual to see detail drawings showing insulation carefully placed on both sides of the duct, below it, and even above it, as shown in figure 8-24. This insulation arrangement is considered to be important because the air in the duct has a much higher temperature than the room air; therefore, a higher temperature differential exists between the duct air temperature and the outside temperature. The temperature differential directly affects the heat loss. Many of these insulation arrangements are labor intensive and, thus, relatively expensive.

If the earth mass below the slab is insulated from exterior cold at its perimeter as shown in figure 8-24, not all of the heat lost to the ground from the duct will be completely lost since the heat is trapped somewhat by the exterior insulation. Although more research is needed on the heat flow in this situation, a directly insulated duct will maintain better heating distribution, particularly at the ends of the duct runs where distribution air temperatures could be considerably cooler for an uninsulated duct. Factory-insulated ducts, however, may be more economical than installing insulation around the duct at the site. In any event, the earth mass below the slab should be separated from the exterior cold by insulation.

Some additional study on duct placement may also be well warranted because of the different conditions that exist in passively heated earth sheltered homes. In most houses built to date, it has been customary to supply warm air below high-loss areas such as windows and to place the return air in the highest part of the house, which frequently is also located above windows. Preliminary studies are beginning to suggest that this arrangement may adequately serve only the areas near the windows; it leaves the north part of the house, which is usually located away from the windows, inadequately supplied with warm circulating air. An alternative configuration that bears further study is a convection loop that would supply warm air at the bottom of the north wall (away from the windows). The air would then rise by convection to a high point near the windows. This process would cool the air, and thereby cause it to drop to the floor, where a cold air return would collect it and circulate it back to the furnace.

Cooling Systems

Similar to heating requirements, both the peak demand for cooling and the total amount of cooling required are lower for a properly designed earth sheltered house than for most conventional structures. In addition, earth sheltered structures can incorporate other strategies besides energy-consuming mechanical air-conditioning to lower temperatures (removing sensible heat) and dehumidify the house (removing latent heat). For example, ventilation not only increases the opportunity for conductive and convective loss of sensible heat, but also promotes evaporation, which absorbs latent heat, providing further cooling. Some cooling strategies, such as dehumidification and evaporative cooling, obviously conflict. A review of the climate conditions in different parts of the country will indicate the relative importance of each strategy for the various regions (see chapter 2).

In many areas, carefully designed ventilation alone will keep an earth sheltered house comfortable. In other

SHEETROCK
VAPOR BARRIER
2 x 6 STUD WALL WITH FIBERGLASS INSULATION
TILE FLOOR
CONCRETE FLOOR SLAB
SAND OR GRAVEL
VAPOR BARRIER
RIGID INSULATION
HEATING DUCT

WOOD SIDING
SHEATHING
ANCHOR BOLT
PROTECTION BOARD OR METAL FLASHING OVER INSULATION
RIGID INSULATION
CONCRETE BLOCK FOUNDATION

8-24: Heating Duct Beneath Floor at Building Perimeter

areas dehumidification may actually be the main concern. The designer of houses in these regions must be careful not to oversize air-conditioning units. An earth sheltered house, which realizes a substantial amount of cooling from earth contact, may need relatively little mechanical cooling but will need the same amount or possibly more dehumidification than a conventional house. In many instances a dehumidifier alone may be adequate for meeting cooling needs. In other situations a small air-conditioning unit that produces a small amount of cooling and is run much of the time may provide the best combination of cooling and dehumidification by itself. Of course, running such a unit for more time than is necessary for cooling reduces the economy of earth cooling. A central air-handling ventilation system incorporating a dehumidifier may be best in some cases.

Earth sheltering cools in three ways: by reducing heat gain; by radiant cooling, which occurs when cool surfaces are in contact with the earth; and by conductive heat loss to the large, cool mass of the soil. Although a variety of heat sources can be combined with earth sheltering to keep inhabitants warm, electricity is by far the most common type of energy used to mechanically assist any passive cooling measure, both for conventional and earth sheltered houses. Cooling is normally distributed through the same duct system that is used for heating. The optimum placement of supply and return openings is not necessarily the same for heating and cooling; however, the compromises required to make dual use of the system are generally minor enough so that both heating and cooling can be adequately provided.

Air Purity

Every house has a substantial amount of pollutants from the occupants, their activities, and the materials within the house. Even the simple boiling of vegetables in a stone fireplace pollutes the indoor air with odors from the vegetables, steam from the boiling, carbon monoxide from the fire, and radon from the stone of the fireplace. In the past, high infiltration has diluted and dissipated the pollution before it could do any harm. Now it is possible to build a house so tight that the pollution is not dissipated, but instead will build up over a period of time if it is not dealt with properly. The many different types of pollutants come from a variety of sources [8.9, 8.10, 8.12].

Dust and particulates can be made up of smoke, soot, mists, fibers, clay, silica, organic and mineral lints, decayed biological material, and metallic fragments. While the larger particles are filtered out by the upper respiratory tract, the smaller particles may be retained in the lungs. These types of pollutants are usually considered to be a relatively insignificant health hazard. As might be expected, higher levels of particulates have been found in homes where heavy smokers reside; however, these levels rarely exceed recommended standards. Curiously, houses in which small children live also appear to have higher levels of particulates.

Microorganisms and allergens are the most epidemiologically important pollutants. This group includes viruses, bacteria, plant pollen, spores, molds, fungi, and particles to which microorganisms cling. Where tobacco is smoked, the smoke is the greatest contributor to particulate matter in the air. While these more commonly

known pollutants may not be as frightening as carcinogens or some of the less familiar gases, they are a major cause of upper respiratory infection. The frequency of these infections, and the fact that they can be quite serious for those weakened by age or other health problems, make them as significant as some of the more feared but less common illnesses.

Gases from various sources are a third major group of pollutants. The principal gases are formaldehyde (CH_2O), carbon monoxide (CO), nitric oxide (NO), and nitrogen dioxide (NO_2). Formaldehyde is emitted from numerous products found in a home, including plywood, particle board, urea formaldehyde foam insulation, adhesives, and fabrics; a small amount also comes from combustion sources and cigarette smoke. Excessive formaldehyde can irritate the eyes, throat, and skin, and can cause allergies and respiratory problems. Carbon monoxide is also a product of combustion. Although it can be harmful or even fatal if concentrations are high enough, the concentrations found in monitored houses were not found to be high enough to be considered a health hazard. Nitric oxide and nitrogen dioxide levels are closely related to the amount of gas heating and cooking taking place within a space. Other gases may also be present. Because carbon dioxide (CO_2) is exhaled by occupants, its concentration level is directly related to the number and activity of people present in a given space. It is not unusual for most residences to exceed the ASHRAE standards for acceptable CO_2 levels. Small amounts of sulfur dioxide, ozone, water-soluble sulfate, and water-soluble nitrates are also found; however, in some cases concentrations were smaller inside the house than outside.

Although water vapor in the air is necessary for health and comfort and is also important in slowing the drying out of many materials within a house (for example, food and furniture), too much water vapor is undesirable. Excess water vapor can promote the growth of mold, mildew, and other microorganisms that can be detrimental to health, cause discomfort related to cold, damp conditions, or hot, humid conditions, and can cause condensation on cooler surfaces. If the house is not properly sealed, it may absorb water vapor from the soil through the building envelope. Even if the house is well sealed, water vapor is generated by the breathing and perspiration of the occupants, as well as by many of their activities, such as washing and cooking.

A final pollutant of particular concern in earth sheltered houses is radon. Radon is a very common component of our environment and was present long before human activity started to change the environment. It is a gas produced by the decay of radium 226, which in turn is a decay product of uranium 238. Because radium is a trace element in most soil and rock, it is present in many building materials, such as stone, concrete, and brick, and is also present in the soil around any building. Radon moves through the spaces between particles of soil until it escapes into the atmosphere or meets some dense barrier. It can also be transported by natural gas or water, especially water from deep wells. More radon is released when it is windy, the atmospheric pressure is low, or a shower sprays well water into the air; less is released when rain or frost make it more difficult for the radon to reach the surface. Cracks or openings in a foundation make

it easier for radon to enter a house; good waterproofing and sealing techniques make it more difficult; and good drainage helps provide radon with an alternate route of escape. Radon released from masonry, plaster, and gypsum board occurs even on upper floors of conventional houses. Radon will accumulate at a higher concentrations in an enclosed space. The more tightly sealed the building, the less the radon can dissipate.

Assuming that radon is present in some quantity, the first concern is understanding its potential harm. Radon has a short half-life of 3.8 days before it decays into short-lived daughter products, which emit alpha particles. These daughter products are solids. It is suspected that because of their atomic charge, the daughter products may attach themselves to dust particles that may be inhaled and retained by the lungs, thereby exposing them to alpha radiation. Some estimates of the potential impact of background exposure to radon and its daughters hypothesize that such exposure could account for up to 10 to 20 percent of lung cancer cases in the United States for nonsmokers; this figure translates into 1 to 4 percent of all lung cancers [8.12, 8.13]. It should be noted that this background exposure level applies to the entire population and is not related solely to an earth sheltered environment.

A different evaluation of the health effects of radon came from an epidemiological study of uranium miners cited by Harold May in "Ionizing Radiation Levels in Energy Conserving Structures" [8.14]. In a study of more than 4,000 miners exposed to less than 120 WLM of radon, statistical evidence of malignancy was slight, although some cases may develop later. (A WLM is a combination of radon decay

product concentrations, which will ultimately release 1.3×10^5 MEV of alpha energy per liter of air over a 170-working-hour month.) A person living in an average .01-WL atmosphere (the approximate level found in basements and earth sheltered homes that have been monitored) for fifteen hours per day, forty-nine weeks per year, would accumulate 3 WLM in ten years. Using currently available estimated environmental radon levels, May estimated the risk of cancer to be on the order of a few cases per million person years; the present risk of lung cancer for all males in this country is about six hundred times as great as this risk figure. The significance of radon will undoubtedly be debated further. For the present, designers should be aware that adequate ventilation can reduce the level of radon in an earth sheltered house to the same level as that found in a conventional house and that this ventilation would be necessary for a healthy environment even if radon did not exist.

strategies to reduce pollutants

As mentioned above, there are three basic strategies for dealing with the various pollutants. Some pollutants can be controlled at their source, by preventing them from entering or being formed, whereas others can be diluted with fresh air or exhausted from the space. The third strategy is to remove the pollutant within the space. The effectiveness of each strategy depends on the type of pollutant; the importance of the strategy depends on the degree of hazard associated with the pollutant.

Controlling or eliminating the source of pollution has two components—construction and life-style modifications. The practicality of both types of control will vary from situation to situation, depending on the type and nature of the pollutant. Construction modifications include using wood-frame construction rather than masonry or concrete in order to reduce radon buildup; having the structure tightly sealed and the exterior well drained in order to prevent radon from entering; selecting electric heating and cooking devices in order to eliminate products of combustion of gas, oil, or wood; and selecting building materials and furnishings that do not contain significant amounts of formaldehyde. Life-style modifications include decisions to prohibit smoking in the house; limit use of aerosols, solvents, cleaners, paints, and varnishes within the space; limit dust-producing activities, for example, sanding wood; and cover cooking pots and limit showering times in order to reduce humidity and radon levels.

A more common and often more practical strategy is to dilute the pollutants with fresh air from the outside or to remove the polluted air. In the past, conventional houses accomplished this by infiltration through cracks in the building and around doors and windows, drafts through vents and chimneys, and air entering and leaving as people opened doors to come and go. But all of these conditions and situations waste energy. In addition, development and use of better-fitting doors and windows, weatherstripping, tighter wall construction, and air-lock entries have made it possible to reduce the energy lost from a structure—and, concomitantly, the amount of fresh air that enters it. A problem results because an energy-efficient house must still have an adequate capacity to eliminate pollutants and replace the exhausted air with fresh air. It is possible to do this in a more controlled way, rather than by ventilating the house with whatever amount of air happens to flow through the cracks in the structure. Exhaust fans over ranges and in bathrooms, as well as vents and flues for clothes dryers, furnaces and fireplaces, remove many pollutants directly at their sources, before they can spread to the rest of the house. Such devices may, however, be too specialized in their function, too small for an entire house, or not operated frequently enough.

Determining how much fresh air is needed is a complex issue. Some pollutants, such as formaldehyde and radon, are generated regardless of the number or activities of occupants, whereas others, such as carbon dioxide, are directly related to these factors. Still other pollutants—carbon monoxide and nitrogen dioxide—are generated in some situations but not in others. A performance standard for air quality would simply limit the level of pollutants allowed; however, the designer and even the occupants may have no means of knowing how much of which pollutants are present. A prescriptive standard would set a definite amount of fresh air to be introduced and might establish limits on the number of occupants, their activities, or the size of the space. The consensus seems to be that approximately .5 air changes per hour is appropriate. It is important to note that this rate of exchange assumes a distribution and mingling of the fresh air so that most of the air is changed during a two-hour period; changing one-tenth of the air ten times over two hours is mathematically—but not functionally —equivalent.

Methods of increasing the energy efficiency of this process by the use of such devices as heat exchangers and earth tempering tubes are being studied and are discussed in more detail later in this chapter. Some type of automatic control may be necessary to achieve such a specific ventilation rate, as the residents may have no way of determining when ventilation is adequate or may neglect to operate the system manually. Development of a low-cost device that would detect pollutants, much as a thermostat detects cold or a smoke detector detects combustion, would enhance the efficiency of such a system.

The third method of enhancing air purity is to extract the pollutants from the air within the space. This can involve devices such as air filters or electronic cleaners, which remove particles, or devices to remove vapor and gas with sorbents such as activated charcoal or activated alumina. Abundant plants in a large greenhouse may be helpful in removing carbon dioxide.

Elements of any or all of the strategies to purify air can be used in combination. As with energy efficiency, probably the most effective method is that which attacks the problem on all fronts, using parts of whatever strategies are appropriate. Combining air purification strategies with energy and conservation strategies adds another layer of sophistication and complexity but should be considered in terms of achieving an effective end product. Two of these strategies, heat exchangers and earth tempering tubes, are discussed below. Heat exchangers are included because they represent a major emerging technique to solve the air purity problem. Although little is known about the cost efficiency of earth tempering tubes, they are discussed because they are closely related to earth sheltering.

Heat Exchangers

Exhausting pollutants and introducing fresh clean air from the outside involves exhausting conditioned air that has used energy to be warmed or cooled to a comfortable temperature and replacing it with air from the exterior that requires additional energy to bring it to comfort level. In order to maximize energy conservation while meeting health standards for indoor air, it is desirable to replace the polluted indoor air with fresh outside air without losing the heat contained in the exhausted air. The device for accomplishing this is the heat exchanger.

The principle behind a heat exchanger is quite simple. Heat is taken out of the air going through the exchanger in one direction (to the outside environment) and is transferred to the air going in the opposite direction (to the interior of the space). Under ideal, completely efficient conditions, given 70°F air in a room and 30°F air outside, air exhausted through a heat exchanger would be used to heat air drawn into the space from 30°F to 70°F; in this process, the air being exhausted would be cooled from 70°F to 30°F. Although, in reality, total efficiency is impossible to achieve, a heat exchanger will improve energy efficiency to some degree because any heat that can be salvaged from the air being exhausted is heat that does not have to be replaced by some other, more energy-intensive means. Efficiencies of 60 percent or better in this energy transfer are not difficult to achieve. (For the sake of simplicity, this discussion of exchangers assumes that the exterior air is cold and that the intake air requires heating, even though most of the same principles apply equally if the interior air has been cooled and the exterior air is hot.)

Several different principles have been used to develop different kinds of heat exchangers [8.15]. The first type is the rotary heat exchanger. In the past, this type of device was primarily made in larger sizes aimed at the commercial and industrial market; however, smaller, residential units are now becoming available. The heat-exchanging element is a rotating disc, half of which is located in the exhaust duct and half in the intake duct. The rotating disc has many small passages running through it parallel to the axle. The warm exhaust air must go through these passages; as it does so, it gives up heat from the air, warming the disc material surrounding the passage. The disc rotates whenever the exchanger is in operation, so that the warmed passages are rotated into the cold intake air passages. This process cools the disc and warms the incoming air as it goes through the passages. The disc continues to rotate so that the cooled part of the disc then returns to the warm air exhaust duct, where it is reheated while cooling more exhaust air, and the cycle repeats itself.

A few degrees of the circle may be blocked off from the ductwork in order to prevent polluted exhaust air from being in transit through the passage when the passage is moving from the exhaust to the intake duct. Thus, any given passage has exhaust air flowing out through it slightly less than half the time and intake air flowing in through it slightly less than half the time; in the balance of the time, the air between the exhaust and intake is purged in order to prevent cross-pollution. With this system, if frost is formed during half of the cycle, it should be immediately and automatically removed during the other half of the cycle, rather than continuing to build up until the air passage is blocked by the accumulated frost.

A second type of heat exchanger uses evacuated, sealed, refrigerant-filled tubes. One end of the tube is placed in the warm exhaust duct and the other end in the cool intake duct; an airtight partition is placed between the two ducts. The warm air causes the refrigerant to evaporate, thereby absorbing heat from the air and cooling the exhaust. Because the tube is slightly tilted, the evaporated refrigerant rises to the other end of the tube, where the cold intake air cools the refrigerant, causing it to condense and then release its latent heat to warm the incoming air. The refrigerant, now cooled and condensed into a liquid, then runs back down the sloped tube to the lower end, located in the exhaust duct. Here, as the refrigerant is again warmed, it absorbs latent heat to evaporate, and the cycle repeats itself. The slope of the tubes can be adjusted or even reversed to change from a heating to a cooling mode.

In the third, most common type of heat exchanger, incoming and outgoing air simply pass through many passages that are close together but separated by any material that readily transmits heat [8.16]. For example, the exchanging unit of one type of heat exchanger is made of layers of corrugated paper. The corrugations on each layer are perpendicular to those on the layer above and below. Thus, exhaust air enters and leaves the exchanger in one direction and the intake air enters and leaves in the perpendicular direction; the two types of air cross each other in thin, alternating layers to exchange their heat but are always separated by the paper.

Within this type of exchanger, there is a distinction between those exchangers in which a water-permeable material separates the exhaust from the intake, and those that use an impermeable material. A water-permeable material will permit water vapor and the latent heat it contains to pass from one direction to the other. In a heating mode, this process will permit recovery of a greater amount of heat and retention of more humidity in the space and will reduce the likelihood of water vapor condensing and freezing within the exchanger, thus eventually blocking the passageways. In the cooling mode, the permeable material should permit some of the humidity from warm, damp exterior air to be transferred to the dryer, cooler exhausted air and, again, will result in the transfer of a greater total amount of heat. When excessive humidity occurs in a heating mode, however, a permeable filter will be less effective in eliminating the excess moisture. Although, in the past, many homes have suffered from excessive dryness in the wintertime, in a tightly sealed house, it may be important to remove some of the moisture generated by breathing, bathing, cooking, and washing.

There are several general design considerations for heat exchangers, regardless of the specific type used. The first is that intake and exhaust points should not be located too close together on either the exterior or interior of the house. If they are too close together on the exterior, the polluted air may simply be recirculated back into the house. If they are too close together inside, the fresh outside air may simply be immediately exhausted, leaving most of the polluted air inside.

A second consideration involves control of the heat exchanger. If it is manually controlled, the occupants have no way of knowing when it is needed or not needed, as many pollutants are not detectable without special equipment. In addition, it is very easy to forget to turn on or turn off the heat exchanger, or overlook a malfunction, because its results are not noticeable. Therefore, some system of automatic controls and a pilot light or warning light to indicate proper operation of the system are useful. Also, it is best not to include the range exhaust fan in any collection system for the heat exchanger, as the grease can easily clog the system. A final concern is that frost can form from cooling humid air, thus blocking the system. Some heat exchangers introduce a small electric heater into the unit in order to alleviate this problem. Because this measure reduces the energy efficiency of the system, its advantages must be weighed carefully against its drawbacks.

Earth-Tempering Tubes

Another strategy for tempering the air in the house makes use of the thermal mass of the earth. Air enters the house through long, underground tubes. The air is tempered by the relatively constant temperature of the earth around the tube so that fresh intake air is warmed by the earth in the winter and cooled by the earth in the summer. Unfortunately, there is a dearth of hard data available on the actual effectiveness of this type of system. Several rules of thumb have emerged, however. It appears that, because the thermal conductivity of the tube material makes very little difference, system

selection can be based on other criteria. A depth of less than 6 feet seems to subject the tubes excessively to surface temperatures, whereas a depth of more than 12 feet is too difficult to trench safely (although any narrow trench can be a safety hazard). A tube diameter of 4 to 12 inches seems to be most appropriate, and two short tubes seem to work better than one long tube [8.17].

The tube inlet can be located in a shady spot for summertime cooling, or a closed loop that starts and ends within the house can be used. There is some question about how much comfort is enhanced by earth-tempering tubes in a warm, damp climate, because if the amount of water in the air remains the same while the air temperature goes down, the relative humidity is increased. It is difficult to slope a long tube to drain leaks and condensation from it.

Another strategy suggested for tempering fresh air is to use two tubes, one for intake and the other for exhaust. The temperature of the intake tube would tend to approach the outside air temperature, while the exhaust tube temperature would approach the interior air temperature. The functions of the two tubes would be interchanged periodically to take advantage of this phenomenon.

There are two major concerns about earth tubes. The first is whether the benefits gained from the tubes are sufficient to justify the cost involved. The second is a health concern. The humidity and temperature inside the tubes may be ideal for growth of microorganisms. There is also danger of unsanitary conditions developing within the tubes as a result of actions of rodents or pets. Therefore, although sufficient data have not been accumulated to warrant a recommendation for or against earth tubes, caution in installing and using them is advised. An option is to use indirect tempering of intake air by a system of liquid-filled tubes exchanging heat with the earth. This would eliminate the health concerns and possibly provide more efficient heat transfer.

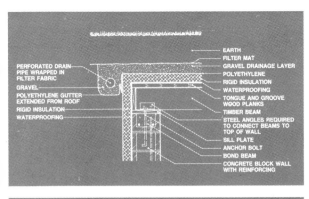

PERFORATED DRAIN PIPE WRAPPED IN FILTER FABRIC
GRAVEL
POLYETHYLENE GUTTER EXTENDED FROM ROOF
RIGID INSULATION
WATERPROOFING

EARTH
FILTER MAT
GRAVEL DRAINAGE LAYER
POLYETHYLENE
RIGID INSULATION
WATERPROOFING
TONGUE AND GROOVE WOOD PLANKS
TIMBER BEAM
STEEL ANGLES REQUIRED TO CONNECT BEAMS TO TOP OF WALL
SILL PLATE
ANCHOR BOLT
BOND BEAM
CONCRETE BLOCK WALL WITH REINFORCING

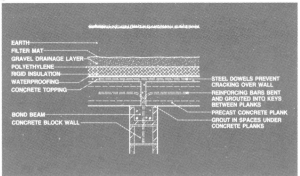

EARTH
FILTER MAT
GRAVEL DRAINAGE LAYER
POLYETHYLENE
RIGID INSULATION
WATERPROOFING
CONCRETE TOPPING

BOND BEAM
CONCRETE BLOCK WALL

STEEL DOWELS PREVENT CRACKING OVER WALL
REINFORCING BARS BENT AND GROUTED INTO KEYS BETWEEN PLANKS
PRECAST CONCRETE PLANK
GROUT IN SPACES UNDER CONCRETE PLANKS

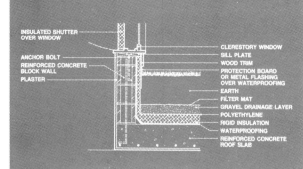

INSULATED SHUTTER OVER WINDOW

ANCHOR BOLT
REINFORCED CONCRETE BLOCK WALL
PLASTER

CLERESTORY WINDOW
SILL PLATE
WOOD TRIM
PROTECTION BOARD OR METAL FLASHING OVER WATERPROOFING
EARTH
FILTER MAT
GRAVEL DRAINAGE LAYER
POLYETHYLENE
RIGID INSULATION
WATERPROOFING
REINFORCED CONCRETE ROOF SLAB

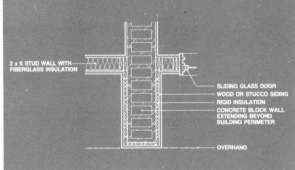

2 x 6 STUD WALL WITH FIBERGLASS INSULATION

SLIDING GLASS DOOR
WOOD OR STUCCO SIDING
RIGID INSULATION
CONCRETE BLOCK WALL EXTENDING BEYOND BUILDING PERIMETER

OVERHANG

CHAPTER 9

LANDSCAPE DESIGN

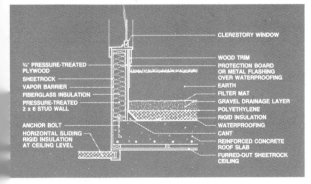

¾" PRESSURE-TREATED PLYWOOD
SHEETROCK
VAPOR BARRIER
FIBERGLASS INSULATION
PRESSURE-TREATED 2 x 6 STUD WALL

ANCHOR BOLT
HORIZONTAL SLIDING RIGID INSULATION AT CEILING LEVEL

CLERESTORY WINDOW

WOOD TRIM
PROTECTION BOARD OR METAL FLASHING OVER WATERPROOFING
EARTH
FILTER MAT
GRAVEL DRAINAGE LAYER
POLYETHYLENE
RIGID INSULATION
WATERPROOFING
CANT
REINFORCED CONCRETE ROOF SLAB
FURRED-OUT SHEETROCK CEILING

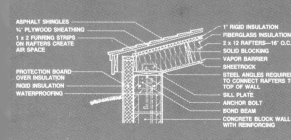

ASPHALT SHINGLES
¾" PLYWOOD SHEATHING
1 x 2 FURRING STRIPS ON RAFTERS CREATE AIR SPACE

PROTECTION BOARD OVER INSULATION
RIGID INSULATION
WATERPROOFING

1" RIGID INSULATION
FIBERGLASS INSULATION
2 x 12 RAFTERS—16" O.C.
SOLID BLOCKING
VAPOR BARRIER
SHEETROCK
STEEL ANGLES REQUIRED TO CONNECT RAFTERS TO TOP OF WALL
SILL PLATE
ANCHOR BOLT
BOND BEAM
CONCRETE BLOCK WALL WITH REINFORCING

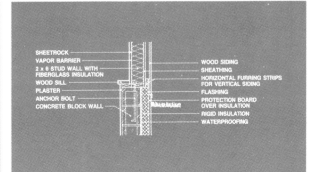

SHEETROCK
VAPOR BARRIER
2 x 6 STUD WALL WITH FIBERGLASS INSULATION
WOOD SILL
PLASTER
ANCHOR BOLT
CONCRETE BLOCK WALL

WOOD SIDING
SHEATHING
HORIZONTAL FURRING STRIPS FOR VERTICAL SIDING
FLASHING
PROTECTION BOARD OVER INSULATION
RIGID INSULATION
WATERPROOFING

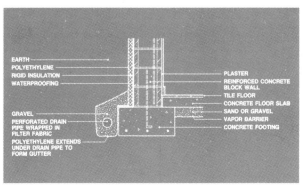

EARTH
POLYETHYLENE
RIGID INSULATION
WATERPROOFING

GRAVEL
PERFORATED DRAIN PIPE WRAPPED IN FILTER FABRIC
POLYETHYLENE EXTENDS UNDER DRAIN PIPE TO FORM GUTTER

PLASTER
REINFORCED CONCRETE BLOCK WALL
TILE FLOOR
CONCRETE FLOOR SLAB
SAND OR GRAVEL
VAPOR BARRIER
CONCRETE FOOTING

Introduction

Landscaping is one component of the total process of building design. Landscape design is not limited to the selection of appropriate plant materials after the building design is complete; rather, it involves attention to site planning and the design of the overall form of the building, as well as to more detailed concerns such as determination of appropriate soils mixes and drainage systems. Many of these aspects—site design, building form, and waterproofing—are discussed in other chapters of this book.

This chapter is concerned with plant materials as they relate to more detailed technical landscape considerations as well as to the total landscape design. In discussing the landscape design for earth sheltered buildings, two aspects deserve special attention. The first is the design of a complete environment that will provide sustained growth for the plant materials. The design of this environment requires the combination of basic landscape technologies—soils, water, nutrients, and the shaping of the container—with building technologies, such as the structural, waterproofing, and insulation systems used in the structure. The second major concern of this chapter is the selection of plants that can best mirror the character of the surrounding natural landscape in order to integrate it with the newly built form of the earth sheltered structure. In earth sheltered building design, these two areas of technology are inseparable.

Determining the key landscape design issues to be resolved for an earth sheltered building is not a routine task. The problems are complex, involving a number of interdependent variables, and the state of the art is still at an early stage of development. It is essential to resolve these problems since reluctance to deal with them will result in missed opportunities at the very least and, in some cases, may have disastrous consequences in terms of both overall cost economies or technical failures.

This chapter represents a first attempt to identify the most important considerations and problems in landscape design of earth sheltered structures. It focuses on rooftop planting, which is the most difficult and unknown aspect of this landscape design application. The first major section of the chapter discusses all of the issues that relate to the physical design of the rooftop container; the second section deals with specific design approaches leading to the selection of plant materials; and the final section includes other more general information on installation and maintenance of plants. Much of this information has been developed with the help of specialists in various fields or through analyses of case studies of existing earth sheltered buildings. Future research may refine and modify some of the information that is presented here.

The Concept of Containerized Planting

The concept of containerized planting is essential to an understanding of the problems of growing and maintaining plant materials on and around earth sheltered buildings. In landscaping terminology the term *container* refers to areas in which the plants or soils that are installed are restricted physically in some manner. In the natural field environment, large depths of soil and/or bedrock underlie and surround the rooting zone. For earth sheltered buildings, the rooftop and the bermed areas, which connect the surrounding ground plane with the roof, restrict growth and therefore form the container (see fig. 9-1). The earth and plant materials on the roof are completely contained by the structure beneath them and, in some places, by parapet walls along the sides of the structure. Although the container environment created by the surrounding berms is more limited in that the earth and plants on the berms are sometimes contained on only one side, it also represents a modification of the natural site.

In the past, most containers for earth sheltered structures have been designed with the emphasis on completing the building in the most economical and convenient way possible. In most cases the amount of soil and the soil mixture used have been designed primarily to lighten the structural load and commercially grown plants have usually been selected, mainly on the basis of their aesthetic appearance and availability. In other cases the field soils that have been removed during excavation have simply been graded back onto the container, and then plant materials were installed. This type of landscaping process seems to be based on the assumption that the container environment does not affect the survival of the plants. In reality, however, the containerized environment is not the same environment that exists under normal field conditions. The special conditions created by heat transfer, containerization of the plant materials, limited soil depths, and potential chemical interactions with other systems such as waterproofing and drainage have resulted in extremely unpredictable plant growth conditions, as well as mechanical failures of waterproofing. Extensive replacements of plants, costly maintenance programs, or both have often been required.

These types of problems point up the need to apply an integrated systems approach to landscaping that implies coordination of the landscape design decisions (including type of plant material, type and depth of soil, and drainage system) with those related to the various building systems designs (structural, waterproofing, and insulation). Ignoring the need for such coordination can affect the success of the entire design. For example, plants or soil mixtures that require extensive watering for normal maintenance repeatedly test the waterproofing system of the building. Commercially grown sod is an example of such a plant material, yet it is the most commonly chosen material for landscaping earth sheltered homes. A number of problems—many of them very costly—related to the maintenance and survival of sod have occurred.

Sod has often been used because home owners have viewed it as an inexpensive, easily installed, low-maintenance material that typically has been used to landscape conventional buildings. On many small earth sheltered structures where sod has been installed without irrigation systems to maintain it, the sod is burning out, especially in areas where the roof meets the walls of the building. When irrigation systems have been installed, severe problems with water buildup and leakage have occurred, necessitating extensive

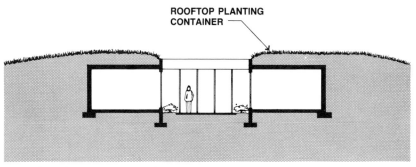

ROOFTOP PLANTING CONTAINER

9-1: Section of Earth-Covered House

repair work. An integrated systems approach to landscape design can help alleviate these kinds of problems. Such an approach is particularly important in designing smaller buildings, for which cost economies are more critical than they are for large-scale structures. Budgets for most houses make no allowance for installation of elaborate mechanical irrigation systems or for extensive replacement of the soils, waterproofing systems, or plant materials.

Basic Determinants of Container Design

The shape of the container is one of the major design components affected by the coordinated systems approach. Therefore, the scale and proportions of the container must be adjusted to optimize both the house design and plant growth potential. Determinants that affect the design of the container shape can be classified into the following categories: the architectural and structural limits; the minimum container depth and area required for ensuring plant survival; and maintaining proper nutrients and moisture balance in the soil for plant growth. To achieve this, the design of the soil mix, watering system and drainage of the container must be integrated. Solutions to potential problems in one of these areas often affects at least one other area.

architectural and structural limitations

The shape of rooftop planting containers can be designed in various ways. When integrated as part of the roof slab, they can be either flush with or recessed into the slab. Recessed planters should be located over structural members that can support the excess loads. Another way to

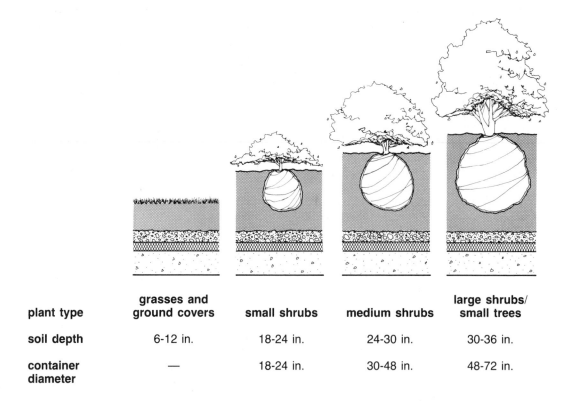

plant type	grasses and ground covers	small shrubs	medium shrubs	large shrubs/ small trees
soil depth	6-12 in.	18-24 in.	24-30 in.	30-36 in.
container diameter	—	18-24 in.	30-48 in.	48-72 in.

9-2: Minimum Topsoil and Drainage Requirements

handle planting containers is to design them as separate, movable planter boxes. For large buildings where extensive plantings include trees, separate planters may be preferable to recessed slab planters; however, they must be placed over structural support columns that can handle the extra loads. Separate planters may also be desirable when plant materials that require specialized soil

conditions or extra insulation are mixed in among those that do not. For example, although plants that thrive in acidic soils should be contained separately from all non-acid-loving plants, through the use of individual planter boxes the two types of plant materials can appear to be growing together naturally.

The structural loading characteristics of the

building design determine the maximum size of the area that can be used for planting. In the past, attempts have been made to lighten the loads of the soils by adding soil-lightening additives to the soils mix. Experience with this procedure suggests that meeting the minimum needs of the plant materials without the use of the additives is generally preferable. A common problem is the tendency of organic matter in the soil to leach out along with the additives as a result of the nearly constant watering that is required to supply the plant needs, given the very sandy soil mixes in which additives are generally used. Moreover, additives have been found to cause some puddling and shifting of the soils.

container depth and area

A second major consideration in determining the shape of the container is the minimum growth requirements of the plants to be used. Adequate soil depths and areas are essential in order to insulate the rooting systems of the plants against extreme cold or heat. The roots of the plants are much less tolerant of these extremes than is the aboveground mass of the plant. Under normal field conditions, the roots are protected by the warming influence of the soils below the root growth zone. The minimum criteria for soil depths and for container diameters in figure 9-2, based on the sizes and/or types of plant materials, have been suggested from the work of Dr. Harold Pellett (Horticulture Science and Landscape Architecture, University of Minnesota) and others.

The recommended minimum soil depth should be provided throughout the slab container. Providing more than the

minimum depths is desirable, especially in areas characterized by severe climate conditions. The soils in the container not only serve to modify the outside temperature with respect to the building interior, but also protect the plant roots from freezing or burning.

soil type

The soil type not only must be appropriate to maximize the growth of the selected plant materials, but also must be coordinated with the watering system to maintain the proper soil moisture balance. Soils are classified into types based on their internal structural characteristics. Sandy soils, for example, are composed of large mineral particles that allow plenty of pore space for air. Although water drains through them quickly, the nutrients in the soil are quickly washed away along with the water. At the other extreme, clayey soils are composed of fine particles that allow little air space and can trap and hold water, thus keeping the soil medium saturated for a long time. These soils are high in nutrient values. Silt particles are larger than particles that constitute clay but smoother than those that constitute sand. They will hold water and nutrients for the plants while still providing substantial air space. Additional information on soils is included in chapter 5.

Field soils (soils found on the site and left unaltered) usually contain all three types of particles. Soil that has equal proportions of the different particle types is called a loam. Technically, a loam is a mixture of sand and silt in which as much as 30 percent of the mix is clay. Loams are characteristically rich, moist soils conducive to good plant growth. Soils that provide too little air space, such as clayey soils,

tend to suffocate the roots of the plants. In excessively sandy or gravelly soils, plants may die of nutrient deficiencies or drought.

The types of minerals from which soils have decomposed over time and the amount of litter that is mixed in with the soil will determine its color and chemical composition. A loamy soil may be many different colors of brown, yet still have the structural characteristics necessary for good plant growth. The chemical composition of a soil will affect different plant materials in different ways. For example, some plants, such as azaleas, rhododendrons, and berries, can tolerate highly acidic soil compositions, whereas many other plants cannot.

The soil borings taken to determine the depth to water table and structural loading characteristics of the field soil can also help determine its suitability for use in rooftop plantings. After the type of soil is determined, a decision should be made about whether or not to create a new mix composed partially of field soil or use the soils as found on site. Testing of the soil by agriculuture extension or soil-testing services is recommended, not only to determine the pH of the soil, but also to determine the amounts and types of fertilizer that will be necessary to supplement the nutrient makeup of the soil.

As different plant materials have adapted genetically over time, they have come to require different amounts of air, available water, and nutrient concentrations from soils. Plants that have adapted to clay soils, for example, are most healthy in these soils and therefore should be selected for use in them. A local agricultural extension service agent, horticulturalist, or landscape architect should be able to help select the appropriate materials for specific soil types. It is important to know the best growth source for all the types of plant materials to be used. Peat-grown sod, for example, requires a very different soil mix than does sod that has been grown in a rich, friable loam.

watering or irrigation systems

Different types of soils vary in their capacities to retain water. The container should be designed to maintain a proper moisture balance in the soil such that the soil is moist enough to supply water to the plants for growth but not so oversaturated as to cause rot or problems with the waterproofing. The coefficient of permeability measures the rate at which soil can discharge water. The coarser the soil texture, the higher the coefficient of permeability. Clay soils, which have a low coefficient of permeability, hold water longer; sandier soils, which have a higher coefficient of permeability, allow water to drain off more rapidly. The type of watering or irrigation system that is selected should be determined primarily by the moisture needs of the plants and the relative ability of the soils to provide that moisture. Other factors to be considered are initial costs and climatic variables, as well as types and costs of maintenance programs.

drainage

The need to provide adequate drainage and to protect the waterproofing to maintain the plant materials is the final concern that affects the design of the soils mix and therefore the container. There are four basic strategies for removing the water from soils in the rooftop or containerized situation. These four methods are: sloping the slab, providing a gravel bed as a drainage layer, providing a subsurface drainage system, and layering of the soils.

The first method to create positive drainage is the form of the roof slab. The basic decision of whether to slope the roof slab in a constant slope from the front to the back of the structure or to leave the roof flat may affect the shape of the living space below it. The minimum slope required is ½ to 1 percent, or approximately ¼ inch per 50 feet. This minimum slope may not be sufficient, however; in fact, a slope of 1 to 2 percent is actually more practical. An important detail related to the form of the roof slab as well as the drainage is the design of the edges of the container. Several alternatives for roof edge details are shown in chapter 10. To avoid puddling where there is a vertical parapet wall, the inside edge of the container should be canted—either by forming the edges during the pour or by adding a curb that is bolted to the structure.

A second method to promote drainage is the addition of a gravel drainage layer beneath the soil layer. This gravel drainage layer is generally recommended for all soil types (see fig. 9-3). For grasses and small and medium shrubs in soil depths up to 30 inches, a 4- to 6-inch gravel layer is recommended. For small trees and large shrubs in soil depths of 30 inches or more, at least a 6-inch gravel layer should be provided. These criteria are minimums; a deeper gravel layer will provide additional protection for the plants. In some clayey soils, it may be necessary to provide perforated drain pipes or drain tiles within the gravel layer as an additional method to enhance drainage.

Finally, a technique known as layering may be used in which thin layers (2 to 4 inches) of different soils are placed over the gravel drainage bed so that the most porous soils are closest to the gravel layer. The layers decrease in porosity as they near the surface and 12 or more inches of rich soil are placed over the thinner layers. Layering in this manner helps to alleviate the problem that occurs when fine-textured soils are overlain directly on the gravel bed. The difference in hydrostatic pressure between the radically different soils does not allow the excess water to pass into the gravel layer, and the soil remains saturated. Layering is a means of reducing the contrasts between soil types so that the water can flow more easily. Specific recommendations concerning all of these measures to promote positive drainage are discussed in the following section of this chapter.

Additional Concerns in Container Design

insulation and waterproofing systems

Although waterproofing and insulation are discussed extensively in other chapters, a few key points relate to their effects on landscape. Because the chemical makeup of waterproofing and insulation materials can adversely interact with the landscaping materials or with the fertilizer used to sustain plant growth, some attention should be given to the compatibility of the various products and chemicals used.

One of the most important concerns with respect to plant survival in rooftop containers is the use of insulation. If the container is not insulated, the heat from the building can keep the soil far warmer than it would be under natural conditions. As a result, the plants do not go into the normal dormant state and, when the outside temperature becomes colder, can be killed by a hard freeze. It is therefore recommended that the container—the sides as well as the base—be completely insulated to ensure good plant growth (see fig. 9-3). This is particularly important in climates characterized by extreme heat and cold, as well as when soil depths are minimal.

filter mats

If a gravel layer is to be used, a decision must be made about whether or not to use a soil filter mat. The purpose of the filter mat is to keep the silty particles in the soils from being carried down with the water into the bottom of the container resulting in improper drainage. A variety of filter mat materials are commercially available including a thin blanket of fiberglass insulation or a geotextile filter fabric. The mat is most commonly installed just above the drainage layer, between the gravel and the soils (see fig. 9-3). Although fiberglass filter mats have not been very successful in retaining the silty

particles, they have successfully provided a barrier against the growth of the rooting system, so that the plants do not grow down into the insulation and waterproofing layers. The use of soil filter mats is recommended because of the total system protection they offer.

impact on energy use

The interrelationship of the building and landscape technologies is important not only to the physical functioning of the building, but also in considering the potential of earth sheltering for energy-efficient design. In *The Climate Near the Ground*, Rudolf Geiger notes that "a vegetative cover exerts a strong influence on the temperature and water content of the soil" [9.1]. Other studies have found that differences in the coarseness of the materials and in height affect the amount of shading provided. In addition, the density of the plant materials affects the amount of energy consumed in evapotranspiration. Finally, the density and type of the plant rooting system affects the total balance of moisture and heat in the soils. With respect to earth sheltered buildings, the most important characteristics appear to be the great reduction in incoming radiation resulting from evapotranspiration of the plant materials and the presence of moisture in the soil, which can significantly affect the conductivity of the soil. At present, however, little quantifiable information has been developed to accurately assess the impact of these choices on building energy use. After more research has been completed, the choice of plant materials can be better integrated into the overall design process to maximize energy conservation.

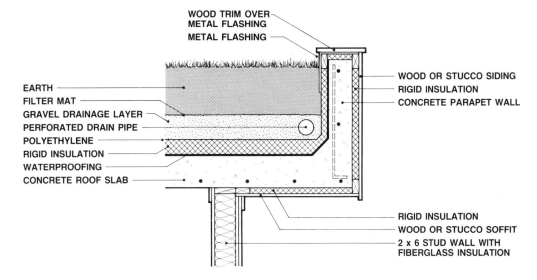

WOOD TRIM OVER METAL FLASHING
METAL FLASHING
WOOD OR STUCCO SIDING
RIGID INSULATION
CONCRETE PARAPET WALL

EARTH
FILTER MAT
GRAVEL DRAINAGE LAYER
PERFORATED DRAIN PIPE
POLYETHYLENE
RIGID INSULATION
WATERPROOFING
CONCRETE ROOF SLAB

RIGID INSULATION
WOOD OR STUCCO SOFFIT
2 x 6 STUD WALL WITH FIBERGLASS INSULATION

9-3: Earth-Covered Roof Detail

Design Approaches Leading to Plant Selection

Integration with the Site

One of the most obvious landscape issues related to earth sheltered building design is the potential integration of the building with the surrounding site landscape. The natural landscape provides a variety of visual settings, which are defined by the contours of the land, the types and forms of vegetation that cover the land, and the relationship of the landforms to other built forms. The special design opportunity that earth sheltering offers is its potential for integrating the built form with the landscape to an extent not possible in conventional building designs. Although some conventional designs have approached total integration through skillful imitation of the landforms in the built forms, the final contact of building with the ground has always separated the two. Earth sheltered design, on the other hand, requires total integration of the building with the ground. For example, in an urbanized setting characterized by small lots and restricted areas, integration is usually best accomplished through repetition of the clean, crisp geometric lines and forms of the surrounding buildings, combined with the selection of plant materials that have crisp, compact, and rather controlled or orderly natural growth forms. The commercially grown and hybridized plants that best serve these needs are commonly available at local nurseries. Larger lots and areas where fewer restrictions are placed on the land allow more flexibility in landscaping. In these settings buildings can be blended into the wild, more natural surrounding landscape through the use of more irregular-shaped materials such as native shrubs, special grass mixes, perennials, and wildflowers.

Three Basic Technical Approaches

It is important to point out that a man-made growth environment such as that described in the preceding section will probably have characteristics dissimilar from those found under natural field conditions. In order to combine the need to integrate the building into the surrounding landscape with the actual growth characteristics of the container, all design approaches should meet the criteria of one of three technical approaches. The three basic approaches are referred to as the nonindigenous planting approach, the indigenous planting approach, and the rock garden approach. The critical factors that distinguish these systems as separate approaches are their basic technical requirements, such as the size and shape of the container, types of soil mixtures, and types of watering and drainage systems required. Their general visual effects can also be different.

All three approaches require some maintenance; no approach can be considered maintenance free. In designing an earth sheltered landscape, it is best to select plants that imitate the surrounding landscape character and in turn to select from the three approaches the one that is most compatible with the natural growth characteristics of the plant materials to be used. Variety may be achieved by alternating selections among the suitable plant materials and by varying the arrangements of the plants.

It must be emphasized that the design approaches discussed here are not based on scientific classifications of plant materials. In practice, one species of plant might be used in several different approaches. Depending on the specific conditions, different varieties of the same species would be selected with varying degrees of hardiness or adaptability. For instance, one type of ground cover could be used with many other ground covers to create a rich, lush effect; it could also be mixed with other small flowering plants in a rocky soil mix to create a rock garden effect. Figure 9-4 compares the variations among the three approaches with regard to soil type, drainage, and irrigation requirements, as well as conditions of the roof slab beneath the planting areas. Following the chart are brief descriptions of the three basic approaches and their variations, as well as information on special plant growth requirements.

Only through careful attention at each design phase can earth sheltering fulfill its potential for the sensitive integration of the built environment with the landscape in a functional, cost-effective manner. In the remainder of this section, a general introduction to each approach is followed by descriptions of several of the adaptations possible for that approach. More technical considerations related to watering systems and soils are also discussed for each approach.

Components of Container Design	Nonindigenous Approach	Indigenous Approach	Rock Garden Approach
Container Shape	cross-sloped to berms at perimeter or to interior drains	cross-sloped to berms at building perimeter	flush
Irrigation System or Watering	spray or trickle tube irrigation	hand watering on regular schedule	natural watering
Drainage System	gravel layer covered with filter mat	gravel layer and layering covered with filter mat	layering covered with filter mat
Soils	rich, loamy soil mixtures (add sand for pedestrian use)	fields soils or mix (rich soils mix for nursery-grown plants)	special soil mix called "scree"
Insulation and Waterproofing	installed as required by building design	installed as required by building design	installed as required by building design
Plants	nursery-grown plants only	native or select nursery plants	special rock garden plants (see fig. 9-8)
Mulch	replace every 1 to 2 years	place in first years until plants spread	place in first years until plants spread

9-4: Basic Landscape Approaches for Rooftop Planting

Nonindigenous Technical Approach

The nonindigenous technical approach, so named because it incorporates plants that are generally not native to the site, is the most mechanically dependent and, therefore, most costly of the three approaches to install. In the life cycle of the building, however, it may not be as costly, as labor intensive, or as energy consumptive in terms of the physical labor, water resources, and materials used as the other approaches. It is the essential system for ensuring the survival of some plants that are generally used to achieve certain design effects. The nonindigenous planting system is appropriate for plant materials that require rich, moist soil environments, such as commercially grown and hybridized sods, seeds, shrubs, and perennial plants. To ensure plant survival, a specially mixed, rich planting soil should be specified and coupled with a mechanical irrigation system that can maintain the soil moisture balance at the necessary critical level.

Preliminary experimentation on hardy materials suggests that at least 12 inches of soil should be installed in the container in order to prevent freezing of the total soil depths in very cold climates which would kill the plants' rooting systems. At these 12-inch depths, the lower layers of soils are protected or insulated by the upper layers of soil. Commercial plants require frequent and regular maintenance for the first two to five years in order to ensure their proper establishment. With the exception of the perennials, the plant materials used in the nonindigenous planting approach are distinguished by their neat, controlled appearance; hence, a good deal of pruning is required to maintain this appearance.

To date, nonindigenous materials rather than native plants have most commonly been used for all types of earth sheltered buildings. But, because they have frequently been installed without the supportive growth conditions described above, many problems and failures have occurred. Although nonindigenous plants do have a special design appeal that is very appropriate to many urbanized settings, they must always be provided with the proper growth environment. Appropriate irrigation techniques for each type of planting are necessary for optimal growth. These are discussed later in this section under *watering systems.*

soils mix

When special rich soil types are required for such planting materials as sods or hybridized nursery-grown plants, a rich loamy soil should be mixed with sand for drainage. If the topsoil on the site fits this description (as determined by the soil boring), it should be stripped and stockpiled for use in the mix. In other cases, special mixes may be required to meet the natural growth requirements of the selected plants. The proportions of various soil mixes are shown in figure 9-5. Sometimes good topsoil (black dirt) may have to be brought to the site. The availability of soils and the costs of preparing a good soil mix that will suit the needs of the plants are basic criteria in deciding whether to use nonindigenous plant materials.

When the area above the soil will receive heavy pedestrian use, the soils mix should include sand. For heavy use areas, sand should comprise as much as 94 percent of the soil. In low-nutrient mixes such as sandy soils, fertilizers should be added on a regular maintenance schedule. Over-feeding or fertilizing of the soil will cause the plants to grow more rapidly, however, and they will then require pruning. It may also contribute to late-season growth that does not get hardy before winter, resulting in winter dieback of the plant material.

drainage

When well-balanced soils or loams are used to support plants that are accustomed to rich growing conditions (as is generally the case for the nonindigenous planting system), adequate drainage can be provided by a combination of a 6- to 8-inch gravel layer and a sloped slab or by a gravel layer placed over a slab that has a network of internal pipes. Sandy soils, which drain fast, need an adequate layer of mulch (approximately 6 inches deep) at the surface to hold moisture for the plants. The addition of the mulch layer may add to the total depth requirements for the container.

watering systems

Sandy soils or soil mixes that have sand added to improve drainage, such as those specified for the commercial systems, require the more controlled maintenance provided by mechanical watering systems (irrigation systems). The specific design of these systems should be planned with assistance from an approved irrigation contractor, as the design will vary with the planting design and soils specifications. As background information, however, some general guidelines can be suggested.

There are two types of irrigation systems: slow-release subsurface systems and conventional sprinklers. The subsurface systems are best suited in conjunction with ground covers and shrubs, whereas sprinklers are better used for grassy areas. The critical limitation of the sprinkler is that sensors are not available to regulate the volume of output according to soil moisture content; rather, the systems are based on automatically timed watering cycles. By contrast, subsurface systems are designed to maintain soil moisture and therefore are preferable. Spacing of the system components is determined by the planting design. For some plant types and in certain climates, the irrigation system may require a deeper than normal cover of soils (greater than 6 inches) to prevent the system from damage from freezing or deterioration from the sun and, of course, all systems should be drained in the winter.

planting approaches

The design effects of the major categories of planting that should be supported by a nonindigenous approach are described below.

- *Commercial Sods*

These sods have the fine-lined, rich look of a highly cultured landscape. For design purposes they are best applied in highly urbanized settings where they can blend with clean-lined architecture and where the design calls for a "minimal" landscape. To achieve this effect, these sods require intensive regular maintenance, not only to look better, but in order to remain healthy as well.

Commercial sods should not be installed on slopes that are steeper than 3:1 because a heavy rainfall can carry the sod downhill, thereby causing extensive erosion to the earth berm. A 6-inch base of topsoil is essential for sods. Sods grown on peat soils should be provided a similar type of soil on a rooftop; those grown on sandy loams may not need as much watering. Sods take up to five years to establish themselves and require much attention during that period. The best sources of commercial sods are plant nurseries or sod farms.

- *Commercial Seeds*

Commercial seed mixes can vary in appearance: some resemble highly cultured sods, whereas others have the mildly weedy look of grasses that grow along highway embankments. Commercial seeds are generally used on steeper, unmowable

Planting soil mixture for shrubs, flowering trees, and groundcovers:		Planting soil mixture for broadleaf evergreen plants:		Planting soil mixture for peat-grown sods (used as a 6-inch layer below grass):	
% Volume	**Material**	**% Volume**	**Material**	**% Volume**	**Material**
25%	screened topsoil	10%	screened topsoil	50%	coarse sand
50%	coarse sand	40%	coarse sand	50%	peat moss
25%	peat moss	40%	peat moss		
		10%	humus		
Nutrients per Cubic Yard		**Nutrients per Cubic Yard**			
5 lbs. bone meal		5 lbs. *Uramite*			
5 lbs. *Uramite* or equivalent		3 lbs. superphosphate			
4 lbs. muriate of potash		1 lb. muriate of potash			
Add lime as necessary to bring pH to 6.0-6.5.		Add lime as necessary to bring pH to 4.5-5.5.			

9-5: Planting Soil Mixtures

This table is based on information from *Landscape Architecture Above Buildings* by Thomas E. Wirth [9.2].

slopes where the design effect calls for a wilder, more natural look than that associated with commercial sods.

The composition of the seed mix should ensure proper combinations of winter or cool season grasses, which are active in cool periods, and subtropical grasses that are dormant during cold periods but active in the dry, hot periods. By using such a mix, it is possible to have a year-round, "full-season" green lawn.

The cool grasses are fescue, bluegrass, rye grasses and redtops; subtropical grasses include zoysias and bermudas. Forbs or flowers such as clover, vetch, and trefoil are often mixed in to help stabilize the other two elements of the mixture during the several years of growth required for the grasses to become established, as well as to help create a more natural, textured look.

In order to provide a properly wet environment for germination, seeded grasses should be covered by mulches. Before germination takes place, mats can be used to help maintain the slope. A 6-inch base of good topsoil should be provided for seed mixtures. Common sources of commercial seeds are grass seed contractors and state highway departments.

● *Commercially Grown Shrubs*

Another common approach to planting on rooftops of earth sheltered houses uses shrubs that are typically available from nurseries. By using commercially grown shrubs, a very formal and controlled landscape design can be integrated with the masses and shapes of the architecture by reinforcing geometric patterns of the built form, thus imparting a highly stylized character to the landscape. Very dramatic

and stimulating effects can be created by carefully selecting colors and textures.

This type of approach differs from the indigenous landscape approach in that the basic design concept is dominance of the art forms, rather than reproduction of the natural look of the native landscape. Integration is accomplished by using plant materials to create textures and patterns that reinforce the lines of the building in the surrounding planes, such as entry areas and other outdoor spaces. The impression of the built form dominates and controls the landscape. In contrast, the landscape approach using indigenous materials (discussed below) is drawn into and even dominates the built form.

Some major technical considerations also distinguish these two landscape approaches. For best plant growth, the nonindigenous approach requires that special loamy soil be brought onto the site or that the field soil be improved unless it is naturally rich loam or sandy loam. The commercial plant materials used in this approach, grown in containers of rich soils, have adjusted their growth requirements to these soil conditions. Small dwarfed shrubs, rather than large plants, should be used unless adequate rooting room is provided. Drought-tolerant species and varieties are preferable to water-loving species.

● *Perennial Gardens*

Plant materials used in the perennial garden approach produce a rather grassy-looking landscape that suggests a very different design character from that of the previously discussed approaches. In these gardens large masses of herbaceous materials contribute to a more cultivated overall appearance than is possible with

grasses or shrubs. The building can be integrated with the site by carrying the mass of materials down from the rooftop area into the surrounding lower planes, for example, at the entry or around the patio area. Through its unique combination of planting materials, the perennial garden takes on a special quality, characterized by a variety of textures and a rhythm of changing colors and accent points that accompany seasonal changes.

Establishing this approach requires considerable care and should be viewed as an opportunity for gardening rather than a maintenance-free situation. Selective cutting of plant materials that have died back over the winter and separating root masses when some plants have spread so extensively as to crowd others are, of necessity, continuing maintenance requirements associated with perennial gardens. In addition, these gardens require frequent regular waterings unless only drought-tolerant materials are used. Local nursery growers and horticulturists can provide more information about caring for specific plant materials that may be selected for the perennial garden landscaping approach.

Initial layout of perennial materials should allow plenty of room for them to spread. Heat from the building probably will force more exterior flowering of materials if they are planted on the rooftop rather than in the ground planes. Soil erosion may occur when perennials are used in a climate that has severe winters. Although the dense root mass of many perennials will hold the slope once the plants are established, the reestablishment of these materials in the spring is often slow; hence, when exposed to heavy spring rains, the soil may erode.

Indigenous Technical Approach

The indigenous planting approach is not mechanically dependent and, therefore, is a less costly landscape system. Because adjustments to the system are made through additional manual labor, this approach may be more labor intensive than the nonindigenous plant materials approach, particularly under conditions of unanticipated or radical changes in climate. In contrast with the nonindigenous planting approach, in which an ecosystem is created to supply the basic needs of the plant materials, the technologies in an indigenous approach balance the conditions of the existing field soils and the effects of the local climate with the selection of plant materials that grow naturally in these environments. The materials selected must also be able to tolerate the special conditions that earth sheltering creates. The indigenous planting approach greatly enhances the potential for integrating a variety of natural landscape settings with the designs of earth sheltered buildings. Special seed mixes, wildflowers, hardy ground covers, vines, native shrubs, and native perennials are design variations of this approach.

Based on the concept of balance, the specifications for soils allow for the use of field topsoils. The soils need to be mulched so that they retain adequate moisture for plants at the root zone. Although planted depths are critical, particularly in extreme climates, this approach generally allows more flexibility for shallower depths when smaller plant materials are used. Plant selection should be based on ecological community principles, taking into consideration the natural growth associations of different plants with different soil types. The native plants often used in this approach may be more difficult to obtain than commercial plants without help from a consultant. The frequent failings of commercial plants have led to a shift toward selecting compatible or native plants, with a corresponding improvement in plant survival. The improved plant survival suggests that the extra effort expended in selecting appropriate plants is cost-effective in the long run.

The indigenous plant materials approach has special potential for smaller earth sheltered structures because it can result in considerable cost savings when it is properly done. This approach is sometimes inappropriate for larger buildings, either because of the design of the building or because of the special maintenance that it may demand (for example, a regular grounds maintenance crew may be necessary). A combination of the indigenous and nonindigenous planting approaches may be appropriate for some buildings, since achieving a design that is integrated with the surroundings is basic to both approaches. Careful selection of all materials is even more critical than usual in a combination approach such as this. This approach should be considered somewhat experimental, as the factors that define the earth sheltered ecosystem are not yet fully understood even for individual systems.

soils

The use of the soils that are found on the site is basic to the indigenous planting approach. A properly planned and prepared indigenous plant system can be much more economical than the nonindigenous plant approach and has good potential for use on earth sheltered houses and other buildings where mixing the soils is not cost-effective.

Field soil can be improved or amended to meet planting conditions. If it is a clayey or clayey-silty mix, more air space can be provided by adding pumice or sandy soils. If the soils are too sandy, organic matter such as ground bark, peat moss, sawdust, leaf mold, or manure can be added. These materials can decay when the soil lacks sufficient nitrogen, however. If the soils test reveals a nitrogen deficiency in the soil, a fertilizer that is high in nitrogen should be added. Coarse organic matter is often added to excessively clayey soils to improve aeration and drainage.

A good growing soil created from a field soil should be composed of two parts field soil (topsoil), one part sand, and one part organic material (peat moss or its equivalent). Bone meal and fertilizer should be added. Mixing, which is usually done by rotary tilling or spading, can be done in place if extreme care is taken to protect the waterproofing. The soil should be mixed evenly over the entire surface of the container to 25 to 35 percent of the container depth. It is usually better to mix the soils on-site before installing them and to place the soil in the container in 6-inch lifts. The first lift should be compacted to 95-percent density and saturated immediately before placement of the second lift. Saturation of the soils at this point will allow for the waterproofing to be tested before the plants are installed. The remaining lifts should then be placed and allowed to settle. Because these layers constitute the root growth zone for the plant materials, they should not be compacted. If compaction occurs after these soils are installed, they should be rototilled and watered before planting begins.

drainage

When field soils are used in their natural condition, as they are in the indigenous plant materials approaches, they hold more moisture and, therefore, require a drainage system. The type of drainage system selected depends on the types of soils used. If the soils are excessively clayey, for example, either a subsurface drain tile system should be installed or the soils should be mixed with sands or layered. Clayey soils can be mixed with sandy soils by rototiller in proportions of approximately one part clayey soil to three parts sandy soil. When fine-textured soils lie directly over the gravel bed, the differences in hydrostatic pressure between the radically different soils does not allow the excess water to pass into the gravel layer; hence, the soils remain saturated. Layering or mixing reduces these contrasts so that the water can flow down through the soil more easily. Layering involves spreading rich layers of soil over more porous layers (each layer is approximately 2 to 4 inches deep), to a total depth of approximately 12 inches (see fig. 9-6). When the layering is complete, the richest soil layer is on top and the most porous layer rests atop the gravel layer at the bottom of the container. A full 12 inches of soils, plus 2 to 4 inches for each layer of gravel, are required; thus, the total minimum depth for proper installation of grasses and other small plants is approximately 20 to 26 inches.

If a drain tile system is to be used, the tiles should be set in a bed of gravel, over which a layer of sand is installed.

The total depth of the container varies with the pipe size used. The 2-inch sand layer should overlay approximately 2 inches of gravel installed above the pipe, and the full depth of soils required for the specified plant types is placed over these layers. The water that is collected should be delivered to collection points at the outer perimeter of the building and dumped into the foundation drain tile system. A qualified landscape architect or civil engineer can assist in determining appropriate drain tile and pipe sizes.

watering systems

When fine soils are used without the addition of sand, as in some indigenous plant materials approaches, the addition of mechanized watering systems may not be necessary. In these cases the hose bibs should be located to facilitate access, and watering can be accomplished by use of hand-adjusted sprinklers and hoses. Watering on a schedule will not only reduce the total time required for maintenance labor, but will also maintain the proper soil moisture balance—neither oversaturated nor dried out.

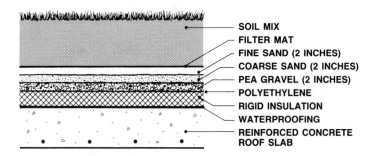

SOIL MIX
FILTER MAT
FINE SAND (2 INCHES)
COARSE SAND (2 INCHES)
PEA GRAVEL (2 INCHES)
POLYETHYLENE
RIGID INSULATION
WATERPROOFING
REINFORCED CONCRETE ROOF SLAB

9-6: Roof Section with Drainage Layering

planting approaches

The design effects of the major categories of planting that can be supported by an indigenous approach are discussed below.

• *Native Shrubs*

The desirable plant materials for the native shrubs approach are those that grow naturally under conditions similar to the field soils condition. Although these materials may be purchased at a nursery, they may also be grown in soils comparable to the field soils, rather than in special soils. Sometimes these plants come in bare-root form.

Native materials are usually mixed with other plants that share their natural ecological associations (e.g., soil and watering needs), rather than mixed for the sake of their art form or texture. These associations tend to build stability into the plant community, thereby reducing the maintenance requirements and improving the resistance of the materials. Native plant materials adjust more readily to variations in watering conditions due to changes in climate, whereas introduced plants will continue to need regular watering to ensure healthy growth. Small dwarfed shrubs, rather than larger plants, should be used unless adequate rooting room is provided. Drought-tolerant species and varieties are preferable to water-loving species.

• *Special Seed Mixes*

In areas where the landscape is grassy, a special seed mix approach may be used to restore the look of the native landscape. Selected species from the prairies of the Great Plain states and the sparse tumbleweed landscapes of the Southwest

are particularly appropriate for this type of landscaping. On-site soils can be prepared for use, and groups of grasses can be selected and mixed to duplicate the effect of grasses growing together by natural selection.

The grass will be healthier and more self-maintaining if seed mixtures compatible with the soil types are used. Although this approach does not require extensive maintenance, several years are required for all grass communities, including sods, to establish themselves. Grasses—especially native grasses—may initially be more critically sensitive than larger plants to their environment but are usually less troublesome once they are properly established.

• *Seed Mixes and Wildflowers*

A more elegant or delicate approach to a native grass landscape uses a mixture containing greater concentrations of wildflowers or forbs than would exist through natural selection. Although grasses alone can have a seasonally changing look, in a special seed mix this change is accentuated by the presence of flowers active in different seasons. The design principle here is to accent the home, to differentiate it from the surrounding landscape while still blending it into its surroundings. This suitable and delightful approach, which increases the concentration of flowering materials, permits both effects.

The work necessary for preparing this landscaping approach is more exacting than that associated with an approach that uses only native flowering plants. It also requires a special willingness to work with the plants over a rather lengthy period of time. If commercially forced perennial

flower seeds are scattered and allowed to grow wherever they may, however, the same effect can often be achieved in a less time-consuming manner.

A local horticulturist or gardener can give good advice about appropriate choices of flowers and seeds. Local authorities should be consulted before digging plants in the wild. Although removing or damaging native plants is often prohibited, collecting seeds is usually permitted. In general, plants transplanted from the wild will not survive as well as nursery stock.

• *Ground Covers and Vines*

Ground cover approaches are characterized by a very thick (12- to 18-inch) mat that creates an insulating surface. These approaches may employ a wide variety of plant materials: very fine-textured leaves and flowers, such as sedums, trefoils, or vetches; rich vining types of materials, such as ivies or berries; evergreen or deciduous materials; and foliage or flowering types of plants.

By using a mixture of materials that have similar soil type requirements, a very sophisticated, rich, lush look can be designed for the rooftop and carried down to the ground planes. The leaf mat can provide an optional third layer of insulation and cooling for earth sheltered houses (in addition to the soil and root mass layers). Like a garden approach, ground covers can be used to create a seasonally changing design.

Although maintenance of this approach is relatively minimal over the long term, requiring only periodic fertilization, a number of maintenance problems may occur unless the initial soil is properly and thoroughly prepared. Such preparation should provide the soils with the textural and chemical characteristics required by the plants selected for use. Conversely, if field soil is to be used, plants compatible with that type of soil should be chosen.

Weed control can be a problem unless the soils are pretreated with short-lived sterilants. Mulching should also be done, both to retain water for the plants to use in their immediate growth zones and to facilitate weed control.

Depending on the total number of plants used and their spacing, a ground cover may take two or more years to achieve full growth. When planting, rows should be staggered across a slope. Early spring and fall seedings are best to ensure establishment of the plant materials. If seeded, plants should be kept moist for three to four weeks, until germination. Many of the plants commonly used for ground covers are available at commercial nurseries or from local garden club sources.

A number of ground cover materials can also serve as vining materials. Although shrublike materials such as raspberries and dwarf honeysuckle may also be used for vining, their mats are much higher, denser, and less easily controlled than mats created by ground covers. An advantage of shrubs, however, is the increased air space for insulation created by the thick netting of the woody branches.

The sources and care of vines are identical to those for ground covers, although the time required for establishment may be longer and the maintenance more difficult because of the pruning required after the dense matting has taken over the surface area.

Rock Garden Technical Approach

As the nonindigenous plant system was based on designing an integrated growth environment around a special selection of plant materials, the rock garden approach is based on designing a growth environment around a radically different type of soils growth medium—a rock garden soils base, or scree—as well as different plant types. The rock garden, which is a variation on the indigenous plant materials landscape approach, can be applied in a number of situations. For example, in the rocky, mountainous areas of Colorado, where re-establishment of large plant materials after they are disturbed is virtually impossible, a scree may be an ideal cover for earth sheltered buildings.

This approach seems most appropriate when the landscape surrounding a building site is rocky and plant materials are scattered. Many of the materials suited for ground cover, seeded, wildflower, and perennial garden approaches may also be used in rock gardens. The overall character of a rock garden, like that associated with Japanese gardens, may be very disciplined and controlled—a study in textures. Conversely, small flowers and ferns can be used to give the garden a very wild, rambling appearance more typical of a Rocky Mountain setting. The types and sizes of rocks selected also will greatly influence the appearance of the finished planting design.

The rock garden approach may be ideal in cases where only minimal soil depths are possible or desirable. Rock garden plants can survive in a minimum of soil,

establishing themselves in niches of soil and organic matter. Some primary technical issues in considering a rock garden approach are the care required to establish and maintain the garden, the necessity for regular watering, and the need to mulch the plants in order to maintain a wet growing area for them. Improperly maintained rock gardens can quickly lose their special character and, instead, look merely weedy and scraggly.

The massive nature of the rocks and the relatively dry environment are likely to have quite different effects on the flow of heat into and out of the structure than does the thick layer of moist soils covered with plant materials that is typical of most of the other approaches. When it is understood more clearly, the interaction of these two properties may be useful in helping to retain or dissipate heat as required by the structure.

The scree, or soil medium, is composed of variations of mixes that include large stones, gravel, and—in smaller proportions—loamy soils and humus. The plant materials have adapted to the minimal soil conditions by developing thickened lobes on the leaves, which store moisture for indefinite periods of time. These plants are also highly adapted to and tolerant of climatic extremes. Depending on the plants selected, watering may be done either by irrigation system or by spray misting from a hose. Mulch is essential in the early plant establishment period. Because 12 inches is an adequate soil depth for plants used in the rock garden approach, shallower containers can be used, except when irrigation systems are installed in the containers or in extremely cold climates. Although establishment of the plants may require

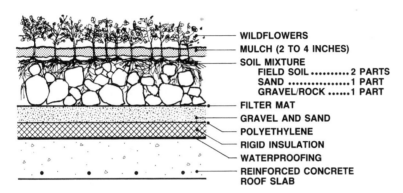

WILDFLOWERS
MULCH (2 TO 4 INCHES)
SOIL MIXTURE
   FIELD SOIL ....2 PARTS
   SAND ....1 PART
   GRAVEL/ROCK ......1 PART
FILTER MAT
GRAVEL AND SAND
POLYETHYLENE
RIGID INSULATION
WATERPROOFING
REINFORCED CONCRETE
ROOF SLAB

9-7: Roof Section with Rock Scree

considerable maintenance, over the long term less maintenance may be required than is necessary for nonindigenous or native plants.

scree

The rock garden approach calls for an entirely different type of growth medium or soil mix than do the other two planting approaches (see fig. 9-7). Plants used in rock gardens can also be grown in native soils. The soil depth for rock gardens can vary; lighter soil can be concentrated into the mix for deeper soils. A general mix for a scree is one part coarse rock or pea gravel to one part coarse sand and two parts field soil. The aim is to create a mix that is porous and drains quickly. A typical rooftop soil profile would include 2 to 3 inches of gravel, 2 inches of sand, and 2 to 4 inches of mulch. The mulch is critical, because water must be held at the growing surface in order for the plants to become established and to sustain growth. The type of garden soil required varies with the desired planting condition. For example, woodland plants in shaded gardens require different planting soil than do desert succulents. Although the proportions of the rocky mixture can be altered, the soil dries out too easily at ratios of four or five parts sand to one part field soil. Finally, the color of rock used in the mix is a very important consideration. The tendency of dark rocks to absorb and store heat is undesirable in the summer; white rocks will reflect heat away from the structure.

drainage

For drainage, a gravel layer is essential, but the slab may be kept flat to hold the water or cross-sloped, depending on the needs of the plants selected.

watering systems

Watering requirements for this approach are related to the depth of the container, which in turn depends on the adaptability of the plants selected. If the plants are genetically adapted to growth under existing climatic conditions, maintenance can be accomplished by hand. In this case no irrigation system or additional drainage layers are required. In deeper containers careful hose maintenance is essential from the time that the plants are first being established until they adapt to their environment. If the plant materials are not adapted to the existing conditions, however, allowance must be made for installing an irrigation system. Slow-release subsurface irrigation systems are recommended when the container depths meet minimum standards.

planting

Wild plants, many of which can be found in the mountains, woodlands, prairies, deserts, and seasides, are most appropriate for rock gardens. Local authorities and owners of private land should be consulted before digging, to make sure that removal of plants from a specific area is permitted. Generally, the best procedure is to buy native plants from a nursery that specializes in them. Some of these plants are listed below by geographic sections of the United States (see fig. 9-8).

Northeast

Cypripedium
Erythronium
Houstonia
Iris cristata
Leiophyllum
Phlox devaricata
Phlox subulata
Silene
Trillium

Northwest

Cornus canadensis ferns, iris
Lewisia
Linnaea
Mahonia
Cxalis oregana
Penstomon
Sedum
Trillium
Vancouvera

Alaska

Andromeda polifolia
Chrysanthemum arcticum
Cypripedium
Dodocatheon
Erigeron
Geranium erianthum
Iris setosa
Loiseleuria procumbens
Rubus arcticus
Silene acaulis

Great Plains and Rocky Mountains

Aquilegia
Dryas octopetalis
Eriogonum
Leucocrinum
Mertensia
Opuntia (and other native cacti hardy in subzero temperatures)
Penstemon
Phlox
Sedum
Viola

California and the Southwest

Arctostaphylos (dwarf species), cacti and succulents
Ceanothus (dwarf), ferns
Heuchera
Penstemon
Phlox
Zauschneria

South

Chrysogonum
Chrysopsis ferns
Galax
Pachysandra procumbens
Phlox
Ruellia
Shortia
Silene
Trillium

9-8: Plant Materials for Rock Garden Approach

Plant Installation and Maintenance

Plant Selection

Although plant selection should not be based solely on current availability at the nursery or on hardiness, both of these factors are certainly important in making decisions about the appropriate landscape design approach. The plants should not be so uncommon that they are not available, and they should be hardy enough to thrive in the region where they will be used. Drought-tolerant plants will help alleviate problems associated with perched, or contained, water tables. Perching of the water table in the soil zone can occur when the hydrostatic pressure builds up between the gravel and soil layers in the container. When this occurs, the roots of the plants receive too much water and not enough air, and gradually suffocate or rot. Highly drought-tolerant materials, which generally are hardy in all climate extremes and can withstand radical changes in weather conditions, should be selected to compensate for this potential problem. Additionally, the plants should be heat resistant, suited to the climate, and ecologically compatible with the soil conditions provided.

All plants grown commercially for outdoor planting are classified and graded, based on their relative healthiness and perfection of form, according to standards set by the American Association of Nurserymen. Grade A plants are guaranteed as healthy (disease-free) and well-formed specimens. Despite their higher cost, only Grade A plants should be used for landscaping earth sheltered structures, in order to ensure their survival under the more stressful conditions of rooftop planting.

Plants used in the various landscaping approaches may be purchased in many forms: as seeds, cuttings, or plugs; bare-root, balled and burlapped; or container grown. Although seeds and cuttings take a long time to establish, they may acclimate to the planting condition better than do transplanted larger plant forms. Shrubs should be selected from among container-grown shrubs in a container environment that replicates the growth conditions that will be provided in the rooftop planting area. Only healthy shrubs—those with a minimum of two years' growth—should be selected; and dwarfed varieties, which require the least maintenance, are recommended. If bare-root plants are to be used, they should be planted in the early, frost-free period of the spring. Care should be taken to protect the fibrous roots when transplanting bare-root material in order to ensure better and faster adaptation of the plants to the new growing conditions. If possible, a small ball of earth should be retained around these plants when they are dropped into the pit. Adequate spacing should be provided for the plants to grow to their desired form. The room required for such plant growth should be taken into consideration in the initial design phases.

Guying

Guying is essential to the survival of any newly planted trees and large shrubs. The purpose of guy wires is to reduce to a minimum the swaying caused by the wind. It is this swaying motion that pulls the young rootlets from their foothold in the fresh soil beyond the original earthball, causing them to dry out and die.

The normal provisions for guying or staking plants also apply to plants used for landscaping earth sheltered structures. Staking is usually less satisfactory because not enough undisturbed soil is available to support the stake. Guying can be anchored to deadmen or to hooks set in the concrete slab. When large trees that will be subjected to heavy winds are to be grown in containers that will severely limit their root growth, permanent guying is desirable. Permanent guying should be made of stainless steel to ensure durability.

Pruning

Pruning is the method by which plants are tended so that they maintain their desired form. To some extent, plants will maintain or contain their own growth when they are forced to grow under minimal or restricted conditions, such as those associated with rooftop or container planting. In addition, the layers of rock or gravel used for drainage, as well as the filter mat, will keep the roots from growing down into the waterproofing zone. Skillful and selective pruning of the aboveground plant mass to contain its size will also prevent excessive growth of the root mass. An annual maintenance program to prune the shrubs, vines, and woody ground covers is essential. Commercial grasses should be mowed—sometimes as often as once a week—to retard root growth.

If plants have been allowed to establish themselves over a long period without pruning, the only method of pruning the root systems is to trench one side of the plant one year and cut the roots, refilling the hole with leaf mold and sandy loam soils. The other side should be trenched, pruned, and refilled the next year. Pruning of the aboveground portion of the plant should be done at the same time the root mass is pruned. Plants can be pruned to three-fourths their former size. Another pruning method involves digging up the whole root ball and pruning it. The plant should be trimmed back and replaced in a pit that has been lined with leaf mold or other organic matter. No chemical systems of root pruning should be considered unless their compatibility with the waterproofing, as well as with the plant materials, has been established.

Mulch

An important component of proper landscaping is choosing and installing the mulching material. For landscaping earth sheltered buildings, mulching is even more important than it is in conventional landscaping, as it provides an additional source of water to compensate for the unbalanced moisture conditions of the container. Mulching should be used in all three earth sheltered landscape approaches. In the indigenous plant materials approaches that use vines and ground covers or perennials, the mulch should be at least 4 inches deep (a 6-inch depth is preferable). Mulch should be reapplied approximately every two years in order to maintain an adequate moisture balance in the soil. The mulching material should not only be chemically compatible with the plant materials, but should also provide the appropriate color and texture to complete the landscape design. The characteristics of various types of mulch are indicated in figure 9-9.

Type of Mulch	Texture	Color	Comments
buckwheat hulls	fine	neutral	

chunk bark
  redwood
  fir
  oak
	coarse	
		red
		beige
		beige/brown
			oak bark is acidic

corn cobs	coarse	light	problems with chemical reaction and odor
hay (legumes)	coarse	light	
hops (spent)	coarse		
lawn clippings	fine		odor problem—do not use if treated with weed killer
leaf mold	medium		needs nitrogen—unattractive
leaves	medium		needs nitrogen
manure			odor problem—do not use if treated for odor reduction
spent mushroom compost	medium		
peanut hulls	medium to coarse	good	
peat moss	medium to coarse		acidic chemical reaction—keep wet at all times
pecan shells	medium	good	good smell
poultry litter	mixed		odor problem
sawdust	fine	neutral	
shredded bark	coarse	mixed	
straw	coarse	neutral	
wood chips	coarse	mixed	chemical reaction is possible

9-9: Characteristics of Various Mulches

This chart based on information from *Weather Wise Gardening* [9.3].

PART THREE:

INTEGRATION OF DESIGN AND TECHNOLOGY

10. TYPICAL DESIGN PROBLEMS AND DETAILS

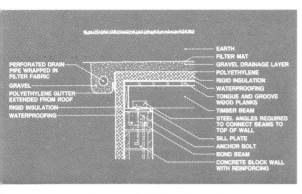

PERFORATED DRAIN PIPE WRAPPED IN FILTER FABRIC
GRAVEL
POLYETHYLENE GUTTER EXTENDED FROM ROOF
RIGID INSULATION
WATERPROOFING

EARTH
FILTER MAT
GRAVEL DRAINAGE LAYER
POLYETHYLENE
RIGID INSULATION
WATERPROOFING
TONGUE AND GROOVE WOOD PLANKS
TIMBER BEAM
STEEL ANGLES REQUIRED TO CONNECT BEAMS TO TOP OF WALL
SILL PLATE
ANCHOR BOLT
BOND BEAM
CONCRETE BLOCK WALL WITH REINFORCING

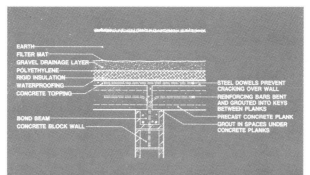

EARTH
FILTER MAT
GRAVEL DRAINAGE LAYER
POLYETHYLENE
RIGID INSULATION
WATERPROOFING
CONCRETE TOPPING

BOND BEAM
CONCRETE BLOCK WALL

STEEL DOWELS PREVENT CRACKING OVER WALL
REINFORCING BARS BENT AND GROUTED INTO KEYS BETWEEN PLANKS
PRECAST CONCRETE PLANK
GROUT IN SPACES UNDER CONCRETE PLANKS

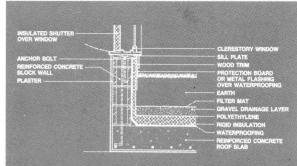

INSULATED SHUTTER OVER WINDOW

ANCHOR BOLT
REINFORCED CONCRETE BLOCK WALL
PLASTER

CLERESTORY WINDOW
SILL PLATE
WOOD TRIM
PROTECTION BOARD OR METAL FLASHING OVER WATERPROOFING
EARTH
FILTER MAT
GRAVEL DRAINAGE LAYER
POLYETHYLENE
RIGID INSULATION
WATERPROOFING
REINFORCED CONCRETE ROOF SLAB

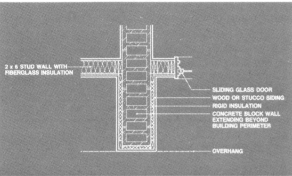

2 x 6 STUD WALL WITH FIBERGLASS INSULATION

SLIDING GLASS DOOR
WOOD OR STUCCO SIDING
RIGID INSULATION
CONCRETE BLOCK WALL EXTENDING BEYOND BUILDING PERIMETER

OVERHANG

CHAPTER 10

TYPICAL DESIGN PROBLEMS AND DETAILS

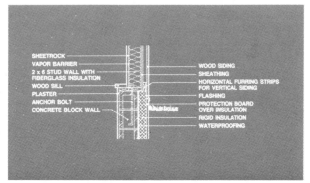

¾" PRESSURE-TREATED PLYWOOD
SHEETROCK
VAPOR BARRIER
FIBERGLASS INSULATION
PRESSURE-TREATED 2 x 6 STUD WALL

ANCHOR BOLT
HORIZONTAL SLIDING RIGID INSULATION AT CEILING LEVEL

CLERESTORY WINDOW

WOOD TRIM
PROTECTION BOARD OR METAL FLASHING OVER WATERPROOFING
EARTH
FILTER MAT
GRAVEL DRAINAGE LAYER
POLYETHYLENE
RIGID INSULATION
WATERPROOFING
CANT
REINFORCED CONCRETE ROOF SLAB
FURRED-OUT SHEETROCK CEILING

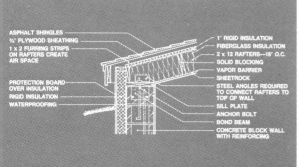

ASPHALT SHINGLES
¾" PLYWOOD SHEATHING
1 x 2 FURRING STRIPS ON RAFTERS CREATE AIR SPACE

PROTECTION BOARD OVER INSULATION
RIGID INSULATION
WATERPROOFING

1" RIGID INSULATION
FIBERGLASS INSULATION
2 x 12 RAFTERS—16" O.C.
SOLID BLOCKING
VAPOR BARRIER
SHEETROCK
STEEL ANGLES REQUIRED TO CONNECT RAFTERS TO TOP OF WALL
SILL PLATE
ANCHOR BOLT
BOND BEAM
CONCRETE BLOCK WALL WITH REINFORCING

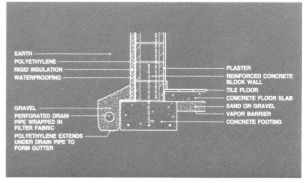

SHEETROCK
VAPOR BARRIER
2 x 6 STUD WALL WITH FIBERGLASS INSULATION
WOOD SILL
PLASTER
ANCHOR BOLT
CONCRETE BLOCK WALL

WOOD SIDING
SHEATHING
HORIZONTAL FURRING STRIPS FOR VERTICAL SIDING
FLASHING
PROTECTION BOARD OVER INSULATION
RIGID INSULATION
WATERPROOFING

EARTH
POLYETHYLENE
RIGID INSULATION
WATERPROOFING

PLASTER
REINFORCED CONCRETE BLOCK WALL
TILE FLOOR
CONCRETE FLOOR SLAB
SAND OR GRAVEL
VAPOR BARRIER
CONCRETE FOOTING

GRAVEL
PERFORATED DRAIN PIPE WRAPPED IN FILTER FABRIC
POLYETHYLENE EXTENDS UNDER DRAIN PIPE TO FORM GUTTER

Introduction

The organization of this manual generally reflects the order in which information is used in the design process. A general assessment of earth sheltered housing (chapters 1 through 3) was followed by design and technical information covering six separate but interrelated subject areas. This chapter, the third major section of the manual, addresses the integration of the design and technical information into actual building design and construction details. The intention here is not to present building layouts suitable for various climates, sites, and programs. Not only is this beyond the scope of this manual, but other publications have already presented a wide range of case studies of earth sheltered houses [10.1, 10.2]. It is important, however, to examine the unique and sometimes conflicting technical and aesthetic concerns that arise in the development of an actual design. This chapter examines key design problems and details found in many earth sheltered structures; for each problem area or detail, design issues and a comparative discussion of various solutions are presented.

In studying the details in this chapter, it is important to remember that earth sheltered construction is still an emerging technology and that the details shown are more experimental than time-tested. They are intended to illustrate methods and concepts and should not be regarded as the only or best solution in every case. The individual designer must determine what is appropriate for each particular situation. Furthermore, most of the details apply to the most common—rectilinear—types of structures. Shell structures and other unique technologies will generate different

design and detailing problems and solutions, although many of the principles are very similar. The details generally reflect the most severe climatic conditions of extreme temperature differentials between inside and outside, which require great care in sealing and insulating. In warmer climates, where the temperature differentials are not as great, the designer may choose to modify these details. No attempt has been made to show details that are similar to those for conventional houses; rather, these details concentrate on applications specific to earth sheltered construction. Finally, the relationship of aesthetics to overall design is discussed in conjunction with the details. Because the details are part of the overall design concept, they must relate to the surrounding context.

Although the emphasis of this chapter appears to be on technical concerns, it should not be concluded that solving all of the technical problems in a house will automatically result in an appealing or livable design. Some architects and builders have set very high design standards for earth sheltered housing; however, many of the early designs are neither attractive nor appropriate to their site or inhabitants. If continued, this situation may lead to a false image—namely, that earth sheltered houses are only achievable through numerous functional and aesthetic compromises. Similar misconceptions exist concerning solar architecture. It is generally understood that a newly emerging building form will not immediately produce ideal results. Nonetheless, there is serious concern that such negative perceptions

could seriously affect the future development of earth sheltered housing.

One of the contributing factors to poorly designed earth sheltered houses is the tendency to solve only one or two key design problems, with little regard for the wide range of concerns that must be addressed to create a house that actually meets the needs of its occupants. For example, in the pursuit of energy efficiency in earth sheltered buildings, it is easy to overlook requirements for natural light, efficient room arrangement, and many of the unique features that reflect the personal needs and life-styles of the inhabitants. It is imperative that a designer review all of the reasons for building a home and examine each design decision to determine whether it enhances or hinders the original design goals. It is important to consider the house as a whole rather than as a series of parts, and to ascertain how it will relate to the people who will live in it.

In addition to the functional shortcomings of some earth sheltered houses, a number of problems associated with many houses can be classified as aesthetic. Because taste and design vary, a successful design element in one situation may be disastrous in another. Nonetheless, some basic design principles remain constant, and adherence to the basic tenets of good design should help designers avoid the worst pitfalls in establishing appropriate designs for earth sheltering.

One of the most frequently breached design principles is that of honesty—making a building look like what it is instead of trying to pretend that it is something else. With regard to earth sheltering, a common example of dishonest design is an attempt to make a flat roof that is constructed with a foot of reinforced concrete, a waterproofing membrane, and 2 feet of earth look like a sloped roof with shingles. Another example is the attempt to make a concrete house constructed underground in the 1980s look like a wood house constructed aboveground in the 1780s. If a designer wishes a house design to bring to mind the warmth and familiarity of other times and situations, the house should be designed carefully, using only those elements that are appropriate to the time and place in which they will be used. Earth-integrated buildings present many unique design opportunities, and thoughtful response to climate may reawaken regional architecture by stressing the similarities of design elements within a region.

Another common problem in earth sheltered design relates to proportion. The size relationships for conventional houses, which have been developed over many years and in thousands of houses, seem almost automatic. The size relationships for a house that has earth up to or over the roof, that may have a 3-foot-thick roof that needs a guardrail, or that may be long and narrow to provide daylight to all rooms, have not become second nature to either the house designer or to those who view the finished product. Hence, more time and care will be required in working out appropriate proportions for earth sheltered buildings.

A third problem is in achieving harmony. In most conventional houses, the front door, back door, garage door, windows for each room, porches, and patios are distributed around all four sides so that not too much is happening on any one side of the house. In an earth sheltered house, because all of these elements may have to be included on one elevation, many different elements are competing with each other for attention on one side of the house, while the bermed sides have a completely different, almost invisible, appearance. Great skill may be required to create a cohesive, harmonious whole. All of these aesthetic problems can be magnified by the fact that, unlike poorly designed conventional houses, which can generally escape into anonymity simply by virtue of being so commonplace, an earth sheltered home almost automatically draws attention to itself. A poorly designed earth sheltered home usually stands out much more than tackiness or inappropriate design or style in a conventional dwelling.

Setting down aesthetic guidelines in a manual such as this is a difficult, if not impossible endeavor. In many cases a good design seems to hinge on very specific principles of proportion, form, and use of materials; however, occasionally a designer can break all the so-called rules and yet create a very successful design solution. It would seem that the most important thing to remember with respect to earth sheltered structures is that they present different technical and aesthetic problems than do conventional structures. Because the building and site are merged and because earth sheltered buildings are generally quite different in appearance from any adjacent conventional structures, relating the design to the surrounding natural and man-made environment is a key element to successful design. Well-designed earth sheltered structures will most likely result when details are developed that both resolve these unique problems and reflect the unique opportunities for aesthetic expression in earth-integrated structures. It is important to emphasize that the major challenge in designing earth sheltered buildings is not just to overcome their liabilities to make them as good as conventional buildings. Instead, it is to use the unique assets of earth integration techniques to create more successful architecture than is possible with conventional building elements.

Edge of Earth-Covered Roof at Exposed Wall

In structures that have earth-covered roofs, one of the most complex and important details is at the edge of the roof over any exposed walls. This very visible detail not only has an important impact on the overall design appearance of the building, but also has implications in the areas of structural design, heat loss, waterproofing, plant growth, sun shading over windows, and provision of protection from falling off the roof. This section includes an examination of the major technical concerns with various solutions, followed by a discussion of aesthetic issues related to this type of detail.

Technical Concerns

In designing an earth sheltered structure, as in the design of many above-grade structures, it seems simplest to extend the roof slab to create an overhang with a vertical concrete parapet wall at the edge to retain the earth (fig. 10-1). Although this approach is relatively easy to apply to a cast-in-place structure, it presents several inherent problems. A primary concern is the heat loss experienced when a highly conductive material, such as concrete, extends from the interior to the exterior of the building. Not only do the overhang and parapet serve as a "wick" for heat loss, but cold spots can occur on the interior ceiling, causing condensation or frost. A second major concern is that a parapet wall can be subjected to high structural stresses, including the lateral forces from the soil and forces caused by the freeze-thaw action of the soil. Because parapets are exposed to the weather more than are other parts of the building and must resist

these structural loads, they must be carefully designed if they are to be used at all.

Special attention should be given to masonry parapet walls, which are subject to cracking at numerous joints unless they are heavily reinforced. Another area of concern is waterproofing and drainage. Because the parapet wall contains the water on the rooftop, a greater concentration of water can occur along the edge of the wall. This can result in higher structural pressures and put more stress at the corners and seams of the waterproofing, where many systems are weakest. A cant (see fig. 10-1) helps to prevent this buildup of water along the edge and for a wood structure, it can significantly increase the strength of the

connection between the roof and the parapet wall. The rest of the slab should be sloped so that the water will run off through the gravel drainage layer.

One solution to the problem of heat loss through a concrete overhang and parapet wall is to insulate around the entire concrete surface, as shown in figure 10-2. A drawback of this approach is the higher cost, as more insulation is required and furring strips and siding are needed to cover the insulation. Also shown in figure 10-2 is a perforated drainpipe running along the edge of the wall. Such a solution can ensure good drainage in this area and perhaps reduce the risk of waterproofing failures and structural damage from freezing and thawing. It is important to remember that any attempt to

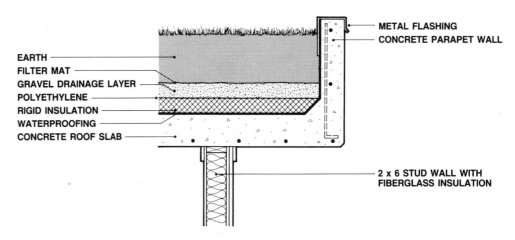

10-1: Roof Edge Detail at Exposed Wall

EARTH
FILTER MAT
GRAVEL DRAINAGE LAYER
POLYETHYLENE
RIGID INSULATION
WATERPROOFING
CONCRETE ROOF SLAB

METAL FLASHING
CONCRETE PARAPET WALL

2 x 6 STUD WALL WITH
FIBERGLASS INSULATION

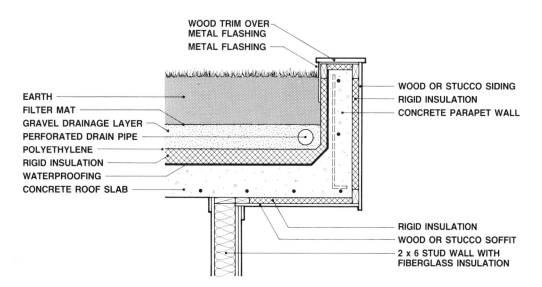

WOOD TRIM OVER METAL FLASHING
METAL FLASHING

WOOD OR STUCCO SIDING
RIGID INSULATION
CONCRETE PARAPET WALL

EARTH
FILTER MAT
GRAVEL DRAINAGE LAYER
PERFORATED DRAIN PIPE
POLYETHYLENE
RIGID INSULATION
WATERPROOFING
CONCRETE ROOF SLAB

RIGID INSULATION
WOOD OR STUCCO SOFFIT
2 x 6 STUD WALL WITH FIBERGLASS INSULATION

10-2: Roof Edge Detail at Exposed Wall

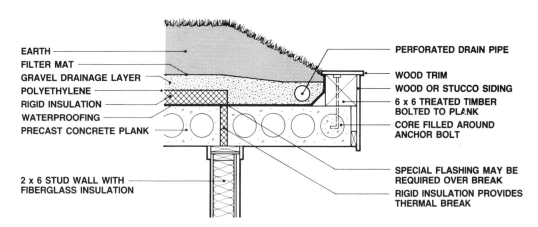

EARTH
FILTER MAT
GRAVEL DRAINAGE LAYER
POLYETHYLENE
RIGID INSULATION
WATERPROOFING
PRECAST CONCRETE PLANK

PERFORATED DRAIN PIPE
WOOD TRIM
WOOD OR STUCCO SIDING
6 x 6 TREATED TIMBER BOLTED TO PLANK
CORE FILLED AROUND ANCHOR BOLT

2 x 6 STUD WALL WITH FIBERGLASS INSULATION

SPECIAL FLASHING MAY BE REQUIRED OVER BREAK
RIGID INSULATION PROVIDES THERMAL BREAK

10-3: Roof Edge Detail at Exposed Wall

extensively drain an area can have a negative effect on plant growth. Thus, the drainage system design must be coordinated with the soil type and plant material selection (see chapter 9 for further discussion of this issue).

Instead of insulating around the entire parapet, an alternative approach to reducing heat loss is to provide a thermal break in the roof structure itself. Rigid insulation can be placed between precast concrete planks as shown in figure 10-3, provided that the planks run parallel to the exposed roof edge. This type of detail can also work in a cast-in-place concrete slab with dowel connections between the two separate portions of the slab. Great care must be taken to ensure proper waterproofing over the thermal break because it is an interruption in the flat roof surface and therefore subject to some movement. Similar to the manner in which a typical building expansion joint is treated, a strip of flexible membrane waterproofing can be used to cover the gap.

Figure 10-3 also illustrates the use of a single timber at the roof edge to diminish the size of the vertical parapet wall. This strategy permits retention of the earth on the roof, while providing the positive benefits of reducing structural forces. It also gives the parapet wall a less massive appearance and allows the plant growth on the roof to be more visible. These aesthetic issues are discussed and a more complete development of these ideas shown under *aesthetic concerns*, below.

The technical concerns for roof edge details are somewhat different when a wood roof structure is used instead of a concrete structure. For example, because wood is not as great a conductor of heat as concrete, heat loss through structural elements that extend both inside and outside the building is of less concern when wood is used. In the example shown in figure 10-4, based on the work of architect Don Metz, the wood beams run parallel to the roof edge and tongue-and-groove planks run perpendicular to it [10.3]. Although no thermal problems are associated with this detail, the masonry bearing walls that extend outside the structure to support the overhang should be examined for heat loss (see *wing walls* section, below). Another very interesting aspect of the detail shown in figure 10-4 is the use of a triangular plywood box to form the roof edge. This shape is very stable structurally and effectively reduces the structural stresses present in typical vertical parapet walls. By tapering the earth near the edge, the load is reduced and any water drains away from the edge.

Architect David Wright, who has designed several earth sheltered houses with wood plank and beam roof structures, has used a similar detail at the roof edge. Wright, however, suggests running the beams perpendicular to the exposed wall and the planks parallel to it resulting in a strong connection between the triangular cant structure and the beams [10.4]. This configuration makes it possible to extend the beams beyond the outside wall to support an overhang. The specific layout of the structural system for an earth covered roof depends not only on the roof edge, of course; it is related to the most efficient means of spanning across the spaces with a support system—bearing walls or columns and beams—that facilitates the plan arrangement and required wall openings.

Aesthetic Concerns

The roof edge detail is an important component of the overall design of the project. A vertical, flat, concrete parapet wall can have a severe, cold, appearance. If the wall extends up to form a solid guardrail around the roof, it can give the house a larger, more predominant form, which people may associate with the negative feeling of being deeper below grade and smaller in scale than is actually the case (fig. 10-5). It also cuts off any view of or connection to the plant growth on the roof. These negative effects can be dealt with in a number of ways. The guardrail is a key element in the scale and appearance of the roof edge. It may

be possible to diminish its effect by designing a more invisible barrier, for example, a brown or green metal rail with shrubs planted along it. In some situations the need for a guardrail at the roof edge may be eliminated by limiting access to the roof (see the *retaining walls* and *guardrails* sections at the end of this chapter). Other techniques used to diminish the negative impact of vertical parapet walls include texturing the concrete or covering it with wood to soften its appearance, and sloping the earth down at the edge to reduce its scale (see fig. 10-3).

One of the more common responses to the aesthetic problems posed by a large parapet wall is the use of a mansard type

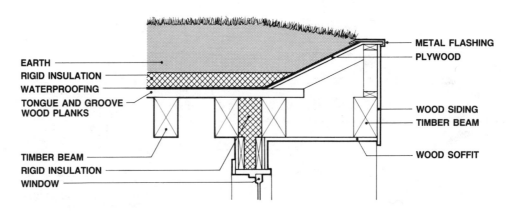

EARTH
RIGID INSULATION
WATERPROOFING
TONGUE AND GROOVE WOOD PLANKS

TIMBER BEAM
RIGID INSULATION
WINDOW

METAL FLASHING
PLYWOOD

WOOD SIDING
TIMBER BEAM

WOOD SOFFIT

10-4: Roof Edge Detail at Exposed Wall

of roof (fig. 10-6). On the positive side, it can be argued that such a roof is an obvious way to create an overhang and that the angle tends to diminish the scale of a tall, vertical parapet wall. In addition, a mansard roof covered with shingles is sometimes seen as a way of making an unconventional structure look more conventional. The negative side to the use of this type of roof is that it is often considered to be a decorative element that attempts to hide the actual structure of the house and the fact that the house is, in reality, partially underground. Many designers feel that the use of this design technique is similar to putting a false front on a building to disguise its actual size, function, or appearance. This negative perception is reinforced by the fact that

the mansard element itself has been used extensively on small commercial structures and apartment buildings, often resulting in a tacked-on appearance. Thus, while some see a mansard roof as a symbol of dishonest architecture, others continue to use it as a familiar and even desirable element.

As stated in the introduction to this chapter, well-designed earth sheltered structures will most likely result when details are developed that both resolve the unique problems and reflect the unique opportunities for aesthetic expression in earth-integrated structures. Because the roof edge is one detail that provides a major focus for these aesthetic concerns, a final example is presented here that

represents an important attempt to develop appropriate new details for earth sheltered architecture.

One of the earliest advocates and leading designers of earth sheltered structures, Malcolm Wells, has given a great deal of attention to the multiple problems to be solved at the edge an earth-covered roof [10.5, 10.6]. Because Wells regards the structural, thermal, and aesthetic problems of parapet walls as quite significant, his designs eliminate the use of parapets completely (fig. 10-7). In addition, he includes no overhangs that are an extension of the interior structure. The separate wood trellis, which serves as a shading device, can be built as a free-standing structure or may be attached to

10-5: Image

10-6: Image

the building wall, depending on the structural system. Insulation is placed outside the structure, thus eliminating any heat loss, and there are none of the structural problems associated with parapets. Wells has used similar details with wood roof structures.

Because there is no curb at the roof edge, water can run off the edge at any point. Eliminating the curb results in a simple waterproofing detail; however, a membrane product that is durable when exposed to the air and sunlight must be used. The earth, which is placed on top of the insulation and waterproofing, is tapered to a point at the edge of the structure. Some designers have expressed concerns over the possibility of erosion at the edge because there is no curb, as well as over the ability to grow plants in the limited depth of soil. Wells has had success with this approach, however. By using just the field soil, covering it with 6 to 12 inches of mulch, and letting natural plant materials take over, Wells has found that very lush plant growth has established itself, imparting a very natural appearance to the rooftop [10.6].

In addition to avoiding some of the technical problems with parapet walls, this detail diminishes the scale of the building wall and maximizes the view of the plant materials on the roof (fig. 10-8). With lush plant growth virtually hanging over the edge of the structure, the building can appear to be very well integrated into the natural landscape of the site. This aesthetic effect is often sought after and associated with building into the earth but is seldom achieved by other design approaches.

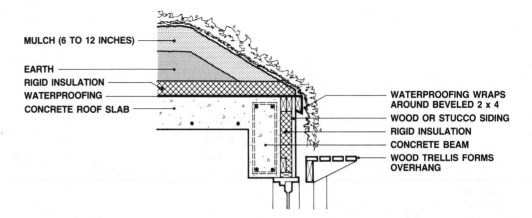

MULCH (6 TO 12 INCHES)

EARTH
RIGID INSULATION
WATERPROOFING
CONCRETE ROOF SLAB

WATERPROOFING WRAPS AROUND BEVELED 2 x 4
WOOD OR STUCCO SIDING
RIGID INSULATION
CONCRETE BEAM
WOOD TRELLIS FORMS OVERHANG

10-7: Roof Edge Detail at Exposed Wall

This drawing based on detail shown in *Underground Plans Book-I* by Malcolm Wells and Sam Glenn-Wells [10.6].

10-8: Image

Roer Edge at Buried Wall

Whereas the roof edges on conventional houses are generally similar in most instances, on earth sheltered houses they may vary significantly as a result of a number of factors. The roof edge over the exposed wall of an earth sheltered house is not only exposed to both view and thermal changes, but must also prevent people and earth from sliding over the edge. The opposite roof edge, which meets a bermed or buried wall, may be subject to entirely different conditions. It is usually inconspicuous on a bermed house and invisible on an earth-covered house. Although the insulation for such walls can be done simply, there are ordinarily substantial lateral forces that must be resisted. The detail drawings shown in this section illustrate some of the possible responses to these concerns.

The case that is most similar to that commonly encountered in conventional houses is the meeting of an exposed wood roof with a bermed wall (fig. 10-9). Although this situation appears similar to that which occurs in a conventional basement, it should not automatically be treated as such unless a structural engineer is consulted. Often the wall is slightly deeper than a typical basement, resulting in higher lateral loads. These lateral loads must be transmitted to the roof, which must act as a diaphragm if the loads are unopposed by a bermed wall on the opposite side of the structure. Thus, it is important that the connection between the roof and wall be adequate to transmit these loads and that the roof structure be capable of acting as a diaphragm.

In the detail shown in figure 10-9, a steel angle makes a strong connection between

the roof rafter and the sill plate anchored to the masonry wall. A structural engineer can determine the necessary size and spacing of such connections for a specific design. Another means of ensuring a good connection in this situation is to notch the bottom of the rafter to hang over the sill plate. This solution, however, may result in the rafter being too narrow at the end to allow sufficient depth for adequate insulation. Notching the roof member to interlock with the wall may be a more satisfactory solution on a flat roof or on a deeper roof structure, such as a truss joist, where greater depth can be maintained for insulation at the end.

In the case of an exposed roof and buried wall, it is important to extend the below-grade insulation on the wall up to meet

the roof insulation so that there is no great heat loss at this point. This problem of above-/below-grade transitions and means of protecting the exposed insulation are discussed later in this chapter. Another important consideration is the necessity of providing a vented space over the roof insulation. In figure 10-9 the opening for the vented space occurs in the minimal overhang; it might be an improvement to have a wider overhang in order to carry rainwater further away from the foundation and to reduce the danger of ice dams in cold climates. Although rain gutters can also be used to channel the rain away, they are often considered to be a maintenance problem.

Figure 10-9 shows ¾-inch plywood sheathing and solid blocking between the

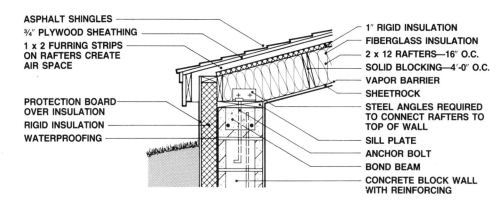

10-9: Roof Edge Detail at Bermed Wall

rafters at 4-foot intervals to create a strong diaphragm to transmit the horizontal wall load to the end walls, where another firm connection is required. A steeper roof pitch may make it more difficult to achieve an effective diaphragm, and the use of trusses instead of rafters may complicate the installation of adequate blocking. Both of these situations, however, can be dealt with through competent engineering.

Figure 10-10 shows a horizontal earth-covered roof that uses angles with anchor bolts for a firm connection of wall to roof because, again, strong lateral forces must be resisted. In this case, wood decking is used to create a diaphragm. Placement of the insulation is much simpler because it is all below grade, and the waterproofing is between the structure and the insulation. Additional protection from water is added by laying polyethylene over the insulation. The polyethylene is extended over the edge of the building and under a drain tile that runs along the top of the wall to catch runoff before too much of it flows into the soil along the wall. The polyethylene is installed with a tuck in it so that settling of the backfill with the resultant sinking of the drain tile will not rupture the polyethylene.

Any precast or cast-in-place concrete roof deck is ordinarily well anchored to the walls below. With a cast-in-place slab, the effects of shrinkage and deflection are not usually much different in adjacent areas. Although techniques have been developed to bond the separate precast planks together, there remain some concerns that deserve careful attention in light of the heavy loads applied with earth cover and the potential for problems because of cracks.

The most thorough method of bonding

precast concrete planks together includes the use of a poured-in-place concrete topping. Whereas the topping does contribute to the structural strength of the deck, its most important role is in increasing the integrity of the waterproofing. The planks are usually relatively rough and have joints between them. The roughness presents a hazard to the waterproofing because of the danger that the waterproofing may be penetrated, thereby permitting water to enter. A topping can make the plank surfaces much smoother. Moreover, if the planks were not bonded together, they might deflect different amounts because of variations in systems, loading, end conditions, or conditions within the planks themselves. It may be necessary for the waterproofing to bridge these differences among the planks, both when the waterproofing is placed and when deflection from loading occurs—

especially if one plank deflects more or less than the adjoining planks. Although one of the criteria in selecting a waterproofing product is its ability to bridge cracks, it is still best to put this feature to the test as infrequently as possible.

In addition to these other advantages, topping adds one more dense, seamless layer to the structure that water would have to penetrate before it could enter the living space. The expense of topping is small when compared to the very important benefits it provides. Topping also provides an opportunity to introduce at least a slight slope to an otherwise flat roof. Some bearing conditions require extra block cutting or forming and pouring an extra element to slope the planks themselves; however, it is possible to introduce as much as 2 or 2½ inches of slope on a small roof by tapering the topping.

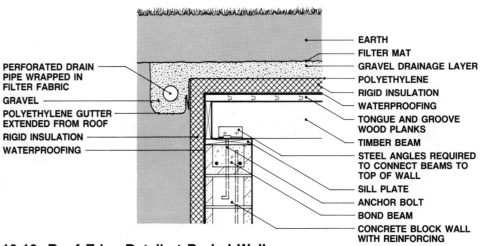

PERFORATED DRAIN PIPE WRAPPED IN FILTER FABRIC

GRAVEL

POLYETHYLENE GUTTER EXTENDED FROM ROOF

RIGID INSULATION

WATERPROOFING

EARTH
FILTER MAT
GRAVEL DRAINAGE LAYER
POLYETHYLENE
RIGID INSULATION
WATERPROOFING
TONGUE AND GROOVE WOOD PLANKS
TIMBER BEAM
STEEL ANGLES REQUIRED TO CONNECT BEAMS TO TOP OF WALL
SILL PLATE
ANCHOR BOLT
BOND BEAM
CONCRETE BLOCK WALL WITH REINFORCING

10-10: Roof Edge Detail at Buried Wall

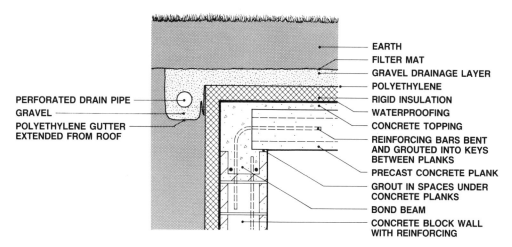

10-11: Roof Edge Detail at Buried Wall

Labels (figure 10-11):
- EARTH
- FILTER MAT
- GRAVEL DRAINAGE LAYER
- POLYETHYLENE
- RIGID INSULATION
- WATERPROOFING
- CONCRETE TOPPING
- REINFORCING BARS BENT AND GROUTED INTO KEYS BETWEEN PLANKS
- PRECAST CONCRETE PLANK
- GROUT IN SPACES UNDER CONCRETE PLANKS
- BOND BEAM
- CONCRETE BLOCK WALL WITH REINFORCING
- PERFORATED DRAIN PIPE
- GRAVEL
- POLYETHYLENE GUTTER EXTENDED FROM ROOF

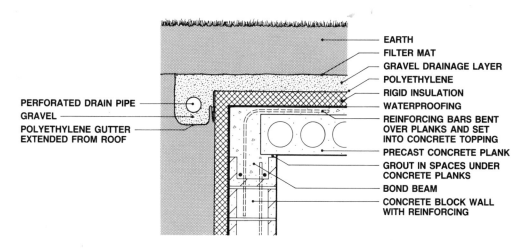

10-12: Roof Edge Detail at Buried Wall

Labels (figure 10-12):
- EARTH
- FILTER MAT
- GRAVEL DRAINAGE LAYER
- POLYETHYLENE
- RIGID INSULATION
- WATERPROOFING
- REINFORCING BARS BENT OVER PLANKS AND SET INTO CONCRETE TOPPING
- PRECAST CONCRETE PLANK
- GROUT IN SPACES UNDER CONCRETE PLANKS
- BOND BEAM
- CONCRETE BLOCK WALL WITH REINFORCING
- PERFORATED DRAIN PIPE
- GRAVEL
- POLYETHYLENE GUTTER EXTENDED FROM ROOF

Roof edge conditions also require special attention. Where the end of the plank bears on the wall, as shown in figure 10-11, a rigid connection is achieved by bending reinforcing that is anchored in the wall into grout-filled keyways between the planks and placing continuous grouting in areas where the planks bear on the wall. The concrete topping is continued down from the top of the planks to close the ends of the planks and top off the outer portion of the wall that is not covered by the planks. These measures should assist in minimizing cracking at the edge of the topping, which would pose potential problems for the waterproofing. The poured concrete also makes it possible to round or taper the corner where the surface changes from horizontal to vertical, so that the waterproofing is not subjected to the stresses of being applied to a sharp corner, where some products are more vulnerable to damage.

When the plank runs parallel to the wall (fig. 10-12), it is again beneficial to grout under the plank bearing. This strategy will help prevent the camber from settling out of the plank when it is fully loaded—a situation that would tend to cause cracking between the edge of the topping, which would move with the plank, and the concrete above the wall, which would not move. The concrete extending into the grout key will also assist in preventing deflection. The steel reinforcing is cast either into the topping or into channels cut into the planks at the job site. It should be emphasized that in all instances the specific installation instructions of the plank manufacturer should take precedence over the general comments presented in this manual concerning installation procedures.

Interior Walls

The waterproofing and structural conditions related to earth sheltered houses can affect the conditions at interior walls. Where an interior wall provides bearing for two bays of concrete planks, as shown in figure 10-13, the downward deflection of the center of the planks tends to widen the top of the crack between the ends of the planks. This in turn puts tensile force on the concrete topping; if not counteracted, this force will promote cracking of the topping. Placing steel reinforcing in the topping in areas where two planks meet will assist the topping in carrying the tensile load.

Some waterproofing systems—sheet membranes, for example—can bridge structural cracks in cases such as this; however, other systems cannot (see chapter 7).

Non-load-bearing partitions may also require special treatment in an earth-covered structure. Because of the extremely heavy loads on an earth-covered roof, even the normal deflection of the roof can place severe stresses on light interior wall construction that has been built tightly against the underside of the roof deck before being loaded completely. Arranging the construction sequence so that interior partitions are not constructed until after the full earth load has been placed on the deck might reduce this problem. The best solution, however, may be to leave a gap proportionate to the anticipated deflection at the top of the wall (fig. 10-14). A compressible filling such as caulking could be used to close the gap for acoustical purposes, and a wood trim piece that is fastened to the ceiling but free to slide by the wall would cover it visually.

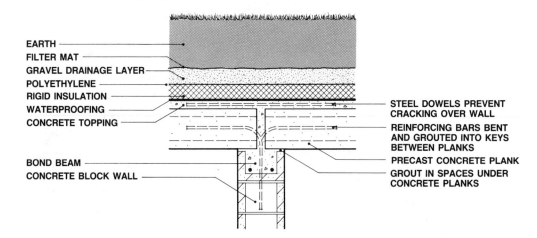

EARTH
FILTER MAT
GRAVEL DRAINAGE LAYER
POLYETHYLENE
RIGID INSULATION
WATERPROOFING
CONCRETE TOPPING

STEEL DOWELS PREVENT CRACKING OVER WALL
REINFORCING BARS BENT AND GROUTED INTO KEYS BETWEEN PLANKS
PRECAST CONCRETE PLANK
GROUT IN SPACES UNDER CONCRETE PLANKS

BOND BEAM
CONCRETE BLOCK WALL

10-13: Interior Bearing Wall Detail

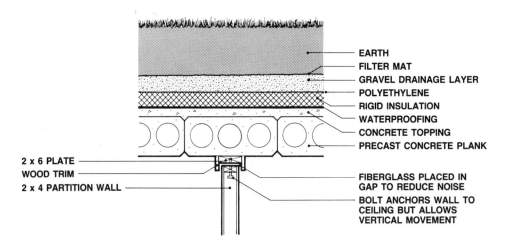

EARTH
FILTER MAT
GRAVEL DRAINAGE LAYER
POLYETHYLENE
RIGID INSULATION
WATERPROOFING
CONCRETE TOPPING
PRECAST CONCRETE PLANK

2 x 6 PLATE
WOOD TRIM
2 x 4 PARTITION WALL

FIBERGLASS PLACED IN GAP TO REDUCE NOISE
BOLT ANCHORS WALL TO CEILING BUT ALLOWS VERTICAL MOVEMENT

10-14: Interior Nonbearing Wall Detail

Roof Penetrations

For earth-bermed houses that have conventional wood-frame roof structures, there are standard, well-known methods of penetrating the roof for various functions, including chimney flues and plumbing and exhaust vents. Standard details also have been developed for skylights on either flat or sloping roofs. On an earth-covered structure, however, special attention must be given to these details because the conditions are different from those for an above-grade roof and problems with waterproofing and increased heat loss may result. In addition, because these roof penetrations may be more visible and predominant on an underground structure than they are on an above-grade building, the aesthetic effects of these elements are particularly worthy of consideration. Experienced designers usually try to minimize roof penetrations.

Vent Pipes and Ducts

It is possible to extend the pipe or duct for a typical exhaust or plumbing vent through a small opening in the roof structure, as shown in figure 10-15. An opening of this size (4 to 6 inches in diameter) is not a problem structurally and presents only minor heat loss problems that are unavoidable in the case of plumbing vents. The heat loss from vents for exhaust fans from dryers or from bathrooms and kitchens can be reduced in various ways. For example, dampers can be installed in the duct so that air cannot escape when the vents are not actually in use. Electric clothes dryers can be vented to the inside in winter, thereby only

expelling heat during the summer, when it is unwanted. Finally, various types of heat-exchange devices can be used in conjunction with exhaust vents to decrease the heat loss caused by the exchange of inside and outside air (see chapter 8 for a discussion of heat exchangers).

The major concern with a small vent or duct penetrating an earth-covered roof in this manner is adequate provision of long-term waterproofing. Although these types of penetrations can be sealed with virtually any of the acceptable waterproofing systems, the projections create points of greater stress than the flat parts of the roof. The cylindrical shape of the pipe and the temperature differentials that may occur around it can affect the adhesion and durability of some products; however, other

products should be able to handle this condition when properly applied (see chapter 7).

The greatest difficulty associated with roof penetrations is the possibility of movement, which most waterproofing systems can tolerate only to a limited degree without failing. Precast concrete planks, for example, can deflect considerably (½ inch or more) when loaded with earth after the waterproofing is installed and can deflect even more over time. If the pipe is held rigid while the structure is moving, usually the waterproofing will give first. One possible solution to this problem is to allow for movement by installing a separate segment of pipe into the roof deck that fits into a slightly larger pipe below that acts as a sleeve (fig. 10-15).

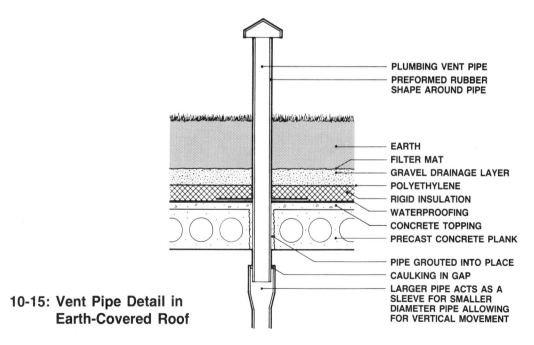

10-15: Vent Pipe Detail in Earth-Covered Roof

PLUMBING VENT PIPE
PREFORMED RUBBER SHAPE AROUND PIPE

EARTH
FILTER MAT
GRAVEL DRAINAGE LAYER
POLYETHYLENE
RIGID INSULATION
WATERPROOFING
CONCRETE TOPPING
PRECAST CONCRETE PLANK

PIPE GROUTED INTO PLACE
CAULKING IN GAP
LARGER PIPE ACTS AS A SLEEVE FOR SMALLER DIAMETER PIPE ALLOWING FOR VERTICAL MOVEMENT

The space between the pipes is caulked but will allow movement without damaging the waterproofing. Another approach is to bond the pipe to the roof and to load the roof before connecting the pipe to the interior plumbing or ductwork so that it is close to its final position. A bend can then be placed in the pipe beneath the roof so that some downward movement can occur if there is any long-term deflection. A final solution to these problems is simply to avoid them by running vent pipes and ducts out through exposed vertical walls or through larger roof penetration structures (discussed later in this section).

Flues

Flues from fireplaces, wood-burning stoves, and furnaces can be classified into two types: masonry and metal. In both cases they are typically designed to pass through a wood roof as well as a concrete structure without creating a fire hazard. The details and special concerns for both masonry chimneys and metal pipe chimneys are very similar to those previously discussed and illustrated for skylights and vent pipes. A small masonry chimney could be treated exactly like a masonry enclosure around a skylight. A metal chimney could be treated similarly to a vent pipe or duct; however, it also presents the same possibility for waterproofing failures because of structural movement and thermal expansion. To avoid these problems, it is generally advisable to enclose a metal flue in a masonry or wood box, similar to a skylight enclosure. Perhaps the best solution is to minimize penetrations by combining the flue with other roof penetrations for reduced costs, ease of construction, and possibly, aesthetic benefits (explained in the following section).

Skylights and Clerestory Windows

In discussing the details of skylight and clerestory window openings in earth-covered roofs, it should be remembered that these openings can have several functions that must be reflected in the overall design, placement, and sizing of the roof penetration. A skylight is important not only for providing natural light in earth sheltered structures, but can also be used to increase solar heat gain in winter, as well as to provide natural ventilation in summer to a structure that may lack cross-ventilation. Conversely, it is desirable to design skylights so that they do not admit excessive solar heat in summer.

As an example, figure 10-16 illustrates a clerestory structure that incorporates vertical south-facing glass to maximize solar collection in winter in more northerly latitudes, while the overhang provides shade from the higher summer sun. In addition, the window opens to allow for naturally induced ventilation. An alternative or an addition to an operating window in this position would be mechanically or naturally induced ventilation through a separate opening in the roof penetration structure. This separate ventilation system could be operated in conjunction with a heat exchange device in winter as well; however, care should be taken to locate

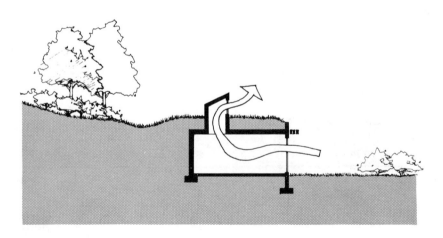

10-16: Section

exhausts and intakes far enough apart to prevent the pollution of fresh incoming air with exhausts.

The details that follow are for the base of the clerestory enclosure shown in figure 10-16. Not only are there thermal benefits associated with vertical or sloping glazing on skylights, but typical horizontal skylights are notorious for problems with water leaks and condensation that can be handled more easily with vertical glazing. Also, horizontal skylights that operate to provide ventilation can be expensive and do not seal particularly tightly compared to vertical windows. In spite of these differences, the design problems and details associated with these larger and more complex roof penetrations are generally quite similar to those for a simple, flat skylight.

Skylights present technical issues that are somewhat different from those for vent pipes and ducts. For example, the larger opening that must be created in the roof structure for a skylight may require additional reinforcing or other support. To raise the skylight above the level of the earth, a 2- to 3-foot deep shaft (usually rectangular) must be constructed of concrete, masonry, or wood walls. In figure 10-17, a basic cast-in-place concrete wall at the edge of a skylight opening is shown. This detail, which appears very similar to the parapet walls discussed previously, poses many of the same technical concerns. Waterproofing and drainage are special concerns because corners are often the weak points of a system; this larger, boxlike structure may act as a dam on a slightly sloping roof, collecting water on one side of it. The cant at the base is helpful in this regard, as is meticulous application of appropriate waterproofing products.

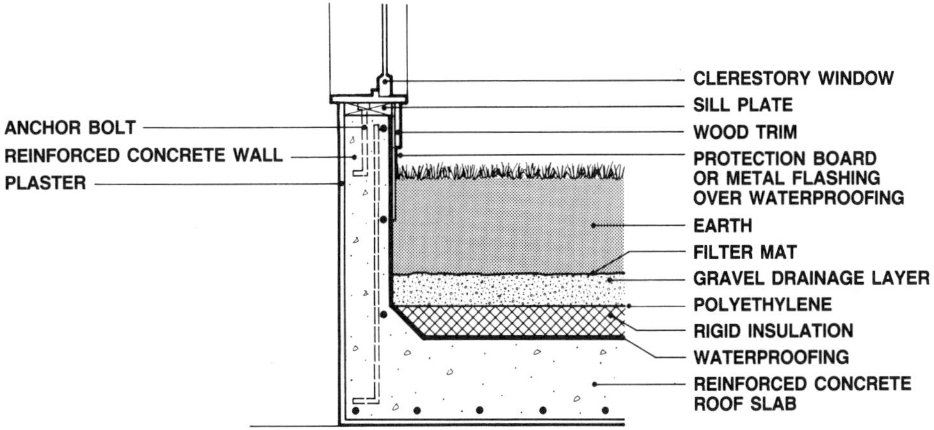

Because the wall extends above grade, the detail at this above-/below-grade transition is also critical. Usually a flashing material that extends below grade is required to cover and protect the waterproofing material. With larger roof penetration structures that are directly attached to the roof, it is likely that the whole assembly will move with the deck, making deflection less of a problem. This makes waterproofing failures at the base of a skylight less of a problem than at the base of a vent pipe or duct. Although keeping the skylight as low to the ground as possible may be aesthetically desirable, it is generally advisable for the walls of the shaft to extend at least 8 inches above grade. Many leaks have occurred when the water or snow level has risen above the level of the skylight during periods of heavy rains or melting snow.

Another problem that these light shaft structures share with parapet walls is the potential for considerable heat loss. The detail shown in figure 10-17 illustrates an undesirable situation in this regard because heat can easily be conducted through the concrete structure and around the insulation, to the outside air and the soil close to the surface. In figure 10-18, the insulation placement shown for the masonry skylight will reduce these high conductive losses through the wall.

Even with extensive insulation around the

ANCHOR BOLT
REINFORCED CONCRETE WALL
PLASTER

CLERESTORY WINDOW
SILL PLATE
WOOD TRIM
PROTECTION BOARD OR METAL FLASHING OVER WATERPROOFING
EARTH
FILTER MAT
GRAVEL DRAINAGE LAYER
POLYETHYLENE
RIGID INSULATION
WATERPROOFING
REINFORCED CONCRETE ROOF SLAB

10-17: Clerestory Window Detail

223

walls, the skylight itself represents the potential for even more serious heat loss—and possibly heat gain. To alleviate this problem, it may be desirable to use some type of movable insulation. Insulating shutters can be placed on the outside of the vertical glazing or various types of insulating panels or shades can be placed over the glazing on the inside (partially shown in fig. 10-18). Another approach, shown in figure 10-19, is to place horizontal sliding insulation at the ceiling level [10.7]. Not only is the insulation more accessible for easier operation, but it is thermally superior since it reduces the volume of the house and places insulation between the heated space and the entire clerestory enclosure.

In addition to concrete and masonry structures that commonly form the skylight enclosure, it is also possible to use a wood-frame structure covered with pressure-treated plywood (see fig. 10-19). This approach helps to solve the heat loss problem in two ways. Not only is the wood structure less conductive than the concrete, but less expensive fiberglass insulation can be easily placed within the wall. Such a wood structure has the advantage of being relatively fast and easy to construct, in comparison to a cast-in-place concrete shaft.

One of the reasons that a wood-frame wall is a reasonable alternative to concrete and masonry for roof penetrations is that the structural problems are not so great a concern as they are with a long, unbraced parapet wall along the edge of a roof. Although the skylight shaft is exposed to stresses from freeze-thaw cycles in the earth, the relatively small, boxlike structure is much more rigid and restrained than the typical parapet wall.

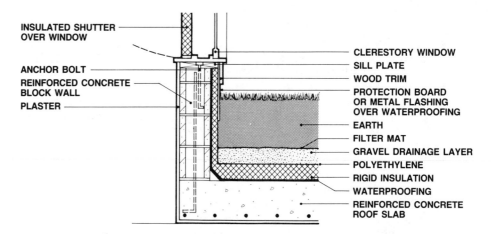

10-18: Clerestory Window Detail

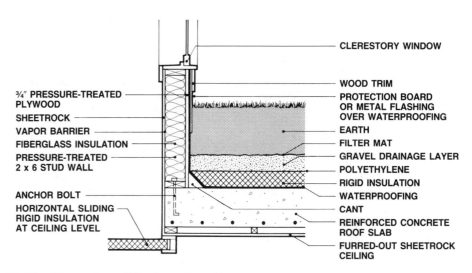

10-19: Clerestory Window Detail

Coordination of Roof Penetration Elements

In typical above-grade construction, roof penetrations for chimney flues, vents, and skylights generally occur wherever they are most convenient. With few exceptions, these elements cause no structural or waterproofing difficulties in conventional roofs and usually do not make very much difference aesthetically. This is particularly true on flat-roof structures, where the roof elements are often not visible. If this generally casual regard for placement of roof penetration elements is followed for earth sheltered structures, however, there can be some drawbacks. Not only is the multiple interruption of the waterproofing more expensive and often difficult to

accomplish without risk of failures, but an earth-covered roof is often more visible from the street. The contrast between the natural ground cover that blends with the surrounding landscape and the various pipes, chimneys, and boxes emerging from the structure below can be aesthetically awkward at the very least (see fig. 10-20). If the roof is accessible and intended for outdoor use, these elements may even pose a safety hazard.

One solution to this problem is simply to avoid it by designing a structure without skylights, in which the necessary vents and flues are brought out through exposed walls. Because this solution can place some severe limitations on room arrangements and often cannot be done, an alternative solution is to consolidate the

various minor elements into one or two major roof penetrations. For example, a skylight structure that provides ventilation could also house a chimney, plumbing vents, and exhaust ducts. With this type of arrangement, as shown in figure 10-21, the overall appearance of the rooftop is less chaotic than that shown in figure 10-20, and the rooftop structure becomes an attractive architectural element. This larger rooftop structure should be compatible in form and materials with the rest of the house and should not be too dominant in size. Otherwise it could look like an ugly shed sitting on top of a house. If this solution places excessive limitations on the interior layout—if all elements cannot be combined at one location—two smaller, compatible structures could be used instead.

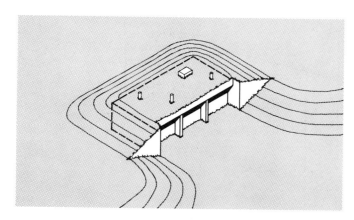

10-20: Aerial View

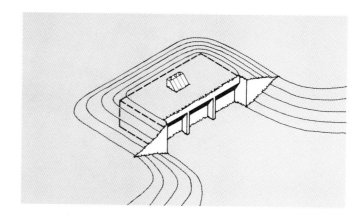

10-21: Aerial View

Wing Walls

In this discussion the term *wing wall* refers to a vertical wall, usually a bearing wall, that extends from the inside to the outside of the structure (fig. 10-22). In earth sheltered buildings, this condition often arises at points of transition from exposed walls to buried walls where a retaining wall is typically required. Extending the buried wall beyond the envelope, as shown for a cast-in-place concrete wall in figure 10-23, can tie the retaining wall to the building both structurally and aesthetically. In addition, it can serve to support the overhang and add depth to an otherwise flat facade. In a similar manner, wing walls occur in the middle of exposed walls where bearing walls extend out, to support the overhang as well as add visual interest, as shown in figure 10-24 for a masonry wall.

10-22: Image

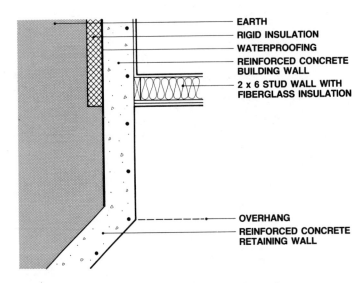

EARTH
RIGID INSULATION
WATERPROOFING
REINFORCED CONCRETE BUILDING WALL
2 x 6 STUD WALL WITH FIBERGLASS INSULATION

OVERHANG
REINFORCED CONCRETE RETAINING WALL

10-23: Detail at Building Corner (Plan)

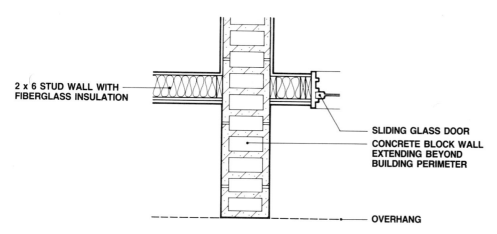

2 x 6 STUD WALL WITH FIBERGLASS INSULATION

SLIDING GLASS DOOR

CONCRETE BLOCK WALL EXTENDING BEYOND BUILDING PERIMETER

OVERHANG

10-24: Detail at Extended Bearing Wall (Plan)

The major problem associated with concrete and masonry retaining walls is that they can conduct a great amount of heat from inside to outside if they are left in the condition shown in figures 10-23 and 10-24. This temperature differential in the wall can also create cold spots on the interior wall, resulting in comfort, frost, and condensation problems. Assuming that a concrete or masonry wing wall is necessary for structural or aesthetic reasons, two basic solutions can prevent the thermal conduction problem. The first is to cover the entire exterior surface of the wing wall with insulation, as shown in figure 10-25 for a wing wall along an exposed wall. This solution requires the additional expense of furring out and covering the insulation with siding.

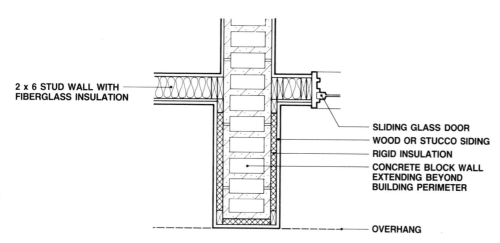

2 x 6 STUD WALL WITH FIBERGLASS INSULATION

SLIDING GLASS DOOR

WOOD OR STUCCO SIDING

RIGID INSULATION

CONCRETE BLOCK WALL EXTENDING BEYOND BUILDING PERIMETER

OVERHANG

10-25: Detail at Extended Bearing Wall (Plan)

The second solution is to provide some type of thermal break to separate the exterior portion of the wall from the interior. As shown in figure 10-26, rigid insulation can be placed in a cast-in-place wall with steel dowels connecting the two portions of the wall. Although the steel is also highly conductive, the area required for it is insignificant in comparison to the amount of concrete. The reinforcing must be carefully designed in a case such as this in order to maintain the structural integrity of the wall.

Like problems associated with parapet walls and overhangs, the problems created by wing walls can be dealt with by eliminating them. If overhangs are required for sun shading, they can be built of wood and supported by a free-standing structure or cantilevered from the exterior wall, thereby eliminating thermal conduction problems. Similarly, retaining walls built of wood can be both structurally and thermally separated from the concrete structure of the building (see fig. 10-27).

Although the fact that the retaining walls are not directly tied to the building would seem to be undesirable structurally, the freedom of movement provided to the walls by this solution may actually be an advantage, provided they are properly designed and constructed. It may be possible to avoid the cracking that often occurs in exterior concrete retaining walls that extend from the interior of a structure, caused by differential settling and the differing load patterns and thermal environments on different parts of the same wall.

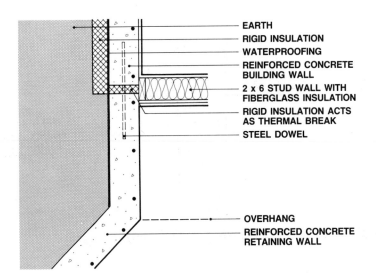

EARTH
RIGID INSULATION
WATERPROOFING
REINFORCED CONCRETE BUILDING WALL
2 x 6 STUD WALL WITH FIBERGLASS INSULATION
RIGID INSULATION ACTS AS THERMAL BREAK
STEEL DOWEL

OVERHANG
REINFORCED CONCRETE RETAINING WALL

10-26: Detail at Building Corner (Plan)

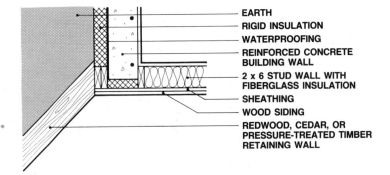

EARTH
RIGID INSULATION
WATERPROOFING
REINFORCED CONCRETE BUILDING WALL
2 x 6 STUD WALL WITH FIBERGLASS INSULATION
SHEATHING
WOOD SIDING
REDWOOD, CEDAR, OR PRESSURE-TREATED TIMBER RETAINING WALL

10-27: Detail at Building Corner (Plan)

Above-/Below-Grade Transitions on Walls

All earth sheltered houses have fully exposed and/or partially bermed walls. Often the below-grade and above-grade portions of these walls are constructed of different materials and are insulated in different ways. Thus, at the grade line on these partially or fully exposed walls, a transition must be made that does not allow excessive heat loss while maintaining structural integrity, adequate waterproofing, and an acceptable appearance.

In order to illustrate the problem at the base of an exposed wall, the detail in figure 10-28 shows a typical slab with no insulation at the edge. Although the frame wall is well insulated, the dense concrete provides a path to conduct heat out of the house. It can function much like a wick, channeling heat out and then absorbing more heat to carry to the outside. This process also makes the floor cold, which in turn cools the room by radiation and makes the occupants of the room feel even colder, especially if their feet are not insulated by carpeting or warm footwear.

In addition to the potential energy loss associated with a building element in contact with the outside cold, condensation can occur on the surface of the element. Whereas older construction usually permitted enough infiltration to limit the buildup of humidity within a house, tighter, energy-efficient construction may result in greater accumulation of humidity, especially if the house is not adequately ventilated. The combination of a cool surface and humid air can result in condensation.

Although a layer of rigid foam insulation on the outside of the floor slab and footing can solve the thermal problem, the additional thickness on the outside of the

foundation must be dealt with in order to provide a solution that is functionally and aesthetically satisfactory. The most direct approach is to place rigid insulation outside the exposed foundation wall even though the face of this insulation extends beyond the face of the siding (see dashed lines in fig. 10-28). Since the insulation cannot be left exposed, a Z-shaped

flashing material that extends under the siding can be placed over the insulation. Such flashing is commercially available for certain thicknesses of insulation or it can be custom formed for individual applications. One concern with this approach is the appearance, which will vary depending on the insulation thickness and the color of the flashing.

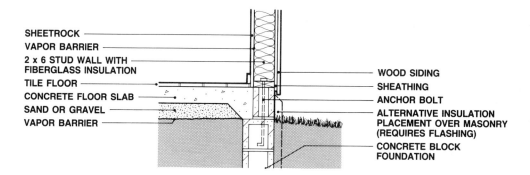

SHEETROCK
VAPOR BARRIER
2 x 6 STUD WALL WITH FIBERGLASS INSULATION
TILE FLOOR
CONCRETE FLOOR SLAB
SAND OR GRAVEL
VAPOR BARRIER

WOOD SIDING
SHEATHING
ANCHOR BOLT
ALTERNATIVE INSULATION PLACEMENT OVER MASONRY (REQUIRES FLASHING)
CONCRETE BLOCK FOUNDATION

10-28: Base of Exposed Wall

Figure 10-29 shows another method of dealing with the thickness of foundation insulation. For this strategy to work, the frame wall above is constructed of two-by-sixes instead of two-by-fours, thereby permitting the framing to extend out 2 inches beyond the foundation while maintaining the same bearing area as a standard wall. Thus, 2 inches of insulation can be installed and yet remain flush with the outer face of the framing. The additional insulation in the thicker frame wall that this strategy permits will also reduce heat loss.

The wall in figure 10-29 gains additional thickness for insulation by using a rigid foam insulation as sheathing under the siding. The foam insulation is continued on down over the foundation, in addition to or instead of insulation under an overhanging two-by-six wall above. The insulation should be used as sheathing only if other diagonal structural bracing is provided, a vapor barrier is installed on the interior side of the innermost insulation, and the thermal and humidity resistance of the sheathing are compatible with the siding to be used.

Another method of reducing heat loss is to insulate inside the foundation (see dashed line in fig. 10-29). The advantage of this technique is that any desired thickness of insulation can be installed inside the foundation without causing the problems of flashing and finishing that thick insulation on the outside could cause. Insulation in this location will significantly cut down on the heat transfer from the floor down through the soil beneath it (which also acts as a heat sink) and out through the foundation to the soil that is near the cold air. It will also help protect any heating

ducts located under the floor slab from excessive heat loss to the outside. One potential disadvantage of this technique is that if the insulation is stopped at the base of the slab, the heat can still be conducted to the outside through the slab. On the other hand, if the insulation extends up to the floor surface, the slab is no longer attached to the foundation wall, possibly allowing for more settling and movement. Also, since the foundation wall is usually thicker than the wood frame wall, there may be a seam 1 to 4 inches wide in the floor where the insulation is exposed. These problems can be resolved with good compaction and careful detailing of the floor surface.

Exterior foam insulation is subject to deterioration from the sun's ultraviolet rays, as well as to damage from being bumped or pierced by lawn equipment, children, workers, animals, etc. Protection for the insulation can be provided by a painted or anodized metal flashing, which will avoid adding thickness to the assembly (fig. 10-29). A thicker layer of protection may be provided by asbestos board, stucco, or a factory-formulated cement plaster that has been designed specifically for application directly to rapid foam insulation. This protective layer can be aligned with the sheathing, as shown in figure 10-31, or flush with the siding with a Z-shaped flashing, as shown in figure 10-30.

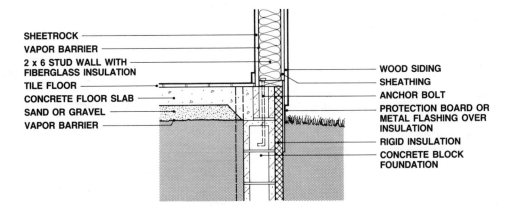

SHEETROCK
VAPOR BARRIER
2 x 6 STUD WALL WITH FIBERGLASS INSULATION
TILE FLOOR
CONCRETE FLOOR SLAB
SAND OR GRAVEL
VAPOR BARRIER

WOOD SIDING
SHEATHING
ANCHOR BOLT
PROTECTION BOARD OR METAL FLASHING OVER INSULATION
RIGID INSULATION
CONCRETE BLOCK FOUNDATION

10-29: Base of Exposed Wall

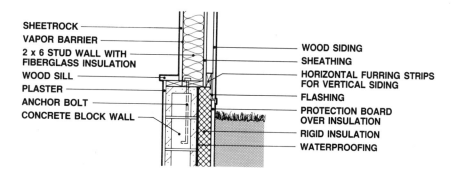

SHEETROCK
VAPOR BARRIER
2 x 6 STUD WALL WITH FIBERGLASS INSULATION
WOOD SILL
PLASTER
ANCHOR BOLT
CONCRETE BLOCK WALL

WOOD SIDING
SHEATHING
HORIZONTAL FURRING STRIPS FOR VERTICAL SIDING
FLASHING
PROTECTION BOARD OVER INSULATION
RIGID INSULATION
WATERPROOFING

10-30: Bermed Wall Detail

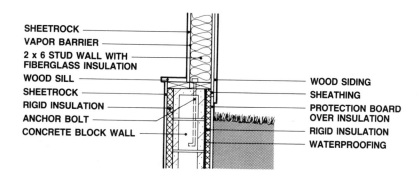

SHEETROCK
VAPOR BARRIER
2 x 6 STUD WALL WITH FIBERGLASS INSULATION
WOOD SILL
SHEETROCK
RIGID INSULATION
ANCHOR BOLT
CONCRETE BLOCK WALL

WOOD SIDING
SHEATHING
PROTECTION BOARD OVER INSULATION
RIGID INSULATION
WATERPROOFING

10-31: Bermed Wall Detail

In some instances the earth will be bermed part of the way up the wall, so that the potential weak point in the thermal envelope is not at the floor slab, but rather at the point where a masonry wall emerging from the earth meets an exposed wood-frame wall, which is often windowsill height. When treated wood is used as the foundation material, no transition must be made; thus, there is no problem to be solved. When wood does meet masonry, the problem is solved in much the same way as in the floor slab.

In figure 10-30, one approach is illustrated in which horizontal nailing strips are provided for vertical siding; however, rather than being flush with the framing or sheathing, they are surface mounted to add their thickness to the depth available for insulation. Although any of the measures that thicken the wall will require extension jambs on doors and windows to finish off the added depth, the jambs are readily available now that energy-conserving construction is becoming more common. When adequate insulation cannot be installed on the outside face of the masonry wall, it can be supplemented on the interior face, as shown in figure 10-31. Fire safety requires that when foam insulation is used, it must be protected by a material such as gypsum board in order to provide adequate fire resistance.

Footings

The design principles for footings are essentially the same for both earth sheltered and conventional houses (fig. 10-32). Footing sizes and the amount of reinforcing may need to be greater for an earth sheltered home, however, because of the greater loads, or because the footings may be designed to cantilever the wall so that it can resist lateral pressure. These structural considerations are discussed more thoroughly in chapter 6.

Waterproofing must run down below the floor level and is usually safeguarded by insulation or protection board. Drain tile is used to channel away excess water so that it does not build up against the wall at a higher level. Gravel is placed around the drain tile to promote drainage. Filter fabric placed over the drain tile is recommended to prevent the earth from entering and clogging the drainage system.

In designing and constructing a wood foundation, the recommendations of the manufacturer of the treated wood assembly should be followed. All members must be carefully sized to ensure that they are adequate for the anticipated loads. Wood foundations usually rest on a wood plate, which in turn rests on a bed of gravel (fig. 10-33). The gravel serves to distribute the load over the soil below and also provides a medium to permit moisture to drain away from the foundation. Some wood foundation manufacturers recommend placement of the drain tile beneath the footing and floor, as shown in figure 10-33. Because of the much higher foundation loads, concrete footings are generally recommended for use with earth-covered roofs unless test structures have proven satisfactory.

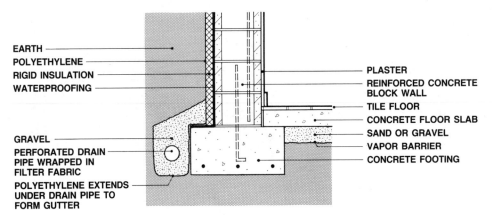

10-32: Concrete Foundation Detail

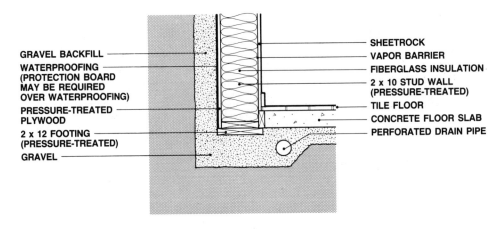

10-33: Wood Foundation Detail

Retaining Walls

In earth sheltered structures, retaining walls outside the structure itself are usually required, especially in buildings with earth-covered roofs where large changes in grade level occur at the transition between buried and exposed walls. In some cases the vertical difference in grade is 12 feet or more; on a two-story structure, it may be over 20 feet. The design and construction of retaining walls is relatively well known. The basic characteristics of various types of retaining walls are discussed in chapter 6.

Although it is beyond the scope of this summary discussion of design problems to illustrate the wide variety of materials and details that could be used for retaining walls, two important design considerations should not be overlooked. First, the size of the required retaining walls may be relatively large, compared to the scale of the house itself. If the retaining walls in

fact represent the predominant form of the house, they must be designed with great care either to diminish their scale or to be compatible with the materials and forms used on the house structure itself. The second consideration is that the lateral loads against high, flat retaining walls induce relatively high stresses in the wall compared to those in an exterior building wall below grade that is held rigid at the top and base. This means that they require substantial structural strength and thus can be quite costly. In order to deal with both the structural/cost concerns and the aesthetic considerations for large retaining walls, it is useful to understand that a wide variety of design solutions exist. Six of the most common design solutions are discussed below and shown in the adjacent illustrations for a one-level earth-covered house that has one exposed elevation.

The most basic and possibly the most common approach is a flat, vertical wall. As shown in figure 10-34, these walls are often splayed out at an angle in order to avoid restricting view and sunlight. This type of wall can have a very flat appearance and, in some cases, is large enough to dominate the form of the house. Assuming the wall height to be 12 feet or more near the house, relatively high stresses on the wall will be induced. A flat-shaped wall such as this has little inherent resistance because of its form and thus must either be heavily reinforced or tied back into the earth. One approach to reducing the scale of the wall is to raise the grade level on the retaining wall itself (fig. 10-35). Not only does the wall appear smaller than in the previous example, but the structural stress is not as great in most places along the wall because the height is reduced. This

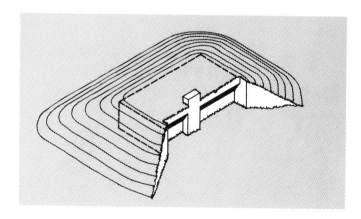

10-34: Aerial View

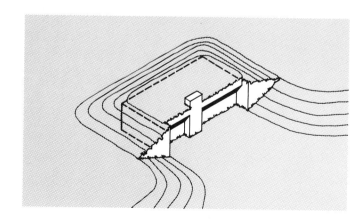

10-35: Aerial View

solution depends on being able to fit the grade level around the retaining wall into the topography on the site. In addition, sloping earth toward the house can cause problems if drainage is not properly handled.

Another means of reducing stress in a tall, vertical retaining wall is to replace it with a series of shorter walls, 4 to 6 feet high (fig. 10-36). This approach not only results in a series of tiers or steps on which plant materials can be placed; it may also reduce or eliminate the perception of the retaining walls as a predominant form. In addition, the structure may blend into the site more easily, as a result of both the stepping-down form and the introduction of plant materials in the retaining structure itself.

The heavy structural requirements in retaining walls can be reduced by modifying the shape of the wall to a form that can resist loads more efficiently than a flat wall. As shown in figure 10-37, a curving form can be used to resist lateral loads, similar to the way in which a shell structure used on a roof resists vertical loads more efficiently than does a flat roof. A folded plate type of form, such as that illustrated in figure 10-38, is far more rigid than a flat wall because of its numerous corners. Although both of these approaches permit more efficient structural design, they may not necessarily represent great cost savings because the curving wall may be more difficult to build and the folded plate actually requires more surface area than a flat wall. Thus, the costs and benefits of these techniques must be analyzed on an individual basis. Another concern related to these two approaches is their aesthetic impact on the structure. Rather than diminishing the scale and

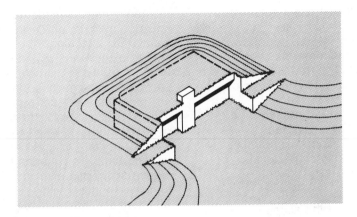

10-36: Aerial View

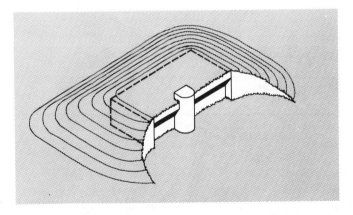

10-37: Aerial View

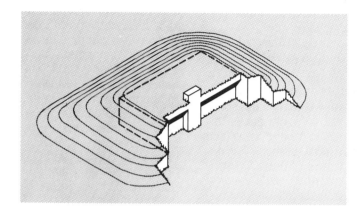

10-38: Aerial View

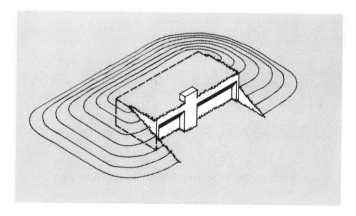

10-39: Aerial View

importance of the retaining wall, they call attention to it. Therefore, if either the curving or folded wall is to be used, the forms and materials used for the wall should be integrated into the design of the entire structure so that they do not appear to be separate, inharmonious appendages to the house.

In attempting to diminish the scale and, consequently, the structural loads and costs of retaining walls, the walls of the building itself can be used to do some of the retaining. As shown in figure 10-39, the exterior building walls can be partially exposed so that the grade change is reduced at the corner of the building. Although this technique reduces the earth cover on the walls slightly, it may create some rather complex detailing problems on the end walls. The appearance of the building in this case is quite different from any of the previous examples. Not only are the retaining walls reduced to minor elements, but the volume of the building is more visibly set into the earth.

In addition to the approaches discussed above, there are various alternatives that, when properly handled, can diminish the scale and appearance of the retaining walls even further. These include natural sloping and the use of rocks to retain steep slopes. By integrating appropriate plant materials into these slopes and forms, they appear to be more a part of the natural site rather than an extension of the building structure. On any of the retaining wall structures and forms discussed in this section, the selection of building materials and plants will have a strong effect on their overall appearance as well as their relationship to the house and the site.

Guardrails

Guardrails can be necessary for houses that have earth-covered roofs, to reduce the likelihood of people falling off the edge along exposed walls and retaining walls. In some circumstances guardrails are essential—for example, an easily accessible roof in an urban setting; in other circumstances, they are not. Interpretations of building code requirements for guardrails differ, and clarification and revisions of codes have been proposed (see chapter 4 and reference 4.1). Nevertheless, when a guardrail is deemed necessary, it presents some unique design problems. The actual guardrail itself can be constructed of metal, wood, or concrete and can appear to be an extension of the facade of the structure or a more separate element placed on top

of it. The numerous methods by which guardrails can be attached to the roof edge are generally similar to those that apply to conventional building details.

One of the most important design considerations related to guardrails is the height they add to the exposed elevations and the retaining walls. In some cases this added height can have the negative effects of exaggerating the height of these walls and destroying the image of the building blending into the landforms and vegetation on the site. Whereas these effects may not be a great concern in an urban setting, on a more open, natural site, the guardrails may be an unfortunate addition (fig. 10-40).

A few alternative design approaches have

been devised to overcome the potential aesthetic problems of adding guardrails to earth-covered structures when necessary. It has been suggested that a row of shrubs could serve as a sufficient deterrent to getting too close to the roof edge. Although it would have aesthetic benefits, such an approach may be too open to individual interpretation, resulting in shrubs that are not dense enough or large enough to provide safety. Shrubs could, however, be used along with a metal guardrail painted green, brown, or black to minimize its appearance. Other proposals to minimize the scale of the guardrail include allowing a shorter rail (18 inches) set back a few feet from the edge or relying on the overhang on the exposed wall to act as a safety net in place of the

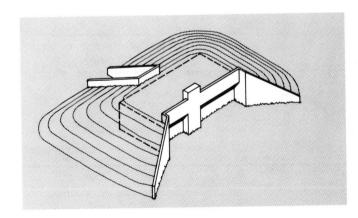

10-40: Aerial View

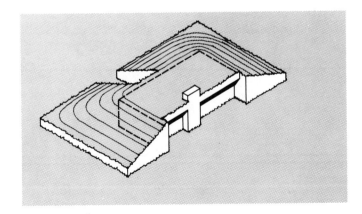

10-41: Aerial View

guardrail. Both of these alternatives would require approval from local code authorities.

In order to eliminate the guardrail along the roof edge for aesthetic reasons, the best solution may be to prevent access to the roof entirely. Two methods of doing so are shown in the figures 10-41 and 10-42. In figure 10-41, the retaining walls are extended around the perimeter of the site, thereby enclosing the berms and providing a barrier to the roof. This alternative requires additional retaining walls; however, it can reduce the land area required for berming, which can be an asset on restricted sites. Although a fence would serve much the same purpose, it is likely to have the same tacked-on appearance as a guardrail.

In figure 10-42, the walls of the structure are only partially bermed, rather than fully bermed, thus creating a barrier to the roof at the perimeter of the building. Because this approach reduces the amount of earth contact and creates a different set of design problems and opportunities than those associated with the previous examples, it is usually not done primarily to resolve the guardrail problem. Nevertheless, the elimination of the guardrail is a consequence of this approach. Both of these alternatives—the retaining wall at the site perimeter and the partial berming of the walls—have another unique aesthetic effect aside from eliminating the guardrails. They define all four sides of the building with at least a minimal architectural element—a narrow horizontal strip of building or retaining wall. Such an element can help resolve the sometimes awkward appearance of a building that looks completely conventional from one side and totally invisible from the other.

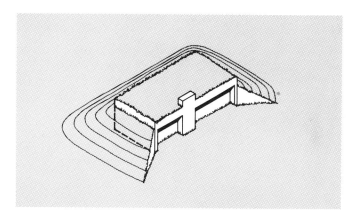

10-42: Aerial View

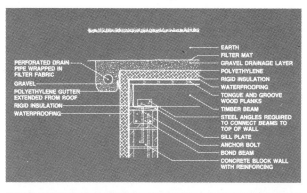

EARTH
FILTER MAT
GRAVEL DRAINAGE LAYER
POLYETHYLENE
RIGID INSULATION
WATERPROOFING
TONGUE AND GROOVE WOOD PLANKS
TIMBER BEAM
STEEL ANGLES REQUIRED TO CONNECT BEAMS TO TOP OF WALL
SILL PLATE
ANCHOR BOLT
BOND BEAM
CONCRETE BLOCK WALL WITH REINFORCING

PERFORATED DRAIN PIPE WRAPPED IN FILTER FABRIC
GRAVEL
POLYETHYLENE GUTTER EXTENDED FROM ROOF
RIGID INSULATION
WATERPROOFING

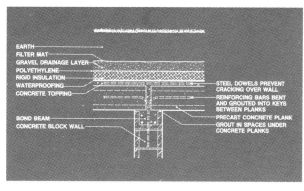

EARTH
FILTER MAT
GRAVEL DRAINAGE LAYER
POLYETHYLENE
RIGID INSULATION
WATERPROOFING
CONCRETE TOPPING

BOND BEAM
CONCRETE BLOCK WALL

STEEL DOWELS PREVENT CRACKING OVER WALL
REINFORCING BARS BENT AND GROUTED INTO KEYS BETWEEN PLANKS
PRECAST CONCRETE PLANK
GROUT IN SPACES UNDER CONCRETE PLANKS

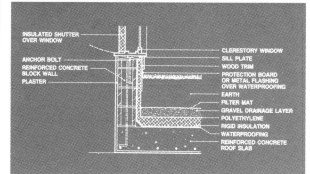

INSULATED SHUTTER OVER WINDOW

ANCHOR BOLT
REINFORCED CONCRETE BLOCK WALL
PLASTER

CLERESTORY WINDOW
SILL PLATE
WOOD TRIM
PROTECTION BOARD OR METAL FLASHING OVER WATERPROOFING
EARTH
FILTER MAT
GRAVEL DRAINAGE LAYER
POLYETHYLENE
RIGID INSULATION
WATERPROOFING
REINFORCED CONCRETE ROOF SLAB

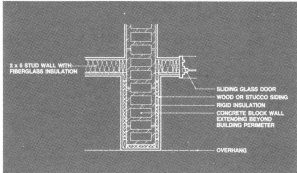

2 x 6 STUD WALL WITH FIBERGLASS INSULATION

SLIDING GLASS DOOR
WOOD OR STUCCO SIDING
RIGID INSULATION
CONCRETE BLOCK WALL EXTENDING BEYOND BUILDING PERIMETER

OVERHANG

REFERENCES AND BIBLIOGRAPHY

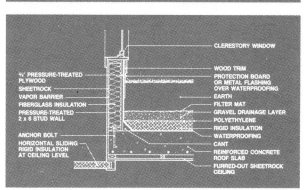

¾" PRESSURE-TREATED PLYWOOD
SHEETROCK
VAPOR BARRIER
FIBERGLASS INSULATION
PRESSURE-TREATED 2 x 6 STUD WALL

ANCHOR BOLT
HORIZONTAL SLIDING RIGID INSULATION AT CEILING LEVEL

CLERESTORY WINDOW
WOOD TRIM
PROTECTION BOARD OR METAL FLASHING OVER WATERPROOFING
EARTH
FILTER MAT
GRAVEL DRAINAGE LAYER
POLYETHYLENE
RIGID INSULATION
WATERPROOFING
CANT
REINFORCED CONCRETE ROOF SLAB
FURRED-OUT SHEETROCK CEILING

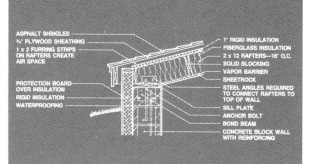

ASPHALT SHINGLES
¾" PLYWOOD SHEATHING
1 x 2 FURRING STRIPS ON RAFTERS CREATE AIR SPACE

PROTECTION BOARD OVER INSULATION
RIGID INSULATION
WATERPROOFING

1" RIGID INSULATION
FIBERGLASS INSULATION
2 x 12 RAFTERS—16" O.C.
SOLID BLOCKING
VAPOR BARRIER
SHEETROCK
STEEL ANGLES REQUIRED TO CONNECT RAFTERS TO TOP OF WALL
SILL PLATE
ANCHOR BOLT
BOND BEAM
CONCRETE BLOCK WALL WITH REINFORCING

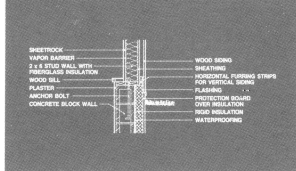

SHEETROCK
VAPOR BARRIER
2 x 6 STUD WALL WITH FIBERGLASS INSULATION
WOOD SILL
PLASTER
ANCHOR BOLT
CONCRETE BLOCK WALL

WOOD SIDING
SHEATHING
HORIZONTAL FURRING STRIPS FOR VERTICAL SIDING
FLASHING
PROTECTION BOARD OVER INSULATION
RIGID INSULATION
WATERPROOFING

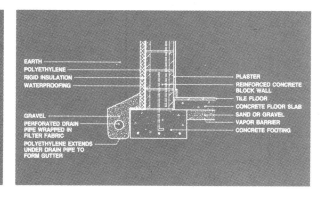

EARTH
POLYETHYLENE
RIGID INSULATION
WATERPROOFING

GRAVEL
PERFORATED DRAIN PIPE WRAPPED IN FILTER FABRIC
POLYETHYLENE EXTENDS UNDER DRAIN PIPE TO FORM GUTTER

PLASTER
REINFORCED CONCRETE BLOCK WALL
TILE FLOOR
CONCRETE FLOOR SLAB
SAND OR GRAVEL
VAPOR BARRIER
CONCRETE FOOTING

References

Chapter 1

1.1. Underground Space Center, University of Minnesota, *Earth Sheltered Housing Design: Guidelines, Examples, and References* (New York: Van Nostrand Reinhold Co., 1978).

1.2. Joe R. Engleman, Vincent Muirhead, and Nicolas Willems, *Thunderstorms, Tornadoes and Building Damage* (Lexington, MA: Lexington Books, D.C. Heath & Company, 1975).

Chapter 2

2.1. David Wright, *Natural Solar Architecture: A Passive Primer* (New York: Van Nostrand Reinhold Co., 1978).

2.2. Vivian Loftness, *Identifying Climatic Design Regions and Assessing Climatic Impact on Residential Building Design* (A.I.A. Research Corporation, Technical Paper No. 1, Winter 1977).

2.3. A.I.A. Research Corporation, *Regional Guidelines for Building Passive Energy Conserving Homes* (Washington, D.C.: U.S. Department of Housing and Urban Development).

2.4. Victor Olgyay, *Design with Climate: A Bioclimatic Approach to Architectural Regionalism* (Princeton: Princeton University Press, 1963).

2.5. Donald Watson and Kenneth Labs, *Climatic Design for Home Building* (Washington, D.C.: NAHB Research Foundation and U.S. Department of Housing and Urban Development, 1980).

2.6. Kenneth Labs, *Regional Analysis of Ground and Above-Ground Climate* (Oak Ridge, TN: Oak Ridge National Laboratory, 1981).

2.7. Baruch Givoni, *Man, Climate and Architecture, 2nd edition* (London: Applied Science Publishers, Ltd., 1976).

2.8. W.T. Grondzik, T.L. Johnson, and L.L. Boyer, Monitoring of Earth Sheltered Residences in Oklahoma: Project Report for Control Data Corporation (Stillwater, OK: Oklahoma State University, 1981).

2.9. Richard E. Peterson, ed., *Symposium on Tornadoes: Assessment of Knowledge and Implications for Man,* June 22-24, 1976 (Lubbock, TX: Institute for Disaster Research, Texas Tech University, 1976).

2.10. Insurance Information Institute, *Insurance Facts, 1980-81 edition* (Chicago: Insurance Information Institute, 1981).

2.11. International Conference of Building Officials, *Uniform Building Code* (Whittier, CA: International Conference of Building Officials, 1976).

Chapter 3

3.1. J.B. Langley and J.L. Gay, *Sun Belt Earth Sheltered Architecture, Part One* (Winter Park, FL: Sun Belt Earth Sheltered Research, 1980).

3.2. Conversation with Dr. John B. Langley, A.I.A., Winter Park, Florida.

3.3. Underground Space Center, University of Minnesota, *Earth Sheltered Housing: Code, Zoning, and Financing Issues* (New York: Van Nostrand Reinhold Company, 1982).

Chapter 4

4.1. Underground Space Center, University of Minnesota, *Earth Sheltered Housing: Code, Zoning, and Financing Issues* (New York: Van Nostrand Reinhold, 1982).

4.2. Building Officials & Code Administrators International Inc., *The BOCA Basic Building Code/1978* (Chicago: BOCAI, Inc., 1978).

Chapter 5

5.1. R.W. Brown, *Residential Foundations: Design, Behavior and Repair* (New York: Van Nostrand Reinhold Co., 1979).

5.2. Center for Natural Energy Design, Oklahoma State University, *Building in Expansive Clays* (Oak Ridge, TN: U.S. Department of Energy Innovative Structures Program, Earth Sheltered Structures Fact Sheet No. 11, 1981).

5.3. M.S. Kersten, *Thermal Properties of Soils* (Minnesota Engineering Experiment Station Bulletin No. 28, Vol. LII, No. 21, June 1, 1949).

5.4. B.K. Hough, *Basic Soils Engineering, 2nd edition* (New York: Ronald Press Company, 1969).

5.5. Underground Space Center, University of Minnesota, *Earth Sheltered Community Design: Energy-Efficient Residential Development* (New York: Van Nostrand Reinhold Co., 1981).

5.6. J.P. Gould, "Lateral Pressures on Rigid Permanent Structures," *Proceedings of the 1970 ASCE Specialty Conference on Lateral Stresses in the Ground and Design of Earth Retaining Structures* (New York: American Society of Civil Engineers, 1970).

5.7. Setter, Leach & Lindstrom, Inc., *Energy, Cost and Design Evaluation of Non-residential Buildings: Phase 2 Report for the U.S. Naval Facilities Engineering Command* (Minneapolis: Setter, Leach & Lindstrom, Inc., 1981).

Chapter 6

6.1. International Conference of Building Officials, *Uniform Building Code, 1976 edition* (Whittier, CA: International Conference of Building Officials, 1976).

6.2. American Iron and Steel Institute, *Handbook of Steel Drainage and Highway Construction Products* (New York: American Iron and Steel Institute, 1971).

6.3. Product information, Tectron Corporation, Colorado Springs, Colorado.

6.4. R. Behr, et al., "Thin Shell Roof Systems and Construction Techniques for Earth Sheltered Housing," *Proceedings of the Earth Sheltered Design Innovations National Technical Conference,* April 18-19, 1980, Oklahoma City, Oklahoma, L.L. Boyer, ed. (Stillwater, OK: Oklahoma State University, 1980).

6.5. Product literature, American Solartron Corporation, Centralia, Ilinois.

6.6. J.B. Langley and J.L. Gay, *Sun Belt Earth Sheltered Architecture, Part One* (Winter Park, FL: Sun Belt Earth Sheltered Research, 1980).

6.7. Product literature, Terra-Dome, Inc., Independence, Missouri.

Chapter 7

7.1. R.B. Peck, W.E. Hanson, T.H. Thornburn, *Foundation Engineering, 2nd edition* (New York: John Wiley and Sons, Inc., 1974).

Chapter 8

8.1. R.K. Maxwell, *Temperature Measurements and the Calculated Heat Flux in the Soil* (M.Sc. Thesis, University of Minnesota, 1964).

8.2. F.C. Houghten, D.I. Taimuty, C. Gutberlet, and C.J. Brown, "Heat Loss Through Basement Walls and Floors," *Transactions American Society of Heating and Ventilating Engineers,* No. 1213, 1942, pp. 369-384.

8.3. Baruch Givoni, *Man, Climate and Architecture, 2nd edition* (London: Applied Science Publishers, Ltd., 1976).

8.4. F.C. Houghten, D.I. Taimuty, C. Gutberlet, and C.J. Brown, "Heat Loss Through Basement Walls and Floors," *Transactions: American Society of Heating and Ventilating Engineers,* No. 1213, 1942, pp. 369-384.

8.5. G.D. Meixel, Jr., P.H. Shipp, and T.P. Bligh, "The Impact of Insulation Placement on the Seasonal Heat Loss Through Basement and Earth Sheltered Walls," *Underground Space,* July/August 1980, Vol. 5, No. 1, pp. 41-47.

8.6. F.J. Dechow and K.A. Epstein, "Laboratory and Field Investigations of Moisture Absorption and Its Effects on Thermal Performance for Various Insulations," prepared for A.S.T.M. Symposium on Advances in Heat Transmission Measurements, Philadelphia, 1977.

8.7. W. Tobiasson and J. Ricard, "Moisture Gain and Its Thermal Consequence for Common Roof Insulation," *Proceedings, 5th Conference on Roofing Technology,* April 19-20, 1979.

8.8. J.L. Severson, "Thermal Performance of Various Insulations in Below-Earth-Grade Perimeter Application," presented at DOE-ORN/ASTM Conference in Clearwater Beach, FL, Dec. 8-11, 1981.

8.9. D.J. Moschandress, et al., *Indoor Air Pollution in the Residential Environment, Volume I, Data Collection, Analysis and Interpretation* (Gaithersburg, MD: Environmental Protection Agency and U.S. Department of Housing and Urban Development, December 1978).

8.10. W. Fuller, "What's in the Air for Tightly Built Houses?" *Solar Age,* June 1981, pp. 30-32.

8.11. Underground Space Center, University of Minnesota, *Earth Sheltered Homes: Plans and Designs* (New York: Van Nostrand Reinhold Co., 1981).

8.12. D. Lord, "Interior Environment Quality in Earth Shelters," *Earth Shelter Performance and Evaluation,* L.L. Boyer, ed., Proceedings of the 2nd National Technical Conference on Earth Sheltered Buildings, Tulsa, OK, Oct. 16 and 17, 1981 (Stillwater, OK: Oklahoma State University, 1981).

8.13. Conversation with Cancer Information Service, Dec. 30, 1981.

8.14. Harold May, "Ionizing Radiation Levels in Energy Conserving Structures," *Underground Space,* May/June 1981, Vol. 5, No. 6, pp. 384-391.

8.15. W.A. Shurcliff, *Air-to-Air Heat Exchangers for Houses* (W.A. Shurcliff, Cambridge, MA, 1981).

8.16. "Clearing the Air: Heat Exchangers in Energy Efficient Houses," *Soft Energy Notes,* Feb. 1980, Vol. 3, No. 1, pp. 24-25.

8.17. "Earth Cooling Tubes: Practical Passive Cooling Technique?" *SSEC News,* March 1981, Vol. 2, pp. 12-13.

Chapter 9

9.1. Rudolf Geiger, *The Climate Near the Ground* (Cambridge, MA: Harvard University Press, 1965).

9.2. Thomas Wirth, "Landscape Architecture Above Buildings," *Underground Space,* August 1977, Vol. 1, No. 4, pp. 339-340.

9.3. *Weather-Wise Gardening for Midwest and Northwest Region,* ORTHO Book Series (San Francisco: Chevron Chemical Co., 1974).

Chapter 10

10.1. Underground Space Center, University of Minnesota, *Earth Sheltered Housing Design: Guidelines, Examples and References* (New York: Van Nostrand Reinhold Co., 1978).

10.2. Underground Space Center, University of Minnesota, *Earth Sheltered Homes: Plans and Designs* (New York: Van Nostrand Reinhold Co. 1981).

10.3. Underground Space Center, University of Minnesota, *Earth Sheltered Homes: Plans and Designs* (New York: Van Nostrand Reinhold Co. 1981). See section on Earthtech Houses.

10.4. Correspondence with David Wright, January 1982.

10.5. Malcolm Wells, *Underground Designs* (Malcolm Wells, Brewster, MA, 1977).

10.6. Malcolm Wells, and Sam Glenn-Wells, *Underground Plans Book-1* (Malcolm Wells, Brewster, MA, 1980).

10.7. Correspondence with David Wright, January 1982 (see *Natural Solar Architecture: A Passive Primer,* David Wright, New York: Van Nostrand Reinhold Co., 1978).

Bibliography

General References

Boyer, L.L., "Earth Sheltered Structures," *Annual Review of Energy,* Vol. 7, Annual Reviews, Inc., Palo Alto, CA, 1982.

Campbell, S., *Underground House Book,* Garden Way Publishing, Charlotte, VT. 1980, 210 pages.

Labs, K., *Regional Analysis of Ground and Above-Ground Climate.* Prepared for U.S. Dept. of Energy ORNL/SUB-81/40451/1, Dec. 1981, 192 pages (Includes microfiche tables). Available from the Underground Space Center.

Langley, J.B. and Gay, J.L., *Sun Belt Earth Sheltered Architecture: Part One.* Sun Belt Earth Sheltered Research, P.O. Drawer 729, Winter Park, FL 32790, 1980.

Moreland Associates, *Earth Covered Buildings: An Exploratory Analysis for Hazard and Energy Performance.* Prepared for the Federal Emergency Management Agency, No. 1981, 302 pages, FEMA Unit #4411E, Contract 81-600091.

Scalise, J.W., ed., *Earth Integrated Architecture—An Alternative Method for Creating Livable Environments with Emphasis on Arid Regions,* College of Architecture, Arizona State University, Tempe, AZ, 1975, 284 pages.

Tri/Arch Associates, *The Earth Shelter Handbook,* Tech/Data Publications, Milwaukee, WI, 1980, 244 pages.

Underground Space Center, University of Minnesota, Sterling, R., Carmody, J., Elnicky, G., *Earth Sheltered Community Design: Energy-Efficient Residential Development,* Van Nostrand Reinhold Co., New York, 1981, 270 pages.

Underground Space Center, University of Minnesota, *Earth Sheltered Housing Design: Guidelines, Examples and References,* Van Nostrand Reinhold Co., New York, 1978.

Underground Space Center, University of Minnesota, *Earth Sheltered Housing: Code, Zoning and Financing Issues,* Van Nostrand Reinhold Co., New York, 1982.

Underground Space Center, University of Minnesota, *Earth Sheltered Homes: Plans and Designs,* Van Nostrand Reinhold Co., New York, 1981.

Wells, M., *Underground Designs,* M. Wells, P.O. Box 1149, Brewster, MA 02631, 1977, 87 pages.

Wells, M. and Glenn-Wells, S., *Underground Plans Book-I,* M. Wells, P.O. Box 1149, Brewster, MA 02631, 1980, 44 pages.

Major Conference Proceedings

Bowen, A., Clark, E., Labs, K., eds., *Passive Cooling,* Proceedings of the International Passive and Hybrid Cooling Conference, Miami Beach, 1981, Presented by American Section/International Solar Energy Society, 1052 pages.

Boyer, L.L., ed., *Earth Sheltered Building Design Innovations,* Proceedings of a National Technical Conference held in Oklahoma City, Conducted by Oklahoma State University, April 1980.

Boyer, L.L., ed., *Earth Shelter Performance and Evaluation,* Proceedings of a National Technical Conference held in Tulsa, Oklahoma, Conducted by Oklahoma State University, Oct. 1981.

Holthusen, T.L., ed., *The Potential of Earth Sheltered and Underground Space,* Proceedings of the Underground Space Conference and Exposition, Kansas City, June 1981, Pergamon Press, 1981, 503 pages.

Moreland, F., ed., *Alternatives in Energy Conservation: The Use of Earth Covered Buildings,* Proceedings of Conference, Fort Worth, Texas, July 1975, Government Printing Office, Stock No. 038-000-00286-4, NSF-RA-760006, 353 pages.

Fact Sheets

U.S. Department of Energy: Earth Sheltered Structures Fact Sheets, Prepared by Underground Space Center, University of Minnesota, Sept. 1981.

No. 01 *Site Investigation* ORNL/SUB-7849/01

No. 02 *Planting Considerations* ORNL/SUB-7849/02

No. 03 *Waterproofing Techniques* ORNL/SUB-7849/03

No. 04 *Waterproofing Considerations and Materials* ORNL/SUB-7849/04

No. 05 *Insulation Principles* ORNL/SUB-7849/05

No. 06 *Insulation Materials and Placement* ORNL/SUB-7849/06

U.S. Department of Energy: Earth Sheltered Structures Fact Sheets, Prepared by Center for Natural Energy Design, School of Architecture, Oklahoma State University, August 1981.

No. 07 *Daylighting Design* ORNL/SUB-6974IV-01

No. 08 *Indoor Air Quality* ORNL/SUB-6974IV-02

No. 09 *Earth Coupled Cooling Techniques* ORNL/SUB-6974IV-03

U.S. Department of Energy: Earth Sheltered Structures Fact Sheets, Prepared by Center for Natural Energy Design, School of Architecture, Oklahoma State University, Sept. 1981.

No. 10 *Disaster Protection* ORNL/SUB-6974IV-04

No. 11 *Building in Expansive Clays* ORNL/SUB-6974IV-05

No. 12 *Passive Solar Heating* ORNL/SUB-6974IV-06

Bibliographies

Keehn, P.A., *Earth Sheltered Housing: An Annotated Bibliography and Directory,* Jan. 1981, Council of Planning Librarians, 1313 East 60th St., Chicago, IL 60637, 61 pages, $11.00

Sterling, R.L., ed., *Annotated Bibliography on Earth Contact Systems: Heat Transfer and Soil Temperature References.* Prepared for Passive Cooling Division, U.S. Dept. of Energy, Dec. 1981, 92 pages. Available from the Underground Space Center.

Periodicals

Earth Sheltered Living. Bimonthly magazine on design and construction of earth sheltered homes. Published by WEBCO Publishing, Inc., St. Paul, Minnesota.

Underground Space. Interdisciplinary professional journal on underground space use and earth sheltered construction. Published by Pergamon Press; also available through American Underground-Space Association (see below).

Other Sources of Information

Active and Passive Solar Conservation/ Information. For information sources and bibliographies contact Conservation and Renewable Energy Inquiry and Referral Service (CAREIRS), P.O. Box 8900, Silver Spring, MD 20907, Toll-Free Phone 800/523-2929.

American Underground-Space Association. Department of Civil and Mineral Engineering, University of Minnesota, Minneapolis, Minnesota 55455.

Oklahoma State University. Obtain bibliography and publications list from: Architectural Extension, 115 Architecture Building, Oklahoma State University, Stillwater, Oklahoma 74078.

Texas Tech University. Obtain publications list and information from: Department of Civil Engineering or Department of Family Management, Housing and Consumer Science, Texas Tech University, Lubbock, Texas 79409.

Underground Space Center. Obtain publications list and ordering information from: Underground Space Center, 128 Pleasant St. S.E., 28 Appleby Hall, Minneapolis, Minnesota 55455.

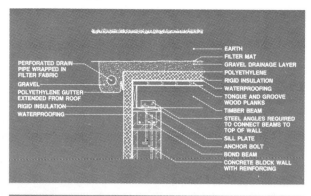

EARTH
FILTER MAT
GRAVEL DRAINAGE LAYER
POLYETHYLENE
RIGID INSULATION
WATERPROOFING
TONGUE AND GROOVE
WOOD PLANKS
TIMBER BEAM
STEEL ANGLES REQUIRED
TO CONNECT BEAMS TO
TOP OF WALL
SILL PLATE
ANCHOR BOLT
BOND BEAM
CONCRETE BLOCK WALL
WITH REINFORCING

PERFORATED DRAIN
PIPE WRAPPED IN
FILTER FABRIC
GRAVEL
POLYETHYLENE GUTTER
EXTENDED FROM ROOF
RIGID INSULATION
WATERPROOFING

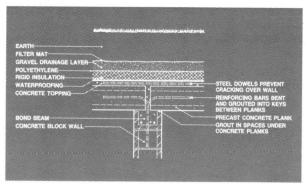

EARTH
FILTER MAT
GRAVEL DRAINAGE LAYER
POLYETHYLENE
RIGID INSULATION
WATERPROOFING
CONCRETE TOPPING

BOND BEAM
CONCRETE BLOCK WALL

STEEL DOWELS PREVENT
CRACKING OVER WALL
REINFORCING BARS BENT
AND GROUTED INTO KEYS
BETWEEN PLANKS
PRECAST CONCRETE PLANK
GROUT IN SPACES UNDER
CONCRETE PLANKS

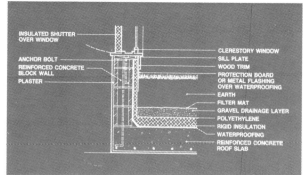

INSULATED SHUTTER
OVER WINDOW

ANCHOR BOLT
REINFORCED CONCRETE
BLOCK WALL
PLASTER

CLERESTORY WINDOW
SILL PLATE
WOOD TRIM
PROTECTION BOARD
OR METAL FLASHING
OVER WATERPROOFING
EARTH
FILTER MAT
GRAVEL DRAINAGE LAYER
POLYETHYLENE
RIGID INSULATION
WATERPROOFING
REINFORCED CONCRETE
ROOF SLAB

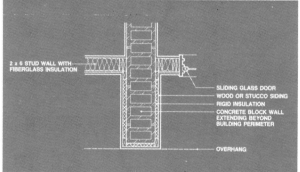

2 x 6 STUD WALL WITH
FIBERGLASS INSULATION

SLIDING GLASS DOOR
WOOD OR STUCCO SIDING
RIGID INSULATION
CONCRETE BLOCK WALL
EXTENDING BEYOND
BUILDING PERIMETER

OVERHANG

INDEX

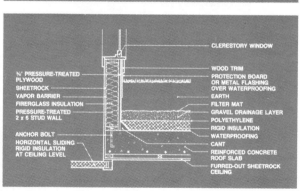

CLERESTORY WINDOW

¾" PRESSURE-TREATED
PLYWOOD
SHEETROCK
VAPOR BARRIER
FIBERGLASS INSULATION
PRESSURE-TREATED
2 x 6 STUD WALL

ANCHOR BOLT
HORIZONTAL SLIDING
RIGID INSULATION
AT CEILING LEVEL

WOOD TRIM
PROTECTION BOARD
OR METAL FLASHING
OVER WATERPROOFING
EARTH
FILTER MAT
GRAVEL DRAINAGE LAYER
POLYETHYLENE
RIGID INSULATION
WATERPROOFING
CANT
REINFORCED CONCRETE
ROOF SLAB
FURRED-OUT SHEETROCK
CEILING

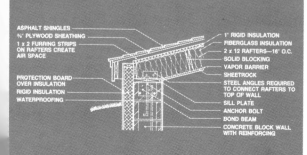

ASPHALT SHINGLES
¾" PLYWOOD SHEATHING
1 x 2 FURRING STRIPS
ON RAFTERS CREATE
AIR SPACE
PROTECTION BOARD
OVER INSULATION
RIGID INSULATION
WATERPROOFING

1" RIGID INSULATION
FIBERGLASS INSULATION
2 x 12 RAFTERS—16" O.C.
SOLID BLOCKING
VAPOR BARRIER
SHEETROCK
STEEL ANGLES REQUIRED
TO CONNECT RAFTERS TO
TOP OF WALL
SILL PLATE
ANCHOR BOLT
BOND BEAM
CONCRETE BLOCK WALL
WITH REINFORCING

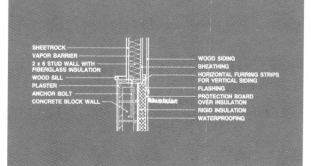

SHEETROCK
VAPOR BARRIER
2 x 6 STUD WALL WITH
FIBERGLASS INSULATION
WOOD SILL
PLASTER
ANCHOR BOLT
CONCRETE BLOCK WALL

WOOD SIDING
SHEATHING
HORIZONTAL FURRING STRIPS
FOR VERTICAL SIDING
FLASHING
PROTECTION BOARD
OVER INSULATION
RIGID INSULATION
WATERPROOFING

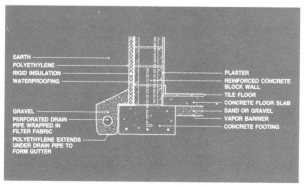

EARTH
POLYETHYLENE
RIGID INSULATION
WATERPROOFING

PLASTER
REINFORCED CONCRETE
BLOCK WALL
TILE FLOOR
CONCRETE FLOOR SLAB
SAND OR GRAVEL
VAPOR BARRIER
CONCRETE FOOTING

GRAVEL
PERFORATED DRAIN
PIPE WRAPPED IN
FILTER FABRIC
POLYETHYLENE EXTENDS
UNDER DRAIN PIPE TO
FORM GUTTER

Italicized numbers refer to photographs

A

B

C

D